Curiosity

ALBERTO MANGUEL

Curiosity

Yale

UNIVERSITY PRESS

New Haven & London

Published with assistance from the foundation established in memory of
Amasa Stone Mather of the Class of 1907, Yale College.

Yale University Press books may be purchased in quantity for educational, business,
or promotional use. For information, please e-mail sales.press@yale.edu (U.S. office)
or sales@yaleup.co.uk (U.K. office).

Designed by Sonia L. Shannon.
Set in A Gos type by Integrated Publishing Solutions.
Printed in the United States of America.

Library of Congress Cataloging-in-Publication Data
Manguel, Alberto.
  Curiosity / Alberto Manguel.
    pages cm
  Includes bibliographical references and index.
  ISBN 978-0-300-18478-5 (hardback)
  1. Manguel, Alberto—Books and reading. 2. Literature—Appreciation. I. Title.
  PR9199.3.M34845C87 2015
  814'.54—dc23
  [B]   2014034697

A catalogue record for this book is available from the British Library.

This paper meets the requirements of ANSI/NISO Z39.48–1992
(Permanence of Paper).

10 9 8 7 6 5 4 3 2 1

To Amelia who, like the Elephant's Child,
is so full of 'satiable curtiosity.
With all my love.

CONTENTS

Curiosity

INTRODUCTION

On her death bed, Gertrude Stein lifted her head and
asked: "What is the answer?" When no one spoke, she smiled
and said: "In that case, what is the question?"

—Donald Sutherland, *Gertrude Stein:*
A Biography of Her Work

I am curious about curiosity.

One of the first words that we learn as a child is *why*. Partly because we want to know something about the mysterious world into which we have unwillingly entered, partly because we want to understand how the things in that world function, and partly because we feel an ancestral need to engage with the other inhabitants of that world, after our first babblings and cooings, we begin to ask "Why?"[1] We never stop. Very soon we find out that curiosity is seldom rewarded with meaningful or satisfying answers, but rather with an increased desire to ask more questions and the pleasure of conversing with

(Opposite) Virgil explains to Dante that Beatrice sent him to show Dante the right path. Woodcut illustrating Canto II of the Inferno, *printed in 1487 with commentary by Cristoforo Landino. (Beinecke Rare Book and Manuscript Library, Yale University)*

others. As any inquisitor knows, affirmations tend to isolate; questions bind. Curiosity is a means of declaring our allegiance to the human fold.

Perhaps all curiosity can be summed up in Michel de Montaigne's famous question "Que sais-je?": "What do I know?" which appears in the second book of his *Essays*. Speaking of the skeptic philosophers, Montaigne remarked that they were unable to express their general ideas in any manner of speech, because, according to him, "they would have needed a new language." "Our language," says Montaigne, "is formed of affirmative propositions, which are contrary to their thinking." And then he adds: "This fantasy is better conceived through the question 'What do I know?,' which I carry as a motto on a shield." The source of the question is, of course, the Socratic "Know thyself," but in Montaigne it becomes not an existentialist assertion of the need to know who we are but rather a continuous state of questioning of the territory through which our mind is advancing (or has already advanced) and of the uncharted country ahead. In the realm of Montaigne's thought, the affirmative propositions of language turn on themselves and become questions.[2]

My friendship with Montaigne dates back to my adolescence, and his *Essays* have since been for me a kind of autobiography, as I keep finding in his comments my own preoccupations and experiences translated into luminous prose. Through his questioning of commonplace subjects (the duties of friendship, the limits of education, the pleasure of the countryside) and his exploration of extraordinary ones (the nature of cannibals, the identity of monstrous beings, the use of thumbs), Montaigne maps out for me my own curiosity, constellated at different times and in many places. "Books have been useful to me," he confesses, "less for instruction than as training."[3] That has been precisely my case.

Reflecting on Montaigne's reading habits, for example, it occurred to me that it might be possible to make some notes on his "Que sais-je?" by following Montaigne's own method of borrowing ideas from his library (he compared himself as a reader to a bee gathering pollen to make his own honey) and projecting these forward into my own time.[4]

As Montaigne would have willingly admitted, his examination of what we know was not a new venture in the sixteenth century: questioning the act of questioning had much older roots. "Whence then cometh wisdom?" asks Job in his distress, "and where is the place of understanding?" Enlarging on

Job's question, Montaigne observed that "judgment is a tool to use on all subjects, and comes in everywhere. Therefore in the tests that I make of it here, I use every sort of occasion. If it is a subject I do not understand at all, even on that I essay my judgment, sounding the ford from a good distance; and then, finding it too deep for my height, I stick to the bank."[5] I find this modest method wonderfully reassuring.

According to Darwinian theory, human imagination is an instrument of survival. In order better to learn about the world, and therefore be better equipped to cope with its pitfalls and dangers, *Homo sapiens* developed the ability to reconstruct outer reality in the mind and to conceive situations that it could confront before actually encountering them.[6] Conscious of ourselves and conscious of the world around us, we are able to build mental cartographies of those territories and explore them in an infinite number of ways, and then choose the best and most efficient. Montaigne would have agreed: we imagine in order to exist, and we are curious in order to feed our imaginative desire.

Imagination, as an essential creative activity, develops with practice, not through successes, which are conclusions and therefore blind alleys, but through failures, through attempts that prove to be mistaken and require new attempts that will also, if the stars are kind, lead to new failures. The histories of art and literature, like those of philosophy and science, are the histories of such enlightened failures. "Fail. Try again. Fail better," was Beckett's summation.[7]

But in order to fail better we must be able to recognize, imaginatively, those mistakes and incongruities. We must be able to see that such-and-such a path does not lead us in the aspired direction, or that such-and-such a combination of words, colors, or numbers does not approximate the intuited vision in our mind. Proudly we record the moments in which our many inspired Archimedes shout "Eureka!" in their baths; we are less eager to recall the many more in which those, like the painter Frenhofer in Balzac's story, look upon their unknown masterpiece and say, "Nothing, nothing! . . . I'll have produced nothing!"[8] Through those few moments of triumph and those many more of defeat runs the one great imaginative question: Why?

Our education systems today by and large refuse to acknowledge the second half of our quests. Interested in little else than material efficiency and financial profit, our educational institutions no longer foster thinking for its own sake and the free exercise of the imagination. Schools and colleges have become training camps for skilled labor instead of forums for questioning and discussion, and colleges and universities are no longer nurseries for those inquirers whom Francis Bacon, in the sixteenth century, called "merchants of light."[9] We teach ourselves to ask "How much will it cost?" and "How long will it take?" instead of "Why?"

"Why?" (in its many variations) is a question far more important in its asking than in the expectation of an answer. The very fact of uttering it opens numberless possibilities, can do away with preconceptions, summons up endless fruitful doubts. It may bring, in its wake, a few tentative answers, but if the question is powerful enough, none of these answers will prove all-sufficient. "Why?," as children intuit, is a question that implicitly places our goal always just beyond the horizon.[10]

The visible representation of our curiosity—the question mark that stands at the end of a written interrogation in most Western languages, curled over itself against dogmatic pride—arrived late in our histories. In Europe, conventionalized punctuation was not established until the late Renaissance when, in 1566, the grandson of the great Venetian printer Aldo Manutius published his punctuation handbook for typesetters, the *Interpungendi ratio*. Among the signs devised to conclude a paragraph, the handbook included the medieval *punctus interrogativus,* and Manutius the Younger defined it as a mark that signaled a question which conventionally required an answer. One of the earliest instances of such question marks is in a ninth-century copy of a text by Cicero, now in the Bibliothèque nationale in Paris; it looks like a staircase ascending toward the top right in a squiggly diagonal from a dot at the bottom left. Questioning elevates us.[11]

Throughout our various histories, the question "Why?" has appeared under many guises and in vastly different contexts. The number of possible questions may seem too great to consider individually in depth and too varied to assemble coherently, and yet some attempts have been made to gather a few according to various criteria. For instance, a list of ten questions that "science must answer" (the "must" protests too much) was drawn up by scientists and philosophers invited by the editors of the *Guardian* of London in 2010. The questions were: "What is consciousness?" "What happened before

Example of *punctus interrogativus* in a ninth-century manuscript of Cicero's
Cato maior de senectute. (Paris, Bibliothèque nationale, MS lat. 6332, fol. 81)

the Big Bang?" "Will science and engineering give us back our individuality?" "How are we going to cope with the world's burgeoning population?"
"Is there a pattern to the prime numbers?" "Can we make a scientific way of
thinking all-pervasive?" "How do we ensure humanity survives and flourishes?" "Can someone explain adequately the meaning of infinite space?"
"Will I be able to record my brain like I can record a programme on television?" "Can humanity get to the stars?" There is no evident progression in
these questions, no logical hierarchy, no clear evidence that they *can* be answered. They proceed by branching out from our desire to know, creatively
sifting through our acquired wisdom. And yet, a certain shape might be
glimpsed in their meandering. In following a necessarily eclectic path through
a few of the questions sparked by our curiosity, something like a parallel cartography of our imagination may perhaps become apparent. What we want
to know and what we can imagine are the two sides of the same magical page.

One of the common experiences in most reading lives is the discovery,
sooner or later, of one book that like no other allows for an exploration of
oneself and of the world, that appears to be inexhaustible yet at the same time
concentrates the mind on the tiniest particulars in an intimate and singular way.
For certain readers, that book is an acknowledged classic, a work by Shakespeare or Proust, for example; for others it is a lesser-known or less agreed-
upon text that deeply echoes for inexplicable or secret reasons. In my case,
throughout my life, that unique book has changed: for many years it was Montaigne's *Essays* or *Alice in Wonderland,* Borges's *Ficciones* or *Don Quixote,* the *Arabian Nights* or *The Magic Mountain.* Now, as I approach the prescribed three
score and ten, the book that is to me all-encompassing is Dante's *Commedia.*

Introduction

5

I came to the *Commedia* late, just before turning sixty, and from the very first reading, it became for me that utterly personal yet horizonless book. To describe the *Commedia* as horizonless may be simply a way of declaring a kind of superstitious awe of the work itself: of its profundity, its breadth, its intricate construction. Even these words fall short of my constantly renewed experience of reading the text. Dante spoke of his poem as one "in which lend a hand heaven and earth."[12] This is not a hyperbole: it is the impression its readers have had from Dante's age on. But *construction* implies an artificial mechanism, an act dependent on pulleys and cogs which, even when evident (as in Dante's invention of the terza rima, for instance, and accordingly his use of the number 3 throughout the *Commedia*), merely points to a speck in the complexity but hardly illuminates its apparent perfection. Giovanni Boccaccio compared the *Commedia* to a peacock whose body is covered with "angelic" iridescent feathers of countless hues. Jorge Luis Borges compared it to an infinitely detailed engraving, Giuseppe Mazzotta to a universal encyclopedia. Osip Mandelstam had this to say: "If the halls of the Hermitage should suddenly go mad, if the paintings of all schools and masters should suddenly break loose from the nails, should fuse, intermingle, and fill the air of the rooms with futuristic howling and colors in violent agitation, the result then would be something like Dante's *Commedia*." And yet none of these similes captures entirely the fullness, depth, reach, music, kaleidoscopic imagery, infinite invention, and perfectly balanced structure of the poem. The Russian poet Olga Sedakova has noted that Dante's poem is "art that generates art" and "thought that generates thought" but, more important, it is "experience that generates experience."[13]

In a parody of twentieth-century artistic currents, from the *nouveau roman* to conceptual art, Borges and his friend Adolfo Bioy Casares imagined a form of criticism that, surrendering to the impossibility of analyzing a work of art in all its greatness, merely reproduced the work in its entirety.[14] Following this logic, in order to explain the *Commedia,* a meticulous commentator would have to end up quoting the whole poem. Perhaps that is the only way. It is true that when we come across an astonishingly beautiful passage or an intricate poetic argument that had not struck us as forcibly in a previous reading, our impulse is not so much to comment on it as to read it aloud to a friend, in order to share, as far as possible, the original epiphany. To translate the words into other experiences: maybe this is one of the possible meanings of Beatrice's words to Dante in the Heaven of Mars: "Turn around and listen, / because not only in my eyes is Paradise."[15]

Less ambitious, less knowledgeable, more conscious of my own horizons, I want to offer a few readings of my own, a few comments based on personal reflections, observations, translations into my own experience. The *Commedia* has a certain majestic generosity that does not bar entry to anyone attempting to cross its threshold. What each reader finds there is another matter.

There is an essential problem with which every writer (and every reader) is faced when engaging with a text. We know that to read is to affirm our belief in language and its vaunted ability to communicate. Every time we open a book, we trust, in spite of all our previous experience, that this once the essence of the text will be conveyed to us. And every time we reach the last page, in spite of such brave hopes, we are again disappointed. Especially when we read what for want of more precise terms we agree to call "great literature," our ability to grasp the text in all its multilayered complexity falls short of our desires and expectations, and we are compelled to return to the text once again in the hope that this time, perhaps, we will achieve our purpose. Fortunately for literature, fortunately for us, we never do. Generations of readers cannot exhaust these books, and the very failure of language to communicate fully lends them a limitless richness that we fathom only to the extent of our individual capabilities. No reader has ever reached the depths of the *Mahabharata* or the *Oresteia*.

The realization that a task is impossible does not prevent us from attempting it, and every time a book is opened, every time a page is turned, we renew the hope of understanding a literary text, if not in its entirety, at least a little more than on the previous reading. That is how, throughout the ages, we create a palimpsest of readings that continuously reestablishes the book's authority, always under a different guise. The *Iliad* of Homer's contemporaries is not our *Iliad*, but it includes it, as our *Iliad* includes all *Iliad*s to come. In this sense, the Hassidic assertion that the Talmud has no first page because every reader has already begun reading it before starting at the first words is true of every great book.[16]

The term *lectura dantis* was created to define what has become a specific genre, the reading of the *Commedia*, and I am fully aware that, after generations of commentaries beginning with those of Dante's own son Pietro, written shortly after his father's death, it is impossible to be either comprehensively critical or thoroughly original in what one has to say about the poem. And yet, one might be able to justify such an exercise by suggesting that every reading is, in the end, less a reflection or translation of the original text than a portrait of the reader, a confession, an act of self-revelation and self-discovery.

The first of these autobiographical readers was Dante himself. Throughout his otherworldly journey, having been told that he must find a new path in life or be lost forever, Dante is seized by an ardent curiosity to know who he truly is and what it is he experiences along the way.[17] From the first verse of *Inferno* to the last verse of *Paradiso*, the *Commedia* is marked with Dante's questions.

In the whole of his essays, Montaigne quotes Dante only twice. Scholars are of the opinion that he had not read the *Commedia* but knew of it through references in the works of other writers. Even if he had read it, possibly Montaigne might not have liked the dogmatic structure within which Dante chose to conduct his explorations. Nevertheless, when discussing the power of speech in animals, Montaigne transcribes three verses from *Purgatorio* XXVI in which Dante compares the penitent lustful souls to "dark battalions of communicating ants."[18] And again he quotes Dante when discussing the education of children. "Let the tutor," says Montaigne, "pass everything through a filter and never lodge anything in the boy's head simply by authority, at second-hand. Let the principles of Aristotle not be principles for him any more than those of the Stoics or the Epicureans. Let this diversity of judgments be set before him; if he can, he will make a choice: if he cannot then he will remain in doubt. Only fools have made up their minds and are certain." Montaigne then quotes the following line of Dante: "Not less than knowing, doubting [*dubbiar*] pleases me," the words Dante addresses to Virgil in the sixth circle of hell, after the Latin poet has explained to his charge why the sins of incontinence are less offensive to God than those that are the fruit of our will. For Dante, the words express the pleasure felt in the expectant moment that precedes the acquisition of knowledge; for Montaigne, they describe a constant state of rich uncertainty, being aware of various opposing views but embracing none except one's own. For both, the state of questioning is as rewarding as, or even more so than, that of knowing.[19]

Is it possible, as an atheist, to read Dante (or Montaigne) without believing in the God they worshiped? Is it presumptuous to assume a measure of understanding of their work without the faith that helped them bear the suffering, bewilderment, anguish (and also joy) that are the lot of every human being? Is it insincere to study the strict theological structures and subtleties of religious dogmas without being convinced by the tenets on which they are based? As a reader, I claim the right to believe in the meaning of a story beyond the particulars of the narrative, without swearing to the existence of a fairy godmother or a wicked wolf. Cinderella and Little Red Riding Hood don't need to have been real people for me to believe in their truths. The god who walked in the garden "in the cool of the evening" and the god who, agonizing on a cross, promised Paradise to a thief, enlighten me in ways that nothing but great literature can. Without stories all religion would be mere preaching. It is stories that convince us.

The art of reading is in many ways opposed to the art of writing. Reading is a craft that enriches the text conceived by the author, deepening it and rendering it more complex, concentrating it to reflect the reader's personal experience and expanding it to reach the farthest confines of the reader's universe and beyond. Writing, instead, is the art of resignation. The writer must accept the fact that the final text will be but a blurred reflection of the work conceived in the mind, less enlightening, less subtle, less poignant, less precise. The imagination of a writer is all-powerful, and capable of dreaming up the most extraordinary creations in all their wishful perfection. Then comes the descent into language, and in the passage from thought to expression much—very much—is lost. To this rule there are hardly any exceptions. To write a book is to resign oneself to failure, however honorable that failure might be.

Conscious of my hubris, it occurred to me that, following Dante's example of having a guide for his travels—Virgil, Statius, Beatrice, Saint Bernard—I might have Dante himself as a guide to mine, and allow his questioning to help steer my own. Though Dante admonished those who in tiny skiffs attempt to follow his keel, and warned them to turn back to their own shores for fear of becoming lost,[20] I nevertheless trust that he will not mind helping out a fellow traveler filled with so much agreeable dubbiar.

I

What Is Curiosity?

EVERYTHING BEGINS WITH A VOYAGE. One day, when I was eight or nine, in Buenos Aires, I lost my way coming back from class. The school was one of many that I attended in my childhood, and stood a short distance from our house, in the tree-lined neighborhood of Belgrano. Then as now, I was easily distracted, and all sorts of things caught my attention as I walked back home in the starched white pinafore all schoolchildren were obliged to wear: the corner grocery store that before the age of supermarkets held large barrels of briny olives, cones of sugar wrapped in light-blue paper, blue tins of Canale biscuits; the stationer's with its patriotic notebooks displaying the faces of our national heroes and shelves lined with the yellow covers of the Robin Hood children's series; a tall, narrow door with harlequin stained glass which was sometimes left open, revealing a grim courtyard where a tailor's mannequin mysteriously languished; the sweet seller, a fat man sitting at a street corner on a tiny stool, who held, like a lance, his kaleidoscopic wares. I usually took the same way back, counting off the landmarks as I passed them, but that day I decided to change course. After a few blocks, I realized I didn't know the way. I was too ashamed to ask for directions, so I wandered, more astonished than frightened, for what seemed to me a very long time.

(Opposite) Dante and Virgil meet the sowers of discord. Woodcut illustrating Canto XXVIII of the Inferno, *printed in 1487 with commentary by Cristoforo Landino. (Beinecke Rare Book and Manuscript Library, Yale University)*

I don't know why I did what I did, except that I wanted to experience something new, to follow whatever clues I might find to mysteries not yet apparent, as in the Sherlock Holmes stories, which I had just discovered. I wanted to deduce the secret story of the doctor with a battered walking stick, to reveal that the tiptoeing footmarks in the mud were those of a man running for his life, to ask myself why someone would be wearing a groomed black beard that was no doubt false. "The world is full of obvious things which nobody by any chance ever observes," said the Master.

I remember becoming aware, with a feeling of pleasurable anxiety, that I was engaging in an adventure different from the ones on my shelves and yet I experienced something of the same suspense, the same intense desire to find out what lay ahead, without being able (without wanting) to foretell what might take place. I felt as if I'd entered a book and was on the way to its undisclosed final pages. What exactly was I looking for? Perhaps this was when for the first time I conceived of the future as a place that held together the tail-ends of all the possible stories.

But nothing happened. At long last, I turned a corner and found myself on familiar ground. When I finally saw my house, it felt like a disappointment.

*But we hold several threads in our hands, and the odds
are that one or other of them guides us to the truth. We may
waste time following the wrong one, but sooner or later,
we must come upon the right.*

—SIR ARTHUR CONAN DOYLE,
"The Hound of the Baskervilles"

*C*uriosity is a word with a double meaning. The etymological Spanish
dictionary of Covarrubias of 1611 defines *curioso* (it is the same in
Italian) as a person who treats something with particular care and
diligence, and the great Spanish lexicographer explains its derivation *curiosidad* (in Italian, *curiosità*) as resulting because "the curious person is always
asking: 'Why this and why that?'" Roger Chartier has noted that these first
definitions did not satisfy Covarrubias, and in a supplement written in 1611
and 1612 (and left unpublished) Covarrubias added that *curioso* has "both a
positive and a negative sense. Positive, because the curious person treats
things diligently; and negative, because the person labors to scrutinize things
that are most hidden and reserved, and do not matter." There follows a quotation in Latin from one of the apocryphal books of the Bible, Ecclesiasticus:
"Do not try to understand things that are too difficult for you, or try to
discover what is beyond your powers" (3:21–22). With this, according to
Chartier, Covarrubias opens his definition to the biblical and patristic condemnation of curiosity as the illicit yearning to know what is forbidden.[1] Of
this ambiguous nature of curiosity, Dante was certainly aware.

Dante composed almost all, if not all, of the *Commedia* while in exile,
and the account of his poetic pilgrimage can be read as a hopeful mirror of
his forced pilgrimage on earth. Curiosity drives him, in Covarrubias's sense
of treating things "diligently," but also in the sense of seeking to know what
is "most hidden and reserved" and lies beyond words. In a dialogue with his
otherworldly guides (Beatrice, Virgil, Saint Bernard) and with the damned
and blessed souls he encounters, Dante allows his curiosity to lead him on

13

towards the ineffable goal. Language is the instrument of his curiosity—even as he tells us that the answer to his most burning questions cannot be uttered by a human tongue—and his language can be also the instrument of ours. Dante can act, in our reading of the *Commedia,* as a "midwife" of our thoughts, as Socrates once defined the role of the seeker of knowledge.[2] The *Commedia* allows us to bring our questions into being.

Dante died in exile in Ravenna on 13 or 14 September 1321, after having recorded in the last verses of his *Commedia* his vision of the everlasting light of God. He was fifty-six years old. According to Giovanni Boccaccio, Dante had begun writing the *Commedia* sometime before his banishment from Florence, and had been forced to abandon in the city the first seven cantos of the *Inferno.* Someone, Boccaccio says, searching for a document among the papers in Dante's house, found the cantos without knowing they were by Dante, read them with admiration, and took them for inspection to a Florentine poet "of some renown," who guessed that they were Dante's work and contrived to send them on to him. Always according to Boccaccio, Dante was at the time at the estate of Moroello Malaspina in Lunigiana; Malaspina received the cantos, read them, and begged Dante not to abandon a work so magnificently begun. Dante consented and began the eighth canto of the *Inferno* with the words: "I say, carrying on, that long before . . ." So goes the story.[3]

Extraordinary literary works seem to demand extraordinary tales of their conception. Magical biographies of a phantom Homer were invented to account for the power of the *Iliad* and the *Odyssey,* and Virgil was lent the gifts of a necromancer and herald of Christianity because, his readers thought, the *Aeneid* could not have been composed by an ordinary man. Consequently, the conclusion of a masterpiece must be even more extraordinary than its inception. As the writing of the *Commedia* advanced, Boccaccio tells us, Dante began to send the completed cantos to one of his patrons, Cangrande della Scala, in lots of six or eight. In the end, Cangrande would have received the entire work with the exception of the last thirteen cantos of *Paradiso.* For the months following Dante's death, his sons and disciples searched among his papers to see if he had not perhaps finished the missing cantos. Finding nothing, says Boccaccio, "they were enraged that God had not allowed him to live

What Is Curiosity?

The first portrait of Dante to appear in a printed book. Hand-colored woodcut
in *Lo amoroso Convivio di Dante* (Venice, 1521). (Photograph courtesy of
Livio Ambrogio. Reproduced by permission.)

in the world long enough to have the chance of concluding what little remained of his work." One night, Jacopo, Dante's third son, had a dream. He saw his father approach, dressed in a white gown, his face shining with a strange light. Jacopo asked him if he was still alive, and Dante said that he was, but in the true life, not in ours. Jacopo then asked whether he had finished his *Commedia*. "Yes," was the answer, "I finished it," and he led Jacopo to his old bedroom, where, putting his hand on a certain place on the wall, he announced, "Here is what you were searching for for so long." Jacopo woke, fetched an old disciple of Dante's, and together they discovered, behind a hanging cloth, a recess containing moldy writings which proved to be the missing cantos. They copied them out and sent them, according to Dante's habit, to Cangrande. "Thus," Boccaccio tells us, "was the task of so many years brought to its conclusion."[4]

Boccaccio's story, which today is regarded less as factual history than as an admiring legend, lends the creation of what is perhaps the greatest poem ever penned an appropriately magical frame. And yet neither the initial suspenseful interruption nor the final happy revelation suffice, in the reader's mind, to account for the invention of such a work. The history of literature is rich in stories about desperate situations in which writers have managed to create masterpieces. Ovid dreaming his *Tristia* in the hellhole of Toomis, Boethius writing his *Consolation of Philosophy* in prison, Keats composing his great odes while dying of tubercular fever, Kafka scribbling his *Metamorphosis* in the public corridor of his parents' house contradict the assumption that a writer can write only under auspicious circumstances. Dante's case is, however, particular.

In the late thirteenth century, Tuscany was split into two political factions: the Guelphs, loyal to the pope, and the Ghibellines, loyal to the imperial cause. In 1260, the Ghibellines defeated the Guelphs at the Battle of Montaperti; a few years later, the Guelphs began to regain their lost power, eventually expelling the Ghibellines from Florence. By 1270 the city was entirely Guelph and would remain so throughout Dante's lifetime. Shortly after Dante's birth in 1265, the Guelphs of Florence divided into the Blacks and the Whites, this time along family rather than political lines. On 7 May 1300, Dante took part in an embassy to San Gimigniano on behalf of the ruling White faction; a month later he was elected one of the six priors of Florence. Dante, who believed that church and state should not interfere in one another's spheres of action, opposed the political ambitions of Pope Boniface VIII; consequently, when he was sent to Rome in the autumn of 1301 as part of the Florentine embassy, Dante was ordered to stay at the papal court while the other ambassadors returned to Florence. On 1 November, in Dante's absence, the landless French prince Charles de Valois (whom Dante despised as an agent of Boniface) entered Florence, supposedly to restore peace but in fact to allow a group of exiled Blacks to enter the city. Led by their chief, Corso Donati, for five days the Blacks pillaged Florence and murdered many of its citizens, driving the surviving Whites into exile. In time, the exiled Whites became identified with the Ghibelline faction, and a Black priorate was installed to rule Florence. In January 1302, Dante, who was probably still in Rome, was condemned to exile by the priorate. Later, when he refused to pay the fine imposed as penalty, his sentence of two years' exile was changed to that of being burned at the stake if he ever returned to Florence. All his goods were confiscated.

Dante's exile took him first to Forlì, then, in 1303, to Verona, where he stayed until the death of the city's lord, Bartolomeo della Scala, on 7 March 1304. Because the new ruler of Verona, Alboino della Scala, was unfriendly, or because Dante thought he could enlist the sympathies of the new pope, Benedict XI, the exile returned to Tuscany, probably to Arezzo. For the next few years his itinerary is uncertain—perhaps he moved to Treviso, but Lunigiana, Lucca, Padua, and Venice are also possible halting places; in 1309 or 1310 he may have visited Paris. In 1312, Dante returned to Verona. Cangrande della Scala had become, a year earlier, the city's sole ruler, and thereafter Dante lived in Verona under his protection, until at least 1317. Dante's final years were spent in Ravenna, at the court of Guido Novelo da Polenta.

In the absence of irrefutable documentary evidence, scholars suggest that Dante began the *Inferno* either in 1304 or 1306, the *Purgatorio* in 1313, and the *Paradiso* in 1316. The exact dating matters less than the astonishing fact that Dante wrote the *Commedia* during almost twenty years of wandering in more than ten alien cities, away from his library, his desk, his papers, his talismans—the superstitious bric-à-brac with which every writer constructs a working theater. In unfamiliar rooms, amidst people to whom he owed polite gratitude, in spaces that, because they were not his intimate own, must have seemed relentlessly public, always subject to social niceties and the conventions of others, it must have been a daily struggle to find small moments of privacy and silence in which to work. Since his own books were not available, with his annotations and remarks scribbled on the margins, his main recourse was the library of his mind, marvelously furnished (as the countless literary, scientific, theological, and philosophical references in the *Commedia* show) but subject, like all such libraries, to the depletions and blurrings that come with age.

What were his first attempts like? In a document preserved by Boccaccio, a certain Brother Ilario, "a humble monk of Corvo," says that one day a traveler came to his monastery. Brother Ilario recognized him, "for though I had never once seen him before that day, his fame had long before reached me." Perceiving the monk's interest, the traveler "drew a little book from his bosom in a friendly enough way" and showed him some verses. The traveler, of course, was Dante; the verses, the initial cantos of the *Inferno,* which, though written in the vernacular of Florence, Dante tells the monk he had at first intended to write in Latin.[5] If Boccaccio's document is authentic, then Dante had managed to take with him into exile the first few pages of his poem. It would have been enough.

We know that early on in his travels, Dante had begun to send friends and patrons copies of a few of the cantos, which were then often copied and passed along to other readers. In August 1313, the poet Cino da Pistoia, one of Dante's friends in the early years, included glosses of a few verses from two cantos of the *Inferno* in a song he wrote on the death of the emperor Henry VII; in 1314 or perhaps somewhat earlier, a Tuscan notary, Francesco da Barberino, mentions the *Commedia* in his *Documenti d'amore.* There are several other proofs that Dante's work was known and admired (and envied and scorned) long before the *Commedia's* completion. Barely twenty years after Dante's death, Petrarch mentions how illiterate artists recited parts of the poem at crossroads and theaters to applauding drapers, innkeepers, and customers in shops and markets.[6] Cino, and later Cangrande, must have had an almost complete manuscript of the poem, and we know that Dante's son Jacopo worked from a holograph copy to produce a one-volume *Commedia* for Guido da Polenta. Today not a single line in Dante's hand has come down to us. Coluccio Salutati, an erudite Florentine humanist who translated parts of the *Commedia* into Latin, recalled seeing Dante's "lean script" in some of his now lost epistles in the Chancery of Florence, but we can only imagine what his handwriting looked like.[7]

How the notion of writing the chronicle of a journey to the Otherworld came to Dante is, of course, an unanswerable question. A clue may lie at the end of his *Vita nova,* an autobiographical essay structured around thirty-one lyric poems whose meaning, purpose, and origin Dante attributes to his love for Beatrice: in the last chapter, Dante speaks of an "admirable vision" which makes him resolve to write "what has never been written of any other woman." A second explanation may be the fascination felt for popular tales of otherworldly journeys among Dante's contemporaries. In the thirteenth century these imaginary voyages had become a thriving literary genre, born perhaps from anxieties to know what lies beyond the last breath: to revisit the departed and learn whether they require the weak hold of our memory for their continued existence, to find out whether our actions on this side of the grave have consequences on the other. Such questions, of course, were not new even then: ever since we started telling stories, in the days before history, we began to draw up a detailed geography for the regions of the Otherworld. Dante would have been familiar with a number of these travelogues. Homer, for instance, allowed Odysseus to visit the Land of the Dead on his delayed return to Ithaca; Dante, who had no Greek, knew the version of that descent given by Virgil in his *Aeneid.* Saint Paul, in his Second Epistle to the Corinthians, wrote of a man who had been to Paradise and "heard unspeakable words, which it is not lawful for a man to utter" (12:4). When Virgil appears to Dante and tells him that he will lead him "through an eternal place," Dante acquiesces, but then hesitates.

> But why should *I* go? And who allows it?
> I am not Aeneas, nor am I Paul.[8]

Dante's audience would have understood the references.

Dante, voracious reader, would have also been familiar with Cicero's *Scipio's Dream* and its description of the celestial spheres, as well as with the otherworldly incidents in Ovid's *Metamorphoses.* Christian eschatology would have provided him with several more accounts. In the Apocryphal Gospels, the so-called *Apocalypse of Peter* describes the saint's vision of the Holy Fathers wandering in a perfumed garden, and the *Apocalypse of Paul* speaks of a fathomless abyss into which the souls of those who did not hope for God's mercy are flung.[9] Other journeys and visions appear in such best-selling pious compendia as Jacop de Voragine's *Golden Legend* and the anonymous *Lives of the Fathers;* in the imaginary Irish travel narratives of Saint Brendan, Saint Patrick, and King Tungdal; in the mystic visions of Peter Damian, Richard de Saint-Victoire, and Gioachim de Fiore; and in certain Islamic Otherworld chronicles, such as the Andalucian *Libro della Scala* (Book of the Ladder), which tells of Muhammad's ascent to heaven. (We will return to this Islamic influence on the *Commedia* farther on.) There are always models for any new literary venture: our libraries repeatedly remind us that there is no such thing as literary originality.

The earliest verses Dante wrote were, as far as we know, several poems composed in 1283, when he was eighteen years old, later included in the *Vita nova;* the last work was a lecture in Latin, *Questio de aqua et terra* (Dispute on Earth and Water), which he delivered in a public reading on 20 January 1320, less than two years before his death.

The *Vita nova* was finished before 1294: its declared intention is to clarify the words *Incipit Vita Nova,* "Here Begins the New Life," inscribed in the "volume of my memory," and following the sequence of poems written for love of Beatrice, whom he saw for the first time when both were children, Dante nine and Beatrice eight. The book is presented as a quest, an attempt to answer the questions elicited by the love poems, driven by a curiosity bred, Dante says, in "the high chamber where all the sensitive spirits carry their perceptions."[10]

Dante's last composition, the *Questio de aqua et terra,* is a philosophical inquiry into several scientific matters, following the style of "disputes" popular at the time. In his introduction, Dante writes: "Therefore, nourished as I have been since my childhood with the love of truth, I suffered not to leave myself out of the debate, but chose to show what was true therein, and also to dissolve all contrary arguments, as much for love of truth as for hatred of falsity."[11] Between the first mention of a need for questioning and the last lies the vast territory of Dante's masterwork. The entire *Commedia* can be read as the pursuit of one man's curiosity.

According to patristic tradition, curiosity can be of two kinds: the curiosity associated with the *vanitas* of Babel, which leads us to believe ourselves capable of such feats as building a tower to reach the heavens; and the curiosity of *umiltà*, of thirsting to know as much as we can of the divine truth, so that, as Saint Bernard prays for Dante in the *Commedia*'s last canto, "joy supreme may be unfolded to him." Quoting Pythagoras in his *Convivio*, Dante defined a person who pursues this wholesome curiosity precisely as a "lover of knowledge . . . a term not of arrogance but of humility."[12]

Though scholars such as Bonaventure, Siger de Brabant, and Boethius deeply influenced Dante's thought, Thomas Aquinas, above all, was Dante's *maître à penser:* as Dante's *Commedia* is to his curious readers, Aquinas's writings were to Dante. When Dante, guided by Beatrice, reaches the Heaven of the Sun, where the prudent are rewarded, a crown of twelve blessed souls circle around him three times to the sound of a celestial music, until one of them detaches itself from the dance and speaks to him. It is the soul of Aquinas, which tells him that, since true love has at last been kindled in Dante, Aquinas and the other blessed souls must answer his questions out of that same love. According to Aquinas, and following the teachings of Aristotle, the knowledge of the supreme good is such that once perceived it can never be forgotten, and the soul blessed with such knowledge will always yearn to return to it. What Aquinas calls Dante's "thirst" must inevitably be satisfied: it would be as impossible not to try to assuage it "as it is for water not to flow back to the sea."[13]

Aquinas was born in Roccasecca, in the Kingdom of Sicily, heir to a noble family related to much of the European aristocracy: the Holy Roman emperor was his cousin. At the age of five, he began his studies at the celebrated Benedictine abbey of Monte Cassino. He must have been an insufferable child: it is told that after remaining silent in class for many days, his first utterance to his teacher was a question, "What is God?"[14] At fourteen, his parents, wary of political divisions in the abbey, transferred him to the recently founded University of Naples, where he began his lifelong study of Aristotle and his commentators. During his university years, around 1244, he decided to join the Dominican order. Aquinas's choice to become a Dominican mendicant friar scandalized his aristocratic family. They had him kidnapped and held confined for a year, hoping he would recant. He did not, and once set free he settled for a time in Cologne to study under the celebrated teacher Albertus Magnus. For the rest of his life he taught, preached, and wrote in Italy and France.

Aquinas was a large man, clumsy and slow, characteristics that earned him the nickname "Dumb Ox." He refused all positions of power and prestige, whether that of courtier or abbot. He was, above all, a lover of books and reading. When asked for what he thanked God most, he answered, "for granting me the gift of understanding every page I've ever read."[15] He believed in reason as a means of attaining the truth, and constructed, along Aristotelian philosophy, laborious logical arguments to reach some measure of conclusion to the great theological questions. For this he was condemned, three years after his death, by the bishop of Paris, who maintained that the absolute power of God could do without any quibbles of Greek logic.

Aquinas's major work is the *Summa Theologica,* a vast survey of the principal theological questions, intended, he says in the prologue, "not only to teach the proficient, but also to instruct beginners."[16] Aware of the need for a clear and systematic presentation of Christian thought, Aquinas made use of the recently recovered works of Aristotle, translated into Latin, to construct an intellectual framework that would support the sometimes contradictory fundamental Christian canonical writings, from the Bible and the books of Saint Augustine to the works of the theologians of his own time. Aquinas was still writing the *Summa* a few months before his death in 1274. Dante, who was only nine when Aquinas died, may have met some of the master's disciples at the University of Paris if (as legend has it) he visited the city as a young man. Whether through the teachings of Aquinas's followers or his own readings, Dante certainly knew and made use of Aquinas's theological cartography, much as he knew and made use of Augustine's invention of the first-person protagonist to recount his life's journey. And certainly he knew both their arguments concerning the nature of human inquisitiveness.

The beginning point of all quests is, for Aquinas, Aristotle's celebrated statement "All human beings, by nature, desire to know," to which Aquinas refs several times in his writings. Aquinas proposed three arguments for this desire. The first is that each thing naturally desires its perfection, that is to say, to become fully conscious of its nature and not merely capable of achieving this consciousness; this, in human beings, means acquiring a knowledge of reality. Second, that everything inclines to its proper activity: as fire to heating and heavy things to falling, humans are inclined to understanding, and consequently to knowing. Third, everything desires to be united to its principal— the end to its beginning—in that most perfect of motions, that of the circle; it is only through intellect that this desire is achieved, and through intellect we each become united to our separate substances. Therefore, Aquinas concludes, all systematic scientific knowledge is good.[17]

Aquinas remarks that Saint Augustine, in a sort of appendix of corrections to much of his work titled *Retractions,* observed that "more things are sought than found, and of the things that are found, fewer still are confirmed." This, for Augustine, was a statement of limits. Aquinas, quoting from another work by the prolific Augustine, remarked that the author of the *Confessions* had warned that allowing our curiosity to inquire about everything in the world might result in the sin of pride and thereby contaminate the authentic pursuit of truth. "So great a pride is thus begotten," Augustine had written, "that one would think they dwelt in the very heavens about which they argue."[18] Dante, knowing himself guilty of the sin of pride (the sin for which, he is told, he will return to Purgatory after his death), may have had this passage in mind when visiting the heavens in *Paradiso.*

Aquinas took Augustine's concern farther, arguing that pride is only the first of four possible perversions of human curiosity. The second entails the pursuit of lesser matters, such as reading popular literature or studying with unworthy teachers.[19] The third occurs when we study the things of this world without reference to the Creator. The fourth and last, when we study what is beyond the limits of our individual intelligence. Aquinas condemns these species of curiosity only because they distract from the greater, fuller impulse of natural exploration. In this, he echoes Bernard of Clairvaux, who a century earlier had written: "There are people who want to know solely for the sake of knowing, and that is scandalous curiosity." Four centuries before Clairvaux, Alcuin of York, more generously, defined curiosity in these terms: "As regards wisdom, you love it for the sake of God, for the sake of purity of soul, for the sake of knowing truth, and even for its own sake."[20]

Like a reverse law of gravity, curiosity causes our experience of the world and of ourselves to increase with the asking: curiosity helps us grow. For Dante, following Aquinas, following Aristotle, what draws us on is a desire for the good or the apparent good, that is to say, towards what we know is good or appears to us to be good. Something in our capacity to imagine reveals to us that something is good, and something in our ability to question propels us towards that something through an intuition of its usefulness or danger. In other cases, we aim towards that ineffable good simply because we don't understand something and demand a reason for it, as we demand a reason for everything in this unreasonable universe. (In my own case, these experiences come often through reading—for instance, wondering with Dr. Watson about the meaning of a candle burning in the moors on a pitch-dark night, or asking with the Master why one of Sir Henry Baskerville's new boots was stolen from the Northumberland Hotel.)

As in an archetypal mystery, achieving the good is always an ongoing search, because the satisfaction of one answer merely leads to asking another question, and so on into infinity. For the believer, the good is equivalent to the godhead: saints reach it when they no longer seek anything. In Hinduism, Jainism, Buddhism, and Sikhism, this is the state of *moksha,* or nirvana, of "being blown out" (like a candle) and it refers, in the Buddhist context, to the imperturbable stillness of mind after the fires of desire, aversion, and delusion have been extinguished, the achievement of ineffable beatitude. In Dante, as the great nineteenth-century critic Bruno Nardi defined it, this "end of the quest" is "the state of tranquility in which desire has subsided," that is to say, "the perfect accord of human will with divine will."[21] Desire for knowledge, or natural curiosity, is the inquisitive force that impels Dante from within, just as Virgil and, later, Beatrice are the inquisitive forces that lead him onwards from without. Dante allows himself to be led, inside and out, until he no longer requires any of them—not the intimate desire or the illustrious poet or the blessed beloved—as he stands confronted at long last with the supreme divine vision before which imagination and words fall short, as he tells us in the *Commedia*'s famous ending:

To the high fantasy here all power failed;
But already my desire and my will were turned
Just like a wheel in even measure turned
By love that moves the sun and the other stars.[22]

Common readers (unlike historians) care little for the strictures of official chronology, and find sequences and dialogues across the ages and cultural borders. Four centuries after Dante's high peregrinations, in the British
isles a very curious Scotsman imagined a system, "plan'd before [he] was one
and twenty, & compos'd before twenty five," that would allow him to set out
in writing questions that arose from his brief experience of the world.[23] He
called his book *A Treatise of Human Nature.*

David Hume was born in Edinburgh in 1711 and died in 1776. He studied
at Edinburgh University, where he discovered the "new Scene of Thought"
of Isaac Newton and an "experimental Method of Reasoning into Moral
Subjects" by which truth might be established. Though his family wished
him to follow the career of law, he found "an insurmountable Aversion to
every thing but the pursuits of Philosophy and general Learning; and while
they fancyed I was pouring over Voet and Vinnius, Cicero and Virgil were
the Authors which I was secretly devouring."[24]

When the *Treatise* was published in 1739, the reviews were mostly hostile.
"Never literary Attempt was more unfortunate than my Treatise of human
Nature," he recalled decades later. "It fell dead-born from the Press, without
reaching such distinction as even to excite a Murmur among the Zealots."[25]

The *Treatise of Human Nature* is an extraordinary profession of faith in
the capacity of the rational mind to make sense of the world: Isaiah Berlin,
in 1956, would say of its author that "no man has influenced the history of
philosophy to a deeper and more disturbing degree." Decrying that in philosophical disputes "'tis not reason, which carries the prize, but eloquence,"
Hume eloquently proceeded to interrogate the assertions of metaphysicians
and theologians, and to inquire as to the meaning of curiosity itself. Prior to
experience, Hume argued, anything may be the cause of anything: it is experience and not the abstractions of reason which helps us understand life.
Hume's apparent skepticism, however, does not reject all possibility of knowl-

edge: "Nature is too strong for the stupor attendant on the total suspension of belief."[26] The experience of the natural world, according to Hume, must direct, mold and ground all our inquiries.

At the end of the second book of his *Treatise,* Hume attempted to distinguish between love of knowledge and natural curiosity. The latter, Hume wrote, derived from "a quite different principle." Bright ideas enliven the senses and provoke more or less the same sensation of pleasure as "a moderate passion." But doubt causes "a variation of thought," transporting us suddenly from one idea to another. This, Hume concluded, "must of consequence be the occasion of pain." Perhaps unwittingly echoing the previously quoted passage of Ecclesiasticus, Hume insisted that not every fact elicits our curiosity, but occasionally one will become sufficiently important, "if the idea strikes on us with such force, and concerns us so nearly, as to give us an uneasiness in its instability and inconstancy." Aquinas, whose concept of causality raised serious objections in Hume regarding its cogency, had made the same distinction when he had said that "studiousness is directly, not about knowledge itself, but about the desire and study in the pursuit of knowledge."[27]

This keenness to know the truth, this "love of truth" as Hume calls it, has in fact the same double nature that we saw defined in curiosity itself. "Truth," Hume wrote, "is of two kinds, consisting either in the discovery of the proportions of ideas, consider'd as such, or in the conformity of our ideas of objects to their real existence. 'Tis certain, that the former species of truth, is not desir'd merely as truth, and that 'tis not the justness of our conclusions, which alone gives us pleasure." Pursuit alone of the truth is, for Hume, not enough. "But beside the action of the mind, which is the principal foundation of the pleasure, there is likewise requir'd a degree of success in the attainment of the end, or the discovery of that truth we examine."[28]

Barely ten years after Hume's *Treatise,* Denis Diderot and Jean Le Rond d'Alembert began in France the publication of their *Encyclopédie.* Here, Hume's definition of curiosity, explained in terms of its outcome, was cleverly reversed: the sources of the impulse, rather than its goals, were explained as "a desire to clarify, to extend one's understanding" and "not particular to the soul itself, belonging to it from its start, independent of sense, as some persons have imagined." The author of the article, the chevalier de Jaucourt, approvingly referred in it to "certain judicious philosophers" who have defined curiosity as "an affection of the soul brought on by sensations or perceptions of objects that we know but imperfectly." That is to say, for the *encyclopédistes*, curiosity is born from the awareness of our own ignorance and prompts us to acquire, so far as possible, "a more exact and fuller knowledge of the object it represents": something like seeing the outside of a watch and wanting to know what makes it tick.[29] "How?" is in this case a form of asking "Why?"

The encyclopédistes translated what for Dante were questions of causality, dependent on divine wisdom, into questions of functionality, dependent on human experience. Hume's proposed examination of the "discovery of truth" meant, for someone like Jaucourt, understanding how things worked in practical, even mechanical terms. Dante was interested in the impulse of curiosity itself, the process of questioning that led us to an affirmation of our identity as human beings, necessarily drawn to the Supreme Good. Stemming from an awareness of our ignorance and tending towards the (wishful) reward of knowledge, curiosity in all its forms is depicted in the *Commedia* as the means of advancing from what we don't know to what we don't yet know, through a tangle of philosophical, social, physiological, and ethical obstacles, which the pilgrim has to surmount by willingly making the right choices.

One particular example in the *Commedia* richly illustrates, I believe, the complexity of this multifaceted curiosity. As Dante, led by Virgil, is about to leave the ninth ditch of the eighth circle of Hell, where the sowers of discord are punished, an unexplained curiosity draws his gaze back to the obscene spectacle of the sinners who, because of the rifts they caused during their lifetime, are now themselves slashed, beheaded, or cloven. The last spirit who speaks there to Dante is the poet Bertran de Born, holding up by the hair his severed head "like a lantern."

> Because I parted persons who were united
> I carry, alas, my own brain parted
> From its source which is this trunk of mine.[30]

At the sight, Dante weeps, but Virgil reproaches him severely, telling him that he has not grieved as they passed through other ditches of the eighth circle, and nothing warrants his increased attention here. Dante then, almost for the first time, challenges his spirit guide and says to him that had Virgil paid more attention to the cause of his curiosity, he might have allowed Dante to stay longer, because there among the crowd of sinners he thinks he has seen one of his kinsman, Geri del Bello, murdered by a member of another Florentine family and never avenged. This is why, Dante adds, he supposes that Geri turned away without saying a word to him. God's justice must not be questioned, and private revenge is contrary to the Christian doctrine of forgiveness. With this, Dante intends to justify his curiosity.

So where do Dante's tears come from? From pity for the tortured soul of Bertran or from shame at having been given a cold shoulder by Geri? Has his curiosity been prompted by the arrogance of assuming to know better than God himself what is just, by a base passion deviant of his quest for the good, by sympathy for his own unavenged blood, by nothing more than wounded pride? Boccaccio, whose intuition of the sense behind the story is often very keen, noted that the compassion Dante feels at times during the journey is not so much for the souls whose woes he hears but for himself.[31] Dante does not provide the answer.

But earlier on he had addressed the reader:

> Reader, if God allows you to profit
> From your reading, now think for yourself
> How I could keep my face dry.[32]

Virgil does not respond to Dante's challenge but leads him on to the edge of the next chasm, the last before the core of Hell, where falsifiers are punished with an affliction similar to dropsy: fluid accumulates in their cavities and tissues, and they suffer from a burning thirst. The body of one of the sinners, the coin forger Master Adam, is "shaped like a lute," in a grotesque parody of Christ's crucifixion, which, in medieval iconography, was compared to a stringed instrument.[33] Another sinner, burning with fever, is the Greek Sinon, who in the second book of the *Aeneid,* allows himself to be captured by the Trojans and then persuades them to take in the Trojan Horse. Sinon, perhaps taking offense at being named, hits Master Adam in his swollen belly, and the two begin a quarrel to which Dante attends enraptured. It is then that Virgil, as if he had been waiting for an opportunity for summing up his reproof, chides him angrily:

> Just keep looking
> A little longer and it is with you that I will quarrel!

Dante is so overwhelmed with shame that Virgil excuses him and concludes: "the desire to listen to such things is a vulgar desire."[34] That is to say, fruitless. Not all curiosity leads us on.

And yet . . .

"Nature gave us an innate curiosity and, aware of its own art and beauty, created us in order to be the audience of the wonderful spectacle of the world; because it would have toiled in vain, if things so great, so brilliant, so delicately traced, so splendid and variously beautiful, were displayed to an empty house," wrote Seneca in praise of curiosity.[35]

The great quest which begins in the middle of the journey of our life and ends with the vision of a truth that cannot be put into words is fraught with endless distractions, side paths, recollections, intellectual and material obstacles, and dangerous errors, as well as with errors that, for all their appearance of falsity, are true. Concentration or distraction, asking in order to know why or in order to know how, questioning within the limits of what a society considers permissible or seeking answers outside those limits: these dichotomies, always latent in the phenomenon of curiosity, simultaneously hamper and drive forward every one of our quests. What persists, however, even when we surrender to insurmountable obstacles, and even when we fail in spite of enduring courage and best intentions, is the impulse to seek, as Dante tells us (and Hume intuited). Is this perhaps why, of all the possible modes offered to us by our language, the natural one is the interrogative?

2

What Do We Want to Know?

MOST OF MY CHILDHOOD IN TEL AVIV was spent in silence: I hardly ever asked questions. Not that I wasn't curious. Of course I wanted to find out what was kept locked away in my governess's pyrographed box next to her bed or who lived in the curtained trailers stranded on the beach of Herzliya, where I was sternly warned never to wander. My governess would respond to any questions carefully, after what seemed to me unnecessarily long consideration, and her answers were always short, factual, disallowing argument or discussion. When I wanted to know how the sand was made, her answer was "of shells and stones." When I sought out information on the dreadful Erlkönig of Goethe's poem, which I had to learn by heart, the explanation was "It's only a nightmare." (Because the German word for nightmare is *Alpentraum,* I imagined that bad dreams could take place only in the mountains.) When I wondered why it was so dark at night and so light during the day, she drew a series of dotted circles on a piece of paper, meant to represent the solar system, and then made me memorize the names of the planets. She never refused to answer and she never encouraged questioning.

It wasn't until much later that I discovered that questioning might be

(Opposite) Dante and Virgil meet the evil counselors punished by fire. Woodcut illustrating Canto XXVI of the Purgatorio, *printed in 1487 with commentary by Cristoforo Landino. (Beinecke Rare Book and Manuscript Library, Yale University)*

something else, akin to the thrill of a quest, the promise of something that shaped itself in the making, a progression of explorations that grew in a mutual exchange between two people and did not require a conclusion. It is impossible to stress the importance of having the freedom of such inquiries. To a child, they are as essential to the mind as movement is to the physical body. In the seventeenth century Jean-Jacques Rousseau argued that a school had to be a space where the imagination and reflection were given free range, without any obvious practical purpose or utilitarian goal. "The civil man is born, lives, and dies in slavery," he wrote. "At his birth he is sewn into swaddling clothes; at his death he is nailed into a coffin. As long as he retains a human form, he is chained up by our institutions." It is not by training our children to go into whatever trade society requires, Rousseau insisted, that they will become efficient in their tasks. They have to be able to imagine with no constraints before they can bring anything truly valuable into being.

One day, a new history teacher began his class by asking us what we wanted to know. Did he mean what *we* wanted to know? Yes. About what? About anything, any notion that occurred to us, anything we wished to ask. After a startled silence, someone lifted his hand and posed a question. I don't remember what it was (a distance of more than half a century separates me from that brave inquisitor), but I do remember that the teacher's first words were less an answer than the hint of another question. Maybe we began by wanting to know what made a motor run; we ended by wondering how Hannibal had managed to cross the Alps, what gave him the idea of using vinegar to split the frozen rocks, what an elephant might have felt falling to its death in the snow. That night each of us dreamt his own secret Alpentraum.

Ulysses: Know the whole world.

—SHAKESPEARE, *Troilus and Cressida*, 2.3.246

The interrogative mode carries with it the expectation, not always ful-filled, of an answer: however uncertain, it is the prime instrument of curiosity. The tension between the curiosity that leads to discov-ery and the curiosity that leads to perdition threads its way throughout all our endeavors. The temptation of the horizon is always present, and even if, as the ancients believed, after the world's end a traveler would fall into the abyss, we do not abstain from exploration, as Ulysses tells Dante in the *Commedia*.

In the twenty-sixth canto of the *Inferno,* after having crossed the dread-ful snake-infested sands where thieves are punished, Dante arrives at the eighth chasm, where he sees "as many fireflies as the peasant, resting on a hilltop, sees": they are souls who are punished here, eternally consumed in whirling tongues of fire. Curious to know what one particular flame is "that comes so parted at the top," Dante learns that these are the entwined souls of Ulysses and his companion Diomedes (who, according to post-Homeric legend, had helped Ulysses steal the Palladium, the sacred image of Athena on which the fortunes of Troy depended). Dante is so attracted to the horned flame that his body leans involuntarily towards it and he asks Virgil's permission to address the fiery presence. Virgil, realizing that, as Greeks, the ardent spirits may disdain to speak to a mere Florentine, speaks to the flame as a poet who "when on earth wrote lofty verses" and begs that one of the two souls will tell where they met their end. The larger tongue of the flame responds and re-veals itself as Ulysses, whose words, legend has it, could bend the will of his listeners. Then the epic hero whose adventures were the source of Virgil's *Aeneid* (Ulysses left the sorceress Circe at the island of Gaeta, he says, "before Aeneas gave that place its name") speaks to the poet he inspired. In Dante's universe, creators and creations construct their own chronologies.[1]

The character of Ulysses can be seen in the *Commedia* partly as the incarnation of forbidden curiosity, but he begins life on our shelves (though he may be older than his stories) as Homer's ingenious and persecuted King Odysseus. Then, through a series of complex reincarnations, he becomes a cruel commander, a faithful husband, a lying con man, a humanist hero, a resourceful adventurer, a dangerous magician, a ruffian, a trickster, a man in search of his identity, Joyce's pathetic Everyman. Dante's version of the Ulysses story, which is now part of the myth, concerns a man not satisfied with the extraordinary life he has led: he wants more. Unlike Faust, who despairs at how little his books have taught him and feels he has at last reached the limits of his library, Ulysses longs for that which lies beyond the end of the known world. After being freed from Circe's island and Circe's lust, Ulysses senses that there is in him something stronger than his love for his abandoned son, his aged father, his faithful wife back in Ithaca: an *ardore*, or "ardent passion," to gain further experience of the world, and of human vices and virtues. In the course of only fifty-two luminous lines, Ulysses will try to explain the reasons that drove him to undertake his last journey: the desire to go beyond the signposts Hercules set up to signal the limits of the known world and warn humans against sailing farther, the will not to deny himself the experience of the unpeopled world behind the sun, and finally, the longing to pursue virtue and wisdom—or, as Tennyson put it in his version, "to follow knowledge like a sinking star, / Beyond the utmost bound of human thought."[2]

The columns that signal the limits of the knowable world are also, as all professed limits, a challenge to the adventurer. Three centuries after the *Commedia* was completed, Torquato Tasso, a devoted reader of Dante, in his *Gerusalemme liberata* had the goddess Fortune lead the comrades of the unfortunate Rinaldo (who must be rescued before Jerusalem can be reconquered) along Ulysses' path up to the Pillars of Hercules. There an infinite sea stretches out beyond, and one of the comrades asks whether anyone has dared cross it. Fortune answers that Hercules himself, not daring to venture out onto the unknown main, "set up narrow limits to contain all daring inventiveness." But these, she says, "were scorned by Ulysses, / full of longing to see and know." After retelling Dante's version of the hero's end, Fortune adds that "time will come when the vile markings / will become illustrious for the sailor / and the recalled seas, kingdoms, and shores / that you ignore will too be famous."[3] Tasso read in Dante's account of the transgression both the marking of limits and a promise of adventurous fulfillment.

The twinning of the curiosity that leads to travel and the curiosity that seeks recondite knowledge is an enduring notion, from the *Odyssey* to the Grand Tours of the eighteenth and nineteenth centuries. The fourteenth-century scholar known as Ibn Khaldun, in his *Al-Muqaddima,* or *Discourse on the History of the World,* noted that travel was an absolute necessity for learning and for the molding of the mind because it allowed the student to meet great teachers and scientific authorities. Ibn Khaldun quoted the Qur'an: "He guides whom He will to the right path," and insisted that the road to knowledge depended not on the technical vocabulary attached to it by scholars but on the inquisitive spirit of the searcher. Learning from various teachers in different places of the world, the student would realize that things are not what any particular language names them. "This will allow him not to confuse science and the vocabulary of science" and help him understand that "a certain terminology is nothing more than a means, a method."[4]

Ulysses' knowledge is rooted in his language and in his rhetorical ability: the language and the rhetoric bestowed upon him by his creators, from Homer to Dante and Shakespeare, from Joyce to Derek Walcott. Traditionally, it was through this gift of language that Ulysses sinned, first by inducing Achilles, who had been secreted at the court of the king of Scyros to escape the Trojan War, to join the Greek forces, which led to the death from a broken heart of the king's daughter Deidamia, who had fallen in love with him; second, by counseling the Greeks to build the wooden horse by means of which Troy was stormed. Troy, in the Latin imagination inherited by the European Middle Ages, was the effective cradle of Rome, since it was the Trojan Aeneas who, escaping the conquered city, founded what was to become, many centuries later, the core of the Christian world. Ulysses, in Christian thought, is like Adam, guilty of a sin that entails the loss of a "good place" and, consequently, the means of the redemption brought on by the commission of that sin. Without the loss of Eden, Christ's Passion would not have been necessary. Without Ulysses' evil counsel, Troy would not have fallen and Rome would not have been born.

But the sin for which Ulysses and Diomedes are punished is not clearly

What Do We Want to Know?

stated in the *Commedia*. In the eleventh canto of the *Inferno*, Virgil takes time to explain to Dante the nature and place of each sin of fraud punished in Hell, but after locating hypocrites, flatterers, necromancers, cheaters, thieves, simonists, panders, and barrators in their proper places, he dismisses the sinners of the eighth and ninth chasms as simply "the same kind of filth." Later on, in the twenty-sixth canto, describing to Dante the faults committed by Ulysses and Diomedes, Virgil lists three: the trick of the Trojan Horse, the abandonment of Deidamia, and the theft of the Palladium. But none of these leads precisely to the nature of the fault punished in this particular chasm. The Dante scholar Leah Schwebel has provided a useful summary of the "slew of prospective crimes for the fallen hero, running the gamut from original sin to pagan hubris" imagined by successive readers of the *Commedia*, and concludes that none of these plausible interpretations is ultimately satisfactory.[5] And yet if we consider Ulysses' sin as one of curiosity, Dante's vision of the wily adventurer may become a little clearer.

As a poet, Dante must construct out of words the character of Ulysses and the account of his adventures, as well as the multilayered context in which the king of Ithaca tells his story, but he must also, at the same time, refuse his ardent storyteller the possibility of reaching the desired good. Travel is not enough, words are not enough: Ulysses must fail because, driven by his all-consuming curiosity, he has confused his vocabulary with his science.

Because Dante the craftsman has to submit to the adamantine structures of the Christian Otherworld as a framework for his poem, Ulysses' place in Hell might be largely defined as that of a soul who is guilty of spiritual theft: he has used his intellectual gifts to deceive others. But what has fueled this trickster impulse? Like Socrates, Ulysses equates virtue and knowledge, thereby creating the rhetorical illusion that knowing a virtue is the same as possessing that virtue.[6] But it is not in the exposition of this intellectual sin that Dante's interest lies. Instead, what he wants Ulysses to tell him is what drove him, after all the obstacles Neptune set up on the return voyage from Troy, to sail not home to his bed and hearth but onwards into the unknown.[7] Dante wants to know what made Ulysses curious. To explore this question, he tells a story.

What Do We Want to Know?

Throughout our convoluted histories, stories have had a way of reappearing under different forms and guises; we can never be certain of when a story was told for the first time, only that it will be not the last. Before the first chronicle of travel there must have been an *Odyssey* of which we now know nothing, and before the first account of war, an *Iliad* must have been sung by a poet who is for us even fainter than Homer. Since imagination is, as we have noted, the means by which our species survives in the world, and since we were all born, for better or for worse, with Ulysses' "ardore," and since stories are, from the very first campfire evenings on, our way of using imagination to feed this ardore, no story can be truly original or unique. All stories have a quality of *déjà lu* about them. The art of stories, which seems not to have an end, in fact has no beginning. Because there is no first story, stories grant us a sort of retrospective immortality.

We make up stories in order to give a shape to our questions; we read or listen to stories in order to understand what it is that we want to know. On either side of the page, we are driven by the same questioning impulse, asking who did what, and why, and how, so that we can in turn ask ourselves what it is that we do, and how and why we do it, and what will happen when something is done or not done. In this sense, all stories are mirrors of what we believe we don't yet know. A story, if it is good, elicits in its audience both the desire to know what happens next and the conflicting desire that the story never end: this double bind justifies our storytelling impulse and keeps our curiosity alive.

In spite of being aware of this, we are more concerned with beginnings than with endings. Endings we take for granted; we even sometimes wish for them to be eternally postponed. Endings tend to comfort us: they allow us the pretense of conclusion, which is why we require memento mori—to remind us of the need to be conscious of our own end. Beginnings trouble us daily. We want to know where and how things start, we seek wisdom in etymologies, we like being present at the birth, perhaps because we feel that what comes first into this world justifies or explains what comes afterwards. And we dream up stories to give us starting-points towards which we can look back and feel a little more secure, however difficult and questionable the process.

What Do We Want to Know?

Dreaming up endings, instead, has always seemed easier. "The good ended happily, and the bad unhappily," Miss Prism tells us in *The Importance of Being Earnest*. "That is what Fiction means."[8]

The fiction of beginnings is a complex invention. For example, in spite of the countless narrative possibilities offered at the start of the Bible, it is other, more explicit stories that provide the religions of the book with a beginning. Two narratives of creation follow each other in the first pages of Genesis. One tells that "God created man in his own image, in the image of God created he him; male and female created he them" (1:27). The second, how God, in order to provide Adam with "an help meet," made him fall into a deep slumber, took out one of his ribs, and from this "made he a woman" (2:18, 21–25). Implicit in the divine creative act is the subservient function of women. Countless biblical commentators explain that this is the reason why a woman, as an inferior being, must obey a man; fortunately, a number of others reinterpret this patriarchal reading in a more egalitarian light.

In the first century C.E., the Jewish scholar Philo of Alexandria, curious about the double narratives of Genesis, proposed for the earliest biblical narrative a Platonic interpretation, suggesting that the first human created by God was a hermaphrodite ("male and female created he him"), and for the second a misogynistic reading in which the male half is conceived as superior to the female. Philo identified the male half (Adam) with the spirit (*nous*) and the female one (Eve) with the physical senses (*aesthesis*). Severed from Adam, as if she represented sensation severed from reason, Eve is denied, in the act of creation, Adam's primordial innocence, and thus becomes instrumental in the Fall of humankind.[9] Two centuries later, Saint Augustine, in his literal interpretation of the book of Genesis, reinstated Eve's primordial innocence by declaring that in the first narrative, Adam and Eve, still unnamed, were created with all their spiritual and physical characteristics *in potentia,* that is to say, present in a virtual state that would flower into material existence, as described in the second narrative.[10] That is what you call having your original cake and eating it too.

Scholars more or less agree that the book of Genesis was written in about the sixth century B.C.E. Some three centuries earlier, in Greece, Hesiod reported a different version of the story of female culpability. Zeus, Hesiod

Jean Cousin the Elder, *Eva Prima Pandora* (Eve as the First Pandora): an explicit conflation of Eve and Pandora in a painting by a sixteenth-century French artist. (Musée du Louvre, Paris, France. Courtesy Giraudon/ Bridgeman Images.)

tells us, furious at Prometheus for having robbed the gods of the Olympian fire and given it to humankind, decided to avenge himself by sending down to earth a beautiful maiden, crafted by Hephaestus, dressed by Athena, adorned with gold necklaces by Peitho and with garlands by the Horae, and with her heart filled by Hermes with lies and misleading promises. Finally, Zeus bestowed upon her the gift of speech and the name Pandora, and presented her to Prometheus's brother Epimetheus. Forgetting Prometheus's warning never to accept a gift from Olympian Zeus, Epimetheus fell in love with Pandora and took her into his household.

Until that time, humankind had lived unburdened by care and disease, all of which were kept in a covered jar. Pandora, curious to know what the jar contained, took its lid off and unleashed into the world all kinds of pain and suffering, along with the illnesses that haunt us night and day silently because Zeus deprived them of the use of their tongues. Horrified by what had happened, Pandora tried to put the lid back on, but our sufferings had all already escaped, leaving nothing but Hope at the bottom. So central is Pandora's story to our conception of the contradictions implied in our impulse of curiosity that by the sixteenth century Joachim du Bellay was able to compare Pandora to Rome itself, the archetypal Eternal City, and all it stood for, everything that was good and everything that was evil.[11]

Curiosity and punishment for curiosity: the Christian typological readings of the stories of Eve and Pandora date from as early as the second century, in the writings of Tertullian and Saint Irenaeus. According to both authors, the godhead bestowed upon humankind the gift of wanting to know more and then the punishment for trying to do so. Leaving aside for a moment their misogynistic resolutions, both stories concern the question of the limits of ambition. A certain curiosity seems permissible, too much is punished. But why?

As we have noted, Dante's Ulysses seems to have met his end as a punishment not for the fault of evil counsel but for going beyond what God has deemed a permissible curiosity. Like Adam and Eve in the Garden, Ulysses is offered the whole of the knowable world to explore: only past that horizon he must not venture. But precisely because the horizon is the world's visible and material limit, just as the Tree of the Knowledge of Good and Evil is the limit of whatever can be perceived and therefore known, the forbidden horizon and the forbidden fruit implicitly admit that something else can be achieved beyond the commonplace. This is what Robert Louis Stevenson, in the nineteenth century, confronted daily in the Presbyterian Edinburgh of his youth, where the gray facades displayed one after another the Ten Commandments, in a perseverance of *Thou Shalt Nots* that Stevenson was later to call "the law of negatives": that is to say, the pleasurable temptations offered, as in a dark mirror, even to those who have not yet conceived them.[12]

To Ulysses' fateful curiosity, Dante counterpoises that of Jason, captain of the Argonauts, who set off with his companions to collect the Golden Fleece and returned home victorious with his booty. As Dante is approaching the end of his journey in Paradise, when he finally sees the ineffable form of the entire universe, he compares his astonished vision to that of the god Neptune seeing the shadow of Jason's ship gliding by, the first human craft to sail the god's desolate waters.[13] This comparison grants Dante the blessing of a quest that has been allowed and is therefore meritorious, as opposed to the damned quest of the unfortunate Ulysses in search of the forbidden unknown.

Ulysses' quest is physical, material, overly ambitious; the brave words that Tennyson puts in his mouth in his inspired translation of the passage—"to strive, to seek, to find, and not to yield"—are partly wishful thinking. Striving and seeking, as we know all too well, do not always lead to finding, and yielding, in certain cases, may not be offered as a choice. Dante's quest is spiritual, metaphysical, humble. For both men, curiosity is the essential attribute of their human nature: it defines what it is to be human. But while for Ulysses this "to be" means "to be in space," for Dante it means "to be in time" (a distinction that the Italian language conveys much more clearly than the English, with *stare* for being in a certain place and *essere* for existing). Three centuries later, Hamlet tries to solve the problem by blending both in his famous question.

As both Eve and Pandora knew, curiosity is the art of asking questions. What is the knowledge of good and evil? What is my role in the Garden? What lies inside the sealed jar? What am I allowed to know? What am I not allowed to know? And why? And by what or whom? To understand what we are asking, we disguise our curiosity as narratives that put the questions into words and open them to further questions. Literature is in this sense an ongoing dialogue that resembles the Talmudic form of argument known as *pilpul,* a dialectical method for reaching knowledge through ever keener questions (though it is sometimes used merely as a hair-splitting debating exercise). So essential is the art of questioning that in the eighteenth century Rabbi Nahman of Bratslav was able to say that a man who has no questions about God does not believe in God at all.[14]

In a very concrete sense, writing stories, collecting stories, setting up libraries of stories are activities that give roots to the nomadic impulse of curiosity: as mentioned earlier, the curiosity of a reader who seeks knowledge of "what happened" and the curiosity of a traveler are intimately intertwined. Ulysses' quest leads him physically into a maelstrom that swirls his ship around three times and then closes the sea over the crew; Dante's leads him poetically to the final point of coherence.

What Do We Want to Know?

> There in its depths I saw
> gathered with love in a single volume
> the leaves that through the universe have been scattered.[15]

Dante's vision, in spite (or because) of its immensity, prevents him from translating that volume into comprehensible words; he sees it but he cannot read it. Assembling books we mirror Dante's gesture, but because no single human book can fully translate the universe, our quests resemble Ulysses' quest, where the intention counts more than the result. Every one of our achievements opens up new doubts and tempts us with new quests, condemning us for ever to a state of inquiring and exhilarating unease. This is curiosity's inherent paradox.

The late Renaissance materialized this paradox in what could be called "curiosity machines." In printed texts, in charts, in intricate drawings, even in three-dimensional construction kits, these extraordinary mnemonic and didactic devices were designed to reward the questioner's curiosity by means of a mechanical system of associations and information retrieval.

The Renaissance machines, tangible incarnations of our belief that the meaning of things lies within our reach, adopted a variety of ingenious forms. They were either intricate versions of our Excel charts, designed like family trees of many branches, or constructed as wheels that moved one inside the other to elicit couplings between the concepts written on their margins. Sometimes they were even conceived as pieces of furniture, such as the wonderful wheel of books designed by Agostino Ramelli in 1588, meant to stand next to the reader's desk like a three-dimensional version of Windows.[16]

Each of these machines works differently. A labyrinthine machine such as that depicted in Orazio Toscanella's *Armonia di tutti i principali retori* (Harmony of all Main Rhetoricians) was designed to help structure rhetorical arguments stemming from any given premise.[17] The procedure is anything but simple. The initial idea is reduced to a single proposition, which is then divided into subject and predicate. Each of these can then be boxed into one of a number of categories inscribed on one of four wheels of Toscanella's machine. The first wheel is dedicated to subjects, the second to predicates, the third to relationships, the fourth to questions such as who, why, and what.

What Do We Want to Know?

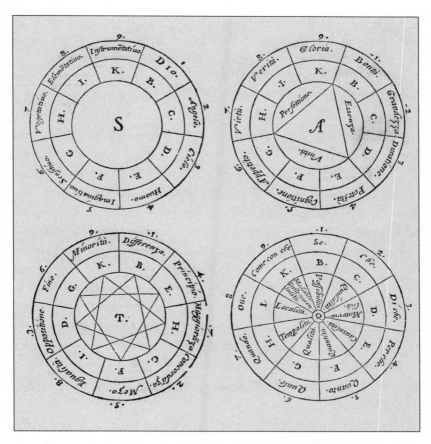

The four wheels of Orazio Toscanella's memory machine, from his
Armonia di tutti i principali retori (Venice, 1569). (*B 6.24 Th.Seld.,*
Sig. I2 recto, Sig. K2 recto, Sig. K3 recto, and Sig. K4 recto.
Courtesy The Bodleian Libraries, The University of Oxford.)

Every point of each wheel can be (or become) the starting place of a new
quest, the beginning of an extraordinary web of connecting thoughts, considerations, musings, inquiries, and illuminations.

These machines are too complex for a nonscholar such as myself to describe accurately; I am not at all sure that, even if I understood the rules better, I would be able to use one effectively. What is obvious, however, is that these machines were concrete representations of the methods of curiosity,

What Do We Want to Know?

and even when supposedly allowing their users to reach the desired conclusion, they continuously suggested different pathways for new explorations. If prehistoric language appeared to humans as aural hallucinations, these machines allowed for voluntary hallucinations, the conjuring up of things projected into the future or recalled from the past. Beyond their use as how-to manuals and cataloguing tools, these machines promised to help the user think. One of their inventors, Ludovico Castelvetro, defined his art as "the science of asking why."[18]

Machines such as Toscanella's are a material representation of Dante's and Ulysses' quests and illustrate the different paths followed by the two travelers, allowing those who learned to use them to follow question after question, from thought to seemingly unconnected thought, privileging the impulse of curiosity over the conscious need to ask. Dante himself, on the beach of Mount Purgatory, compares this impulse to "people who reflect on the path to take / who set forth with the heart, and with the body stand still."[19] Carlo Ossola, in his illuminating reading of the *Commedia,* notes that to Ulysses' *curiositas* Dante opposes his own *necessitas* to act.[20] Ulysses' curiosity is the shadow of Dante's and leads to his tragic death; Dante's necessary quest ends as all comedies end—that is to say, with a happy and successful achievement. But it is an achievement that, as Dante repeatedly tells us, cannot be told in human language.

Much of the otherworldly voyage, many of the terrors and the marvels, even Dante's own wavering undertakings, are expressed in the clearest possible verse, but the actual final vision is ineffable, beyond the scope of human art, partly because he is describing his movement towards the Aristotelian primordial good, and "each thing that moves is in some respect lacking and does not possess its whole being at one time," as Dante noted in one of his epistles. This is the "other path" already mentioned that Virgil recommends when he first addresses Dante, whose first-chosen road is blocked by the three wild beasts at the edge of the dark forest, the "fated path" that Virgil orders Minos not to hinder when the two travelers reach the edge of the second circle of Hell. This is also the "other way" announced to the three Magi in Matthew 2:12 in the dream that leads them away from Herod and towards the birth of their Saviour.[21]

What Do We Want to Know?

The Stoics saw Ulysses' curiosity as exemplary. Seneca, in the early years of the first century C.E., praised the figure of Ulysses for teaching us "how to love fatherland, wife, father, how to navigate to those honourable things even in the midst of storms," but declared himself uninterested in the details of his wanderings, "whether Ulysses was tossed about between Italy and Sicily or beyond the known world." Earlier, Heraclitus, for whom Ulysses' long journey is nothing more than "a vast allegory," argued that Ulysses' "wise decision" to descend into Hades proved that his curiosity "would not leave any place unexplored, not even the depths of Hell." Several decades later, Dio Chrysostom praised Ulysses (pairing him with the sophist Hippias) for being just what a philosopher must be, "exceptional in everything under any circumstances." Dio's contemporary, Epictetus, compared Ulysses to a traveler who does not allow himself to be distracted by the beautiful inns he may find on his way; confronted with the Sirens' song, he leaves his ears unplugged so as to hear them, but at the same time sails on, to pursue his quest successfully. This is Epictetus's advice to all curious travelers.[22]

For Dante, Ulysses' enterprise ends not in success but in disaster. Ulysses' voyage is a tragedy. If by success we mean the full achievement of our endeavors, then failure is an integral part of Ulysses' attempt, as it is an integral part of Dante's all-apprehending poetic project, in that his final vision cannot be put into words. Such failures are, in fact, an integral part of every artistic and scientific enterprise. Art advances through defeat, and science learns mostly from mistakes. What we don't achieve maps our ambitions as much as what we do, and the Tower of Babel stands unfinished, less as a memorial of our shortcomings than as a monument to our exultant chutzpah.

As Dante certainly knew, no human quest is exclusively one or the other, none of our endeavors follows exclusively the adventures of Ulysses or those of Dante. Every investigation, every inquiry, every exploration is choked with an undergrowth of questions—moral, ethical, practical, whimsical— through which we advance and from which we cannot disentangle ourselves. Some progress, of course, is made but always accompanied by swarms of doubts and irresolution, when not by a feeling of guilt and transgression that results in the designation of a scapegoat: Eve and Pandora, the village witch and the heretical thinker, the inquisitive Jew and the nonconformist homosexual, the alienating outsider and the unorthodox explorer. Imaginative researchers in biology and chemistry, brave scholars in unofficial histories, illuminating critics of art and literature, revolutionary writers and composers and visual artists, lucid scientists in every field, even as they seek a truth comparable to the one Dante sought, face again and again the dangers that awaited Ulysses on his final journey. This is how our thinking evolves: trying to see at each turn not only the possible answers to our questions—in other words, the questions that will be conjured up next in our quest—but also the aleatory, sometimes tragic consequences of treading unexplored landscapes.

The question of how to find cures for deadly illnesses elicits the question of how to feed an ever-increasing and aging population; the question of how to develop and protect an egalitarian society elicits the question of how to prevent demagogy and the seduction of fascism; the question of how to create jobs to develop the economy elicits the question of how the creation of these jobs might tempt us to turn a blind eye on human rights and how it might affect the natural world around us; the question of how to develop technologies that allow us to hoard more and more information elicits the question of how to access, refine, and keep from abusing such information; the question of how to explore the unknown universe elicits the uneasy question of whether our human senses are capable of apprehending whatever it is we might discover on earth or in outer space.

Seven centuries after Dante's encounter with Ulysses, on 26 November 2011, an exploring device the size of a small car was launched from Cape Canaveral at 10:02 in the morning. After traveling over 350 million miles, it reached the planet Mars on 6 August 2012 and landed on the desolate plain of Aeolis Palus. The name of the exploratory craft was *Curiosity*, the desire for knowledge that Dante called "ardore" and that drove Ulysses to undertake his one last fatal journey.

The Martian plain chosen as the landing site of *Curiosity* bore the name of the king of the winds, Aeolus, in whose realm Ulysses stopped on his own travels. In the tenth book of the *Odyssey*, Homer tells us, after escaping from the hunger of the Cyclops, Ulysses, who called himself Nobody, which also means Everybody, reaches Aeolus's island. Here he is feasted by the king for a full month and, upon leaving, he is given a sack of oxhide in which Aeolus has bound the winds up tightly with a silver cord, allowing only Zephyr, the West Wind, to help Ulysses on his way. Zephyr, in late medieval iconography, represents the sanguine man: that is to say, the optimist, the constant searcher, someone like Ulysses himself.[23]

After nine days' travel, the crew begins to imagine that Aeolus's sack contains a treasure which Ulysses intends to keep for himself. They loosen the cord, and, in a dreadful gust, all the imprisoned winds escape, provoking a terrible storm that drives the ship back to Aeolus's island. Offended by their carelessness, the king of the winds banishes Ulysses and the crew from his realm and sends them off to sea without the smallest breeze. In the story of the beginning of a new chapter of Ulysses' journey, not a woman but a crew of curious men are to blame for the disaster.

If one cared to construct a typology between the curiosity of Ulysses' companions and the *Curiosity* vessel that landed on Mars, one could create a little cautionary tale about the dangers of discovery. But more interesting, more instructive, more rewarding perhaps, is to read the episode in the context of Homer's entire poem and Dante's illuminating sequel. In that case, the unleashing of the winds is a circumstantial disaster that takes place in mid-adventure, cautionary only in the sense that the outcome of our quests is not entirely dependent on our own actions. Rather than demeaning Ulysses' performance, the episode adds strength to his determination, his thirst for knowing more, his ardore. And if in the end (as Homer has it) Odysseus reaches Ithaca and defeats the suitors and tells Penelope his version of the story, or whether (as Dante imagines) he refuses to bring the story to an end and continues his search until he can seek no more, what matters is that Ulysses never gives up his questioning. Dante, who is ultimately given an answer too vast to comprehend except as an impoverished memory, envies, we sense, Ulysses' fatality, and though for the sake of the poem's logic Dante must condemn him, he lends Ulysses words that, spoken from the hovering flames, seem to transcend his fate and survive his condemnation.

3

How Do We Reason?

MY HIGH SCHOOL WAS THE COLEGIO NACIONAL de Buenos Aires. Among the several professors who taught me Spanish literature, I was fortunate to have, for two of the six school years, Isaias Lerner, a brilliant specialist in the Spanish Golden Age. With him we studied in painstaking detail some of the major classics: the *Lazarillo,* the poems of Garcilaso, *Don Quixote, La Celestina.* Lerner loved those texts and enjoyed reading them, and his love and enjoyment were contagious. Many of us followed the adventures of young Lazarillo with the enthusiasm we reserved for cliffhangers, the love lyrics of Garcilaso with our own saccharine daydreams, the brave endeavors of Don Quixote with a budding sense of the meaning of justice, and the dark, erotic world of *La Celestina* with the physical thrill of what the old bawd calls, cursing the devil, "the flooding of your sad, dark dungeons with light." Lerner taught us to find in literature clues to our identity.

As adolescents we are unique; as we grow older, we realize that the singular being of which we proudly speak in the first-person singular is in reality a patchwork made up of other beings that in a smaller or greater measure define us. To recognize these mirrored or learned identities is one of the con-

(Opposite) Virgil leads Dante to the Noble Castle, to which the good pagans are condemned. Woodcut illustrating Canto IV of the Inferno, *printed in 1487 with commentary by Cristoforo Landino. (Beinecke Rare Book and Manuscript Library, Yale University)*

solations of old age: to know that certain persons long turned to dust still keep on living in us, just as we will live now in someone whose existence perhaps we don't even suspect. I realize that now, in my sixty-sixth year, Lerner is one of those immortals.

When in my last year of high school, in 1966, the military authorities took charge of the university, Lerner and fifteen other professors protested the arbitrary measure and were promptly fired from their posts. His replacement, a barely literate nonentity, accused him of having taught us "Marxist theory." To be able to carry on his professional life, Lerner went into exile in the United States.

Lerner understood something essential in the art of teaching. A teacher can help students discover unknown territories, provide them with specialized information, help create for themselves an intellectual discipline, but, above all, he or she must establish for them a space of mental freedom in which they can exercise their imagination and their curiosity, a place in which they can learn to think. Simone Weil says that culture is "the formation of attention." Lerner helped us acquire that necessary attentive training.

Lerner's method was to have us read out aloud an entire book, line after line, adding his comments as he saw fit. These comments were erudite because he believed in our adolescent intelligence and our persistent curiosity; they were also funny or deeply tragic because for him reading was above all an emotional experience; they were investigations of things of a time long past because he knew that what had once been imagined seeped into whatever we imagine today; they were relevant to our world because he knew that literature always addresses its present readers.

But he would not think for us. Coming across yet another speech in which Celestina, without telling a single lie, twists and distorts the story so that whoever is following her seemingly faultless logic falls into the trap of taking her words for facts, Lerner would stop us and smile. "Gentlemen," he would ask, "do you believe what she's saying?" We were supposed to have read the book beforehand at home, and also some of the relevant criticism. We were usually scrupulous; we dared not disobey him. So one of us, with the urge adolescents have for showing off, would answer, "Well, Sir, Malkiel says . . . ," and begin to quote the opinion of one of *La Celestina's* most prestigious critics. "No, Sir," Lerner would interrupt. "I wasn't asking Dr. Malkiel, whose opinion I've read in her admirable book, as, I'm sure, as a good and faithful student, you have too. I'm asking you, Sir." And so he would force us, step by step, to tease out Celestina's reasoning, to follow the labyrinth of her arguments made up of vulgar wisdom, ancient sayings, commonplace bits of the classics, and other popular lore, woven into a web from which it was difficult to extricate oneself. The star-crossed lovers Calisto and Melibea had fallen for her tale, and so did we, savvy as we thought we were in bluffing and fibbing. That was how we learned about "lying with the truth." Later on, the concept, discovered through the wiles of a sixteenth-century bawd, would help us understand the political speeches delivered with much waving of hands by a succession of uniformed authorities from the balcony of the presidential palace. To our common stock of "Why?" and "Who?" and "When?" Lerner taught us to ask "How?"

To formulate a question is to resolve it.

—KARL MARX, *Zur Judenfrage*

Words are the means by which Dante accomplishes his voyage from the dark wood to the Empyrean along the cartography of the Otherworld (outlined in Chapters 9 and 14, below). Through his own inquisitiveness he advances along the path set out by Virgil, and through the inquisitiveness of others he is allowed the final redeeming vision. Following his itinerant inquiries we, his readers, might also learn how to ask the right questions.

After crossing the first seven heavens, Dante, led by Beatrice, enters the abode of the Fixed Stars. Here Beatrice appeals to the saints to allow Dante to drink from their table since divine grace has already granted him a foretaste of what awaits a soul that is blessed. The saints respond joyfully to her request, and out of the brightest group of stars Saint Peter appears and sings so wonderful a song that Dante can neither recall it nor transcribe it.

> But my pen leaps and I won't write it down:
> Because the images we paint, and our words,
> Are far too garish for such folds.[1]

Then Beatrice addresses Peter and says that even though he truly knows (because nothing is hidden from him) that Dante "loves well, and well hopes and believes," it would be best if Dante now spoke for himself since all citizens of the realm of Heaven must prove that they profess the true faith. And at Beatrice's insistence, Dante must submit to what is, for all effects and purposes, a school examination.

> Just as the student readies himself but doesn't speak
> Until the teacher lays out the question for him,
> To sanction it, not to conclude it,

Just so I readied myself with every argument,
While she was speaking, to be prepared
For such an examiner and such a profession.[2]

Peter proceeds to question Dante, beginning with "What is faith?" and concluding with delighted praise for Dante's answers. In fact, so satisfied is Peter with Dante's discourse that he exclaims:

If everything drawn
From doctrine down there were thus understood,
There'd be no room for the Sophist's wit.[3]

Saint Peter's examination of Dante strictly follows the recognized medieval Scholastic method that guided intellectual curiosity through clearly set-out paths for several hundreds of years. From about the twelfth century until the Renaissance, when humanism changed the traditional teaching methods in Europe, education in the Christian universities was largely Scholastic. Scholasticism (from the Latin *schola,* which originally meant a learned conversation or debate, and only later a school or place of learning) arose from an attempt to achieve knowledge concordant both with secular reason and with Christian faith. The Scholastics, such as Saint Bonaventure, considered themselves to be not innovators or original thinkers but "compilers or weavers of approved opinions."[4]

The Scholastic teaching method consisted of several steps: the *lectio,* or reading of an authoritative text in class; the *meditatio,* or exposition and explication; and the *disputationes,* or discussion of issues, rather than a critical analysis of the texts themselves. Students were expected to know the classic sources and also the approved commentaries; questions were then set for them on particular topics. From all these procedures, the "Sophist's wit" was supposed to be sternly excluded.[5]

The "Sophist's wit" was the ability to propose a false reasoning in such a way that it appeared true (the method favored by Celestina) either because it distorted the rules of logic and had only the semblance of truth or because it reached an unacceptable conclusion. The term and its pejorative meaning

How Do We Reason?

derived from Aristotle, who associated Sophists with slanderers and thieves. The Sophists, Aristotle had taught, were noxious because they labored by means of seemingly logical arguments, using subtle falsities and reaching fallacious conclusions, thus leading others into error. For example, a Sophist might try to convince a listener to concede a premise (even one totally irrelevant to the thesis) that the Sophist knew beforehand how to refute.[6]

Thanks mainly to Aristotle, Plato, and Socrates, the Sophists have rarely enjoyed a happy place in the history of philosophy. Disregarding the Platonic restrictions to the metaphysical and the Aristotelian to the empirical, the Sophists embraced both, proposing an empirical inquiry into metaphysical questions. This, according to the historian G. B. Kerford, condemned them to "a kind of half-life between Presocratics on the one hand and Plato and Aristotle on the other, [where] they seem to wander for ever like lost souls."[7]

Before Plato, the Greek term *sophistes* was a positive denomination, related to the words *sophos* and *sophia,* meaning "wise" and "wisdom," and designating a skilled craftsman or artist, such as a diviner, a poet or a musician. The legendary Seven Wise Men of Greece were called *sophistai* (in Homer's day, a *sophie* was a skill of any kind) and so were the pre-Socratic philosophers. After Plato, the term *sophistry* came to mean "a reasoning that is plausible, fallacious and dishonest," and a sophist discourse, a medley of false arguments, misleading comparisons, distorted quotations, and absurdly mixed metaphors. Paradoxically, this definition of the sophist method presupposed an understanding of a much greater question. "Plato knew he could interpret the sophist as the antipode of the philosopher," wrote Heidegger, "only if he was already acquainted with the philosopher and knew how matters stand with him." For Plato and his followers, it was easier to identify the faulty system of their perceived opponents than to define the features of their own undertaking. In the second century C.E., Lucian of Samosata described the Christians as "worshipping the crucified sophist himself and living under his laws."[8]

Medieval and early Renaissance Europe inherited the scorn and the underlying questions. When in the fifteenth and sixteenth centuries it became necessary to label the practitioners of syllogistic reasoning, pedantic rhetoric, and empty erudition in the universities and cloisters, Erasmus and his followers used *Sophists* to deride them. In Spain, the leading scholar Fray Luis de Carvajal, who first defended and then criticized Erasmus's reading of Scripture, strongly supported the position against what he called the sophistry of many Scholastics. "I, for my part, would wish to teach a theology that is neither quarrelsome nor sophist and impure but free from all contamination."[9]

Though the texts of the ancient Sophists themselves were long lost and only the caricature of their authors survived, many humanists accused the European universities of harboring inefficient teachers and mediocre scholars who were guilty of those same sophist sins that Plato and Aristotle had denounced. By the sixteenth century, François Rabelais, following the now established idea of the Sophist as a dullard, mocked the Scholastic theologians of the Sorbonne by depicting them as "sophist philosophers": drunk, dirty, and money-grabbing. His hilarious creation Master Janotus de Bragomardo delivers in macaronic French, full of Latin distortions and misquotations, a Scholastic oration for the recovery of the bells of Notre Dame, which the giant Gargantua has stolen to hang on his mare. Master Janotus belts out with sophist panache: "A Town without bells is like a blinde man without a staffe, an Asse without a crupper, and a Cow without Cymbals; therefore be assured, until you have restored them unto us, we will never leave crying after you, like a blinde man that hath lost his staffe, braying like an Asse without a crupper, and making noise like a Cow without Cymbals."[10]

It has been noted that Rabelais's refusal to submit to orthodox literary forms (his *Gargantua* is a subversive riot of mock-chronicles, pastiches, fantastic catalogues, and vicious parodies) stems from a profound sympathy for popular lore and belief—or rather increasing unbelief in a time of spiritual crisis—and a knowledge of the undergrowth above which rose the official Christian culture of universities and cloisters.[11] The social order, which in Dante's time was already crumbling, found its image in the sixteenth century as the world of topsy-turvy, where the place of everything is in its antipodes: the donkey is the teacher, the dog, the master.[12] According to the Oracle of the Bottle, which Gargantua's son Pantagruel and his companions consult in the last chapter of the fifth book, "When you come into your World, do not fail to affirm and witness, that the greatest Treasures and most admirable

How Do We Reason?

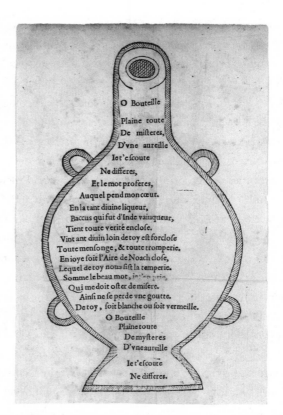

O Bouteille

Plaine toute
De misteres,
D'vne aureille
Iet'escoute
Ne differes,
Et le mot proferes,
Auquel pend mon cœur.
En la tant diuine liqueur,
Baccus qui fut d'Inde vainqueur,
Tient toute verité enclose.
Vint ant diuin loin de toy est forclose
Toute mensonge, & toute tromperie.
En ioye soit l'Aire de Noach close,
Lequel de toy nous fist la temperie.
Somme le beau mot, ie'l en prie,
Qui me doit oster de misere.
Ainsi ne se perde vne goutte,
De toy, soit blanche ou soit vermeille.
O Bouteille
Plaine toute
De mysteres
D'vne aureille
Iet'escoute
Ne differes.

François Rabelais, "La Dive Bouteille" (The Oracle of the Bottle), from *Illustrations du Cinquiesme et dernier livre des faicts et dicts héroïques du bon Pantagruel,* 1565. (Bibliothèque nationale de France.)

Things are hidden under Ground, and not without reason." "All Things Tend Towards Their End," reads an inscription on the wall of the Oracle's temple: both divine and human curiosity, Rabelais seems to be saying, are meant to be pursued to their uttermost reach. Our curiosity is to be rewarded not by looking upwards to the heavens but down to earth. "For all the Ancient Philosophers and Sages have held two things necessary, safely and pleasantly to arrive at the Knowledge of God and true Wisdom: first, God's gracious Guidance, then Man's Assistance."[13] For Rabelais, as for Dante before him, the hapless Sophists were not included among those honest seekers.

How Do We Reason?

In later centuries, there were exceptions to this accepted disparagement of the Sophists, and not all of them were minor. Hegel called the early Sophists "the masters of Greece," who instead of merely meditating on the concept of being (like the philosophers of the Eleatic school) or discoursing on the facts of nature (like the *phisiologoi* of the Ionian school) chose to become professional educators. Nietzsche defined them as men who dared efface the borders between good and evil. Gilles Deleuze praised their ideas because of the interest these awaken in us. "There is no other definition of meaning," he wrote, "but one identical to a proposition's novelty."[14] Novelty, however, was not what the Sophists were after, but rather efficiency of a kind.

Sometime in the early decades of the fifth century B.C.E., perhaps during the fragile peace with Sparta after 421, there arrived in Athens a prominent philosopher from a city-state in the northwestern corner of the Peloponnese, Elis, known for the excellence of its horses and for having organized, three centuries earlier, the first Olympic Games. The name of the philosopher was Hippias, and he was celebrated for his prodigious memory (he could retain over fifty names after a single hearing) and for being able to teach, on demand and for a considerable fee, astronomy, geometry, arithmetic, grammar, music, metrics, genealogy, mythology, history, and, of course, philosophy.[15] He is also credited with the discovery of a curve and the *quadratix,* used in attempts to square the circle, and also for the trisection of an angle.[16] Hippias was a voracious and curious reader, and compiled a sort of anthology of his favorite passages under the title *Synagoge,* "Collection." He also wrote declamations on the classical poets which he offered to recite whenever the occasion arose, poetic productions that probably dealt with lofty moral questions. We must say "probably" because of all of Hippias's extensive work, nothing has come down to us except a few quotations in the works of his critics: Plutarch, Xenophon, Philostratus, and, above all, Plato.[17]

Plato made Hippias the principal interlocutor of Socrates in two of his early dialogues, named, according to their length, *Hippias Minor* (or *Lesser Hippias*) and *Hippias Major.* In neither is the portrait of Hippias flattering. With little sympathy for the character, Plato has Socrates, somewhat tongue in cheek, seek from Hippias an answer to essential questions about justice and truth, knowing well that Hippias will be incapable of providing it. In his tentative responses, Hippias is shown as a pedant, a braggart who boasts that "I have never found any man who was my superior in anything," someone who offers to answer any conundrum put to him (as he is said to have done at the festival of all Hellas),[18] someone easily flattered and yet, at the same time, a curiously naive and trusting man. According to the classicist W. K. C. Guthrie, Hippias must have been someone "with whom it would be difficult to be angry."[19] Because he taught for money all around Greece, he was called a Sophist, a designation that referred not to a sect or a philosophical school but to a profession, that of itinerant teacher. Socrates despised the Sophists because they advertised themselves as purveyors of knowledge and virtue, two qualities that according to him were unteachable. Perhaps a few men, principally men of noble birth, could learn how to become virtuous and wise, but only on their own—and in Socrates' opinion most of humanity was hopelessly incapable of learning how to become either.

The divide between the Sophists and the followers of Socrates was largely a matter of class. Plato was an aristocrat and scorned these wandering pedagogues who set themselves up for hire in the market among the rising middle class of the nouveau riche. This class was composed of merchants and artisans whose newly acquired wealth allowed them to buy weapons and, by enrolling in the infantry, political power. Their goal was to take the place of the old nobility, and for this they needed to learn how to speak effectively in an assembly. The Sophists offered to teach them the necessary rhetorical skills in exchange for money. "The sophists," says I. F. Stone, "are treated with snobbish disdain in the pages of Plato for accepting fees. Generations of classical teachers have echoed this uncritically, though few of them could afford to teach without pay either." However, not all Sophists kept the money they were given. There were those who distributed their pay among the poorer students, and there were others who refused to teach students they deemed hopeless. But because, by and large, they agreed to teach almost anyone for cash, Xenophon argued that the Sophists stripped themselves of their intellectual freedom and became slaves to their employers.[20]

It must be said that Socrates and his followers speak in negative terms not of all Sophists, past and present, but only of the Sophists of their day. Against these contemporaries they advanced not only social and philosophical objections but also accusations of perverting the truth. Xenophon had this to say: "I'm astonished that the men called Sophists today maintain that they often lead young people to virtue, when in fact they do the contrary. . . . They render them skilled with words, but not skilled with ideas."[21]

The Sophists were also criticized because of their ostentatious posturing and contrived manners. In the second century C.E., Philostratus of Lemnos, who admired them and wrote *The Lives of the Sophists* to exalt them, argued that a true Sophist should speak only in a setting prestigious enough for his status: a temple would be acceptable, a theater as well, even an assembly or some place "proper to an imperial audience." Facial expressions and gestures should be carefully controlled. Faces should be cheerful and confident but serious, the eyes steady and keen, though this might vary according to the subject of the declamation. During moments of intensity, a Sophist might stride about, sway from side to side, slap his thigh, and toss his head with passion. A Sophist should be fastidiously clean and exquisitely perfumed; his beard should be well cared for and daintily curled, and his dress scrupulously elegant. A generation earlier, Lucian of Samosata, in his satirical *The Rhetorician's Vade Mecum,* recommends that the Sophist seek "bright colours or white for your clothes; the Tarentine stuff that lets the body show through is best; for shoes, wear either the Attic woman's shape with the open network, or else the Sicyonians that show white lining. Always have a train of attendants, and a book in your hand."[22]

Socrates, however much he believed in justice and truth, did not believe in the equality of all human beings. The Sophists (though one must be careful not to attribute the same opinions to all those grouped under the Sophist label) did. A few, such as Alcidamas, went so far as to challenge the institution of slavery—something Socrates and his disciples never did, any more than they questioned the right of a select enlightened few to govern. Hippias, instead, believed in a kind of practical cosmopolitanism, a universal solidarity that justified opposing even national laws for the sake of a better relationship with all men. One of the sources of this belief may have been the tolerance of foreign cults practiced at Delphos, which resulted in the unity of Greeks and "barbarians" in the age of Alexander, and also to the dissolution of the Greek polis that was so dear to Plato's heart.[23] For Hippias, laws preserved merely by tradition have no value because they are contradictory, allowing for unjust acts; the laws of nature, however, because they are universal, can eventually become the laws of a democratic political life. Hippias defended unwritten against written laws, and argued for the well-being of the individual through the well-being of the community. In Plato's *Republic,* where none of the existing states that are discussed is ultimately chosen as ideal, it becomes clear that Socrates (Plato's Socrates) believes in a society ruled not by democratic laws but by philosophical tyrants trained from their childhood to be "wise and good."[24]

The half-century of Plato and Hippias was also that of Pericles, who for a short, miraculous time fostered in Athens a climate of rare political and intellectual freedom, as well as an effective government administration: even the plan of erecting new buildings on the Acropolis was perhaps devised by Pericles as a way of countering growing unemployment. After Pericles, every Athenian citizen could hope to have a voice in the running of the state, as long as he possessed the gifts of rhetoric and logic. Such an ideal society attracted a variety of people from many other cities, some escaping tyranny, some seeking an outlet for their talents, others looking to ply their trade profitably and freely. Among these immigrants were the Sophists. In contrast to Athens, Sparta, with the excuse of preserving moral order and secrets of state, regularly banished resident aliens from within its walls. Athens never adopted Sparta's xenophobia, though Athenians did banish and even condemn to death those who opposed their way of life, Socrates among them.

In one of the dialogues of Plato's middle period, *Protagoras,* the Sophist of that name, a critic of Hippias and a friend of Pericles who admired the regime Pericles had instituted, tells Socrates a myth to illustrate his conception of an efficient political system. To explain how it came about that irascible humans managed to live in a peaceful society, Protagoras explains that at a time when constant bickering threatened to destroy the entire human race, Zeus sent Hermes down to earth with two gifts that would enable humans to live together in relative harmony: *aidos,* the sense of shame that a traitor might feel on the battlefield, and *dike,* a sense of justice and respect for the rights of others. Together they are the essential components of the art of politics. Hermes asked whether these gifts should be distributed only to a select few who would specialize in the arts, or whether the art of politics should be given to all. "To all" was Zeus's reply, "because cities cannot be formed if only a few posses *aidos* and *dike*." Socrates does not respond to Protagoras's story. He sarcastically dismisses the myth as "a great and fine sophist performance" and then drops the subject altogether in order to grill Protagoras on whether he believes that virtue is teachable. The question of democracy is not something that Socrates would, even for a moment, consider. And neither is the meaning of virtue, supposedly the subject of the dialogue.[25]

Just as *Protagoras* avoids a discussion of virtue itself, *Hippias Minor* is a dialogue about the definition of a truthful man that avoids a discussion of what constitutes truth. Hippias has just finished lecturing on the poets, in particular Homer. One of the listeners asks Socrates whether he has anything to say about such a magnificent speech, either in praise or to point out its errors. Socrates confesses that indeed certain questions have sprung to his mind, and with dangerous meekness he tells Hippias that he can understand why Homer calls Achilles the bravest of men and Nestor the wisest, but he can't understand why Odysseus is called the most wily. Did Homer not make Achilles wily as well? Hippias answers that no, he didn't, and quotes Homer's words proving that Achilles is a truthful man instead. "Now, Hippias," says Socrates, "I think I understand your meaning. When you say that Odysseus is wily, you clearly mean that he is false?"[26] This leads to a discussion on whether it is better to be false intentionally or unintentionally. Socrates gets Hippias to admit that a wrestler who falls purposefully is a better wrestler than one who falls because he cannot help it, and that a singer who sings false deliberately is a better singer than one who has no ear at all. The conclusion is a sophistry to outdo all sophistries:

SOCRATES: And to do injustice is to do ill, and not to do injustice is to do well?
HIPPIAS: Yes.
SOCRATES: And will not the better and abler soul, when it does wrong, do wrong voluntarily, and the bad soul involuntarily?

HIPPIAS: Clearly.

SOCRATES: And the good man is he who has the good soul, and the bad man is he who has the bad?

HIPPIAS: Yes.

SOCRATES: Then the good man will do wrong voluntarily, and the bad man involuntarily, if the good man is he who has the good soul?

HIPPIAS: Which he certainly has.

SOCRATES: Then, Hippias, he who voluntarily does wrong and disgraceful things, if there be such a man, will be the good man?

But here Hippias can no longer bring himself to follow Socrates' reasoning. Something stronger than faith in logic overcomes Hippias at last, and instead of taking the next fatal step in Socrates' tortuous argument, he refuses to submit to what he knows not only to be perfidious but what is worse, absurd. "There I cannot agree with you," says the honest sophist.[27]

"Nor can I agree with myself," is Socrates' surprising answer, "and yet that seems to be the conclusion which, as far as we can see at present, must follow from our argument. As I was saying before, I am all abroad, and being in perplexity am always changing my opinion. Now, that I or any ordinary man should wander in perplexity is not surprising, but if you wise men also wander, and we cannot come to you and rest from our wandering, the matter begins to be serious both to us and to you."[28]

Socrates' intention, to ridicule Hippias's pretensions to wisdom, is of course clear, as is his own position, that the pursuit of knowledge of what is good, true, and just is an ongoing endeavor with no absolute conclusion. But the method by which he exposes Hippias is beneath Socrates' reputed dignity. Of the two, it is Hippias who stands out in the dialogue as the stronger and more serious debater. Certainly, Socrates appears to be more wily, an Odysseus to Hippias's Achilles, thanks to whom the debate on paradox has "turned into slapstick."[29] What emerges too, and very powerfully, is that rather than Socrates demonstrating the vacuity of Hippias's teaching, Hippias ends up showing that the Socratic method of leading an interlocutor through a series of questions to the discovery of a contradiction in his affirmations can be dangerously unsound. Socrates himself recognizes this, aware as he must be of the difference between an unjust action performed justly and a just action performed unjustly.

Montaigne (quoting Erasmus) relates that Socrates' wife, upon learning the verdict of the court condemning him to drink poison, exclaimed, "Those wretched judges have condemned him to death unjustly!" To which Socrates responded, "Would you really prefer that I were *justly* condemned?"[30] But in the *Hippias Minor,* however thick Socrates lays on the irony, the unavoidable conclusion is that his arguments have led to a wrong, humanely unacceptable, conclusion. Probably this is not what Plato intended.

It is important to remember that just as the man called Hippias who has come down to us is almost entirely the interpretation of Socrates, the Socrates that we know is largely the version of Plato. "To what extent," asks George Steiner, "is the Socrates of the major dialogues a partial or largely Platonic fiction, perhaps surpassing in intellectual impact, in both tragic and comic resonance a Falstaff, a Prospero or an Ivan Karamazov?"[31] Perhaps, just as beneath the vast bulk of Falstaff we can glimpse the shadow of a different Prince Hal, and beneath the scholarly Prospero a different kind of Caliban, and even through the brutish Ivan Karamazov (the thought is very disturbing) his younger and compassionate brother Alexei, through Plato's Socrates we can discern, not the Hippias whom the inquisitive philosopher taunts and mocks, but a different, lucid, discriminating thinker, curious about the logic of curiosity.

The society set up by Pericles did not survive the Macedonian armies or, later, the Roman colonists. Nor did the philosophy of the Sophists, except in the quotations of their detractors. Their books vanished, as did most of the details of their lives, but the remaining fragments of their work, and the depictions of their characters in the works of others, reveal a thriving desire to know more in a complex constellation of ideas and discoveries, not the least of which is the refusal to follow the apparent logic of the man who called himself "the midwife of thought" up a particularly devious garden path.[32]

4

How Can We See What We Think?

UNTIL WELL INTO MY ADOLESCENCE, I was unaware of the concept of translation. I was brought up in two languages, English and German, and the passage from one to the other was not, in my childhood, an attempt to convey the same meaning from one language to another but simply another form of address, depending on whom I was speaking to. The same fairy tale by the Brothers Grimm read in my two different languages became two different fairy tales: the German version, printed in thick Gothic characters and illustrated with gloomy watercolors, told one story; the English version, in clear, large type, accompanied by black-and-white engravings, told another. Obviously they were not the same story because they looked different on the page.

Eventually, I discovered that the changing text remains in essence the same. Or, rather, that one text can acquire different identities in different tongues, a process in which every constituent part is discarded and replaced by something else: vocabulary, syntax, grammar, and music, as well as cultural, historical, and emotional characteristics. In *De vulgari eloquentia*, "On the Vernacular Tongue," a linguistic treatise written in Latin but defending the use of endemic speech, Dante lists the constituent parts of language that

(Opposite) Dante and Virgil at the Gate of Hell. Woodcut illustrating Canto III of the Inferno, *printed in 1487 with commentary by Cristoforo Landino. (Beinecke Rare Book and Manuscript Library, Yale University)*

are replaced in passing from one tongue to another: "In the first place, the musical component, in the second place, the disposition of each part in relation to the others, in the third place, the number of verses and syllables."

But how do these ever-changing identities remain a single identity? What allows me to say that different translations of Grimms' *Fairy Tales* or the *Arabian Nights* or Dante's *Commedia* are, in fact, one and the same book? An old philosophical conundrum asks whether a person whose every body part has been replaced by artificial organs and limbs remains the same person. In which of our members lies our identity? In which of a poem's elements lies the poem? This, I felt, was the core mystery: if a literary text is all the various things that allow us to call it Grimms' *Fairy Tales* or the *Arabian Nights,* what remains when every one of these things is exchanged for something else? Is translation a disguise that allows the text to converse with those outside its circle, like the peasant clothes worn by the caliph Haroun Al-Rashid that enabled him to mingle among common folk? Or is it a usurpation, like that perpetrated by the maid in the tale of Fallada, the Speaking Horse, who takes her mistress's place and undeservedly marries the prince? What degree of original identity can a translation claim?

Every form of writing is, in a sense, a translation of the words thought or spoken into a visible, concrete representation. Penning my first words in English with their rounded *n*s and *m*s, or in German, with their *N*s and *M*s sharp-tipped as waves, I became conscious that a text not only changed from one vocabulary to another, but from one materialization to a different one. When I read, in a Kipling story, of a love letter sent as a bundle of objects to be deciphered by the beloved, each object representing a word or a cluster of words, I realized that my scribbles were not the only method of bringing words into material being. Here was another one, made up of stones and flowers and such things. Were there other methods, I wondered. Did words, the representation of our thoughts, make them visibly present in yet other ways?

How Can We See What We Think?

He gave man speech, and speech created thought,
Which is the measure of the universe.

—PERCY BYSSHE SHELLEY, *Prometheus Unbound*

W hether or not a question leads us up the garden path may depend not only on the words chosen to ask it but on the appearance and presentation of those words. We have long understood the importance of the physical aspect of the text, and not only of its contents, to transmit our meanings. In the third- or fifth-century C.E. *Life of Adam and Eve* (a text included in the Apocrypha, of which there are many versions in various languages) Eve asks her son Seth to write down her story and that of his father, Adam. She says to him, "But listen to me, my child! Make tablets of stone and others of clay, and write on them all my life and your father's and all that you have heard and seen from us. If by water the Lord judge our race, the tablets of clay will be dissolved and the tablets of stone will remain; but if by fire, the tablets of stone will be broken up and the tablets of clay will be baked [hard]."[1] Every text depends on the features of its support, be it clay or stone, paper or computer screen. No text is ever exclusively virtual, independent of its material context: every text, even an electronic one, is defined by both its words and the space in which those words exist.

In the Heaven of Mars, Dante's ancestor Cacciaguida tells him of the good old days when Florence was an exemplary, decent place to live in, and in prophetic tones announces the poet's forthcoming exile. Dante, moved by the encounter, is then guided by Beatrice to the Heaven of Jupiter. The souls who greet him there begin to flock together, forming words that Dante slowly and joyfully deciphers:

> Like birds that rise above a riverbank,
> As if rejoicing all over their food,
> And form into a circle or other line,

Just so within the lights the holy creatures
Flying sang, shaping themselves
Into figures now of D, now I, now L.[2]

The souls form thirty-five letters, spelling out the words DILIGITE IUSTI-
TIAM QUI IUDICATIS TERRAM, "Love Justice, you rulers of the earth," which make
up the first line of Solomon's Book of Wisdom. Jupiter's is the heaven of the
lawgivers: the Latin word *lex,* "law," is etymologically related to Latin *lego,*
"read," and the Italian *leggere,* "to read" or "reading." The souls of the lawgivers form the "reading" of the essence of the law, that law which is the object
of human love, and an attribute of the supreme good. Later in the canto, the
closing *M* will transform itself, first into a heraldic lily, then into an eagle. The
eagle, made up of the just souls who formed the words of warning, is the symbol of imperial authority, designated to carry out divine justice. Like the bird
Simurgh in Persian legend, the eagle is all the souls, and each one of the souls
is the eagle.[3] An ancient Talmudic tradition speaks of the world as a book
that we write and in which we are written: the souls in the Heaven of Jupiter
mirror that generous notion. The manifold and singular eagle then tells
Dante that God's justice is not human justice; if we fail to understand the
justice of God's actions, the failing is ours, not God's.

The question of the relationship between the revealed word and human
language is central to the *Commedia.* Language, we know, is our most effective tool for communicating but, at the same time, an impediment to our full
understanding. Nevertheless, as Dante learns, it is necessary to go through
language in order to reach that which cannot be put into words. Visions of
the blessed souls are not enough to foretaste the final revelation: the souls
must themselves become language before Dante can be awakened to the meaning beyond it.

Twice before in the *Commedia* has language materialized into something tangible, as "speech made visible." First, when Virgil leads Dante to
the gate of Hell, depicted as a triumphal arch with an epitaph-like inscription which speaks mutely to the traveler through nine darkly colored lines
of verse:

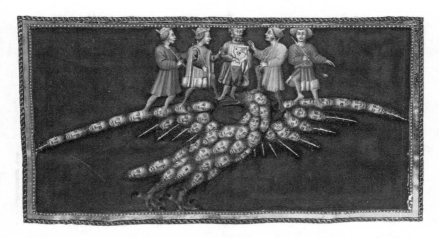

The eagle formed by the souls of the just. Fifteenth-century illumination by Giovanni di Paolo for Canto XX of the *Paradiso*. (© The British Library Board. Yates Thompson MS 36, f.164r.)

> Through me is the way into the doleful city;
> Through me is the way to eternal pain;
> Through me is the way to those who are lost.
>
> Justice moved my High Maker;
> Divine Power made me,
> Wisdom supreme and primal Love.
>
> Before me no things were created,
> Except eternal, and eternal I endure;
> Abandon all hope, you who here enter.[4]

Dante reads these words with feeling but not with understanding, and tells Virgil that he finds them "hard." Virgil advises him to leave here all distrust and faint-heartedness, because in this place he will see "wretched people who have lost the gift of intellect." Dante, Virgil says, must not become one of them. The words on the gate, fashioned from divine thought, are meant, unlike certain of God's actions, to be apprehended by human thought. And Virgil leads Dante on "into the secret things."[5] The journey commences.

The second time language materializes is when the guardian angel of Purgatory inscribes on Dante's forehead with the point of his sword the seven *P*s of the seven deadly sins (*Peccati*). These Dante himself cannot see, but as he climbs the Mount, cornice after cornice, *P* after *P* is wiped off, until he is cleansed enough to reach the summit where stands the Garden of Eden. The inscription of the *P*s and their gradual erasure are part of a necessary ritual that must be accomplished before the heavenly ascension. In front of the entrance are three steps, representing (according to some commentators) contrition of heart, confession of sins, expiation by works; beyond is the steep climb during which, the angel warns Dante, he must not look back. Echoing the warning to Lot's wife, he orders Dante not to yearn for the old sinful ways:

> Enter, but I warn you
> That he returns outside who here looks back.

The *P*s on Dante's forehead, which he himself cannot read but which he knows are there, materialize the cautionary language.[6]

All writing is the art of materializing thought. "When a word is written," wrote Saint Augustine, "it makes a sign to the eyes whereby that which is the domain of the ears enters the mind."[7] Writing belongs to a group of conjuring arts related to the visualizing and transmission of ideas, emotions, and intuitions. Painting, singing, and reading are all part of this peculiar human activity born of the capacity to imagine the world in order to experience it. On an inconceivable afternoon, a very long time ago, a remote ancestor of ours realized for the first time that he or she did not need to perform an action in order to know it; that the action performed itself in the mind and that it could be observed, explored, reflected upon in a time and space of its own making. Imagining something led to naming that something—that is to say, translating the visualized something into an equivalent of sound, so that the enunciation of the sound might conjure back the image of the thing like a witch's charm. In some societies, the sound was given in turn a material representation: markings in a handful of clay, notches in a piece of wood, designs on a polished stone, scribbles on a page. Experience of reality could now be encoded by the tongue or the hand, and decoded through the ear or the eye. Like an illusionist showing a flower in a box, then causing it to disappear, then bringing it back again in front of the public's astonished gaze, our ancestor made it possible for us to perform magic.

Readers belong to societies of the written word and, as every member of such societies must (but not all do), they try to learn the code by which their fellow citizens communicate. Not every society requires the visual encoding of its language: for many, sound is enough. The old Latin tag *scripta manent, verba volant,* which is supposed to mean "what is written endures, but what is spoken vanishes," is obviously not true in oral societies, where the meaning might be "what is written remains dead on the page, but what is said out loud has wings and flies." That is also the meaning readers discover: only when read do the written words come to life.

Two schools of thought offer competing theories of language. A detailed discussion is far beyond the scope of this book, but in general terms, nominalists have long held that only individual things are real—that is to say, things exist independent of the mind, and words cannot refer to something real unless they refer to an individual thing—while realists, though they too maintain that we live in a world that exists independent of us and our thoughts, believe that there are certain kinds of things, called "universals," that do not owe their existence to the individuals of which they are attributes, but can, like these individuals, be named with words. Language generously embraces the two beliefs and names both individuals and universals. Perhaps because in societies of the written word this faith in the syncretic power of language is less strong, its members rely instead on the materialization of the word to affirm language's life-giving power. *Verba* are not enough, they need the *scripta.*

In 1976, the psychologist Julian Jaynes suggested that when language was first developed in humans, it manifested itself in aural hallucinations: the words were generated by the right hemisphere of the brain but they were identified by the left as coming from somewhere in the world outside us. According to Jaynes when written language was invented in the third millennium B.C.E., we "heard" the written signs as voices which we perhaps attributed to communicative gods, and only in the first millennium B.C.E. did these voices become internalized.[8] The earliest readers may have experienced a hallucinatory sense of sound, so that the words read by the eyes acquired in the reading a physical presence in the ear, a second reality outside the mind that echoed or mirrored the primary reality of the written words.

Certainly the passage from spoken to written language was less an improvement in quality than a change in direction. Plato invented a myth in which the Egyptian god Thoth offered the pharaoh the gift of language, but the pharaoh explained to the god that he was obliged to refuse it because if people learned to write they would forget to remember. Plato failed to mention, because it did not suit his story, that thanks to writing speakers were now able to overcome the limitations imposed by time and space. They would not need to be present in order to deliver their speeches and, across the centuries, the dead would be able to converse with the living. Less immediate, less corporeal, less reactive than the art of speech, the art of writing simultaneously strengthened and diminished the power of the wordsmith. This, of course, is true of every contraption or tool in whatever craft we use it. G. K. Chesterton defined a chair as "an apparatus of four wooden legs for a cripple with only two."[9]

Either as the inspiration that led to the invention of writing or as its consequence, the assumption that justifies the existence of writing as an instrument of thought is one of linguistic fatalism. Just as everything in the universe can be given a name to identify it, and every name can be expressed in a sound, every sound has its representation. Nothing can be uttered that cannot be written down and read. Nothing: not even the words of God dictated to Moses, not even the songs of whales transcribed by biologists, not even the sound of silence notated by John Cage. Dante understood this law of material representation: in his Paradise, the souls of the blessed appear to him as faces emerging from a cloudy mirror and gradually take on a clear and recognizable form. In fact, like thoughts, they have no corporeality since in Heaven there is no space or time, but they kindly assume visible features, like written signs, so that Dante can be witness to the experience of the life to come. The spirits themselves don't need crutches; we do.

We know little of the aesthetics of the Otherworld, but in our own, every instrument we create, and everything created by that instrument, is ruled by both an aesthetic and a utilitarian sense. Everything: when a school in Phnom Penh was transformed by the Khmer Rouge into a so-called security prison where more than twenty thousand people were tortured and killed, the authorities decided that the color of the building was not aesthetically pleasing; the walls were therefore repainted in a soft tone of beige.[10]

Aesthetics and utility also shape the representations of language. The most ancient fragment of writing that has come down to us, dating from the fourth millennium B.C.E., is a Sumerian clay tablet from Uruk, the city of King Gilgamesh, and consists of columns of cuneiform signs punctuated by deep indentations. Our romantically inclined souls must accept that the first written texts were the handicraft not of poets but of accountants: that ancient Sumerian tablet does not hold love songs but lists the sale of grain and cattle by farmers long turned to dust. We can suppose that for its readers, such a list had both a practical aspect and a certain, perhaps unacknowledged beauty. For those of us who are incapable of deciphering the meaning, it is this second feature that prevails.

Written language, serving a variety of purposes and obeying a diversity of aesthetic norms, gradually developed almost everywhere in the world. Sumeria and Babylon, Egypt and Greece and Rome, China and India developed their own scripts, which in turn inspired those of other cultures: in Southeast Asia, in Ethiopia and Sudan, among the Inuit people. Other peoples, however, imagined different methods to lend words material visibility. In many parts of the world there is an art of writing that involves not penned or incised markings but other semantic signs: strips of bamboo in southern Sumatra, message sticks among the Australian aborigines, wreaths of twigs in the Torre Straits Islands, wampum belts among the Iroquois, wooden *lukasa* boards among the Luba people of Zaire. It follows then that there must be something equivalent to an art of typography for each of these "other" forms, each with its particular aesthetics and readability. These "typographies" may not be used in printing, but they affect and shape the conveying of meaning through words, in much the same way as a Garamond or a Bodoni affects and shapes a text written in English, Italian, or French.

In the year 1606, there appeared in Madrid a curious book titled *Comentarios reales*.[11] The title played on both meanings of the Spanish word *real,*

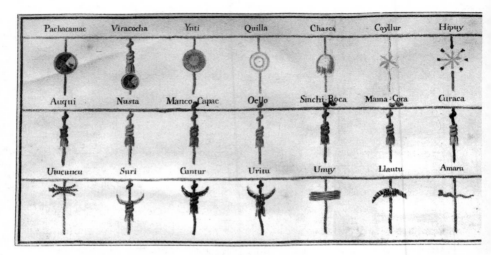

Pachacamac	Viracocha	Ynti	Quilla	Chasca	Coyllur	Hipuy
Auqui	Nusta	Manco-Capac	Oello	Sinchi-Roca	Mama-Cora	Curaca
Uucuncu	Suri	Cuntur	Uritu	Umuy	Llautu	Amaru

Phonetic translation of a *quipu*. Hand-colored illustration from [Raimondo di Sangro,] *Carta Apologetica dell' Esercitato Accademico della Crusca* (Naples, 1750). (By kind permission of Professor José Burucúa)

"royal" and "existing in reality," because these *Comentarios* purported to be the true chronicles of royal Incas of Peru. The author, born of a Spanish captain and an Inca princess, signed his book "Inca Garcilaso de la Vega," thus acknowledging both lineages. He had been brought up by Spanish tutors in his father's house in Cuzco who taught the boy Latin grammar and physical sports, but also by relatives of his mother who taught him Quechua, the language of Peru. At the age of twenty-one, he traveled to Spain, where he began his literary career translating the *Dialogues of Love* of the Spanish neoplatonist Leon Hebreo. Keen on being recognized as a true historian of the Inca culture, he titled the second part of his Inca chronicles, which appeared eleven years after the first, *Historia general del Perú*.

In the *Comentarios reales*, the Inca Garcilaso gives a detailed account of the customs, religion, and government of the Incas, as well as of their language, oral and written. One chapter describes the system of *quipu* ("knot" in the Quechua language), which served, the author tells us, essentially as a counting device. To make quipu, the Incas used threads of different colors, braided and knotted, and sometimes fixed onto a cane. Colors symbolized

How Can We See What We Think?

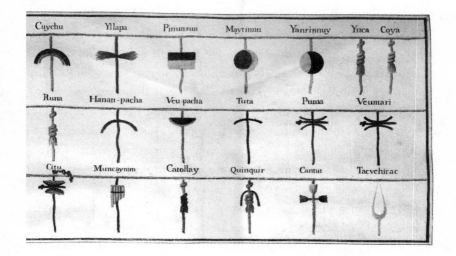

Cuychu	Yllapa	Pinunsun	Maytinnu	Yanrinnuy	Ynca	Coya
Runa	Hanan-pacha	Veu-pacha	Tuta	Puma	Veumari	
Citu	Muncaynim	Catollay	Quinquir	Cantut	Tacvchirac	

categories (yellow for gold, white for silver, red for warriors), and the knots followed the decimal system up to ten thousand. Things that could not be distinguished by their color were placed in order of value, from the most important to the least. For example, if weapons were listed, first would come the noble ones such as spears, followed by bows and arrows, clubs and axes, slingshots, and so on. The lists set down on the quipu were entrusted to a registrar or public reader called a *quipucamaya*, which means "he who looks after the accounts." To keep this power from being abused, the Incas made certain that every town, however small, had a large number of quipucamaya so that, Garcilaso tells us, "they would either all have to be corrupt or none at all."[12]

The Inca Garcilaso de la Vega died in Córdoba, Spain, in 1616, having tried to reconcile the tenets of the all-but vanished culture of his maternal ancestors with the dominant ones of his father's lineage. Almost a century later, in 1710, Raimondo di Sangro, later prince of Sansevero, was born in Torremaggiore, heir to a couple of the most prestigious families of the Kingdom of Naples. Sansevero did so many extraordinary things in the course of his sixty-year life that it is almost impossible to name them all.[13] He began his kaleidoscopic career as a military historian, composing a "Universal Dictionary of the Art of War," unfortunately left unfinished at the letter *O*. His interest in warfare led to his experimenting with gunpowder and pyrotechnics, and in this field he discovered how to achieve several hitherto unobtainable tones of green in firework displays: sea-green, bright emerald, and the color of fresh grass. These discoveries in turn allowed him to invent what he called "pyrotechnic theaters," in which the fireworks created successive scenes depicting temples, fountains, and intricate landscapes. The incandescent set designs inspired in the prince, already a voracious reader, an interest in the designing of printing and casting type; always ingenious, he invented a single-passage method for printing colored images on copper sheets that anticipated Alois Senefelder's lithography by half a century.

In 1750, Sansevero set up in his Neapolitan palazzo the first printing press in the Kingdom of Naples, with characters designed by Nicolas Kommareck and Nicolà Persico under his supervision. The ecclesiastical authorities disapproved of Sansevero's publications, notably of a book on the so-called secret sciences by the abbot Montfaucon de Villars and a defense of Livy's condemnation of superstition by the English pamphleteer John Toland. As a result, two years later, they ordered that the press be closed. To circumvent the proscription, Sansevero cunningly donated both the press and the type to His Majesty Charles III, who, on the basis of the gift, created the Royal Printing-House of Naples.

The press was not Sansevero's last enterprise. The manuscripts and foreign books he perused for possible publication led to an interest in the arts of alchemy; the alchemical experiments in the creation of life inspired him to build exquisite automata; the building of automata took him into a study of the technology of machines and the sciences of metallurgy, mineralogy, and chemistry. In 1753, an accidental fire in Sansevero's laboratory took six hours to extinguish; as a result, the prince announced that he had discovered "a lamp of perpetual or eternal light" fused by powdered human skull mixed with gunpowder.

Other casual combinations led to new and prodigious inventions: a water-resistant cloth, a tapestry not of woven but of superimposed threads that resembled an oil painting in the perfection of its detailed depictions, a linen that would not wrinkle, a paper made of vegetable silk ideal for drawing and writing, a method for cleaning copper that did not require burnishing and left no scratches, a technique for producing brass sheets thinner than any other produced until then, a procedure for making translucent porcelain and the slimmest possible crystal, a system for coloring glass without having to heat it, indelible pastel crayons that required no fixing, an artificial wax and "oleohydric" colors that resembled oil paints but needed no previous preparation of the canvas or wood. He also invented a machine for desalinizing seawater and another for making false agates and lapis lazuli, with which he tricked many a reputable jeweler. He devised a method for hardening marble which allowed sculptors to chisel it down to unheard-of thinness, so that they could now create transparent veils and delicate lacework in stone. He also built two anatomical machines, still visible in the Sansevero family crypt in Naples, that reproduced the circulatory system of a man and a woman, from the heart to the tiniest capillaries. Among his most fanciful creations were a table that laid itself for dinner without the need for servants, and a water chariot adorned with horses made of cork that could cover a fair distance through the waves of the Bay of Naples.

People began to suspect that Sansevero was assisted in his inventions by the devil himself; it was rumored that he had brewed a substance akin to blood, and also that he had been able to bring river-crabs back to life after they had been burnt to cinders in the hearth. It was said that, like Paracelsus, he could make a rose bloom again from its ashes. Neapolitans later believed that the prince had taken his own life after instructing his servants to perform a resurrection procedure which his wife, alerted to this sacrilege, had piously interrupted. The corpse had barely the time to step out of its coffin before it uttered a hideous shriek and crumbled to mortal dust.

Among the books issued from Sansevero's press in the year of its founding, 1750, perhaps the most curious one was the *Apologetic Letter,* composed by Sansevero himself, and accompanied by superb color plates. The subject of the *Letter* was the quipu system of the ancient Incas. Our investigative prince, interested as he was in everything, came to know about the quipu through the books of the Inca Garcilaso but also through a Jesuit treatise on the Inca language illustrated with several colored sketches of a variety of knots accompanied by explanations of their meanings. He also saw the real thing: an original quipu brought from the Spanish colonies. The books and the quipu had come into the hands of a Jesuit father who had been to the New World and had sold the lot to the prince in 1745.

Two years later, in 1747, a French bluestocking, Madame Françoise de Graffigny, following the vogue of epistolary novels begun with Montesquieu's *Persian Letters,* had published *Letters of a Peruvian Lady.* Graffigny's love story concerns two aristocratic Incas, Zilia and Aza, who are engaged to be married. Zilia is kidnapped by Spanish soldiers, and to let her betrothed know of her sad fate, she secretly sends him letters from prison in the form of knotted quipu, using a stock of colored threads that she always carried with her. Poor Zilia is forced to accompany her raptors back to Europe, where she continues to tie her knots, but she is unable to get them to Aza, far across the sea. In the end, her stock of threads runs out and she must learn the European art of writing in ink in order to carry on her lovesick correspondence.

Sansevero was convinced that an efficient writing system based on knots had indeed existed in the Inca Empire, but in the Europe of the Enlightenment such non-European inventions, so different from the traditional Western models, were regarded with more than skepticism. Anxious to engage in a debate on the authenticity and efficacy of the quipu, in which he believed, and unable or unwilling to find among the published detractions a propitious text, Sansevero invented a critical response to the novel of Madame Graffigny, attributing the text to a friend, the Duchess of S***. Thus armed, Sansevero proceeded to debate the nonexistent tract, ending the *Apologetic Letter* with an entreaty to the Duchess of S*** to become herself a quipucumayac, or story-weaver, and write her next book in the knotted script of the quipu.

Sansevero's entangled argumentation in his *Apologetic Letter,* full of distracted asides composed in a deliciously convoluted prose, tackles among its many subjects the universal origins of language, the invention of writing, the hidden truths of the Bible, the meaning of the mark of Cain, the ancestral custom of poets in the Inca Empire, and the detailed analysis of certain quipu texts in the author's possession, a copy of one of which had been quoted and translated in the Inca Garcilaso's book.

Sansevero began with the assumption that the quipu were readable— that is to say, that they were constructed according to a code that allowed both words and numbers to be transmitted by means of the system of colored knots. Anticipating Champollion's methods by half a century, Sansevero began by identifying in the quipu some forty key words common in the Quechua tongue, such as "vassal," "Princess," "Divine Creator," and the like, that the Quechua poets would have dictated to the weavers in charge of knotting the quipu. For these basic concepts, Sansevero believed he could identify certain underlying quipu patterns, equivalent to linguistic signs.

A couple of examples: the Quechua word for "Divine Creator" is *Pachacamac*. According to Sansevero, the core sign would have been a yellow knot symbolizing the Creator's eternal light. This central knot would contain four threads of different colors: red for fire, blue for air, brown for earth, and emerald for water. However, the same central sign could stand for the word for "sun" (*ynti* in Quechua), and though it would dispense with the four colored threads, it would include several yellow threads, knotted from the inside out.

The word for *ñandú*, a small South American flightless bird, is *suri* in Quechua: in the quipu it would be represented by the same knots as those depicting a human being, but the distance between the knots would be greater, to indicate the bird's long neck.

According to Sansevero, the Inca poets would have been able to write all other words they required by dividing them into syllables and looking for corresponding syllables in one of the basic words. Smaller knots were then made following the one for the key word, thus indicating which syllable was meant. For instance, if a word began with the syllable *su,* the knots for *suri* would be tied, followed by one smaller knot. Then, if the second syllable of the word were *mac,* the knot for *Pachacamac* would be tied, followed by four smaller knots. The resulting word is *sumac,* the first word of the poem included in the *Comentarios reales.*

On 29 February 1752, the Augustinian Domenico Giorgi entered the *Apologetic Letter* into the Catholic *Index of Prohibited Books,* branding the text as a Kabbalistic production that mocked the True Faith. Father Giorgi traced Sansevero's interpretation and defense of the quipu to the pagan hieroglyphs of Egypt, the Pythagorean numbers of the Rosicrucians and the *sephirot* of the Jews. The Kabbalists, according to Father Giorgi, maintained

How Can We See What We Think?

that God is our brother, and compared the Almighty and his Adam to knots that are bound on the same piece of string. The quipu, argued Father Giorgi, were the New World representation of this horrendous blasphemy. A year later, Sansevero published a plea in defense of his *Apologetic Letter*. His arguments proved unconvincing, and the Holy See maintained its interdiction. On 22 March 1771, Raimondo di Sangro, prince of Sansevero, died in Naples, his work unredeemed.

For a contemporary reader, Sansevero's *Apologetic Letter* remains an enigma. No doubt the variety, ingenuity, craftsmanship, and beauty of the quipu (many depicted in the superb color sheets of Sansevero's book) are extraordinary. As in traditional Western typography, the art of the quipu, while conveying the meaning of the text it contains, is above all a visual art and, like all writing, born of images.[14] Writing does not reproduce the spoken word: it renders it visible. But the code to that visibility must be shared in the society in which the artist works. "Typography," says the Canadian poet Robert Bringhurst in the introduction to his typographical handbook, "thrives as a shared concern—and there are no paths at all where there are no shared desires and directions."[15] From our distant place, we lack the clues to help us understand what those desires and directions were in the Inca Empire; we must assume that the examples of quipu that have come down to us have features that a reader in that society would have been able to identify as distinct one from the other, some graceful and some clumsy, some clear and others blurry, a few distinctly original and most conventional—if grace, clarity, and originality were qualities that an Inca reader would recognize or care about.

A number of recent scholars are of the opinion that Sansevero's proposed syllabic method for reading the quipu was inspired less by the science of linguistics than by the rebus and charades popular in the European press of the eighteenth century.[16] These scholars believe that, while highly sophisticated, the quipu was no more than a counting system and a mnemonic device such as those used in the Americas from the coast of British Columbia to the tip of the southern Andes. It is true that today, in certain parts of Peru, quipu are used exclusively for storing numerical information, but a number of Spanish documents from colonial times tell of quipucamaya who, using the knots as memory aids, could recite lengthy chronicles and poems and preserve the documentary memory of past events. In other cultures, poets have used rhyme and alliteration for a similar purpose.

In the Inca society, the quipu was also an instrument that facilitated the maintenance of order. "The wars, cruelties, pillages and tyranny of the Spaniards had been such that if these Indians had not been accustomed to order and providence, they would all have perished," wrote Pedro Cieza de Leon in 1553. "After the Spaniards had passed through," the chronicler continues, the Inca chieftains "came together with the keepers of the quipu, and if one had expended more than the others, those who had given less made up the difference, so that all were on equal footing."[17]

"Typography is to literature," says Bringhurst, "as musical performance is to composition: an essential act of interpretation, full of endless opportunities for insight or obtuseness."[18] Except that in the case of the quipu we do not know what is revealing and what is obtuse, and their reading, both aesthetic and hermeneutical, must necessarily consist largely of guesswork. Inspired guesswork, perhaps, but guesswork nevertheless.

There may, however, be a few clues to understanding something of that (to us mysterious) practical and aesthetic sense that ruled the quipu artisans of the Inca Empire. It is a fact that when the Spaniards sacked the Inca cities, the beautifully crafted gold artifacts that they collected from the royal treasuries and private homes were melted down into ingots, for an easier distribution of the loot. Today, engraved in stone over the door of the Museum of Gold in Santafé de Bogotá, the visitor can read the following verses, addressed by a native poet to his Spanish conquerors: "I am marveled by your blindness and folly, that you undo such lovely jewels and turn them into bricks and stones."

5

How Do We Question?

I HAVE ALWAYS KNOWN THAT THE words of others help me to think. Quotations (and misquotations), asides, seemingly dead ends, explorations and rummagings, retracing one's steps and leaping ahead—all seem to me valid instruments for inquiry. I sympathize both with Little Red Riding Hood's inclination to leave the set path and with Dorothy's decision to follow the Yellow Brick Road. My library, in spite of its thematic and alphabetical arrangements, is less a place of order than a benevolent chaos, like one of those magical flea markets where you find treasures that only you can recognize. Anything you need is there, but you won't know what it is until you see it. Recognition is nine-tenths of fulfillment.

Since as long as I can remember, I have believed that my library held every answer to every question. Or if not the answer, then at least a better phrasing of the question that would impel me along the path of understanding. Sometimes I will look for a specific author or book or sympathetic spirit, but often I let chance guide me: chance is an excellent librarian. Readers in the Middle Ages used Virgil's *Aeneid* as a divination tool, asking a question and opening the volume in search of revelation; Robinson Crusoe does much

(Opposite) Dante and Virgil, ascending Mount Purgatory, come across the cleansing of the proud. Woodcut illustrating Canto XII of the Purgatorio, *printed in 1487 with commentary by Cristoforo Landino. (Beinecke Rare Book and Manuscript Library, Yale University)*

the same with the Bible to find guidance in his long moments of despair. Every book can be, for the right reader, an oracle, responding on occasion even to questions unasked, as if putting words to what Joseph Brodsky called "a silent beat." The vast oracle of the Internet is less useful to me; probably because I'm a poor navigator of cyberspace, its answers are either too literal or too banal.

In my library, at the exact height of my arm's reach, are the works of Brodsky. In the early sixties, Brodsky, accused of some imaginary plot by the KGB, was condemned twice to a psychiatric asylum and later to internal exile in a prison camp in the north of Russia, where he was made to work on a state farm in temperatures of below thirty degrees Celsius. In spite of the terrible conditions, and thanks to a benevolent supervisor, he was allowed to send and receive letters, and also to write (he'd later say) "a fair amount" of poetry. Friends sent him books. Four poets became essential for him because of what he called their "uniqueness of soul": Robert Frost, Marina Tsevetaeva, Constantin Cavafy, and W. H. Auden. Auden had once said that Frost's favorite image was that of an abandoned house fallen into ruin. In a conversation with Brodsky, the critic Solomon Volkov reminded him that whereas in European poetry a ruin is usually associated with war or pillaged nature, in Frost it became "a metaphor for courage, an image of man's hopeless struggle for survival." Without reducing the image to an explanation, Brodsky agreed with Volkov's reading, but he preferred this knowledge to lie dormant, not immediately apparent. Brodsky distrusted any account of the events surrounding the creative act: the text should be allowed to speak alone, in an amorous entanglement with the reader. "Circumstances," he said, "may recur—prison, persecution, exile—but the result, in the sense of art, is unrepeatable. Dante was not the only one, after all, to be exiled from Florence."

Years later, after being himself exiled from Russia, sitting outdoors one winter in the Venice he loved, he read the mazes of the city built on water as he had read his poets in the frozen Russian north: as something "in which life speaks to man." Brodsky wrote, "The city, while words are at it, / is akin to attempts to salvage notes from a silent beat."

"O where are you going?" said reader to rider,
"That valley is fatal when furnaces burn,
Yonder's the midden whose odours will madden,
That gap is the grave where the tall return."

—W. H. AUDEN, *Five Songs*, V

Often, the most difficult questioning begins with inspired guesswork. Arriving at the foot of Mount Purgatory, Virgil warns Dante that he must not be curious about everything because not everything lies within human ken.

> Mad is he who hopes that our reason
> may travel along the endless path
> that one substance in three persons takes.
>
> Be content, you human race, with *quia:*
> For if you'd been able to see all
> Mary would not have needed to give birth;
>
> And you have seen the fruitless yearning of those who
> Might have succeeded in contenting their desire
> Given to them eternally to mourn.

To clarify his point, Virgil adds, "I mean Aristotle, Plato too / and many others." Then he bends his head and remains silent, because he too is one of those who tried to content his desire.[1]

Scholasticism insisted on the acceptance of consequences: this tenet was deemed enough to offer substance for thought to the limited capacities of the human mind. Aquinas made the distinction clear between wanting to know why and wanting to know what. "Demonstration is two-fold," he wrote in his *Summa Theologica.* "The one demonstrates by means of the cause, and is called *propter quid* . . . the other by means of the effect, and is called *quia.*" In other words, don't ask *why* something exists, but merely start from the *because* and explore its existence. In the early years of the seventeenth century, Francis Bacon would take the opposite view on human inquiry: "If a man will begin with certainties," Bacon argued, "he shall end in doubts; but if he will be content to begin with doubts, he shall end in certainties."[2]

For inquiring, for reflecting, for reasoning out, for demonstrating, language is obviously the essential tool. Immediately after his exile, as if the loss of his world demanded the reassurance that he still possessed his language, Dante began to write *De vulgari eloquentia,* his treatise on the vernacular tongue and its use in lyric poetry. Boccaccio, as we have mentioned, relates that the *Commedia* was perhaps begun in Latin and then changed to Florentine Italian. *De vulgari eloquentia,* perhaps because Dante felt that a scholarly instrument allowed him better to explore the language deemed vulgar ("of the people"), is written in the elegant Latin of the Scholastics. For several centuries, the text was scarcely read: only three medieval manuscripts survive, and it was not printed until 1577.

De vulgari eloquentia begins with the scandalous statement that the language of the people, learned by infants at their parents' knee, is nobler than the artificial and legislated language learned in school. To justify his claim, Dante traces the history of language from the biblical story to his own time. The first language of the world, Dante says, a God-given gift that allowed humans to communicate with one another, was Hebrew; the first speaker, Adam. After the arrogant attempt to build the Tower of Babel, that single primordial language shared by all people was, as a punishment, divided into many, thus preventing communication and causing confusion. The punishment endures: language separates us not only from our contemporaries in other nations but also from our ancestors, who spoke differently from the way we speak ourselves.

Having reached the Heaven of Fixed Stars, Dante now encounters the soul of Adam, who tells him that "not the tasting of the tree / was of itself the cause of so great a banishment / but the overstepping of the mark." Dante then asks Adam the questions that his contemporaries had long been troubled by: How long was his sojourn in Eden? How long did he afterwards live

How Do We Question?

on earth? How much time did he spend in Limbo before Christ recalled him? And finally, what was the language Adam spoke in Eden? To this last question, Adam answers:

> The tongue I spoke had all died out
> Before the unaccomplishable task
> Was by the people of Nimrod undertaken:

> Never did our mind effect something
> (For all human pleasure is renewed
> As is the sky) that lasts unchanged forever.

> It is Nature's gift that humans speak;
> But if this way or that, Nature allows
> For you to do according to your choice.[3]

Dante's ideas regarding the origins of language have changed here since *De vulgari eloquentia*. In the treatise, he had argued that it was God who both empowered Adam to speak and gave him the language to do so. In the *Commedia*, Adam says that while the gift of speech was indeed bestowed upon him, it was he who created the language he spoke, a first human language that became extinct before Babel. But what was that primordial language? Giving examples of what God was called before the Fall and after, Adam uses Hebrew terms: first "J," pronounced *jah*, then "El," meaning "the Mighty."[4] The reader must conclude therefore that the language spoken in Eden was Hebrew.

In *De vulgari eloquentia*, Dante attempts to justify the preeminence of Hebrew. God had bestowed upon Adam a *forma locutionis,* a "linguistic form." "By this linguistic form spoke all his descendants up to the construction of the Tower of Babel, which has been interpreted as the 'tower of confusion.' This was the linguistic form inherited by the Sons of Eber, who were called Hebrews after him. This remained with them exclusively after the confusion [of tongues], so that our Savior, who because of the human side of His nature had to be born of them, was able to use a language not of confusion but of grace. That was how the Hebrew language was devised by the first being endowed with speech."[5]

But the shattered remains of that first language, the shreds of linguistic forms inherited by Adam's descendants, were insufficient to express the thoughts and revelations that humans conceived and wished to transmit. It was therefore necessary to build, out of the language available to us (in Dante's case, Florentine Italian), a system that might allow a gifted poet to approximate the lost perfection and counteract the curse of Babel.

In the Judeo-Christian tradition, words are the beginning of everything. According to Talmudic commentators, two thousand years before the creation of heaven and earth, God brought into being seven essential things: his divine throne; paradise, placed to his right; hell, to his left; the celestial sanctuary, in front; a jewel with the name of the Messiah engraved upon it; a voice calling out from the darkness, "Return, ye children of men!"; and the Torah, written in black fire on white. The Torah was the first of these seven and it was the Torah that God consulted before creating the world. With some reluctance, because it feared the sinfulness of the world's creatures, the Torah consented to the creation. Learning of the divine purpose, the letters of the alphabet descended from the august crown, where they had been written with a pen of flames, and one by one the letters said to God, "Create the world through me! Create the world through me!" From the twenty-six letters, God chose beth, the first letter in the word *Blessed,* and thus it was that through beth the world came into being. The commentators note that the only letter that did not put forward its claims was the modest aleph; to reward its humility, God gave aleph the first place in the Decalogue.[6] Many years later, Saint John the Evangelist, somewhat impatiently, summed up the lengthy procedure with the declaration "In the beginning was the Word." From this ancient conviction stems the metaphor of God as author and the world as book: a book we try to read and in which we are also written.

Because the word of God is supposed to be all-encompassing and perfect, no part of Scripture can be ambiguous or fortuitous. Every letter, the order of every letter, the placement of every word must have a meaning. To better attempt to read and interpret the word of God, sometime around the first century C.E. the Jews of Palestine and Egypt, perhaps under the influence of Persian religion, began to develop a system of interpretation of the Torah and the Talmud, the Kabbalah, or "tradition," a term appropriated ten centuries later by the mystics and theosophists who became known as Kabbalists. The *Mishnah,* a digest of the oral Torah compiled by Rabbi Judah the Prince around the second century C.E., condemned human curiosity beyond certain set limits: "Whoever ponders on four things, it were better for him if he had not come into the world: what is above, what is below, what was before time, and what will be hereafter."[7] The Kabbalah circumvents such condemnation by concentrating on God's word itself, which necessarily contains all these things in every one of its letters.

In the mid-thirteenth century, a brilliant student of the Kabbalah, the Spanish scholar Abraham Abulafia, inspired perhaps by encounters with Sufi masters during his extensive travels, developed through ecstatic experiences a technique of letter combination and divination by numbers which he called "The Way of Names." Abulafia believed that his method would allow scholars to set down in writing their interpretations and meditations by an almost infinite combination of the letters of the alphabet. Abulafia compared this to the variations played in a musical piece (a simile dear to Sufi teaching): the difference between the letters and the music was that while music is apprehended through the body and the soul, the letters are perceptible only through the soul, the eyes being, as the ancient metaphor has it, the windows of the soul.[8]

For example, Abulafia systematically combined the first letter of the Hebrew alphabet, aleph, with the four letters of the Tetragrammaton, God's unpronounceable name, YHWH, obtaining four columns of fifty words each. Seven centuries later, in a hemisphere and on a continent Abulafia could not have suspected existed, Jorge Luis Borges imagined a library that would contain all these combinations in a countless series of volumes of identical format and number of pages; another name for this library is "Universe."[9]

Abulafia argued that in Hebrew, which, like Dante, he considered the mother of all languages, there was a conventional correspondence, established by God for his prophets, between sounds and the things those sounds named. Because of this, Abulafia mocked those who suggested that an infant bereft of human contact would learn to speak Hebrew spontaneously; this, Abulafia argued, would be impossible because no one would have taught the child the semiotic conventions. He lamented that the Jews had forgotten the language of their forefathers, and looked passionately forward to the coming of the Messiah, when that knowledge would be restored to them by the generosity of God.

A great admirer of the twelfth-century Spanish master Maimonides, Abulafia saw his own work, in particular his *Life in the Other World* and *Treasure of the Hidden Eden,* as a sequel to Maimonides' celebrated *Guide of the Perplexed,* a manual for students of Aristotelian philosophy puzzled by the apparent contradictions between Greek philosophy and biblical texts. To solve these, Abulafia eschewed the traditional techniques of the Kabbalah, based on the *sefirot* (the powers or potencies of the Godhead) and the mitzvoth (the commands or precepts in the Torah): for Abulafia, our understanding of God comes through the interactions among the intellect, that which is intelligible, and the act of achieving intelligence itself.[10] This dynamic triangle allows our curiosity to pursue its endless quest.

For Abulafia, pleasure is the principal fruit of the mystical experience, and also its essential purpose, more important than the attainment of intellectual answers. In this he notoriously strays from both Aristotle and Maimonides, who believed that reaching the superior good was the desired goal. Using a fortuitous etymology between the Hebrew words *ben,* "son," and *binah,* "understanding" or "intellect," Abulafia argued that the conception of ideas was equal to sexual conception.

Dante, attempting to reconcile certain Epicurean principles with the notion of *voluptas,* or erotic pleasure, in the divine vision, has the Roman poet Statius guide him and Virgil through the upper reaches of Purgatory, where, on the sixth terrace, before reaching a tree of strange and forbidden fruit, they see how "a clear water fell from the high rock / and spread itself above over the leaves."[11] This is the water that will purify the waters of Parnassus, the spring of poetry from which Statius says he drank when he discovered the works of Virgil. Statius, who is purging on Mount Purgatory the excessive prodigality shown throughout his life, has said (without knowing that he is speaking to Virgil) that the *Aeneid* "was a mother / to me and was my nurse in poetry."[12] Virgil looks sternly at Dante to keep him from revealing the poet's identity, but a smile on Dante's lips makes Statius ask what the joke is. Virgil gives his ward consent to speak, and Dante tells Statius that he is standing in the presence of the author of the *Aeneid* himself. Then Statius (because shades can be overcome by emotion, too) stoops to embrace the poet's feet. Virgil stops him, saying:

"Brother
Don't, for you're a shade and see a shade.

And Statius apologizes: such was his love for Virgil, he explains, that he forgot that they were both nothing, "treating a shade as a solid thing." For Dante, who like Statius, reveres Virgil as the "glory and light" of all poetry and confesses to the "long care and great love / that made me search out your book," the intellectual joy achieved in reading must now be transmuted into another, higher pleasure.[13]

Abulafia's disciples carried his work to centers of Jewish culture outside the Spanish peninsula, mainly to Italy, which became, in the thirteenth century, an intermittent stronghold of Kabbalistic studies.[14] Abulafia himself had visited Italy several times and lived there for more than a decade: we know that in 1280 he visited Rome with the intention of converting the pope. Dante may have learned of Abulafia's ideas through the learned debates that took place in various cities after Abulafia's visits, especially in the intellectual circles of Bologna. But, as Umberto Eco remarks, it is not likely that before the Renaissance a Christian poet would have wanted to acknowledge the influence of a Jewish thinker.[15]

Two centuries later, the Neoplatonists of the Renaissance, who would further explore Abulafia's combinatory arts in the construction of their memory machines, would also rescue Abulafia's belief in the importance of pleasure—in particular orgasmic pleasure achieved in both mystical and intellectual experiences—and also his notion of the intellect being an early intermediary between the Maker and his creatures. For Dante, the orgasmic experience takes place at the end of his voyage, when his mind is "battered" by the thrust of the ineffable ultimate vision; the role of the intermediary belongs to the poet himself.[16]

If the gift of linguistic forms that God gave Adam coincides, as Abulafia imagined, with God's own linguistic gift in the act of creation, then it is in the act of artistic creation that the poet puts into action the powers bestowed

How Do We Question?

Cima da Conegliano, *Il leone di San Marco* (The Lion of Saint Mark).
(Gallerie dell'Accademia, Venice; courtesy of the Ministero dei beni e delle
attività culturali e del turismo)

by the shared gift. A work of art is, no doubt, as Plato judged it, an imitation that tells lies because it provides "false images"; however, these lies are for Dante "non falsi errori," "not false falsehoods." In other words, poetic truth.[17]

An example of such truth elicited by "false images" is provided by a large painting by Cima da Conegliano dating from 1506–8, now in Venice. It depicts, against a landscape of tower-capped hills and the walls of a seaport, the lion of Saint Mark, standing on both land and water, thus reflecting Venice's amphibious nature as *Stato da terra* and *Stato da mare*.[18] With multicolored wings, his right front paw on an open book, the beast is framed by four saints: facing the lion's haloed features are Saint John the Baptist and Saint John the Evangelist; facing his rump, Saint Mary Magdalene and Saint Jerome. Far behind, at the foot of a cliff on which some of the buildings of a distant city are perched, is a turbaned rider on a white horse. The lion's book is the Bible, its open pages showing the words with which, according to tradition, an angel greeted Mark when he first arrived in Venice: *Pax tibi, Marce, Evangelista meus* (Peace be with you, Mark, my evangelist). The saints are grouped in complementary pairs: John the Baptist and Mary Magdalene are the active ones, reading God's word in the world; John the Evangelist and Jerome, each carrying a codex, are the contemplative ones who read God's word in the books. The lion shares equally in both these readings.

How Do We Question?

Reading is a craft that can never be fully accomplished. Even if every syllable of a text were to be analyzed and interpreted to its fullest extent, the obstinate reader would still be left with the readings of those who preceded him or her and which, like the tracks of animals in the woods, form a new text whose narrative and meaning are also open to perusal. And even if this second reading were successful, there would still remain the text formed by the readings of those first readings, commentaries on the commentary and glosses of the gloss—and so on until the last vestige of meaning has been thoroughly examined. The end of a book is wishful thinking. Like Zeno's demonstration of the impossibility of movement, the paradoxical truth that every reader must accept is that reading is an ever-ongoing but not infinite enterprise and that, on one inconceivably faraway afternoon, the last word of the last text will finally be read. In the eighteenth century, Rabbi Levi Yitzhak of Berdichev, asked to explain why the first page of each of the treatises in the Babylonian Talmud was missing, answered that this was "because however many pages the studious man reads, he must never forget that he has not yet reached the very first page."[19] That tempting page still awaits us.

If the quest to find the first page has not been successful, it is not for want of trying. Sometime in the second half of the fifteenth century, the Portuguese philosopher Isaac Abravanel, who had settled in Spain, later to be exiled and make his exodus to Venice, strict in the principles of his learned reading, raised an unusual objection to Maimonides. In addition to reconciling Aristotle and the Bible, Maimonides sought to extract from the Torah's sacred words the basic principles of Jewish belief.[20] Shortly before his death in 1204, following a tradition of summary exegesis begun by Philo of Alexandria in the first century, he had expanded Philo's list of the five core articles of faith to thirteen.[21] Thus increased, these thirteen articles were to be used, according to Maimonides, as a test of allegiance to Judaism, separating true believers from the goyim. Abravanel, arguing against Maimonides' dogma, remarked that since the Torah was a God-given whole from which no syllable could be dispensed, the attempt to read the sacred text in order to choose from it a series of axioms was disingenuous if not heretical. The Torah, Abravanel asserted, was complete unto itself and no single word of it was more or less important than any other. For Abravanel, even though the art of commentary was a permissible and even commendable accompaniment to the craft of reading, God's word admitted no double entendres but manifested itself literally, in unequivocal terms. Abravanel was implicitly distinguishing between the Author as author and the reader as author. The reader's job was not to edit, either mentally or physically, the sacred text but to ingest it whole, just as Ezekiel had ingested the book offered to him by the angel, and then to judge it either sweet or bitter, or both, and work from there.

Abravanel belonged to one of the oldest and most prestigious Jewish families of the Iberian Peninsula, which claimed to be descended from King David: his father served the Infante of Portugal as a financial adviser, and his son was Leon Hebreo, the author of the Neoplatonist classic *Dialogues of Love,* which the prince of Sansevero later printed in Naples. Abravanel was a voracious bookworm, and he pursued readings of the word of God, not just those written on tomes of parchment and paper, but also those inscribed in the vast book of the world. In the Jewish tradition, the notion that the natural world is the material manifestation of the word of God stems from an apparent scriptural contradiction. The book of Exodus states that after Moses received God's commandments on Mount Sinai, he "came and told the people all the words of the Lord, and all the judgments, and all the people answered with one voice, and said, 'All the words which the Lord hath said will we do.' And Moses wrote all the words of the Lord" (24:3–4; see also Deuteronomy, Leviticus, and Numbers). But the *Abot* treatise in the *Mishnah* declares that "Moses received the Torah on Mount Sinai and transmitted it to Joshua, Joshua to the elders, the elders to the prophets, the prophets to the members of the Great Assembly" (1:1). How to hold together these statements since both must be true? Like Maimonides' and Abulafia's attempts to hold together Aristotelian philosophy and the Word of God, Abravanel pondered how the apparently contradictory divine texts could be reconciled.

In the first years of the ninth century there appeared a collection of biblical commentaries attributed to the second-century master Eliezer ben Hyrcanus, *The Chapters of Rabbi Eliezer,* which proposes an answer to the conundrum: "Moses spent forty days on the Mountain before the Lord, blessed be His name, as a student sits before his master, reading the precepts of the written Torah during the day and learning the precepts of the oral Torah

Detail of the 1933 RCA building mosaic "Intelligence Awakening Mankind," by Barry Faulkner, at Rockefeller Center, New York, showing "Thought" with "the Written Word" on one side and "the Spoken Word" on the other, a modern depiction of God's oral and written books. (Photograph © Christopher Murphy. Reproduced by permission.)

during the night."[22] The Torah was thus presented as a double book, written and oral, the written Torah being the immutable core made of God's words and bound in the book that came to be called the Bible, the oral Torah an ongoing dialogue between God and his creatures, set down in the commentaries of inspired teachers and materialized for all in the hills and rivers and woods of the world itself. In the seventeenth century, Baruch Spinoza recognized God's double manifestation in the famous maxim: *God sive natura,* "God or [in other words] Nature." For Spinoza, God and Nature were two editions of the same text.

Perhaps because Abravanel understood that our duty is strictly to read the text, not add to it our own words, the learned man of the world mistrusted the concept of divine inspiration and was skeptical of prophets. He preferred the philologist's task of comparing different editions, and used his political and philosophical skills to decipher the book of the world in the light of the written Torah. Since God, by means of one of his curious instruments, the Catholic crown, had decreed the expulsion of Jews and Arabs from Spain and led him, Don Isaac Abravanel, into painful exile, he would profit from this adversity by transforming his enforced wanderings into an experience of learning: he would prepare himself to study the pages of God's other volume as they now unfolded before him in time and space.

After disembarking in Venice in 1492, Abravanel applied his knowledge of Scripture to the new society that confronted him on every minor and major occasion. He asked himself, for instance, in the light of the Torah, how the doge's government, given the lukewarm welcome he himself had experienced, could be compared to the brutal and exclusionary rule of the Catholic kings. Deuteronomy 17:14–20 set down the manner in which a ruler should be chosen in order to rule well; according to Abravanel, the Spanish king had disobeyed these sacred precepts. Ferdinand did not, as Deuteronomy instructed, "write in a book a copy of the law," nor did he read it faithfully "all the days of his life, that he [might] learn to fear the Lord his God, by keeping all the words of this law and these statutes, and doing them." Stretching his exegetical rule, Abravanel argued that, according to the Talmudic commentary of this passage, Jews were not obliged to be governed by a king or an emperor. However, if they chose to be, the monarch's powers would certainly fall under the Deuteronomical limitations. King Ferdinand had evidently refused to comply with these. Therefore, Abravanel concluded, the Venetian doges were closer to the Torah's law, and even though they manifestly disdained another Deuteronomical prohibition—that no ruler should "greatly multiply for himself silver and gold"—by and large it could be said that they submitted faithfully to the sumptuary regulations of the Venetian Republic.

Abravanel became the head of the exiled Jewish community in Venice, using his political skills to help his brethren. He was, above all, a faithful and exacting reader, a rationalist, a practical man, a scientific scholar confident enough even to criticize the "prophetic leanings" of Jeremiah and Ezekiel, and he probably knew of Dante and his *Commedia,* since several Jewish scholars had read and discussed the poem in Rome, Bologna, and Venice. The scholar Yehuda Romano lectured on the *Commedia* to his community, and transliterated it into Hebrew script, and the poet Immanuel de Roma (who was perhaps Romano's half-brother) attempted to write his own version from a Jewish perspective.[23]

How Do We Question?

The core of Jewish faith is the belief in the promised coming of the Messiah. Based on his close readings of the Torah and using his mathematical knowledge, Abravanel concluded that the Messiah would arrive in the year 1503 (a date postponed by Abravanel's contemporary, the learned medical doctor Bonet de Lattes, to 1505). In this expectation Abravanel was to be disappointed: he died in 1508, without witnessing any of the marvels that were said to announce the Messiah's arrival. A literalist to the end, he assumed that the error was in his own reading, never in the sacred texts from which his conclusions had been drawn. It may be supposed that, if anything, his failure confirmed his conviction concerning the dangers of exegetical temptation.

As so many times in the history of human intentions, a grand ambitious curiosity was overshadowed by aleatory failure. Abravanel's struggle to restore hermeneutical confidence in the totality of the sacred texts and in the mirror of the world was forgotten in the light of his failure to date the Messiah's coming. If he had not been able to accomplish the latter, what faith could anyone have in the former?

Abravanel had argued that the proper reading of the Torah was one in which reason and logic must prevail over poetic and visionary disquisitions. But within the ever-constraining limits of the ghetto walls, the Jews of Venice, who by 1552 were to number over nine hundred souls, longed for something more than a strict reading of the Talmud: they longed for a reading that would offer if not magical assistance at least magical hope. In the early twentieth century, Rainer Maria Rilke described the Venice ghetto as a self-contained city which, instead of spreading out by the sea, because of the constricted space the Jews were allowed, grew into the heavens like a new Babel, a place for storytelling. The stories they chose to tell were tales of magic.[24]

Rather than profit from the rigorous lessons of the lost master, the majority of the Jews preferred to recall his (however inexact) auguries. In order better to understand, to assist, or even to refute the failed predicted chronology, the Jews of Venice began to show a thirst for occult learning and ancient conjuring that might help them establish a new date for the certain coming, and a flood of Kabbalistic books, from apocalyptic visions to manuals of divination (such as those by Abulafia), flowed from the Venetian presses under

How Do We Question?

97

the fluctuating tolerance of the Inquisition, which intermittently allowed and prohibited the printing of Jewish books.[25]

Among the many titles, the Talmud, above all, was considered a book of both natural and magical knowledge. Though in the *Mishnah,* Rabbi Shlomo Yitzhaki, known as Rashi, the greatest of all Talmudic scholars, had declared that magicians (*mekhasheph*) who performed a "real" act of magic were to be stoned, the text distinguished clearly between the learning of the occult craft and its performance. Close to his death in 120, Rabbi Eliezer, wise in even the most humble things but forbidden to teach them for having disobeyed the rulings of the Sanhedrin (the council of Jewish leaders), bemoaned like Faust that all his knowledge was now useless. "I know," he said, "three hundred rulings—and some say, three thousand rulings—concerning the planting of cucumbers, and no man has ever asked me about it, except for Akiva ben Yoseph. On one occasion, I and he were walking down the road: he said to me, Master, teach me about the planting of cucumbers. I said one thing, and the whole field was filled with cucumbers. He said, Master, you have taught me how to plant them, now teach me how to uproot them. I said one thing, and they were all gathered in one place." On this magical performance, the Talmud comments: "It says, 'You shall not learn to do' (Deuteronomy 18:9)—to do you may not learn, but you may learn to understand and to teach."[26] The Talmud underscores the difference between the act imagined and the act performed, between what is permissible in literature and the imagination but not permissible in life.

To reflect on such weighty matters, access to the Talmud was of the essence: the *Shulkhan Arukh,* or Code of Jewish Law, demands that time be set aside for frequent study of the Talmud. Prior to the invention of printing, yeshiva students either themselves copied individual tractates or commissioned scribes for the task, but "the system was slow and prone to error."[27] A solution for this problem needed to be found.

Venice, in the early years of the sixteenth century, had already become the undisputed center of publishing in Europe, both because of the skill of its printers and because of the extent of its book trade. Though the first Hebrew book printed in Venice, Ya'akov ben Asher's *Arba' ah Turim* (The Four Orders), had issued from the press of Rabbi Meshullam Cusi and sons, the

Venetian printing business was almost exclusively in the hands of gentiles such as Daniel Bomberg, Pietro Bragadin, and Marco Giustiniani, all of whom employed Jewish artisans when printing Hebrew books "to compose the letters and assist in the corrections."[28] In spite of this, what mattered was not who printed the books but the mere fact that Hebrew books were now easily available, and in this sense Gutenberg's invention changed the relationship of the Jews to their books. Until the late fifteenth century, few Jewish communities could afford to have a good library, and much effort was spent on editing faulty copies to obtain correct texts. With the invention of the press, printers throughout Europe quickly recognized that there was a market for books in Hebrew not only in the Jewish communities but also among the gentiles. Numerous editions of the Hebrew Bible, the prayer book, the rabbinical commentaries, and works of Jewish theology and philosophy poured forth and reached every class of reader, facilitating among Jews the obligatory study of the Torah. A hundred and forty Hebrew volumes were printed during the incunabula period (before 1501) in Europe until Venice established its remarkable supremacy in the international market.[29]

Arguably, the masterpiece of the Venetian Hebrew book production was the first complete edition of the Babylonian Talmud, printed some fifty years after Abravanel's death, by Daniel Bomberg. Born Daniel van Bomberghen and originally from Antwerp, Bomberg established himself in Venice in 1516, where he translated his name into Hebrew and, during his three decades in Venice (he returned to his hometown in 1548, dying there a year later), produced some of the best and most important editions of Jewish books, among them the *Biblia rabbinica* (the Hebrew Bible with translations into Aramaic and commentaries by noted medieval scholars), which he astutely dedicated to Pope Leo X. Though Bomberg was, above all, a businessman and published only what he believed would sell, he was also a man driven by what some scholars have called "missionary intentions," a bookmaker who loved the work in which he was engaged. Probably to divert the censors, together with the Jewish books Bomberg printed in 1539 an anti-Semitic tract, *Itinera deserti de judaicis disciplini* (The Desert Wanderings of the Jewish People), by Gerard Veltwyck. It was his only anti-Semitic publication.[30]

Assisted by a friar, Felice da Prato, Bomberg began his catalogue of books printed in Hebrew characters with the Pentateuch, followed by a selection of the Prophets and later by both the Babylonian and the Palestinian Talmuds, including the eleventh-century commentaries of Rashi. For his edition of the Talmud, Bomberg employed a group of Jewish and non-Jewish scholars assembled for this purpose, thus setting a model for editing Jewish works that would later be followed by most other printing houses in Europe.

The Babylonian Talmud, printed in sets of twelve volumes, was a gigantic enterprise that took Bomberg three years to complete. Bomberg disliked ornamentation: the title page of each volume lacks any hint of a family crest or printer's mark. The title page of the *Pesahim* tractate (in the third volume) reads:[31]

> TRACTATE PESAHIM PESACH RICHON AND SHENI WITH THE COMMENTARY of Rashi, Tosafot, Piskei Tosafot, and the Asheri free from all impediments and precise for the purpose of study. As the hand of the Lord has favoured us, for this has never been printed, may the Lord enable us to complete all six orders as is the intent of Daniel Bomberg from Antwerp, in whose house this was printed, here in VENICE

Though a number of individual Talmudic tractates had appeared earlier in other cities, this was the first time that the entire corpus was printed as a scholarly whole. Bomberg relied for his text on the only extant manuscript, known as the Munich codex, of 1334. The layout of Bomberg's edition is remarkable both for its efficiency and its originality: the text of the Talmud itself appears in square Hebrew type in the center of each page, Rashi's commentary is on the inside margin, and the *tosafot,* or "additions" (other critical remarks by various commentators), are on the outer, both set in the semi-cursive Gothic lettering known as "rabbinical" or "rashi." All subsequent editions of the Babylonian Talmud followed Bomberg's layout, maintaining the disposition of text and commentary, as well as the exact position of words and letters.

It has been suggested by the French scholar Marc-Alain Ouaknin that the layout for Bomberg's Talmud was inspired by the layout of Venice itself; it could also be said that it was inspired by the position of the ghetto within the city, a Jewish core nestled within Venice, the city itself boxed in by land

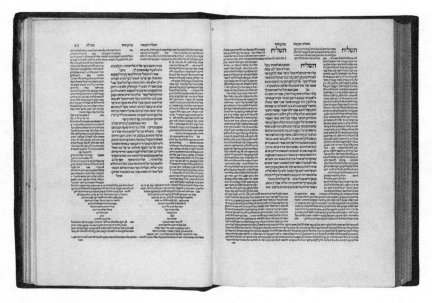

Pages from Daniel Bomberg's Talmud (Venice, 1519–23). (Photograph courtesy of Sotheby's, Inc., and the Valmadonna Library Trust ©)

and water, a frame within a frame within a frame. Less than a decade after Abravanel's death, on 29 March 1516, the Jews of Venice were ordered for the first time to stay within the walls of the ghetto. To prevent them from "roaming about at night," the two gates were locked at midnight by a couple of guards whose salaries the Jews themselves were obliged to pay. The prescribed enclosure is already notable in a perspective map of Venice printed in 1500 by Jacopo de' Barbari: it shows the ghetto enclosed by canals and rows of buildings, like an island of text in the middle of an annotated page.[32]

Like every visitor to Venice, Bomberg must have been struck by its inlaid, convoluted structure. Whether inspired by the city itself and its web of canals and islands or by the enclosed ghetto seen as a microcosm of the larger urban design, it seems likely that, consciously or unconsciously, the printer's imagination mirrored on the page the mazelike contours of the place in which he had settled. Turn a map of Venice and its ghetto sideways and something akin to a page of the Talmud appears, its clean lines twisted and broken like

How Do We Question?

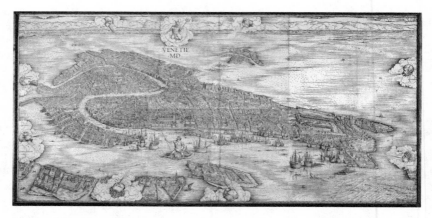

Jacopo de' Barbari, "Perspective Plan of Venice," 1500. (Palazzo Ducale, Venice, Cameraphoto Arte, Venice/Art Resource, NY)

a picture in a dream. The singular, unreal city that every visitor discovers is thus echoed in a book that is, like the city, a commentary on God's work: the Talmud glossing the Torah mirrors Venice glossing the book of nature. Just as the Talmud surrounds with its learned annotations the word delivered to Moses for the people, the Venice of fire and air is surrounded by God's earth and water, which gloss the flaming castles floating between land and sea with the responding breath of an enraptured speaker.

G. K. Chesterton once remarked that "perhaps God is strong enough to exult in monotony. It is possible that God says every morning, 'Do it again' to the sun; and every evening, 'Do it again' to the moon."[33] On the scale of the stars or of the universe, God's book is at the same time unique and repetitive, and we, its footnotes, try to follow suit, so that while the invisible and singular core of Venice is forever framed by a cacophony of commentaries—geographical and architectural, poetic and artistic, political and philosophical—the Talmud (aided by Gutenberg's invention) reproduces its established wake of commentaries again and again, in copy after printed copy and in the very design of each of its pages. And because no design is fortuitous, both the layout of Venice and the layout of its Talmud allow readers to test their intuitive intelligence and cultural memory by means of these cartographies.

As any visitor to the city knows, maps are useless in Venice. Only the repeated experience of its pavements and bridges, its *campi* and glimmering facades, its Arsenal guarded by stone lions from different ages that Dante must have seen allow a small degree of knowledge of its meandering coherence. Getting to know Venice entails losing yourself in it as the Romantics spoke of losing yourself in a book. True Venice connoisseurs, if led blindfolded through the city, will always know where they find themselves, recognizing by touch or smell or sound, reading the city with their mind's eye, its every twist and every turn.

The Talmud too is mapless, and yet a constant and wise reader will know what lies on every page, both through memory and force of habit. In a yeshiva reading test known as *Shass Pollak* (from *Shass,* an abbreviation of "Talmud" in Hebrew, and *Pollak,* "Polish"), the Talmud is opened at random and a pin is placed on a word. The reader undergoing the examination is asked what word is in that same place on any other page. Once the reader has given his answer, the pin is pressed through the book until it reaches the page mentioned. If the reader is a true scholar, someone who has "lost himself in the Talmud" and is therefore capable of visualizing the whole text in his head, the answer proves to be correct. A true reader of the Talmud knows always where he finds himself.[34]

In the thirteenth century, Saint Bonaventure noted that after God created the world through the Word, he perceived that it appeared dead on the page, and "He found it therefore necessary that another book should illuminate the first in order to show the meaning of things." Bonaventure concludes: "This is the Book of Scripture that shows the similarities, the properties and the meaning of things as they are written in the Book of the World."[35] For Bonaventure, as for the Talmudists, one book (the Bible) enables the reading of the other book (the world), and both contain in essence the same text. The Talmudic commentaries continue to copy that text, clarifying and expanding, and producing in time a layering of readings that recognizes in the book of the world a vast, ongoing palimpsest. In this manner, reading advances in two directions: burrowing towards the universal core text in an attempt to fathom it, and reaching out to the generation of readers to come with an ever new individuated text which adds itself endlessly to the pile.

Perhaps without acknowledging this process of individuation as its own,

Venice too exists in the tension between the two reading impulses. On one hand, few cities are so blatant about their mythology and their history. Venice demands at first sight an exploration of its imaginative roots, in earth and water and in stone and deeds, a deep retracing of every step a visitor takes, following its canals down into its legendary beginnings. On the other, it is through the succession of historical readings that Venice wants to identify itself in the present, discarding every new reading (which at first might appear illuminating) as repetitive, banal, and commonplace, and asking for yet another. There is no satisfying Venice. Pulling the reader in opposite directions at the same time, towards the theoretical city of history books and the imaginary city of the stories and pictures, all too often in the process Venice (like the world itself) is itself lost.

The story of how Venetian zealots stole Saint Mark's remains from his tomb in Alexandria in the year 828 is well known. As a result of this *furta sacra,* or "holy theft," Saint Mark and his lion replaced Saint Theodore and his dragon as the city's patron, though both saints tower today, in amiable companionship, above Saint Mark's Square. Sometimes with the book open to indicate prosperity, other times with it closed to signal a period of war, often with a sword or with a halo, the literate lion constantly alters or enriches his own emblematic significance. Though this symbolism has been questioned, these are still the popular readings.[36]

Maimonides, in his *Hilkhot Talmud Torah* (Laws for the Study of the Torah), notes that "the time for study is divided in three parts: one third for the written Torah, one third for the oral Torah, and the last third for reflecting, drawing conclusions from certain premises, deducing one meaning from another, comparing one thing to another, judging the rules by which the Torah must be studied, until one reaches the knowledge that the Torah is the foundation of the rules, thus learning to understand what is forbidden and what is permitted in that which is learned through hearing. This then is what is called Talmud." For Maimonides, a scholar who becomes wise need no longer dedicate himself to reading the written Torah (the words of the prophets) or listening to the oral one (the learned commentaries) but can devote himself exclusively to studying "according to the measure of his mind and the maturity of his intellect," pursuing his curiosity.[37]

How Do We Question?

Conegliano's lion is, of course, a commonplace in Venice. Bas- and haut-reliefs, gargoyles, banners, coats of arms, fountain decorations, mosaics, stained-glass windows, capitals, wellheads, embrasures, keystones, single sculptures like the ones lining the Arsenal, and paintings in every museum: hardly anything in the city is deemed unfit for the lion's presence. *Andante,* with his head shown frontally or foreshortened, or sitting on his haunches like an expectant domestic animal; reduced like the Cheshire Cat to almost nothing but his grin, or crowding his entire muscled body inside a gilded and opulent frame; stamping his outline in official ex libris or enshrined in plastic bells with artificial snow made in China, the lion is everywhere in Venice. And in every case, whether in his own beastly presence or metonymically reflected in his trappings and surroundings, the lion of Saint Mark always stands for more than any single reading presumes. Caught between God's two books, as Conegliano's lion stands between the saints of active and contemplative life, the almost invisible rider explores the solid landscape beyond the visible emblems of reading, book and world. It is as if, intuiting that neither book suffices unto itself (as Maimonides bravely argued), the artist has placed a third option in the picture, the emblem of something equivalent to Abulafia's intermediary.

Psalm 32 advises: "Be ye not as the horse, or as the mule, which have no understanding: whose mouth must be held in with bit and bridle." To which Psalm 33 adds: "An horse is a vain thing for safety: neither shall he deliver any by his great strength." Curbing the beast's ignorance, knowing that it will not grant protection from harm, directing its "great strength" towards a firm and certain purpose, in Conegliano's painting the rider escapes the strictures of Scripture and of gloss, and creates a new landscape of phrases as yet unwritten, evolved in memory and thought, a text permitted to change and transform itself as the remembered pages of words and world are turned and annotated in the curious imagination. Whether exploring the city or exploring the book, between the Word of God spoken and written and the human world, the rider is allowed the freedom to seek that every reader must be allowed to claim. In the untranslatable, conventional language of ancestral symbols, perhaps this unanswerable questioner has his function.

6

What Is Language?

A WEEK BEFORE CHRISTMAS 2013, in the early evening, I sat down at my desk to answer a letter. But as I was about to write the words, I felt as if they were escaping me, vanishing into air before reaching the paper. I was surprised but not concerned. I decided that I was very tired, and promised myself to stop work after finishing the note. Trying to concentrate harder, I attempted to form in my mind the sentence I was supposed to write. However, while I knew the gist of what I wanted to say, the sentence would not take shape in my mind. The words rebelled, refused to do as I asked them; unlike Humpty Dumpty, I felt too weak to show them "which is to be the master." After much mental strain, I managed, painfully, to string a few words together and set them down coherently on the page. I felt as if I had been groping in an alphabet soup, and as soon as I put in my spoon to grab one, it would dissolve into meaningless fragments. I went back into the house and tried to tell my partner that something was wrong, but I realized that as well as write them, I was unable to mouth the words except in a painfully protracted stutter. He called an ambulance, and an hour later I was in the Emergency Room being treated for a stroke.

To prove to myself that I had not lost the capacity of remembering

(Opposite) Dante and Virgil come across the giants trapped in the ice. Woodcut illustrating Canto XXXI of the Inferno, *printed in 1487 with commentary by Cristoforo Landino. (Beinecke Rare Book and Manuscript Library, Yale University)*

words, only that of expressing them out loud, I began to recite in my head bits of literature I knew by heart. The flow was easy: poems by Saint John of the Cross and Edgar Allan Poe, chunks of Dante and Victor Hugo, doggerel by Arturo Capdevila and Gustav Schwab echoed clearly in the darkness of my hospital room. The ability to read never left me, and a few hours later, I found that I was again able to write. However, when I tried to speak to the nurses, the stammer persisted. After four or five weeks of hesitant speech, it gradually disappeared.

The experience, while terrifying, made me reflect on the relationship between thought and language. If thought, as I believe, forms itself in our mind by means of words, then, in the first fraction of a second, when the thought is sparked, the words which instantaneously cluster around it are not clearly distinguishable to the mind's eye: they constitute the thought only in potentia. Their verbal cluster allows the mind to perceive the presence of a shape under water, but not in full detail. Caused to emerge by the language of its speaker (and each language produces particular thoughts which can only be imperfectly translated into another language), the mind selects the most adequate words in that specific language to allow the thought to become intelligible, as if the words were metal shavings gathering around the magnet of thought.

A blood clot in one of the arteries that feeds my brain had blocked for a few minutes the passage of oxygen. As a consequence, some of the neural passages were cut off and died, presumably the ones dedicated to transmitting electric impulses that turn words conceived into words spoken. Unable to go from thought to the expression of thought, I felt as if I were groping in the dark for something that dissolved itself at the touch, preventing my thought to form itself in a sentence, as if its shape (to carry on with the image) had been demagnetized and were no longer capable of attracting the words intended to define it.

This left me with a question: What are these thoughts that have not yet achieved their verbal state of maturity? This, I suppose, is what Dante meant when he wrote, "My mind was struck / by lightning bringing me what it wished": the desired thoughts not yet expressed in words. Aristotle spoke of *phantasia* as the capacity to make present to the mind something which it has not previously perceived; perhaps in humans, phantasia is the capacity to make this presentation through language. Under normal circumstances, the progress from the conception of a thought in the specific linguistic field of the thinker to its verbal constellation and on to its expression in speech or in writing is instantaneous. We don't perceive the stages of the process, except in half-dreams and hallucinatory states (I experienced this when, in my twenties, I experimented with LSD). In this process, as in all our conscious processes, what drives us is desire.

Torn between my desire to put my thoughts into specific words and my inability to do so, I tried to find synonyms for what I knew I was trying to say. Again, a simile might help: it was as if, floating down a stream, I had come to a dam that blocked my way and sought a side canal to allow my passage. In the hospital, finding it impossible to say "my thinking functions are fine, but I find speaking difficult," I managed to say "I have words." I experienced the expression of negatives as especially difficult. In my sloweddown mental process, if I wanted to say, in answer to the nurse's question, "I don't feel pain," I found myself thinking "I feel pain" and adding "no" to the words. Then, accustomed to my normal rhythm of speech, I would try to answer all at once, but the words would come out as "of course" or "yes" before I had time to frame my thought in the negative. Apparently, in my mind, the stage of affirmation precedes that of negation. (This process of asserting something in order then to negate it is in fact a "prototype of narration." Don Quixote is presented as a feeble old man in order to deny that he is a feeble old man and affirm that he is a valiant knight errant, and then to deny that he is a valiant knight errant and affirm that he is a feeble old man.)

Perhaps, I said to myself afterwards, this is how one's literary style works: selectively finding the right waterway, not because of any blockage of the verbal expression but because of a particular aesthetic sense that chooses not to take the commonplace main course ("the cat is on the mat") but a personal side canal ("the cat slumbers on the mat").

Lying in the hospital, allowing my brain to be scanned in coffinlike machines, I reflected on the fact that our age has allowed our curiosity that which medieval theologians believed impossible except for God: the observation of our observing, drawing a chart of our own thinking, enjoying the privilege of being both audience and performer of our intimate mental acts—holding, as it were, our brain in our hands, like Dante's Bertram de Born, who must carry his severed head about as punishment for having parted two who were meant to be united forever.

"The World is like the impression left by the telling of a story."

—VALMIKI, *Yoga Vasistha*, 2.3.11

Asking unanswerable questions serves a dialectical function, as when a child asks "Why?" not in order to receive a satisfactory explanation (it may merely elicit an exasperated "Because!") but in order to establish a dialogue. Dante's motives are obviously more complex. Under Virgil's supervision, Dante is confronted with the souls of his fellow men and women, sinners like himself, whose stories he wishes to learn, perhaps because of prurient curiosity (for which Virgil chides him) or to mirror his own condition (of which Virgil silently approves).[1] Some of the souls want to be remembered on earth and tell their story so that Dante may retell it; others, like the traitor Bocca degli Abati, scorn the idea of posthumous fame. The encounters all take place through speech, through that poor and ineffectual instrument whose feebleness Dante laments.

> Certainly every tongue would fall short
> because our speech and our memory have,
> for so much understanding, so little wit.[2]

And when finally Dante is ready to tell his readers his experience of the glories of Paradise, he prays to Apollo. Up to this point the inspiration of the Muses has sufficed, but now he must have the assistance of the god himself, however painful it will be—because the presence of a god is always terrible. Dante compares the process to the flaying of Marsyas, the flute player who presumed to challenge Apollo to a contest and after having lost was tied to a tree and flayed alive. Dante invokes the fearsome god:

> Enter my breast and blow your breath
> As when you drew Marsyas out
> From within the sheath of his limbs.[3]

Melchior Meier, *Apollo and Marsyas: The Judgment of Midas* (or *The Flaying of Marsyas*), 1581. (The Metropolitan Museum of Art, New York. Bequest of Phyllis Massar, 2011 [2012.136.725]. Image copyright © The Metropolitan Museum of Art. Image source: Art Resource, NY.)

With (or generally without) the help of Apollo, we use words to try to recount, describe, explain, judge, demand, beg, affirm, allude, deny—and yet in every case we must rely on our interlocutor's intelligence and generosity to construe from the sounds we make the sense and meaning we wish to convey. The abstract language of images helps us no farther, because something in our constitution makes us want to translate into words even these shadows, even that which we know for certain is untranslatable, immanent, unconscious. Dante's initial forest, for instance, is its own ineffable definition, and yet he tries to render it for our comprehension as "dark" (*oscura*), "wild" (*selvaggia*), "rough" (*aspra*), "strong" (*forte*), "bitter" (*amara*).[4] But semantic innocence is beyond us.

In the final leg of their frightful descent to the pit of Hell, crossing the bank that separates the last chasm of the Malebolge from the ninth circle,

where the traitors are punished, Dante hears the loud sound of a horn blow-
ing in the thick gloom. Dimly he discerns tall shapes which he takes to be the
towers of a city, but Virgil explains that the shapes are those of giants en-
sconced in the chasm up to the waist.[5] They are the biblical Nephilim, who
according to the book of Genesis were the offspring of the daughters of men
and the sons of God in the days before the Flood. One of them cries out a
few unintelligible words: *Rafel mai amech zabi almi.* Virgil explains:

> He accuses himself;
> This is Nimrod, through whose ill whim
> a single language is not still used worldwide.
>
> Let's leave him here and not speak in vain;
> for every language is like this to him,
> as his to others, that no one understands.[6]

Nimrod's speech "that no one understands" has long been debated by
Dante scholars. Though most commentators argue that Dante intended the
line to be read as gibberish, some have proposed ingenious solutions to the
decipherment of the words. Domenico Guerri has suggested that Dante,
following the tradition according to which Nimrod and the giants spoke
Hebrew, combined five Hebrew words found in the Vulgate. Guerri argues
that the original phrase conceived by Dante was made up of the words *ra-
phaïm* (giants), *man* (what is this?), *amalech* (people who touch lightly, who
feel their way), *zabulon* (dwelling) and *alma* (sacred, secret), distorted, as
they might have been by the curse God put on Babel, into the unintelligible
Rafel mai amech zabi almi. The hidden meaning of the phrase would then be:
"Giants! What is this? People feeling their way into the secret place!"[7]

Perhaps Guerri's explanation is correct, but it is scarcely satisfying. (Borges,
in his detective story "Death and the Compass," has a police inspector offer
to the investigator a certain hypothesis that might explain the crime. "Your
hypothesis is possible, but not interesting," is the investigator's response. "You
will reply that reality has not the least obligation to be interesting. To which
I will reply that reality can forgo that obligation, but hypotheses can't.")[8]

Dante may have used Hebrew words because according to biblical scholarship Nimrod would have spoken Hebrew, and Dante may have distorted these words because Nimrod's speech is condemned to be incomprehensible. But Dante may also have wished Nimrod's speech to be not only secret but dreadfully so because he knew that an enigma that suggests an unsatisfactory solution is more terrible that one that can be dismissed as signifying nothing. Nimrod and his workers on their ambitious Tower were cursed with speaking a language whose meaning had been rendered confused—but not inexistent, incomprehensible but not entirely lacking an original sense. That meaning, distantly glimpsed but beyond the full discernment of Nimrod's audience, will be eternally taken for gibberish. Nimrod's curse is that he is condemned not to silence but to delivering a revelation never to be understood.

Nimrod's speech is not unique. Once before, during their descent, Dante and Virgil have heard incomprehensible words, and once before, Virgil has dismissed them. As they enter the fourth circle, where misers and spendthrifts are punished, the travelers come upon Pluto, god of riches and guardian of the circle, who cries out at them in a hoarse and strident voice: "Pape Satàn, pape Satàn aleppe!" Pluto's words have been interpreted as a demonic invocation to Satan: most commentators, beginning with the earliest ones, have understood *pape* and *aleppe* to be exhortations, the former derived from the Greek *papai* and the latter from the Hebrew *aleph*. Pluto's cry, however, is lost on the two poets, and Virgil, with scornful words, causes the ancient god to fall to the ground like "a mast that breaks."[9]

A language can be incomprehensible because we have never learned it or because we have forgotten it: either case presupposes the possibility of an original communal understanding. The search for this primordial tongue long engaged scholars worldwide. Centuries before Dante's era, the Egyptian pharaoh Psammetichus, according to Herodotus, tried to determine who were the first people on earth, and conducted an experiment that was later copied by a number of other rulers. He took two newborn infants from an ordinary family and gave them to a shepherd to bring up in his cottage, with strict orders that no one should utter a word in their presence, though he was to look after them in any other way that was necessary. Psammetichus wanted to discover what words the infants would first speak after their initial babbling. The experiment, Herodotus tells us, was successful. Two years later, the shepherd was greeted by the children with the word *becos,* Phrygian for "bread." Psammetichus concluded that it was not the Egyptians but the Phrygians who were the first people on earth, and the primordial tongue was Phrygian.[10]

In the twelfth century, following the example of Psammetichus, the Holy Roman emperor Frederick II (whom Dante condemned to the sixth circle of Hell among the heretics) tried to determine which was the first natural human language. He arranged for a number of nurses to suckle and wash the children in their charge, but not to speak to them, in order to discover whether the children's first words would be in Hebrew, Greek, Latin, Arabic, or the language of their biological parents. The experiment failed because all the children died.[11]

Not to be able to communicate with one's fellow human beings has been compared to being buried alive. In his now classic *Awakenings,* Oliver Sacks describes the plight of a forty-six-year-old patient whom he calls Leonard L., a victim of the sleeping-sickness epidemic (*encephalitis lethargica*) which spread through America in the mid-twenties. In 1966, the year Sacks first met him at Mount Carmel Hospital in New York City, Leonard was completely speechless and incapable of voluntary motion, except for minute movements of his right hand. With these he could spell out messages on a small letter-board, his only means of communication. Leonard was an avid reader, though the pages of his books had to be turned by someone else, and he even managed to write book reviews, which were published in the hospital magazine every month. At the end of their first meeting, Sacks asked Leonard what it was like to be the way he was. What would he compare it to? Leonard spelt out for Sacks the following answer: "Caged. Deprived. Like Rilke's 'Panther.'" Rilke's poem, written either in the fall of 1907 or the spring of the next year, captures the trapped sense of the wordless:

His vision, from the constantly passing bars,
has grown so weary that it cannot hold
anything else. It seems to him there are
a thousand bars, and behind the bars, no world.

What Is Language?

As he paces in cramped circles, over and over,
the movement of his powerful soft strides
is like a ritual dance around a center
in which a mighty will stands paralyzed.
Only at times, the curtain of the pupils
lifts, quietly——. An image enters in,
rushes down through the tensed, arrested muscles,
plunges into the heart and is gone.[12]

Like the "mighty will" of Rilke's panther, like the persistent will of Leonard, Nimrod's rebellious will is condemned to verbal immobility.

After the encounter with Nimrod, Virgil and Dante come upon Antaeus, one of the several giants who rebelled against Zeus. The son of the gods of the sea and the earth, Antaeus grew stronger whenever he touched his mother, but he was defeated when Hercules held him aloft and crushed him to death. Virgil treats Antaeus very differently from Nimrod: he addresses the giant politely and asks him to help them descend into the ninth and last circle. To persuade Antaeus (as Beatrice resorted to flattery, Virgil resorts to bribery), he points to Dante and offers:

He can restore your fame on earth;
because he lives and a long life still awaits him,
Unless grace call him to her before his time.

Virgil promises Antaeus Dante's speech: the giant's physical action will be repaid with a future verbal one, communication in space is bartered against communication in time. Antaeus accepts (even in Hell we are left certain choices), scoops the travelers up in one enormous hand, and sets them down again "in the deep that devours / Lucifer and Judas." Then he rises "like the mast of a ship."[13]

Antaeus is a bridge, a transport, a ship, but it is Nimrod and his incomprehensible words that tower over the final cantos of the *Inferno*, because the encounter with Nimrod foreshadows the meeting with Lucifer, the arch-fiend who chose to place himself beyond the redemptive power of God's Word.

According to Jewish legend, Nimrod was a descendant of Ham, one of Noah's three sons. From his father, he inherited the clothes God had given Adam and Eve before their expulsion from Eden, which made the wearer invincible; beasts and birds fell down before Nimrod, and no man could defeat him in combat. His clothes made his fortune: because people supposed Nimrod's strength was his own, they made him their king. Victorious in all battles, Nimrod conquered land after land until he became the sole ruler of the world, the first mortal to possess universal power. This gift, however, corrupted him, and Nimrod became a worshiper of idols and later demanded that he himself be worshiped. Nimrod became known as "the Mighty Hunter of Men and Beasts." Inspired by Nimrod's blasphemy, the people no longer trusted God but came to depend on their own powers and abilities. And yet Nimrod's ambition was not satiated. Not content with his conquests on earth, he decided to build a tower that would reach the heavens and claim them as his domain. In the construction, Nimrod employed six hundred thousand men and women loyal to his cause: the first third were willing to wage war against God, the second proposed to set up idols in heaven and worship them, the last third wanted to attack the heavenly hosts with arrows and spears. Many years were spent building the tower, which reached so great a height that it took a worker twelve months to climb to the top. A brick was considered more precious than a human being: if a worker fell, none took notice of it, but if a brick was dropped, they wept because it would take a year to replace it. A woman was not allowed to interrupt work even to give birth: she would bring her child into the world while molding bricks and, after tying it around her waist with a swaddling cloth, she would continue her molding.[14]

According to the book of Genesis, "the Lord came down to see the city and the tower, which the children of men builded. And the Lord said, Behold, the people is one, and they have all one language; and this they begin to do; and now nothing will be restrained from them, which they have imagined to do. Go to, let us go down, and there confound their language, that they may not understand one another's speech. So the Lord scattered them abroad from thence upon the face of all the earth; and they left off to build the city" (11:5–8). Implicit in the Genesis account is the skill of the builders of Babel, whose work required even God to descend from the heavens in order to admire it. The unfinished tower, Talmudic commentators say, was destroyed. A third of it sank into the earth, a third was consumed by fire, and the third that was left standing in ruins was cursed with the power of making passersby forget everything they knew.[15]

The notion of a primeval single common language that was fragmented into a plurality of languages bears a symbolic relationship to contemporary theories about the origins of our verbal capacities. According to one of these theories (the "gesture first" theory as opposed to the "speech first" theory), we are mimetic animals and the complex imitation of manual actions (copying a hammering gesture in order to request a hammer, for instance) evolved from such pantomimes to early forms of sign language. These proto-signs, in turn, developed into proto-speech, and both the imitative gestures and the utterances gave birth to proto-languages that became the link between the communications of our earliest ancestors and the first recognizable human languages. In the "gesture first" theory, the reason humans have language (and other creatures do not) is because "the human brain is language-ready, in the sense that a normal human child will learn a language—an open-ended vocabulary integrated with a syntax that supports the hierarchical combination of words into larger structures which freely express novel meanings as needed—while infants of other species cannot. Indeed, humans not only can learn an existing language but can take an active role in the shaping of new languages."[16]

Chimpanzees, who share 98.8 percent of the human DNA, possess brains that differ from human brains not only in size but also in the range and relative extent of their regions in connectivity and in details of cellular function. Though chimpanzees can be taught to understand spoken words, all attempts to teach them to speak have failed: chimpanzees (and all other apes) lack the neural control mechanisms that regulate the vocal apparatus. Because of their manual dexterity, they can, however, be taught sign language, as well as a symbolic visual language consisting of so-called lexigrams, a reading and writing method "akin to moving magnetized symbols on the door of a fridge." A bonobo ape called Kanzi was able to master 256 of these lexigrams and arrange them in novel combinations. And yet these combinations, however remarkable, are not equivalent to possessing and using a syntax: Kanzi's extraordinary ability was compared by scientists to that of a two-year-old child exposed to an ordinary linguistic environment: there it stops.[17] But what experience does a bonobo like Kanzi communicate, as opposed to that, however rudimentary, of a human child? What experience of the world is he trying to transmit?

In April 1917, Franz Kafka sent his friend Max Brod a collection of prose pieces that included one he titled "A Report to an Academy." It is the first-person account of an ape captured on the Gold Coast and transformed, through training, into something resembling a human being, whose language ranges from conventional gestures (handshakes, for instance, that "denote openness") to speech. "Oh, one learns when one has to, when one seeks a way out," the ape explains to the learned members of the Academy, "one learns at all costs." But though the ape can recount, clearly and precisely, the details of his five-year-long education, he nevertheless knows that what he is putting into words is not his experience as an ape but an experience translated into the observation of that experience by his human persona. "What I felt then as an ape," he says to his expectant audience, "I can only represent now in human terms, and therefore I misrepresent it." As Kafka intuited, if the ape's brain is not biologically "language-ready," as a human one is, any transformation into a human "language-ready" brain—in a literary, symbolic, even perhaps (in a Dr. Moreau future) medical sense—must render the verbalization of the world seen through the eyes of the ape impossible to communicate, much as it is impossible for the human brain (in Dante's system of belief) to grasp the Word of God and put it in human terms.[18] In both these cases, translation is betrayal.

"To go beyond the human is impossible / to put into words," Dante says of his experience of Paradise, an opinion confirmed by Thomas Aquinas. "The faculty of seeing God," Aquinas argues, "does not belong to the created intellect naturally, but is given to it by the light of glory, which establishes the intellect in a kind of *deiformity*."[19] In other words, divine grace can make the human brain "God's Word–ready" just as education can make Kafka's ape "human language–ready." In either case, however, the authentic original experience is necessarily lost in the attempt to utter it.

The progress from proto-languages to languages such as we speak today may have gone through a phase of fragmenting conventionalized verbal expressions or communicative gestures, as an utterance became divided into its component parts or a complex gesture into simpler significant gestures. An utterance that signified, for instance, "there is a stone with which we can crack this coconut" would, according to this theory, be broken up over time into sounds signifying "there," "stone," "crack," and "coconut"—a counterintuitive assumption since it is simpler to suppose that the separate words came first and their combination into a sentence followed later (an assumption perhaps influenced by the single-word speech of Johnny Weissmuller in the early *Tarzan* films).

The "gesture-first" theory is only a few decades old. More than fifteen centuries ago, in India, a Sanskrit poet and religious thinker known as Bhartrihari developed a theory of language that somewhat foreshadowed these modern findings. Information about Bhartrihari's life is vague. Even the dates of his birth and death are doubtful: he is thought to have been born around 450 C.E. and to have lived for some sixty years. Popular stories about Bhartrihari are many. One has it that he was a king who, after discovering the infidelity of his mistress, like King Shahryar in *The Arabian Nights,* renounced the throne and took to wandering in the world. Another says that he was offered the fruit of immortality by a Brahman priest; Bhartrihari, as an amorous gesture, gave the fruit to his queen, who in turn gave it to her lover, who passed it on to Bhartrihari's mistress, who brought it again to Bhartrihari. Discovering what had happened, Bhartrihari retired to the forest and wrote a poem that ends with these words:

Damn her, damn him, damn the god of love,
The other woman, and myself![20]

Bhartrihari's fame as a philosopher spread quickly to other cultures. Just over a century after his death, I-Tsing (Yi Jing), a Chinese scholar and itinerant, who believed that his homeland was the model for all societies ("Is there anyone in any part of India who does not admire China?" he asked), cited Bhartrihari as one of the luminaries of universal culture.[21] Perhaps led astray by his own beliefs, I-Tsing mistakenly portrayed Bhartrihari as a defender of the Buddhist faith. In fact, Bhartrihari's beliefs were rooted in the sacred Sanskrit texts, the Vedas (a Sanskrit word that means "knowledge"), supposed to have been received by certain elected scholars directly from God and then passed on to the following generations by word of mouth. The Vedas consist of four texts composed in India over a millennium, from approximately 1200 to 200 B.C.E.: the *Rig-Veda,* or Veda of Hymns; the *Sama-Veda,* or Veda of Chants; the *Yajur-Veda,* or Veda of Sacrifices; and the later *Athra-Veda,* or Veda of Magical Charms. Each Veda is in turn divided into three sections; the third sections, the Upanishads, are speculative treatises on the nature of the universe, the nature of the self, and the relationship between the two.[22] All the Vedas are rooted in the belief that the individual soul is identical to Brahman, the sacred power which informs all reality and is equal to it. "Brahman is the vast ocean of being," it says in the Upanishads, "on which rise numberless ripples and waves of manifestation. From the smallest atomic form to a Deva or an angel, all spring from that limitless ocean of Brahman, the inexhaustible source of life. No manifested form of life can be independent of its source, just as no wave, however mighty, can be independent of the ocean." Ralph Waldo Emerson translated the idea for a Western audience in his poem "Brahma":

They reckon ill who leave me out;
When me they fly, I am the wings;
I am the doubter and the doubt,
And I the hymn the Brahmin sings.[23]

The fifth-century India of Bhartrihari was, for the most part, a prosperous and happy society ruled by the Gupta dynasty. In the early decades of the century, Chandra Gupta II, who took the title "Sun of Valor," made his reputation not only as a warrior but as a patron of the arts. Under his protection, the great Sanskrit poet Kalidasa became a member of the imperial entourage, and the literary and philosophical court gatherings were famous beyond the empire's borders. During the reign of Gupta's son Kumara Gupta, India was threatened by Huns from Central Asia. Having occupied Bactria in the previous century, the Huns for decades tried to enter the Indian Empire, mainly through the Hindu Kush; when at last the invasion occurred, the Hun army had become weakened by the endless skirmishes, and India was able to hold them off. But in the climate of constant threat, the authority of the Gupta dynasty declined, and their powerful empire fragmented into a number of smaller, battling kingdoms.[24] It was at this period between the wane of the Gupta rulers and the rise of the Indian Huns that Bhartrihari developed his theory of language.

Several fundamental books have been attributed to Bhartrihari: the *Vâkyapadîya*, a philosophical treatise on sentences and words; the *Mahâbhâshyatîkâ*, a commentary on the great yoga scholar Patanjali's *Vâkyapadîyavrtti*, a series of notes on his own linguistic treatise; and the *Shabdadhâtusamîksha*. Bhartrihari began by developing a more or less traditional commentary or exegesis of the Vedas derived from older linguistic theories, but eventually he developed a philosophical linguistic theory of his own. Some of the early masters, such as the seventh-century B.C.E. grammarian Pânini, had proposed a series of rules governing the Sanskrit language that could be applied to the text of the Vedas; in the second century C.E., Patanjali, following Pânini, argued that grammar was the study of the truth of the Vedas and a guide to their recitation. Bhartrihari moved these arguments into the philosophical arena: grammar, he said, could be considered an intellectual instrument to investigate not only the sacred Vedas but also the Brahman, total reality. He postulated that human language was like the Brahman itself, not subject to the avatars of temporal events but something that embraces a timeless and spaceless whole which it names in its entirety and also in each of its component parts. The first lines in the first stanza of his *Vâkyapadîya* announce Bhartrihari's conclusion: language is "the beginningless and endless One, the imperishable *Brahman* of which the essential nature is the Word, which manifests itself at the Creation of the Universe."[25] Without indulging in facile translations, we can note that Bhartrihari's thesis is in essence much the same as that announced by John in the first line of his Gospel.

Language was for Bhartrihari both the divine creative seed and its resulting creations, both the eternal regenerative force and the plurality of things issuing from it. According to Bhartrihari, one cannot speak of language as being created (either by a divine being or by humans) because there is no time previous to language. As one Sanskrit scholar has it, "Language [for Bhartri-hari] is continuous and co-terminus with human existence or the existence of any sentient being."[26]

We know that language expresses itself in verbal representations of objects and actions, and in sounds that can be combined in almost infinite ways to name the multiplicity of the universe, and even in that which has no cogent universal existence. Jorge Luis Borges's Universal Library, the Library of Babel, is a container for this quasi-infinity of words, though the vast majority of them are meaningless: in a note appended to the story, he suggested that a library was not necessary for this colossal project—one volume composed of an infinite number of infinitely thin pages would suffice. In a short essay that predates this fiction by two years, Borges quoted Cicero, who, in *Concerning the Nature of the Gods*, wrote, "If a countless number of copies of the one-and-twenty letters of the alphabet, made of gold or what you will, were thrown together into some receptacle and then shaken out on to the ground, it would be possible that they should produce the *Annals* of Ennius, all ready for the reader. I doubt whether chance could possibly succeed in producing even a single verse!"[27]

Cicero and Borges (and many others) noted that the combinatory art of the alphabet allows for a complete nomenclature of existing and nonexisting things, even unintelligible utterances such as those of Nimrod. Bhartrihari, however, argued that language does not just name things and the meaning (or lack of meaning) of things, but that all things and their attendant meanings derive from language. Things perceived and things thought, as well as the relationships among them, are determined, according to Bhartrihari, by the words that language lends them. This is obviously true of metaphysical concepts. Alice, speaking to the White Queen in *Through the Looking-Glass*, argues against Bhartrihari that "one *can't* believe impossible things." "I daresay you haven't had much experience," the Queen, siding with Bhartrihari, objects. "When I was your age, I always did it for half-an-hour a day. Why, sometimes I've believed as many as six impossible things before breakfast."[28]

Bhartrihari's arguments opposed both those of traditional Buddhists and the Brahmin Nyâyas (members of one of the six orthodox schools of Hindu thought). The former hold that meaning is a social convention, and the scope of a certain meaning is the projection of a collective imagination of that convention. The word *tree* designates a type of woody perennial plant because the speakers of English have agreed that the sound *tree* will denote a plant and not a body of water, and the scope of its meaning includes an oak, a cypress, a peach tree, and others because collectively and conventionally these things are each imagined as a tree. The Nyâyas argue that words have meaning only in reference to external existing things, and combine into sentences just as things relate to one another in the world. *Tree* denotes that type of woody perennial plant because such a thing as a tree exists in reality, and language allows us to construct the phrase "the tree is in the forest" because in reality a tree and a forest form a real relationship.[29]

Bhartrihari argued that meaning happens in the act of using language, both in the utterances of the speaker and in the recognition of those utterances by the listener. In implicit agreement with Bhartrihari, later theorists of the art of reading suggest that the meaning of the text emerges from the interaction of the text with the reader. "Reading," wrote Italo Calvino, "means approaching something that is just coming into being."[30] Bhartrihari called this "coming into being" *sphota,* a term dating back to Pânini signifying "spoken language," and in Bhartrihari's theory it defines the act of "bursting forth," spouting, as it were, meaningful sounds. Sphota does not depend on the user's manner of speaking (or writing, so style or accent is not of the essence) but carries a definite meaning in the particular combination of words in a sentence. This meaning is not reducible to its component parts: only those who have not learned a language properly divide a sentence into words in order to understand it. In most cases, meaning is apprehended by the listener (or the reader) as a whole, in an instantaneous illumination of what is being conveyed. This illumination is conveyed by the sphota, but, Bhartrihari argues, it is already present in the hearer's (or reader's) brain. In modern terms, the illumination happens when the sphota is received by a brain that is language-ready.

Bhartrihari goes farther. If perception and understanding are innately verbal, the anguished chasm between what we see and what we believe we see, between what we experience and what we know to be true or false in our experience, becomes illusory. Words create the total existing reality, and also our particular visions of that reality; that which we call our world "bursts forth" from the Brahman in verbal, communicative form. This is what Dante, struggling to express what he witnessed in Paradise, described as a "flaying" of appearance to reveal the meaning of experience in human words.

Dante believed that language was the supreme human attribute, given by God to no other of his creatures, neither to animals nor to angels, in order to allow human beings to express what is formed in their God-given language-ready minds. Language, according to Dante, is the instrument that rules human society and makes possible our communal living. The language we use is made up of conventional signs which allow us, within our linguistic circle, to represent ideas and experiences. Language, for Dante, gives existence to the things it names merely by naming them, because "nothing can produce what itself is not," as he says in *De vulgari eloquentia*.[31] Perhaps for that reason, as a symbol of the unresolvable quest Dante left *De vulgari eloquentia* unfinished, in the middle of this sentence: "Words that deny must always be placed at the end; all others will gradually arrive at the conclusion with appropriate slowness . . ."[32]

7

Who Am I?

I HAVE IN FRONT OF ME A PHOTO taken sometime in the early sixties. It shows an adolescent boy lying on his belly on the grass, looking up from a pad of paper on which he has been drawing or writing. In his right hand is a pencil or a pen. He is wearing a sort of cap and hiking boots, and tied around his waist is a sweater. He is lying in the shade of a brick wall next to what seem like stumpy apple trees. A short-legged dog is close behind him, reminiscent of the dogs that lie on stone tombs at the feet of dead crusaders. I am that boy, but I don't recognize myself in the picture. I know it is me, but that is not my face.

The photo was taken half a century ago, somewhere in Patagonia, during a camping holiday. When I look into the mirror today, I see a tired, puffed-up face circled by gray hair and a jovial white beard. The small eyes, lined with wrinkles and framed by narrow glasses, are olive brown with a few orange flecks. Once, when I tried to cross into England with a passport that stated that the color of my eyes was green, the immigration officer, staring me in the face, told me I should change that to blue, or next time I would not be allowed in. I know that sometimes my eyes look gray. Maybe their color changes from moment to moment, like those of Madame Bovary, but

(Opposite) Virgil and Dante meet Cato on the shores of Mount Purgatory. Woodcut illustrating Canto I of the Purgatorio, *printed in 1487 with commentary by Cristoforo Landino. (Beinecke Rare Book and Manuscript Library, Yale University)*

Photograph of the author in early adolescence. (Courtesy of the author)

I'm not sure if that change of color, as in her case, has a meaning. Nevertheless, the face in the mirror is me, it has to be me. But it is not my face. Others recognize me in my features; I don't. When, inadvertently, I catch sight of myself reflected in a shop window, I wonder who that fat elderly man is walking by my side. I have a vague fear that if I truly saw myself one day on the street, I wouldn't know myself. I'm convinced that I would not be able to pick myself out in a police line-up, nor would I easily identify myself in a group portrait. I'm not sure whether this is because my features age too rapidly and too drastically or because my own self is less grounded in my memory than the printed words I've learned by heart. This thought is not completely unpleasant; it is also somehow comforting. To be myself, to be so utterly and absolutely myself that no particular circumstance or point of view can impeach the recognition, grants me a happy sense of freedom from the obligation of following the conditions of being who I am.

According to Dante, Christian dogma decrees that after we die we shall regain our earthly bodies again at the Last Judgment: all of us except suicides, "for it is not just that a man have what he has taken from himself." Science teaches us that the human body commits a kind of periodic suicide. Each of our organs, each of our bones, each of our cells dies and is reborn every seven years. None of our features is the same today as it was in the past, and yet we say, with blind confidence, that we are who we were. The question is, what do we mean by "being" ourselves? What are the identifying signs? Something that is not the shape of my body, not my voice or my touch, my mouth, my nose, my eyes—something there is that is me. It lies, like a timorous little animal, invisible behind a jungle of physical trappings. None of the disguises and masks that I wear represent myself to myself except in uncertain hints and tiny forebodings: a rustle in the leaves, a scent, a muffled growl. I know it exists, my reticent self. In the meantime, I wait. Perhaps its presence will be confirmed but only on my last day, when it will suddenly emerge from the undergrowth, will show itself full-faced for an instant, and then will be no more.

The shadow of a fat man in the moonlight
Precedes me on the road down which I go;
And should I turn and run, he would pursue me:
This is the man whom I must get to know.

—JAMES REEVES, "Things to Come"

To allow his words not to deny but "gradually to arrive at the conclusion with appropriate slowness," throughout his journey, Dante, much like any curious traveler, asks questions about the customs and beliefs, the geography and history of the places he traverses. He is especially keen on knowing who the people are whom he meets, and from his first encounter, with the soul of Virgil, he asks the poet to tell him "whatever you might be, shade or real man!"[1] Some of the souls, like Virgil's, answer him directly; others refuse and must be bribed with the promise of having their story told when Dante returns to earth; still others are forced to submit; several more are questioned by Virgil for Dante's sake. On a number of occasions, Dante recognizes the soul as someone he knew when alive; at other times the transformation in the Otherworld is such that the recognition fails, and the poor soul must tell him who it was.

But the journey is not, of course, a mere exercise in reconnoitering: Dante is here to learn about himself and to discover in the mirror of others his own wretchedness and possibility of salvation. The Otherworld is not impermeable: its punished and purged sins, as well as the divine beatitudes, seep sometimes into the visitor and affect him for good or ill. Dante feels in his own heart the anger of the wrathful and the scorn of the proud; in the heavens of Paradise, a glimmer of the divine light shining on the elect is enough to dazzle and transform him. The three-act vision through which Virgil and Beatrice guide him is like an ongoing performance played out for his benefit, in which his own faults, fears, and hesitations, his temptations, errors, and falls, and even his moments of enlightenment are all displayed before his eyes and ears. The entire *Commedia* is presented to an audience of one, but that single spectator is also the main protagonist. This, in a different context, is what the Jungian analyst Craig Stephenson defines as a place where "still resides the multifaceted ambiguous living archetype of the theatre, with its architecture of memory and liminality, in which are housed the epistemological opposites of acting and observing, of knowing ourselves from within and knowing our world by looking without."[2]

Not only by the souls' stories does Dante discover who they are or once were. Not far from the summit of Mount Purgatory, walking behind Virgil and the poet Statius, Dante reaches the Cornice of the Gluttonous, where the excess of love for the things of this world must be purged through unrelieved starvation. While the ancient poets talk about their craft, Dante, now cleansed of the sin of pride that made him accept Homer's welcome to the Noble Castle, walks meekly behind his masters, learning from their dialogue:

> They went ahead, and I alone
> Behind, listening to their discourse
> Taught me by discussing poetry.

The three poets are greeted by a throng of pale and silent spirits, their skin stretched over their bones, their eyes dark and hollow like gemless rings. Perhaps it is Virgil and Statius's talk of poetry that brings to Dante's mind the idea that things are metaphors of themselves, that in an effort to translate the experience of reality into language, we sometimes see things as the words that name them, and the features of things as their incarnated script. "Who reads *OMO* in the face of man," says Dante, "would clearly have recognized there the *M*." Pietro Alighieri, Dante's son, in his commentary to the *Commedia*, noted that the image evoked was well known in his time: in Gothic script, *O*s are like human eyes, while *M* depicts the eyebrows and the nose.[3] This accords with the tradition of Genesis by which all creatures carry their name inscribed in their appearance, thus allowing Adam to identify them correctly when God orders him to name them immediately after their creation (Gen. 2:19–20).

Socrates, in Plato's *Cratylus,* also believes that names are manmade: to

The letters *OMO* depicting a human face, copied from a tenth-century Spanish manuscript (British Library, add. ms. 30844). (Photograph courtesy of the author)

suggest that the first words were given to us by the godhead is, for Socrates, not an explanation but merely an excuse for not having an explanation. The discussion about names in the Platonic dialogue is proposed by two friends of whom we know almost nothing except that they may have been, like Socrates himself, Plato's teachers. Cratylus believes that the names of things contain "a truth or correctness" derived from nature. Hermogenes, the other participant in the dialogue, disagrees and takes the Sophist position that language is a human creation. "Any name which you give, in my opinion, is the right one, and if you change that and give another, the new name is as correct as the old," he says. "For there is no name given to anything by nature; all is convention and habit of the users." Socrates argues (or at least, puts forward the suggestion) that "names rightly given are the likenesses and images of the things which they name," but goes on to say that it is nobler and clearer to learn from the things themselves rather than from their images. In the *Cratylus,* as in so many of the dialogues, the question under debate remains undecided.[4]

A name defines us from outside. Even if we choose a name to call ourselves, the identity purported by the name is exterior, something we wear for the convenience of others. Names, however, sometimes encapsulate an individual's essence. "Caesar I was, and now I am Justinian," proclaims the emperor who codified the Roman system of law in the sixth century, and who in Dante's Paradise sums up the history of Rome for his listener's benefit. In another instance, later, in the Heaven of the Sun, Bonaventure the Franciscan praises the founder of the Dominican order and notes that Dominic (meaning "belonging to the Lord") was given this name by his parents when "a spirit from up here moved them to call him / by the possessive adjective of him whose he was all." And of the names of Dominic's parents themselves, Felice (Happy) and Giovanna ("Grace of the Lord," according to Saint Jerome), Bonaventure notes, echoing the creed in the *Cratylus:*

> Oh, his father, truly Felice!
> Oh, his mother, truly Giovanna
> If, translated, it means what they say![5]

A name, however, does not entirely satisfy the question "Who am I?" and it is not through the knowledge of his name that Dante reaches an answer at the end of his quest. The question of this final identity merits further inquiry.

At the exact midpoint of the *Commedia,* in the thirtieth canto of *Purgatorio,* as the chariot drawn by the Gryphon appears in the Garden of Eden, three essential things take place simultaneously: Virgil vanishes, Beatrice reveals herself, and Dante is named for the first and only time in the entire poem. Between the disappearance of his poet guide and the humiliating scourging to which Beatrice will submit him, Dante's name is pronounced and makes him turn in recognition: "when I turned to the sound of my own name, / which out of necessity is here set down." Then Beatrice orders him to look at her:

> Look at me well: indeed I am, I am Beatrice.
> However did you dare approach this mountain?
> Did you not know that here a man is happy?[6]

Contrary to Narcissus, who remained enraptured by his own image in the water, when Dante glances down into the river Lethe he cannot bear the sight of himself, and looks away mortified.

Who Am I?

My eyes dropped down to the clear fountain;
But beholding myself in it, I drew them back to the grass,
So great a shame weighed down my brow.[7]

After having gone down to the depths of Hell and ascended the cornices of
Purgatory, Dante discovers his identity, yet this is revealed to him not by the
utterance of his name but by the reflection of his image. Up to this point,
guided by Virgil, he has only seen others enact failings that he sometimes
recognizes as his, but now, for the first time, Dante is conscious of witnessing
his own dramatic performance. Dante must weep, he now learns, not for
things outside him but for his innermost being, not over the departure of his
beloved Virgil, not for love of the beloved Beatrice, but for his own sins, knowing at last who he is so that he may repent of who he was. Then he can drink
of the waters of Lethe and forget. In Paradise, there is no memory of sin.

The question "Who am I?" is no more fully answered by a name than a
book is revealed fully by its title. The cowardly soldier Parolles in *All's Well
That Ends Well* carries a name that (as Shakespeare's audience, with a smat-
tering of French, must have understood as an intentional pun) points to his
use of words for lying and bragging. Parolles is overheard by two lords as he
speaks to himself, seeking a way to escape humiliation, and for the first time
in the play, everything he says about himself to himself is true. "Is it possible
that he know that he is, and be that he is?" asks one of the lords, amazed that
this fool can reason truthfully. He can and he does, because what Shakespeare is attempting with the person of Parolles is to find behind the mask
whatever it is that makes him who he is. That is why, when shortly afterwards, the final disgrace comes upon him, Parolles sheds his role of *miles
gloriosus* and becomes utterly his own person: "Captain I'll be no more," he
says, "But I will eat and drink, and sleep as soft / As captain shall: simply the
thing I am / Shall make me live."[8] "The thing I am": Parolles's sudden illumination answers the underlying sense of Hamlet's much-abused question, and
involuntarily echoes the tremendous answer of the godhead to Moses: "I Am
That I Am."

Partly, what we are may be what we believe we once were and lost. "I'm
looking for the face I had," says a woman in a Yeats poem, "before the world

was made." Sometimes the shadow of an identity seems like that face, half-remembered, now forgotten, as in those early states of Alzheimer's in which we lose some part of the assurance of being whatever it is we are. Aristophanes, in Plato's *Symposium,* proposed that human beings were of three sexes, males born from the sun, females from the earth, and hermaphrodites from the moon, which partakes of either sex. The hermaphrodites were the strongest and in their vanity tried (like the builders of Babel) to scale the heights of heaven and attack the gods. To prevent this, Zeus split each hermaphrodite in half, causing the male half to desire to be reunited with the female half, and the female half with the male. This resulted in three kinds of couplings: the sun-males desired the sun-males, the earth-females desired the earth-females, the lunar hermaphrodites, now cloven in two, became the heterosexual humans who long for the half they had lost. "And so," Aristophanes concludes, "we are all like pieces of the coins that children break in half as keepsakes, making two out of one, like the flatfish, and each of us is forever seeking the half that will tally with himself." For Plato's Aristophanes, love is the impulse bred from these longings, the desire to know who we are by recalling who we have been.[9]

The first inkling of our identity comes early. In Jacques Lacan's description of what he called the "mirror stage," typically between the ages of six and eighteen months, a child, still unable to speak and control its motor activities, is confronted with an image of itself in a mirror. Its reaction is one of jubilation because the image shows the child a functional unity which it has yet to achieve. The child identifies with that which it will become, but at the same time the image is an illusion, since the reflection is not the child. The child's realization of who it is begins as both recognition and misrecognition, as the physical apprehension of identity and also an imaginary creation. The mirror, like the imagination, sets upon a stage a character who uses our first person singular. Rimbaud intuited that paradox when he wrote: "Car *Je* est un autre," "Because *I* is another." Alonso Quijano is both an old infirm gentleman with a taste for novels of chivalry and a courageous and just knight whose name is Don Quixote; when at the end of the book he allows himself to be convinced that his literary incarnation is a delusion, he dies. We are all, in this sense, *Doppelgängers:* seeing our double and rejecting it signals our end.[10]

Who Am I?

In order to know who we are integrally, in all our components, even that part of ourselves we call the unconscious (and which Carl Gustav Jung defined as "reality *in potentia*"), we question ourselves throughout our lives, seeking for clues. The unconscious, according to Jung, feeds us with such clues in our dreams, "backward-looking dreams or forward-looking anticipations," which, he says, have always, in all cultures, been read as intimations of the future. As images from the unconscious become conscious, telling us something about ourselves, they add to our sense of who we are, like the pages that are already read in a book. In the third century, Augustine compared the process to the recitation of a psalm. "Suppose that I am going to recite a psalm I know," he suggests in the *Confessions*. "Before I begin, my faculty of expectation is engaged by the whole of it. But once I have begun, as much of the psalm as I have removed from the province of my expectation and relegated to the past, now engages my memory, and the scope of the action which I am performing is divided between the two faculties of memory and expectation, the one looking back to the part which I have already recited, the other looking forward to the part which I have still to recite. But my faculty of attention is present all the while, and through it passes what was the future in the process of becoming the past. As the process continues, the province of memory is extended in proportion as that of expectation is reduced, until the whole of my expectation is absorbed. This happens when I have finished my recitation and it has passed into the province of memory." Unlike the psalm, however, the fathoming of the unconscious is never exhausted. That lifelong quest, the embodiment of intuitions and revelations about ourselves, Jung calls "individuation."[11]

In a 1939 essay published originally in English under the title "The Meaning of Individuation," and later rewritten in German and much revised, Jung defined individuation as "the process by which a person becomes a psychological 'in-dividual,' that is, a separate, indivisible unity or 'whole'" of all parts assembled and coherent, including those that feel unfathomable and unfamiliar to the person. Jung's first definition of individuation was given when he was sixty-four. Almost two decades later, five years before his death, he put together, partly in conversation with an acquaintance and partly in chapters written by himself, a kind of intellectual autobiography. Towards the end of the book, Jung takes up again the idea of individuation, but this time it is not the knowable and painfully known self that interests him but that other vast uncharted space of his own cartography. "The more uncertain I have felt about myself," he writes, "the more there has grown up in me a feeling of kinship with all things. In fact it seems to me as if that alienation which so long separated me from the world has become transferred into my own inner world, and has revealed to me an unexpected unfamiliarity with myself."[12]

"The meaning of my existence," Jung wrote, "is that life has addressed a question to me. Or, conversely, I myself am a question which is addressed to the world, and I must communicate my answer, for otherwise I am dependent upon the world's answer."[13] The quest to find out who we are, as whole and singular human beings, the attempt to answer life's question is responsible, in some measure, for our delight in the stories of others. Literature is not "the world's answer" but rather a trove of more and better questions. Like the tales told to Dante by the souls he meets, our literatures provide more or less efficient mirrors for discovering our own secret features. Our mental libraries are composite maps of who we are (or believe we are) and who we are not (or believe we are not). To admire, as did Freud, the early scenes of Goethe's *Faust,* or to be drawn to the inconclusiveness of *Faust*'s ending, as was Jung, to prefer Conrad to Jane Austen, as did Borges, or to choose Ismail Kadare over Haruki Murakami, as did Doris Lessing, is not necessarily to take a critical position in literary theory but more likely to respond to a question of reflective sympathy, of empathy, of recognition. Our readings are never absolutes: literature disallows dogmatic tendencies. Instead, we shift allegiances, prefer for a time a certain chapter of a certain book and later other chapters; one or two characters hold our fancy, but then others take their place. The enduring love of a reader is a rarer thing than we imagine, though we like to believe that our most considered literary tastes change little with the passing of the years. But we change, and our tastes change as well, and if we recognize ourselves in Cordelia today, we may call Goneril our sister tomorrow, and end up, in days to come, kindred spirits with Lear, a foolish, fond old man. This transmigration of souls is literature's modest miracle.

Who Am I?

137

Of all the miracles, however, that pinpoint the histories of our literatures, few are as astonishing as that of the birth of *Alice in Wonderland*. The
well-known story is worth repeating. On the afternoon of 4 July 1862, the
Reverend Charles Lutwidge Dodgson, accompanied by his friend the Reverend Robinson Duckworth, took the three young daughters of Dr. Liddell,
dean of Christ Church, on a three-mile boating expedition up the Thames,
from Folly Bridge, near Oxford, to the village of Godstow. "The sun was so
burning," Alice Liddell recalled many years later, "that we landed in the mead-
ows down the river, deserting the boat to take refuge in the only bit of shade
to be found, which was under a new-made hayrick. Here from all three came
the old petition of 'Tell us a story' and so began the ever-delightful tale. Sometimes to tease us—and perhaps being really tired—Mr. Dodgson would stop
suddenly and say, 'And that's all till next time.' 'Ah, but it is next time' would
be the exclamation from all three: and after some persuasion the story would
start afresh." When the boating party returned, Alice asked Dodgson to
write out the adventures for her. He said he would try, and sat up nearly the
whole night putting down the tale on paper, adding a number of pen-and ink
illustrations; afterwards, the little volume, *Alice's Adventures Underground*, was
often seen on the drawing-room table at the Deanery. Three years later, in
1865, the story was published by Macmillan in London under the pseudonym
of "Lewis Carroll" with the title *Alice's Adventures in Wonderland*.[14]

Reverend Duckworth recalled the excursion precisely: "I rowed *stroke*
and he rowed *bow* in the famous Long Vacation voyage to Godstow, when
the three Miss Liddells were our passengers, and the story was actually composed and spoken *over my shoulder* for the benefit of Alice Liddell, who was
acting as 'cox' of our gig. I remember turning round and saying, 'Dodgson,
is this an extempore romance of yours?' And he replied, 'Yes, I'm inventing
as we go along.'" Inventing Alice's adventures "as we go along": the truth is
unbelievable. That Alice's fall and explorations, her encounters and her discoveries, the syllogisms and puns and wise jokes should, in all their fantastic
and coherent development have been made up then and there in the telling
seems almost impossible. Osip Mandelstam, commenting on the composition of Dante's *Commedia*, says that it is naive of readers to believe that the
text they have in front of them was born full-fledged from the poet's brow

without a long mess of drafts and trials in its wake. No literary composition, says Mandelstam, is the fruit of an instant of inspiration: it is an arduous process of trial and error, helped along by experienced craft.[15] But in the case of *Alice* we know it wasn't so: precisely such an impossibility seems to have been the case. No doubt Carroll, in the back of his mind, had previously composed many of the jokes and puns that pepper the story, since he loved puzzles and word games, and spent much of his time inventing them for his pleasure and that of his child friends. But a bagful of tricks is not enough to explain the strict logic and joyful avatars that govern the perfectly rounded plot.

Alice's Adventures was followed six years later by *Through the Looking-Glass,* a story that did indeed benefit from the usual desk time, and yet the looking-glass chess game of the latter is not better constructed than the mad card game of the former, and all the wonderful nonsense in both stories obviously stems from that single invented "extempore" fantasy told on the primordial afternoon. Mystics are said to receive in full dictation from the godhead, and the history of literature boasts of a few celebrated examples of such in toto compositions—Caedmon's "Hymn of Creation" and Coleridge's "Kubla Khan" are two examples—but we almost never have an unbiased witness of these poetic miracles. In the case of *Alice's Adventures in Wonderland,* Reverend Duckworth's testimony seems unimpeachable.

No miracle, however, is entirely unexplainable. Carroll's tale has deeper roots in the human psyche than its nursery reputation might suggest. *Alice's Adventures in Wonderland* does not read like another children's story: its geography has the powerful reverberations of other established mythical places, such as Utopia and Arcadia. In the *Commedia,* Matilda, the guardian spirit on the summit of Mount Purgatory, explains to Dante that the Golden Age of which poets have sung is a forgotten memory of a paradise lost, a vanished state of perfect happiness; perhaps Wonderland is the unconscious memory of a state of perfect reason, a state which, seen now through the eyes of social and cultural conventions, appears to us as utter madness.[16] Whether archetypal or not, Wonderland seems always to have existed in some form or other: one never follows Alice down the rabbit hole and through the Red Queen's labyrinthine kingdom for the first time. Only the Liddell sisters and Reverend

Duckworth can be said to have been present at the creation, and even they must have felt a sense of déjà vu: after that first day, Wonderland entered the universal imagination much like the Garden of Eden, a place we know exists without ever having set foot in it. Wonderland ("it is not down in any map; true places never are," as Melville noted of another archetypal location)[17] is the recurrent landscape of our dream life.

Because Wonderland is, of course, our world, or rather a stage on which the things of our world are played out for us to see—not in unconscious symbolic terms (in spite of Freudian readings), not as an allegory of the anima (according to Jungian interpretations), not as a Christian parable (in spite of the serendipity of names on the storyteller's journey, from Folly Bridge to Godstow, "God's Place"), not as a dystopian fable like those of Orwell or Huxley (as certain critics have argued). Wonderland is simply the place in which we find ourselves daily, mad as it may seem, with its quotidian ration of the heavenly, the hellish, and the purgatorial—a place through which we must wander as we wander through life, following the instructions of the King of Hearts: "Begin at the beginning," he tells the White Rabbit, "and go on till you come to the end: then stop."[18]

Alice (as we have said of Dante) is armed with only one weapon for the journey: language. It is with words that we make our way through the Cheshire Cat's forest and the Queen's croquet ground. It is with words that Alice discovers the difference between what things are and what they appear to be. It is her questioning that brings out the madness of Wonderland, hidden, as in our world, under a thin coat of conventional respectability. We may try to find logic in madness, as the Duchess does by finding a moral to everything, but the truth is, as the Cheshire Cat tells Alice, that we have no choice in the matter: whichever path we follow, we will find ourselves among mad people, and we must use language as best we can to keep a grip on what we deem to be our sanity. Words reveal to Alice that the only indisputable fact of this bewildering world is that under an apparent rationalism we are all mad. Like Alice, we risk drowning ourselves (and everyone else) in our own tears. We like to think, as the Dodo does, that no matter in what direction or how incompetently we run, we should all be winners and we are all entitled to a prize. Like the White Rabbit, we give orders left and right, as if others were obliged (and honored) to serve us. Like the Caterpillar, we question the identity of our fellow creatures but have little idea of our own, even on the verge of losing that identity. We believe, with the Duchess, in punishing the annoying behavior of the young, but we have little interest in the reasons for that behavior. Like the Mad Hatter, we feel that we alone have the right to food and drink at a table set for many more, and we cynically offer the thirsty and hungry wine when there is no wine and jam every day except today. Under the rule of despots like the Red Queen, we are forced to play mad games with inadequate instruments—balls that roll away like hedge-hogs and sticks that twist and turn like flamingoes—and when we don't suc-ceed in following the instructions, we are threatened with having our heads chopped off. Our education methods, as the Gryphon and the Mock-Turtle explain to Alice, are either exercises in nostalgia (the teaching of Laughing and Grief) or training courses in the service of others (how to be thrown with the lobsters into the sea). And our system of justice, long before Kafka described it, is like the one set up to judge the Knave of Hearts, incomprehensible and unfair. Few of us, however, have Alice's courage, at the end of the book, to stand up (literally) for our convictions and refuse to hold our tongue. Be-cause of this supreme act of civil disobedience, Alice is allowed to wake from her dream. We, unfortunately, are not.

Fellow travelers, we readers recognize in Alice's journey, as we do in Dante's, the themes ever present in our lives: pursuit and loss of dreams, the attendant tears and suffering, the race for survival, being forced into servi-tude, the nightmare of confused self-identity, the effects of dysfunctional families, the required submission to nonsensical arbitration, the abuse of authority, perverted teaching, the impotent knowledge of unpunished crimes and unfair punishments, and the long struggle of reason against unreason. All this, and the pervading sense of madness, are, in fact, a summary of the book's table of contents.

"To define true madness," we are told in *Hamlet*, "what is't but to be nothing else but mad?" Alice would have agreed: madness is the exclusion of everything that is not mad, and therefore everyone in Wonderland falls under the Cheshire Cat's dictum ("We're all mad here"). But Alice is not Hamlet. Her dreams are not bad dreams, she never mopes, she never sees herself as the hand of ghostly justice, she never insists on proof of what is crystal clear, she believes in immediate action. Words, for Alice, are living creatures, and thinking (contrary to Hamlet's belief) does not make things good or bad. She certainly does not want her solid flesh to melt, any more than she wants it to shoot up or shrink down (even though, in order to pass through the small garden door, she wishes she could "shut up like a telescope"). Alice would never have succumbed to a poisoned blade or drunk, like Hamlet's mother, from a poisoned cup: picking up the bottle that says "DRINK ME" she first looks to see whether it is marked *poison* or not, "for she had read several nice stories about children who had got burnt, and eaten up by wild beasts, and other unpleasant things, all because they *would* not remember the simple rules their friends had taught them." Alice is much more reasonable than the Prince of Denmark and his family.[19]

Like Hamlet, however, Alice must have wondered, crammed in the White Rabbit's house, if she too might not be bounded in a nutshell, but as to being king (or queen) of infinite space, Alice does not merely fret about it: she strives for the title, and in *Through the Looking-Glass,* she works hard to earn the promised dream-crown. Brought up on strict Victorian precepts rather than lax Elizabethan ones, she believes in discipline and tradition, and has no time for grumbling and procrastination. Throughout her adventures, like a well-brought-up child, Alice confronts unreason with simple logic. Convention (the artificial construct of reality) is set against fantasy (the natural reality). Alice knows instinctively that logic is our way of making sense of nonsense and uncovering its secret rules, and she applies it ruthlessly, even among her elders, whether confronting the Duchess or the Mad Hatter. And when arguments prove useless, she insists on at least making the unjust absurdity of the situation plain. When the Red Queen demands that the court give the "sentence first—verdict afterwards," Alice quite rightly answers "Stuff and nonsense!" That is the only answer that most of the absurdities in our world deserve.[20]

However, Alice's journey is one from which she emerges not with answers but with an open question. In her underground adventures and later through the looking-glass, Alice will be tortured with the thought of not being who she thinks she is, or even of ceasing to be, which leads ineluctably to the terrible conundrum posed by the Caterpillar: "Who are *You?*" "I—I hardly know, Sir, just at present," she answers shyly. "At least I know who I *was* when I got up this morning, but I think I must have changed several times since then." The Caterpillar sternly tells her to explain herself. "I can't explain myself, I'm afraid, Sir," she says, "because I'm not myself, you see." To test her, he asks her to recite things from memory, but the words come out "different." Alice and the Caterpillar know that we are defined by what we remember, since our memories are our biographies and hold our image of ourselves.[21]

Waiting to see the effect produced by the beverage in the bottle that says "DRINK ME," Alice asks herself whether she might end by "going out altogether, like a candle. I wonder what I should be like then?" The answer is given in *Through the Looking-Glass* by Tweedledee and Tweedledum, when they point to the Red King asleep under a tree. "And what do you think he's dreaming about?" asks Tweedledee. Alice says that no one can know that. "Why, about *you!*" Tweedledee exclaims. "And if he left off dreaming about you where do you suppose you'd be?" "Where I am now, of course," Alice answers confidently. "Not you!" Tweedledee retorts contemptuously. "You'd be nowhere. Why you're only a sort of thing in his dream!"[22]

Alice wonders if she might not be Ada or Mabel (but "*she's* she, and I'm *I*," she reflects, distraught); the White Rabbit takes Alice for someone called Mary Ann; the Pigeon believes she's a serpent; the Live Flowers take her for a flower; the Unicorn believes that she is a fabulous monster, and proposes that, if she'll believe in him, he'll believe in her. Our identity seems to depend on the belief of others. We gaze into the screens of our electronic gadgets with the intensity and constancy of Narcissus gazing into the pool of water, expecting to be restored or affirmed in our identity not by the world around us, not in the workings of our interior life, but through the often inane messaging of others who virtually acknowledge our existence and whose existence we virtually acknowledge. And when we die, and our fleeting communications are inspected for clues of who we were, a little fable imagined by Oscar Wilde will become pertinent:

When Narcissus died the pool of his pleasure changed from a cup of sweet waters into a cup of salt tears, and the Oreads came weeping through the woodland that they might sing to the pool and give it comfort.

And when they saw that the pool had changed from a cup of sweet waters into a cup of salt tears, they loosened the green tresses of their hair and cried to the pool and said, "We do not wonder that you should mourn in this manner for Narcissus, so beautiful was he."

"But was Narcissus beautiful?" said the pool.

"Who should know that better than you?" answered the Oreads. "Us did he ever pass by, but you he sought for, and would lie on your banks and look down at you, and in the mirror of your waters he would mirror his own beauty."

And the pool answered, "But I loved Narcissus because, as he lay on my banks and looked down at me, in the mirror of his eyes I saw ever my own beauty mirrored."[23]

Alice conceives of a different way of deciding for herself who she might be. Trapped down the rabbit hole, Alice asks herself who she really is and refuses to be anyone she doesn't want to be. "It'll be no use their putting their heads down and saying, 'Come up again, dear!' I shall only look up and say, 'Who am I, then? Tell me that first, and then, if I like being that person, I'll come up: if not, I'll stay down here till I'm somebody else.'"[24] If things don't appear to have meaning, then Alice will make sure that she chooses a meaning (an identity that will denote that meaning) for herself. She might be echoing Jung: "I must communicate my answer, for otherwise I am dependent upon the world's answer." Alice must make the Caterpillar's question her own.

And yet, in spite of its apparent madness, our world, like that of Wonderland, tantalizingly suggests that it *does* have a meaning and that if we look hard enough behind the "stuff and nonsense" we will find something that explains it. Alice's adventures proceed with uncanny precision and coherence, so that we, as readers, have the growing impression of an elusive sense in all the surrounding absurdity. The entire book has the quality of a Zen koan or a Greek paradox, of something meaningful and at the same time inexplicable, something on the verge of revelation. What we feel, falling down the rabbit hole after Alice and following her through her journey, is that Wonderland's madness is not arbitrary, nor is it innocent. Half epic and half dream, Carroll's invention lays out for us a necessary space somewhere between solid earth and fairyland, a vantage point from which to see the universe in more or less explicit terms, translated, as it were, into a story. Like the mathematical formulas that fascinated Carroll, Alice's adventures are both hard fact and lofty invention.

This is true of the *Commedia* as well. Guided by Virgil's hand through the treacherous terrain of Hell or by the momentous smile of Beatrice through the adamantine logic of Heaven, Dante undertakes his voyage on two planes simultaneously: one which grounds him (and us, his readers) in the reality of flesh and blood and one in which that reality can be reconsidered and transformed. This double reality is like that of the Cheshire Cat perched on its branch, drifting from something bewilderingly visible to the miraculous (and reassuring) ghost of a Beatrician smile.

8

What Are We Doing Here?

THE YEAR I WORKED FOR A newspaper in Buenos Aires, in my early twenties, I was sent into the countryside to interview a priest, Domingo Jaca Cortejarena, of the parish of Mones Cazón, who had translated the nineteenth-century Argentine national poem *Martín Fierro*, by José Hernández, into Basque under the title *Matxin Burdín*. He was a small, fat, smiling man who had come to Argentina in the late thirties and had entered orders during his exile. Out of gratitude towards the country that had welcomed him, he had decided to undertake the translation, but his passion, like that of the elderly Sherlock Holmes, was beekeeping. Twice during our interview he excused himself and went towards the hives that sat in humming rows under the jacaranda trees, and there he performed certain rituals which I didn't understand. He spoke to the bees in Basque. When he answered my questions in Spanish, he gestured vehemently; with the bees his movements were gentle and also his voice. He said that their humming reminded him of falling water. He seemed utterly unafraid of being stung. "When you collect the honey," he explained, "you must always leave some for the hive. Industrial collectors don't do that, and the bees resent it and become avaricious. Bees respond to generosity with generosity." He was worried because many

(Opposite) Dante and Virgil in the Wood of the Suicides. Woodcut illustrating Canto XIII of the Inferno, *printed in 1487 with commentary by Cristoforo Landino. (Beinecke Rare Book and Manuscript Library, Yale University)*

of his bees were dying, and he accused the neighboring farmers of using pesticides that were killing not only the bees but also the songbirds. It was he who told me that when a beekeeper dies, someone must go tell the bees that their keeper is dead. Since then I've wished that when I die someone will do the same for me, and tell my books that I will not come back.

Walking through his untidy garden (he said he liked weeds), the little priest observed that Hernández had committed a curious error in his poem. *Martín Fierro* is the story of a gaucho who deserts the army after being forcibly conscripted. He is hunted down by a sergeant who, after having him surrounded and seeing that Fierro will fight alone to the death, says he will not allow a brave man to be killed, and, turning against his own soldiers, allies himself with the deserter. The priest said that in the poem the gauchos give a description of the land and the sky, and this is the mistake: that was something city people did, not men of the country, for whom the landscape was unremarkable because it was simply there. Hernández, a city intellectual, would have been curious about the natural surroundings; the gaucho Martín Fierro would not.

I was taught in school that the model for Hernández's bucolic interests was Virgil, whose landscapes were not those of the Po valley of his youth (as Peter Levi has observed) but a much more deliberately artificial picture of amorous shepherds and beekeepers inherited perhaps from Theocritus. Virgil was the preferred classical author in the schools of the Spanish colonies, along with Cicero; Hernández would not have studied Greek, a culture neglected in Catholic countries because of its uncomfortable proximity to that of the scholars of the Reformation. In spite of the bucolic convention, Virgil's woods, streams, and glades are conceivable as authentic landscapes, and his advice about beekeeping and farming is, I am told, perfectly sound. Hernández prefers to eliminate any sense of artificiality, and in spite of lending his gauchos philosophical ruminations and invocations to all the saints (as Virgil invoked Apollo and the Muses), he manages to ground his characters in a believable place. Martín Fierro's pampas are immediately recognizable: the vastness, the sudden appearance of a hut or a tree, the endless horizon, which the French writer Drieu La Rochelle described as inducing "horizontal vertigo." If Hernández fell into the mistake my Basque priest pointed out, it was because he must have felt, like La Rochelle, an outsider, a city dweller for whom it was impossible to stand in these empty spaces under an uninterrupted sky without being overcome by the whirling immensity. When Martín Fierro, in his loneliness, stares up at the stars, he sees them as a mirror of his emotions:

> It's sad, in the open countryside
> To spend night after night
> Gazing up at the slow courses
> Of the stars that God created,
> Without any other company
> Than one's loneliness and the wild beasts.

The observer is human, and the landscape he observes becomes contaminated with human aspirations and regrets: the underlying question is "What am I doing here?" In classical bucolic poetry, the landscape mirrors the nostalgia for a blissful Golden Age invented perhaps by the Greeks; in Hernández, the nostalgia is, of course, a literary conceit, but it is also historically true. When Hernández has his hero say the following lines, he is describing not a wishful magical age but the memory of Fierro's own life, or what he felt his life was before the army hauled him away:

> I have known this land
> Where the peasant lived
> And where he had his home
> And his children and wife . . .
> It was such pleasure to see
> How he spent day after day.

The word *gaucho*, used as an insult by the Spanish colonists towards the locals, was adopted with pride by those who fought against the Spanish crown, but soon after independence the word relapsed into its pejorative connotation to label those who lived off the land without attempting to congregate in cities. A gaucho was seen by the urban dwellers as a barbarian who refused civilization, as Domingo Faustino Sarmiento made clear in the title of his classic *Facundo: Civilization and Barbarism*. Superb horsemen and herders, settling wherever they chose, far away from the sprawling metropolis, the gauchos lived off small crops and stray cattle, and worked occasionally as hired hands for the wealthy *hacendados* who had bought or had been given titles to vast extensions of virgin land. Obligatory conscription, expropriation of their homes by the government, and the increasingly frequent incursions of native raiders changed all that, and Martín Fierro incarnated the change. The pampas were no longer an open space where anyone could live without benefit of deed of sale or real estate contract: it had now become, for the gauchos, an alien place that allowed no roots except to those who claimed to have bought it and felt entitled to exploit it. For the gaucho, he and the land were vitally entwined, and what affected the one affected the other; for the landowners, the land was property, to be used as effectively as possible in order to extract the greatest economic profit. "What do you think we're doing here on this earth?" my priest asked, without expecting an answer. "All I know is that whatever it is we're doing, the bees are dying."

Vladimir: What are we doing here? That is the question.

—SAMUEL BECKETT, *Waiting for Godot,* act 2

Two planes of existence are explicit in all three of Dante's realms, that of reality and that of reflection on that reality. Dante's land-scapes, as well as the souls he encounters in them, are simultaneously real and imaginary. No detail in the *Commedia* is arbitrary: the reader retraces Dante's voyage following the path Dante followed and seeing the things he saw. Darkness and light, smells and sounds, rock formations, rivers, water that falls with the sound of humming bees (as my Basque priest had remarked), open spaces and chasms, crags and hollows carefully constitute the worlds beyond the world. Or, rather, the first two: in Heaven there are sensible presences but no tangible geography, since in Heaven there is no time and no space.

Three main woods grow in the *Commedia:* the dark forest from which Dante emerges before the encounter with Virgil, the awful Wood of Suicides in Canto XIII of the *Inferno,* and the Garden of Eden on the summit of Mount Purgatory. Heaven is devoid of vegetation, except for the monstrous rose that congregates the souls in the Empyrean. All three forests exist in relation to their inhabitants: they are defined by that which takes place under their boughs, as settings for the story. As always in Dante, our actions determine our geography.

John Ruskin, commenting on the discovery of what he calls "the laws of beauty" in the thirteenth century, remarks that "these discoveries of ultimate truth are, I believe, never made philosophically, but instinctively." No doubt a vast library of learning underpins the *Commedia,* but as Ruskin rightly warns us, not every detail can be the result of a scholarly process: the total creation is too precise to have been consciously justified word by word. "Milton's effort," Ruskin notes, "in all that he tells us of his Inferno, is to make it indefinite; Dante's, to make it *definite.*" For this reason, Ruskin says, upon reaching the Garden of Eden after daring to cross the purgatorial wall of flames, Dante enters a lovingly described "dense wood" which reminds the reader of the "dark forest" of the poem's beginning. And the "pathlessness of the wood, the most dreadful thing possible to him in his days of sin and shortcoming, is now a joy to him in his days of purity. And as the fenceless-ness and thicket of sin led to the fettered and fearful order of eternal punish-ment, so the fencelessness and thicket of the free virtue lead to the loving and constellated order of eternal happiness."[1]

An even more poignant example is given at the Wood of Suicides. After being guided by the centaur Nessus across the River of Blood in which those guilty of murder are punished, Dante and Virgil reach a gloomy wood where, again, no path is visible. This wood is made of negatives, punctuated by a hail of *no*s that begin each of the first three tercets of the canto, and all the verses of the second. This is a place where being itself is denied.

> No, Nessus had not yet returned
> When we moved deep into a wood
> That was not marked by any path.
>
> No green foliage, but of a murky hue,
> No smooth branches, but all knotted and warped,
> No apples were there, but dry and poisoned twigs.
>
> No undergrowth so rough and thick
> Have the wild beasts that loathe the farmer's plots
> Between Cecina and the Cornetto.

Upon these ghastly thorny trees the Harpies make their nests. These mon-strous creatures of wide wings and human necks and faces, with feet like claws and feathered bellies, endlessly utter woeful shrieks that announce the sor-rows to come.[2]

Before advancing farther, Virgil tells Dante that they are now in the second cornice of the seventh circle and instructs him to pay attention so as to see "things that will strip away belief from my speech" because in this place of shadows speech is disembodied: Dante hears wailings but sees no one, and he wonders whether there are souls hiding in the undergrowth. To dispel his doubts, Virgil instructs him to break off a small shoot from one of the trees around him. Dante obeys, and the tree cries out in pain, "Why do you rend me?" From the stump, dark blood begins to flow.

It said again: "Why do you tear me?
Have you no single breath of pity?

"Men we were, and now we're become stumps:
Truly your hand should have been more merciful
If we had been the very souls of snakes."

As Dante steps back in horror, blood and words gush out together from the broken splint. In the *Aeneid,* Virgil had described how Aeneas, after leaving the coast of Troy, seeking to honor his mother, Venus, and the other gods with a sacrifice, tears up cornel bushes and myrtle to deck the altar. Suddenly, he sees with amazement that the stumps begin to ooze drops of black blood, and a voice from below the ground tells him that this is the tomb of Polydorus, treacherously killed by the Thracian king to whom his father, Priam, had entrusted him.[3] Virgil, realizing that Dante has forgotten this episode from his epic (on the imaginary plane), has thought it necessary to prove to him empirically the prodigious fact that trees can bleed (on the plane of factual reality). Doing so, Virgil reminds Dante that both planes are necessary to experience existence fully.

However, "to make amends," Virgil now asks the wounded spirit to say who he is so that Dante might later restore his fame in the world of the living. (Throughout Hell, Virgil, whose own fame on earth is assured, assumes that the dead care about what the living think of them.) The weeping tree proves to be the politician and poet Pier delle Vigne, chancellor of the Two Sicilies and minister to Frederick II, the emperor who so disastrously conducted linguistic experiments with children. Delle Vigne committed suicide after being falsely accused of treachery, and is now punished because his soul, thinking it could escape shame through death, "made me unjust against my just self."[4]

The trees can speak only as long as their blood flows. Having had no pity on themselves, they now beg it of Dante, and seeing them Dante feels a pity as strong as the one he felt only once before in this pitiless realm, after hearing Francesca's story in the circle of the lustful. Since pity is always in some measure pity for oneself, Dante the poet, throughout his own painful exile, may have considered the possibility of suicide and rejected it. Certainly the question of suicide was for him a troubled one. Within the dogma of the Catholic Church, suicide was clearly a sin committed against the body as temple of the soul. Saint Augustine had reduced suicide to a simple equivalence to murder, forbidden in the Sixth Commandment: "It remains that we take the command 'You shall not kill' as applying to human beings, that is, other persons and oneself. For to kill oneself is to kill a human being."[5] But among Augustine's (and Dante's) beloved pagan authors, suicide was often considered a noble and honorable act.

In a profound meditation on this episode, Olga Sedakova asks what Pier della Vigne means when he says, "men we were," and suggests that to be human is to be heard, to be able to speak. "Man is first and foremost a message, a sign," she writes. But what sign? Certainly one that links blood with language, suffering with the need to express the suffering in words. This is perhaps why, taking Sedakova's remarks a step farther, we could say that, considering the ancient metaphor of the world as book, the writing in nature's book mirrors both human suffering and the suffering inflicted by humans upon nature. Suffering, whether of a human being or of the earth itself, must be translated into words of revolt, repentance, or prayer. (Some years ago, a poster in British Columbia depicted a landscape devastated by clear-cutting overlaid with a quotation from Shakespeare's *Julius Caesar*: "O pardon me, thou bleeding piece of earth, / That I am meek and gentle with these butchers," equating the land with Caesar's butchered body.) Dante, in *De vulgari eloquentia,* remarks that after the expulsion from Eden, every human being begins a life of suffering uttering a word that denotes pain: "Ahi!"[6]

Sedakova believes that for Dante life and violence are two absolute opposites, and violence, in every sense, belongs to the realm of death. If this is true, then we can argue that when violence erupts in life, it translates the

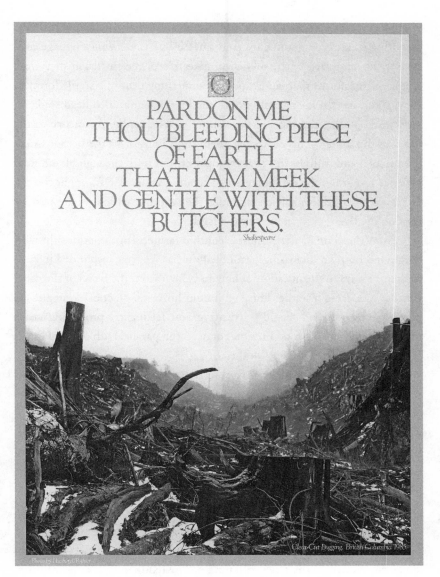

Anti-logging poster from British Columbia.

vital, creative human vocabulary into one that denotes its shadow side, the loss of what has been granted us. And since in the *Commedia* language constructs the landscape where all action takes place, the intrusion of violent language transforms that landscape into something deadly, a sterile forest fit for the Harpies. In the ancient world, the Harpies embodied dead souls intent on despoiling the souls of the living.[7] Consequently, if violence to the self robs the sinner of his or her own being and transforms the suicide into a tongue-tied and fruitless tree that can only express itself through blood, then violence to nature, the deliberate act of creating such a forest, might be seen as a form of collective suicide that kills the world of which we are part by turning the living ground into a wasteland.

From the time of the earliest Neolithic farmers, our relationship with nature has been an increasingly troubled one, as we have responded in contradictory ways to the question of how to benefit from the fruits of the earth without rendering it sterile. Throughout our histories, practical strategies for plowing, sowing, and reaping, irrigating and fertilizing, protecting crops from pests and storing food for times of need run parallel with poetical imaginings of nature as the Great Mother.

In the ancient world, noted Ruskin, forests were considered "sources of wealth and places of shelter," sacred, haunted sites that were by and large benevolent towards humans.[8] In the Middle Ages, this vision changed and was reimagined as a dichotomy: the countryside was now seen either as dangerous, the demonic shadow of the civilized city, or as a place of ascetic cleansing, opposed to the vices of Babylon. It was depicted both as a savage place of refuge for criminals and wild beasts, outlawed sects and unspeakable practices, and as a paradisiacal realm, home to a lost Golden Age, a sanctuary from the sordid business of everyday life. This dichotomy was reflected in the visual arts. In the early Middle Ages, many artists, concerned with obeying as far as possible the tenets of faith and the requirements of portraiture, gradually abandoned certain mundane genres popular in Hellenistic Rome such as decorative landscape painting and turned to allegorical scenes and biblical stories, with depictions of daily life appearing as background. Dante himself, a keen observer of the cycles and changes in nature and knowledgeable about the techniques of agriculture and animal husbandry, describes the landscapes through which he passes in startling detail: they are stages for human events and examples of the inspired creation of the godhead. Whether in the gloom of Hell, where the whiteness of the naked bodies reveals with excruciating clarity their torments, or in the earthly Purgatory, with its dawn, dusk, dark night, and brilliant sunlight illuminating or shading the painful ascent of souls, the landscapes Dante describes are both intensely real and deeply symbolic, form and meaning revealing each other throughout the journey.

For Dante, all possible wisdom, all knowledge of one's own being, all intuition of God's will is made explicit in nature itself, in the stones and stars, "when divine love / first set in motion these lovely things." The experience of nature is the experience of God's hand in the world, and knowing how to interact with all other living things is a way of recognizing our own place in the cosmos. What we do to ourselves, we do to the world; therefore, following Dante's method of *contrapasso*, what we do to the world, we do to ourselves.[9] Dante's moods and doubts, fears and revelations are echoed in the everyday life of the landscapes he crosses; the broken rocks of Malebolge, the agonized trees of the Wood of Suicides and the exultant vegetation in Matilda's grove, the burning sands of the seventh circle of Hell, and the breeze-swept meadow of Eden affect Dante in body and in spirit.

Virgil too understood the complexity of our relationship to nature, and how our behavior determines nature's fate and our own. Virgil had lost his family farm after the defeat of Brutus and Cassius at Philippi in 42 B.C.E., but his farming experience is evident throughout the *Georgics,* which could be read as an agricultural manual in verse. Describing the pests and weeds that attack the crops, for example, Virgil admonishes the farmer: "Therefore, unless time and again your hoe assail the weeds, your voice affright the birds, your knife check the shade of the darkened land, and your vows invoke the rain, vainly, alas! will you eye your neighbour's big store, and in the woods shake the oak to solace hunger."[10]

Virgil's views harked back to those of ancient Greece, where two ideas prevailed regarding the responsibility of humans towards the natural world.

One, proclaimed by the followers of Pythagoras for instance, maintained that trees had souls. In the third century C.E., the philosopher Porphyry wrote: "Why should the slaughter of an ox or sheep be a greater wrong than the felling of a fir or oak, seeing that the soul is implanted in trees also?" The other, following Aristotle, taught that animals and plants existed solely to serve humankind. Echoing Aristotle's judgment, Pliny the Elder, in the first century C.E., pronounced: "It is for the sake of their timber that Nature has created . . . the trees."[11]

In the mid-second century B.C.E. in Rome, it became clear that the peasant families who had long cultivated their small plots were being forced out by powerful landowners, who employed slaves for investment farming. In order to revive the traditional agricultural mentality, in 133, the Gracchi brothers, then serving as tribunes, set up laws to control land reform. At the same time, agricultural manuals became popular throughout the Roman republic: a few were translations, such as that of the Carthaginian Mago, while others were original works by Cato, Columella, and Varro. Later, the emperor Augustus encouraged poets to take on agricultural themes so as to foster the notion that farming in the traditional way was a Roman gentleman's true occupation. Whether giving practical advice on how to farm, reworking the myths of nature, or comparing the delights of country life with the arduous business of the city, the Latin poets adopted the theme, and echoes of their work persisted for centuries.[12]

Not much documentation has come down to us regarding the development of agricultural methods in the Middle Ages. In places where two-field rotation was used, more labor and irrigation were required than in ancient Greece and Rome, and this led to the invention of more efficient instruments. The Arab conquests brought into Europe a number of new crops and cereals that required no irrigation: above all, hard wheat (which became the staple in most of the Mediterranean region) and sorghum. Though times of hardship were mainly due to natural causes such as floods and droughts, human factors, including over-cultivation and excessive logging, contributed to creating frequent periods of famine. In the Arab world, over-grazing and over-cultivation were minimized by a system called *hima,* which gave tribes in some regions collective rights over certain lands, but the system proved impractical in Europe. By the tenth or eleventh century, much of the land had been laid waste, rural security had waned, the monetary economy had failed to provide assistance to farmers, and a succession of plagues had led to a general decline of agriculture in Europe. Dante has Virgil say that certain souls in the seventh circle are being punished because they lived "disdaining Nature and her goodness."[13] Of the opposing notions of how we should behave regarding the natural world, Aristotle's had become obviously prevalent.

The Aristotelian attitude towards nature has had long-lasting consequences. In 1962, an American marine biologist who had been writing since the early fifties about the noxious effects of human activity on nature published a book, *Silent Spring,* that was to change the health policies of many countries and initiate the environmental movement around the world. Rachel Carson's early work at the U.S. Fish and Wildlife Service had made her aware of the effects of dumping atomic waste into the sea, as well as the then still undetected phenomenon of global warming; her research into the misuse of pesticides revealed that the agricultural industries were both dangerously inefficient and untruthful in their reports to the public. As her biographer Linda Lear noted, with *Silent Spring* "Carson did more than challenge the scientific establishment, or force the implementation of new pesticide regulations. The hostile reaction of the establishment to Carson and her book was evidence that many government and industry officials recognized that Carson had not only challenged the conclusions of scientists regarding the benefits of the new pesticides, but that she had undermined their moral integrity and leadership." Dante might have judged them sinners against nature, like the woeful souls in the seventh circle who, because they never recognized their responsibility to the natural world, must run eternally on the burning sand, in a desecrated landscape, looking towards that which they have offended. "In these circles of the Violent," noted Charles Williams, "the reader is peculiarly conscious of a sense of sterility. The bloody river, the dreary wood, the harsh sand, which compose them, to some extent are there as symbols of unfruitfulness."[14]

Carson conceived the danger of chemical use as one bred from the stubborn unwillingness to look at consequences other than those desired by the practitioner. She understood (as Dante intuited) that deliberate ignorance of collateral lethal results implied a willful blindness towards the "cose belle," the "beautiful things" that nature offers, and is simply a form of self-destruction resulting from lack of humility and overwhelming greed. "Control of nature," wrote Carson, "is a phrase conceived in arrogance, born of the Neanderthal age of biology and philosophy, when it was supposed that nature exists for the convenience of man."[15]

This was, as noted, Aristotle's supposition. For Aristotle, property, not work, provides the means of making a living, and entitles a man to be called a citizen. Property consists of that which nature offers for human sustenance: cattle driven by nomad farmers, game taken by hunters, fish and birds caught by fishermen and trappers, and the fruits of harvest. "We must believe," he wrote, "first that plants exist for the sake of animals, second that all other animals exist for the sake of man." (Also slaves, since Aristotle argued that capturing "inferior people" and making them slaves was a natural human activity.)[16]

Aristotle's entwined arguments—our right to exploit nature and our right to exploit other "inferior" human beings—run throughout our economic histories to this day. In 1980, the United Nations Environmental Programme (UNEP) reported that desertification caused by deforestation threatened 35 percent of the world's land surface and 20 percent of the world's population. The vast process of deforestation in the Amazon, for instance, which after a steady decline spiked again in 2012 by more than a third, employs today tens of thousands of people working under slavelike conditions. A report from the World Wildlife Fund notes, "Poor people, lured from villages and deprived neighbourhoods, are brought to remote soy estates [planted after the trees have been cut down] where they are put to work in barbaric conditions— often at gunpoint and with no chance of escaping. . . . Those who fall sick are abandoned and replaced by others."[17]

In recent years, a new branch of psychology has explored the relationship between the human psyche and the natural surroundings. Under the somewhat fanciful name of ecopsychology (first used in 1992 by the historian Theodore Roszak, who also coined the term *counterculture*), it is the study of a phenomenon that poets have understood since they first associated storms with the raging of passion and flowering fields with moments of happiness; John Ruskin characterized it as the "pathetic fallacy." Attempting to analyze our mirroring in nature, ecopsychologists argue that because we are an intricate part of the natural world, separation from it (through neglect, indifference, violence, fear) results in something like psychological suicide. With a possible reference to Aristotle, the psychologist and poet Anita Barrows says, "It is only by a construct of the Western mind that we believe ourselves to be living in an 'inside' bounded by our skin, with everyone and everything else on the outside."[18]

In order to explain his own state of mind and his fantastic encounters, Dante will often describe a memory of natural surroundings. Reaching the stone bridge that would have allowed them to pass from the Cornice of the Hypocrites to the Chasm of the Thieves, Dante and his guide discover that it has been shattered, and a feeling of anguish overwhelms them. To explain to the reader what he felt, Dante conjures up a memory:

> During that period of the boyish year,
> When the sun tempers his locks under Aquarius
> And the nights already wane towards half the day,
>
> When the hoar frost copies out onto the ground
> The image of his sister white as snow,
> Though only a short while his pen holds out,
>
> The peasant, whose supplies now are gone,
> Rises and looks, and sees the fields
> All white, at which he slaps his thigh,
>
> Goes back into the house, and grumbles to and fro,
> Like a poor fool who knows not what to do.
> Then he comes out again and hope returns,
>
> Observing how the world has changed its face
> In such short while; so he picks up his staff
> And chases out his lambs to go and feed.

What Are We Doing Here?

In passages such as this, Dante is recalling, not Aristotle's utilitarian view of nature, but Virgil's, not the lyrical artifice of the *Eclogues* but the considered reflections of the *Georgics,* where Virgil abandoned the idyllic vision of country life and concentrated instead on the hardships and rewards of farming, and the farmer's responsibilities towards the natural world. "Toil conquered the world," Virgil wrote, "unrelenting toil, and want that pinches when life is hard." But, he continued, "Nature has ways manifold for rearing trees. For some, under no man's constraint, spring up of their own free will, and far and wide claim the plains and winding rivers. . . . But some spring from fallen seed, as tall chestnuts, and the broad-leaved tree, mightiest of the woodland, that spreads its shade for Jove, and oaks, deemed by the Greeks oracular." This natural generosity, as both Virgil and Dante understood, entails an obligation.[19]

On 31 March 2014 the Intergovernmental Panel on Climate Change (IPCC) issued a report about the effects of "man-made climate change around the world." A total of 309 specialized writers drawn from 70 countries were selected to produce the report, with the help of a further 436 contributing authors, and a total of 1,729 expert and government reviewers. Their conclusion was that since the nature of the risks brought on by climate change have become increasingly clear, governments need immediately to make drastic choices between suffering the consequences of these changes and forgoing or decreasing the financial profits sought by our national economies. The report identified vulnerable people, industries, and ecosystems worldwide and found that the risks from a changing climate come from our societies' vulnerability and lack of preparation in the face of future catastrophes. The risks from a changing climate depend strongly on how fast and how intensely those changes will occur; these will determine whether they are irreversible. "With high levels of warming that result from continued growth in greenhouse gas emissions, risks will be challenging to manage, and even serious, sustained investments in adaptation will face limits," said one of the chairmen of the panel, adding that climate change has already severely affected agriculture, human health, ecosystems on land and in the oceans, water supplies, and people's livelihoods from the tropics to the poles, from small islands to large continents, and from the wealthiest countries to the poorest.[20] Once again, we have been warned.

Dante may have considered Aristotle the supreme thinker, "master of those who know," as he calls him, but throughout the undergrowth of the *Commedia* creeps the intuitive suspicion that, with regard to our relationship to God's other book, the "maestro di color che sanno" was wrong.[21]

9
Where Is Our Place?

ON MY FIFTIETH BIRTHDAY, I stopped counting the places in which I had lived. Sometimes for just a few weeks, sometimes for a decade or more, the map of the world consisted for me not of its conventional representation on a globe, like the one that sat by my bed when I was a child, but of a personal cartography in which the largest masses of land were the places in which I spent the longest periods, and the islands the ones of briefer passage. Like the model of oneself designed by physiologists in which the size of each feature is given according to the importance we lend it in our mind, my model of the world is the map of my experience.

It is difficult to answer the question where is my home. My house and my library are like the shell of a crustacean, but along what seabed am I slowly crawling? "I had no nation now but the imagination," wrote Derek Walcott. This is as true for me today as it was in my childhood. I remember as a child trying to imagine from where I stood indoors the garden outside, then the street, the neighborhood, the city, enlarging the space of vision circle after circle until I thought I could see all around me the pinpointed darkness of the cosmos depicted in my natural sciences book. Stephen Dedalus had the same impulse when he inscribed on the flyleaf of his geography

(Opposite) Virgil and Dante see the traitors trapped in the ice. Woodcut illustrating Canto XXXII of the Inferno, *printed in 1487 with commentary by Cristoforo Landino. (Beinecke Rare Book and Manuscript Library, Yale University)*

book his name and then "Class of Elements, Clongowes Wood College, Sallins, County Kildare, Ireland, Europe, The World, The Universe." We want to know the full extent of that which is supposed to embrace us.

The place I live in defines me, at least in part, at least during the time I'm there. The presence of a market or a forest, the knowledge of certain events and certain customs, one language spoken by those around me rather than another, all change a multitude of my actions and reactions. Goethe observed, "No one wanders under palm-trees unpunished, and certainly one's way of thinking alters in a country where elephants and tigers are at home." The local fauna and flora shape my features. Where I am and who I am intertwine, and one questions the other. After leaving a place, I ask myself what is different in me now, what quality of taste or touch, what intonation, what subtle shift in the phrasing of a thought.

Memory, too, of course, is different. In Lawrence Durrell's *Constance; or, Solitary Practices,* a certain Mrs. Macleod, in her diary titled *An Englishwoman on the Nile,* makes this observation: "In Egypt one acts upon impulse as there is no rain to make one reflect." For a Sudanese in England the contrary is true: Mustafa Sa'eed, the enigmatic stranger who confides in the narrator of *Season of Migration to the North,* says that in soggy London "my soul contained not a drop of sense of fun." Places define us as we define them. Cartography is an art of mutual creation.

The places we name don't exist spontaneously: we conjure them up. The universe is blind to its own measures, its dimensions, its speed and duration, and as in the medieval definition of the godhead, the world is a circle whose center is everywhere and whose circumference is nowhere. We, however, carry our center within us and from our secret corner call out to the universe and say, "You orbit around me." Home patch, township, province, fatherland, continent, hemisphere are our necessary inventions, like the unicorn and the basilisk. As the Bellman says in *The Hunting of the Snark:*

> "What's the good of Mercator's North Pole and Equators,
> Tropics, Zones, and Meridian Lines?"
> So the Bellman would cry: and the crew would reply,
> "They are merely conventional signs!"

Where Is Our Place?

Faithful to his assertion, the Bellman provides his crew with the best and most accurate map: a perfect and absolute blank—the exact definition of our universe unobserved. Within this blank, we draw squares and circles, and trace paths from one place to another in order to have the illusion of being somewhere and someone. Northrop Frye tells the story of a doctor friend who, crossing the Arctic tundra with an Inuit guide, was caught in a blizzard. In the icy dark, outside the boundaries he knew, the doctor cried out, "We are lost!" His Inuit guide looked at him thoughtfully and answered, "We are not lost. We are here."

We are cartographers at heart and we parcel and label our "here" and believe that we move about, towards alien territory, perhaps merely in order to shift our grounding and our sense of identity. And so we believe that in one place we are alone and look out onto the world, and in another we are among our brethren and look back upon our self, lost somewhere in the past. We pretend to travel from home to foreign countries, from a singular experience to a communal alien one, from whom we once were towards whom we'll one day be, living in a constant state of exile. We forget that, wherever we find ourselves, we are always "here."

*Never ask the way of someone who knows it, because then you
won't be able to get lost.*

—RABBI NAHMAN OF BRATSLAV, *Tales*

F ar from the Aristotelian notion of a subservient nature, on the morning of Easter Friday 1300, the year of Christendom's first jubilee,
Dante emerged from a dark forest. The attempt to describe it to his
readers renewed in him the fear he had felt: it was "wild and rough and
strong," and so "bitter" that death could scarcely be worse. He could not
remember how he had entered the forest because he was full of sleep at the
time, but as he finally came out of the darkness he saw before him a mountain rising at the end of the valley, and above the mountain the rays of the
Easter sun. In his text the exact location of the forest is not given: it is everywhere and nowhere, the place into which we enter when our senses are
blurred, and the place from which we emerge when the rays of the sun wake
us, the dark place Saint Augustine called "the bitter forest of the world."
Dark things happen in the darkness, as our fairy tales tell us, but it may be
that, since our expulsion from the forest that was also a garden, the path
through the other terrible forest is almost certainly our promised path into
the light. It is only when Dante has crossed the forest where "I spent the
night so piteously" that he can begin the journey that will lead him to an
understanding of his own humanity.[1]

The entire *Commedia* can be read both as an exodus from the forest and
as a pilgrimage towards the human condition. (Dante himself stresses the
importance of reading correctly the biblical verse "When Israel went forth
from Egypt.")[2] And not only towards a perception of the pilgrim's singularity: also, and most important, towards his condition as a member of the
human fold, contaminated and redeemed by what others have done and
what others are. Not once during his voyage after leaving the forest is Dante
alone.[3] Met by Virgil or by Beatrice, speaking with souls condemned or saved,

addressed by demons or angels, Dante progresses through constant dialogue with others: he advances through conversation. Dante's voyage coincides with the telling of that voyage.

As noted earlier, conversation is the reason the dead have not lost the gift of language: it enables them to communicate with the living. This is why their physical form, shuffled off on this earth, is apparent to Dante when he meets them, so that he might know he speaks with humans and not merely with intangible spirits. In the dark forest he is alone, but after that, never again.

Dante's forlorn forest is a place through which we must all pass in order to emerge more conscious of our humanity. It rises in all its awful darkness as a long succession of forests: some older, like the demon forest through which Gilgamesh must journey at the beginning of our literatures, or like the one that first Odysseus and then Aeneas must traverse on their quests; others more recently sprung up, like the live forest that moves forward to defeat Macbeth, or the black forest in which Little Red Riding Hood and Tom Thumb and Hansel and Gretel lose their innocent way, or the blood-soaked forest of the marquis de Sade's unfortunate heroines, or even the pedagogical forests to which Rudyard Kipling and Edgar Rice Burroughs entrust their young. There are forests on the edge of other worlds, forests of the night of the soul, of erotic agony, of visionary threat, of the final totterings of old age, of the unfolding of adolescent longing. It is of such forests that Henry James's father wrote in a letter addressed to his adolescent sons: "Every man who has reached even his intellectual teens begins to suspect that life is no farce; that it is not genteel comedy even; that it flowers and fructifies on the contrary out of the profoundest tragic depths of the essential dearth in which its subject's roots are plunged. The natural inheritance of everyone who is capable of spiritual life is an unsubdued forest where the wolf howls and the obscene bird of night chatters."[4]

Such unsubdued forests are always duplicitous: they lend us the illusion that it is here, in the darkness, that the action takes place, and yet we know the forests are defined not only by their trees and filtered light but also by their frame, the land that surrounds them and lends them context. Into a forest we are lured, but we are never allowed to forget that there is another world waiting outside. Inside may be darkness (even Milton's over-quoted "darkness visible") and yet a web of shapes and shadows outline the promise of a twilight sky. There we must stand each alone, in this preparatory stage, an initiation ground for that which is still to come: the encounter with the other.

Thirty-two cantos away from the shadows of the forest, almost at the end of Dante's descent into Hell, he reaches the frozen lake where the souls of traitors are trapped up to the neck in ice. Among the dreadful heads that shout and curse, Dante hits his foot against one and then thinks he recognizes in the shivering features a certain Bocca degli Abati, who in Florence betrayed his party and took arms on the side of the enemy. Dante asks the angry soul his name and, as has been his custom throughout the magical journey, promises to bring the sinner posthumous fame by writing about him when he returns among the living. Bocca answers that he wishes for the exact opposite, and orders Dante to leave him to his unrepentance. Furious at the insult, Dante grabs hold of Bocca by the scruff of the neck and threatens to tear out every hair on his head unless he gets an answer.

> Then he to me: "Even if you leave me bald,
> I will not tell you my name, nor show you my face,
> even if you pound my head a thousand times."

Hearing this, Dante tears out "more than one fistful," making the tortured sinner howl in pain. (Another condemned soul cries out to him, "What ails you, Bocca"—thus revealing his name.)[5]

Some way farther, Dante and Virgil encounter more souls embedded in the ice whose "very weeping allows them not to weep": their eyes are sealed with frozen tears. Hearing Dante and Virgil speak, one of them begs that the strangers remove from his eyes "the hard veils" before his weeping freezes them again. Dante agrees to do so, swearing, "If I do not extricate you, may I go to the bottom of the ice," but in exchange the soul has to tell him who he is. The soul agrees and explains that he is Friar Abrigo, condemned for murdering his brother and nephew, who had insulted him. Then Abrigo asks Dante to reach out his hand and fulfill his promise, but Dante refuses:

"and to be rude to him was courtesy." All the while, Virgil, Dante's heaven-appointed guide, remains silent.[6]

Virgil's silence can be read as approval. Several circles earlier, as both poets are ferried across the River Styx, Dante sees one of the souls condemned for the sin of wrath rise from the filthy waters, and, as usual, asks him who he is. The soul doesn't give his name but says that he is merely one who weeps, for which Dante, unmoved, curses him horribly. Delighted, Virgil takes Dante in his arms and fulsomely praises his ward with the same words Saint Luke uses in his Gospel in praise of Christ ("blessed be she who bore you").[7] Dante, taking advantage of Virgil's encouragement, says that nothing would give him greater pleasure than to see the sinner plunged back into the ghastly swill. Virgil agrees, and the episode ends with Dante giving thanks to God for granting his wish. Outside the forest, the rules of engagement do not follow our own code of ethics: they are not exclusively our own.

Over the centuries, commentators have tried to justify Dante's actions as instances of what Thomas Aquinas identified as "noble indignation" or "just anger," not the sin of wrath but the virtue of being roused by the "right cause."[8] The other punished souls gleefully call out to Dante the sinner's name: he is Filippo Argenti, Dante's fellow Florentine and one of his former political enemies, who acquired some of Dante's confiscated property after Dante was banished. Argenti received his nickname (Silver) for having shod his horses with silver rather than iron; his misanthropy was such that he rode through Florence with his legs outstretched so that he could wipe his boots on the passersby. Boccaccio described him as "thin and strong, scornful, easily drawn to wrath and eccentric."[9] Argenti's history seems to bring a sense of private vindictiveness to mingle with whatever loftier sentiments of justice may have driven Dante to curse him in the name of "the right cause."

The problem, of course, resides in the reading of "right." In this case, "right" refers to Dante's understanding of the unquestionable justice of God. "Shall mortal man be more just than God?" asks one of Job's friends. "Shall a man be more pure than his maker?" (Job 4:17). Implicit in the question is the belief that to feel compassion for the damned is "wrong" because it means setting oneself against God's imponderable will and questioning his justice.

Only three cantos earlier, Dante was able to faint with pity when hearing the tale of Francesca, condemned to whirl forever in the wind that punishes the lustful. But now, advanced in his progress through Hell, Dante is less of a sentimentalist and more a believer in the higher authority.[10]

According to Dante's faith, the legal system decreed by God cannot be mistaken or wicked; therefore, whatever it determines to be just must be so, even if human understanding cannot grasp its validity. Aquinas, discussing the relation between truth and God's justice, argued that truth is a pairing of mind and reality: for human beings, this pairing will always be incomplete, since the human mind is by nature faulty; for God, whose mind is all-embracing, the apprehension of truth is absolute and perfect. Therefore, since God's justice orders things according to his wisdom, we must consider it to be equivalent to the truth. This is how Aquinas explains it: "Therefore God's justice, which establishes things in the order conformable to the rule of His wisdom, which is the law of His justice, is suitably called truth. Thus we also in human affairs speak of the truth of justice."[11]

This "truth of justice" that Dante seeks (his deliberate infliction of pain on the prisoner in the ice, and his prurient desire to see the other prisoner tortured in the mire) must be understood (his supporters say) as humble obedience to the law of God and acceptance of his superior judgment. But for most readers, such neatness is not satisfactory. An argument similar to that of Aquinas is put forward today by those who object to the investigation and prosecution of official murderers and torturers who are said to act under government orders. And yet, as almost any reader of Dante will admit, however cogent the theological or political arguments may be, these infernal passages leave a bad taste in the mouth. Perhaps the reason is that if Dante's justification lies in the nature of divine will, then instead of Dante's actions being redeemed by the religious dogma, the dogma is undermined by Dante's actions, and human nature is debased, not elevated, by the divine. Much the same way, the implicit condoning of torturers merely because their abuses are said to have taken place in the unchangeable past and under the superior law of a previous administration, instead of encouraging faith in the present administration's policies, undermines that faith and those policies. And worse still: left unchallenged, the worn-out excuse "I merely obeyed orders,"

Where Is Our Place?

tacitly accepted, acquires new prestige and serves as precedent for future exculpations.

There is, however, another way to view Dante's actions. Sin, theologians say, is contagious, and in the presence of sinners, Dante becomes contaminated by their faults: among the lustful he pities the weak flesh to the point of fainting, among the wrathful he is filled with bestial anger, among the traitors he betrays even his own human condition, because no one, certainly not Dante, is incapable of sinning as others have sinned. Our fault lies not in the possibility of evil but in our consent to do evil. In a landscape where a certain evil flourishes, consent is easier to give.

Landscape is of the essence in the *Commedia:* where things happen is almost as important as what happens there. The relationship is symbiotic: the geography of the Otherworld colors the events and the souls lodged therein, and these color the chasms and cornices, the woods and the water. For centuries Dante's readers have understood that the places of the afterlife are supposed to conform to a physical reality and this precision lends the *Commedia* no small measure of its power.

For Dante, broadly following Ptolemy, whose model of the universe he corrected under the stronger influence of Aristotle, the earth is a motionless sphere in the center of the universe, around which run nine concentric heavens that correspond to the nine angelic orders. The first seven spheres are the planetary heavens: of the moon, Mercury, Venus, the sun, Mars, Jupiter, and Saturn. The eighth is the heaven of the fixed stars. The ninth, the crystalline heaven, is the Primum Mobile, the invisible source of the diurnal rotation of the heavenly bodies. Surrounding this is the Empyrean, wherein blooms the divine rose in the center of which is God. The earth itself is divided into two hemispheres: the northern hemisphere, inhabited by humankind, whose midpoint is Jerusalem, equidistant from the Ganges to the east and the Pillars of Hercules (Gibraltar) to the west; and the southern, a watery realm forbidden to human exploration, at the center of which rises the island mountain of Purgatory, sharing the same horizon as Jerusalem. At the top of Purgatory is the Garden of Eden. Beneath Jerusalem is the inverted cone of Hell, at the core of which is embedded Lucifer, whose fall pushed up the land that formed Mount Purgatory. The two rivers, the holy city, and the southern mountain form a cross within the earth's sphere. Hell is divided into nine decreasing circles, reminiscent of the grades in an amphitheater. The first five circles constitute Upper Hell, the following four Lower Hell, which is a city fortified with iron walls. The waters of Lethe have opened a crack in the bottom of Hell, offering a path that leads to the base of Mount Purgatory.

So detailed is Dante's geography that in the Renaissance several scholars undertook an analysis of the information provided in the poem to determine the exact measurements of Dante's realm of the damned. Among these was Antonio Manetti, a member of the Platonic Academy of Florence and friend of the Academy's founder, the great humanist Marsilio Ficino. An ardent reader of Dante, Manetti used his political connections to influence Lorenzo de' Medici to assist in the repatriation of the poet's remains to Florence, and his extensive knowledge of the *Commedia* to write a preface for an important annotated edition of the poem edited by Cristoforo Landino and published in 1481, which included Landino's reflections on the measurements of Hell. In his preface, Manetti discussed the entire *Commedia* mainly from a linguistic point of view; in a text published posthumously, in 1506, Manetti centered his investigations on the geography of the *Inferno*.

In the literary as in the scientific realm, every original argument seems to elicit its contrary. In opposition to Manetti, another humanist, Alessandro Vellutello, a Venetian by adoption, decided to write a new geography of Dante's *Inferno*, mocking Manetti's "Florentine" views and arguing for more universal considerations. According to Vellutello, Landino's measurements were faulty and the Florentine Manetti, basing his own calculations on those of his predecessor, was nothing but "a man who is blind seeking guidance from a man who is one-eyed."[12] The members of the Florentine Academy received the comments as an insult and swore revenge.

In 1587, to counter the perceived indignity, the Academy resolved to invite a talented young scientist to rebut Vellutello's arguments. The twenty-year-old Galileo Galilei was then an unlicensed mathematician who had made his name in intellectual circles with his studies of the movements of the pendulum and his invention of hydrostatic scales. Galileo accepted. The full title of his talks, given in the Hall of the Two Hundred in the Palazzo Vecchio,

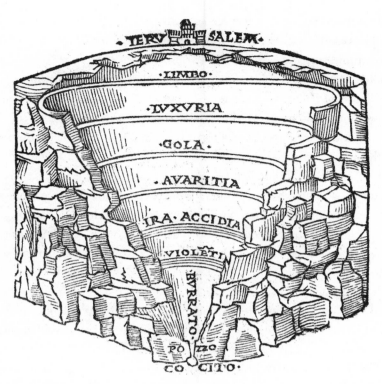

A depiction of the terraces of Hell from Antonio Manetti's *Dialogo* (Florence, 1506). Reading from top to bottom, after Limbo are the terraces of the Lustful, the Gluttonous, the Avaricious, the Wrathful and Sullen, the Violent, and Barrators. The Well leads down to the Frozen Lake. (Photograph courtesy of Livio Ambrogio. Reproduced by permission.)

was *Two Lessons Read Before the Academy of Florence Concerning the Shape, Location and Size of Dante's Hell.*[13]

In the first lesson, Galileo follows Manetti's description and adds to it his own calculations, with learned references to Archimedes and Euclid. To measure the height of Lucifer, for instance, he takes as his starting point Dante's statements that the face of Nimrod is as long as the bronze pinecone of Saint Peter's in Rome (which in Dante's time stood in front of the church and measured seven and a half feet) and that Dante's height is to a giant as the giant's is to Lucifer's arm. Using for his calculations Albrecht Dürer's chart to measure the human body (published in 1528 as *Four Books on the Human Proportions*), Galileo concludes that Nimrod was 645 fathoms tall. Based on that figure, he calculates the length of Lucifer's arm which in turn allows him, using the rule of three, to determine Lucifer's height: 1,935 fathoms. Poetic imagination, according to Galileo, obeys the laws of universal mathematics.[14]

In the second lesson, Galileo exposes (and refutes) the calculations of Vellutello, which was the conclusion the members of the Florentine Academy were waiting for. Surprisingly, for those who read them from the distance of five centuries, in both these lessons Galileo embraces Ptolemy's geocentric model of the universe, perhaps because in order to deny Vellutello and side with Manetti, he found it more convenient to take Dante's view of the universe for granted.

Retribution, once obtained, is often quickly forgotten. The members of the Academy never mentioned the lectures again, and neither were the hellish explorations of the young Galileo collected by his last disciple, Vincenzo Viviani, in his edition of his master's works, published after Galileo's death in 1642. But certain texts are infinitely patient. Three centuries later, in 1850, the Italian scholar Octavo Gigli was researching the work of a minor sixteenth-century philologist when he came across a thin manuscript wherein he believed he could recognize the handwriting of Galileo, which he had seen once by chance on a piece of paper in the house of a sculptor friend (such are the miracles of scholarship). The manuscript proved to be that of Galileo's *Lectures on Dante,* which the over-scrupulous secretary of the Academy at the time had not entered into the official registry because the young mathematician was not an elected member but merely a guest (such are the abominations of bureaucracy).

Long ago, Copernicus's discoveries shifted the self-centered vision of our world to a corner that has since constantly shifted farther and farther towards the margins of the universe. The realization that we, human beings, are aleatory, minimal, a casual convenience for self-reproducing molecules is not conducive to high hopes or great ambitions. And yet what the philosopher

Nicola Chiaromonte called "the worm of consciousness" is also part of our being, so that, however ephemeral and distant, we, these particles of stardust, are also a mirror in which all things, ourselves included, are reflected.[15]

This modest glory should suffice. Our passing (and, on a tiny scale, the passing of the universe with us) is ours to record: a patient and bootless effort begun when we first started to read the world. Like the geography of what we call the world, what we call the history of the world is an ongoing chronicle which we pretend to decipher as we make it up. From the beginning, such chronicles purport to be told by their witnesses, whether they be true or false. In book 8 of the *Odyssey*, Odysseus praises the bard who sings the misfortunes of the Greeks "as if you were there yourself or heard from one who was."[16] The "as if" is of the essence. If we accept this, then history is the story of what *we say* has happened, even though the justifications we give for our testimony cannot, however hard we try, be justified.

Centuries later, in a severe German classroom, Hegel would divide history into three categories: history written by its assumed direct witnesses (*ursprüngliche Geschichte*), history as a meditation upon itself (*reflektierende Geschichte*) and history as philosophy (*philosophische Geschichte*), which eventually results in what we agree to call world history (*Welt-Geschichte*), the never-ending story that includes itself in the telling. Immanuel Kant had earlier imagined two different concepts of our collective evolution: *Historie* to define the mere recounting of facts and *Geschichte,* a reasoning of those facts—even an a priori Geschichte, the chronicle of an announced course of events to come. Hegel pointed out that in German the term *Geschichte* comprised both the objective and subjective sense and simultaneously meant *historia rerum gestarum* (the history of the chronicle of events) and *res gestae* (the history of exploits or the events themselves). For Hegel, what mattered was the understanding of (or the illusion of understanding) the entire flow of events as a whole, including the riverbed and its coastal observers, and in order to better concentrate on the main, from this torrent he excluded the margins, the lateral pools and the estuaries.[17]

In an essay admirably titled *Dostoyevsky Reads Hegel in Siberia and Bursts into Tears,* the Hungarian scholar László Földényi suggests that this is the horror Dostoyevsky discovers in his Siberian prison: that history, whose victim he knows he is, ignores his existence, that his suffering goes on unnoticed or, worse, serves no purpose in the general flow of humankind. What Hegel proposes, in Dostoyevsky's eyes (and in Földényi's) is what Kafka would later say to Max Brod: there is "no end of hope, only not for us." Hegel's caveat is even more terrible than the illusory existence proposed by the idealists: we are perceived but we are not seen.[18]

Such an assumption is, for Földényi (as it must have seemed to Dostoyevsky) inadmissible. Not only can history not dismiss anyone from its course, but the reverse is true: the acknowledgement of everyone is necessary for history to be. My existence, any person's existence, is contingent on your being, on any other person's being, and both of us must exist for Hegel, Dostoyevsky, Földényi to exist, since we (the anonymous others) are their proof and their ballast, bringing them to life in our reading. This is what is meant by the ancient intuition that we are all part of an ineffable whole in which every singular death and every particular suffering affects the entire human collective, a whole that is not limited by each material self, a whole that Dante knows he must attempt to understand through a few of its individual parts. The worm of consciousness mines but also proves our existence; it is no use denying it, even as an act of faith. "The myth that denies itself," says Földényi wisely, "the faith that pretends to know: this is the gray hell, this is the universal schizophrenia with which Dostoyevsky stumbled on his way."[19]

Our imagination allows us always one hope more, beyond the one shattered or fulfilled, one as yet seemingly unattainable frontier that we'll eventually reach, only to propose another lying farther away. Forgetting this limitlessness (as Hegel tried to do by trimming down his notion of what counts as history) may grant us the pretty illusion that what takes place in the world and in our life is fully understandable. But it reduces the questioning of the universe to catechism and that of our existence to dogma. As Földényi argues, and Dante would have agreed, what we want is not the consolation of that which seems reasonable and probable but the unexplored Siberian regions of the impossible, the "here" always present beyond the horizon.

If "beyond" implies an open question, it also implies a center from which we conceive the world, a position that enables us to claim superiority over the alien others out there. The Greeks saw Delphi as the center of the universe, the Romans claimed that it was Rome, whose secret name is "Love" (*Roma* read backwards is *Amor*).[20] For Islamic people, the center of the world is Mecca, for the Jewish people it is Jerusalem. Ancient China recognized that center in Taishan, at an equal distance from the four sacred mountains of the Middle Kingdom. Indonesians see that center in Bali. While the assumed geographical center lends an identity to those who assume it, whatever lies "out there" has identifying properties as well that are too often perceived as potentially threatening or dangerously infectious.

Through cultural and commercial contacts, through imagistic and symbolic dialogues, what happens beyond affects travelers who leave their home center. Not all show the openness and understanding of the Persian polymath Abū al-Rayhān Muhammad ibn Ahmad al-Bīrūnīas, known in English simply as Al-Biruni, who in the tenth century visited India and, after observing the local religious rituals remarked, "If the beliefs they hold differ from ours and even seem abominable to Muslims, I have only this to say: This is what Hindus believe, and this is their own way of seeing things." A long tradition of imperialistic thought holds that the only methods for converting the beyond are enslavement or assimilation. Virgil makes this explicit in the words of Anchises to his son, Aeneas:

Let others fashion from bronze more lifelike, breathing images—
For so they shall—and evoke living faces from marble;
Others excel as orators, others track with their instruments
The planets circling in heaven and predict when stars will appear.
But, Romans, never forget that government is your medium!
Be this your art:—to practice men in the habit of peace,
Generosity to the conquered, and firmness against aggressors.[21]

In 1955, Claude Lévi-Strauss published a book that would become famous as an attempt to overcome the imperialist view of how to enter into dialogue with peoples beyond the limits of one's own culture. Among the Caduveo people, the Bororo, the Nambikwara, and the Tupi-Kawahib, Lévi-Strauss found a way of communicating and learning without overbearing or translating these people's thoughts into his own system of beliefs. Commenting on his reaction to a simple Buddhist rite, Lévi-Strauss wrote: "Every effort to understand destroys the object studied in favour of another object of a different nature; this second object requires from us a new effort which destroys it in favour of a third, and so on and so forth until we reach the one lasting presence, the point at which the distinction between meaning and the absence of meaning disappears: the same point from which we began. It is 2,500 years since men first discovered and formulated these truths. In the interval, we have found nothing new, except—as we have tried in turn all possible ways out of the dilemma—so many additional proofs of the conclusion that we would have liked to avoid." To this, Lévi-Strauss adds, "This great religion of non-knowledge is not based on our inability to understand. It bears witness to that ability and raises us to a pitch at which we can discover the truth in the form of a mutual exclusiveness of being and knowledge. Through an additional act of boldness, it reduces the metaphysical problem to one of human behaviour—a distinction it shares only with Marxism. Its schism occurred on the sociological level, the fundamental difference between the Great and the Little Ways being the question of whether the salvation of a single individual depends, or does not depend, on the salvation of humanity as a whole."[22]

Dante's *Commedia* seems to answer the question in the negative. The salvation of Dante depends on Dante himself, as Virgil at the very beginning of the journey upbraids him: "What is it then? Why, why do you stand back? / Why do you nurse so much cowardice in your heart? / Why don't you show courage and determination?"[23] Dante's will and Dante's will alone will allow him to reach the final blessed vision after having seen the horrors of the damned and been cleansed of the seven deadly sins. And yet . . .

The first image that confronts Dante when he ascends into Paradise is that of Beatrice gazing at God's sun. Comparing himself to the fisherman Glaucus, who, according to Ovid, having tasted magic grass that grew on the shore was seized with a longing to plunge into the deep, Dante is filled with longings of the divine. But at the same time he realizes that the place he comes from is necessarily the human commonwealth—that to be human is not a singular state but one pertaining to a plurality. Personal will and sensations and thoughts are not, for all their individuality, isolated experiences. In the words of Lévi-Strauss: "Just as the individual is not alone in the group, nor any one society alone among others, so man is not alone in the universe." And using the same rainbow image that Dante describes at the end of his vision, Lévi-Strauss concludes: "When the spectrum or rainbow of human cultures has finally sunk into the void created by our frenzy; as long as we continue to exist and there is a world, that tenuous arch linking us to the inaccessible will still remain, to show us the opposite course to that leading to enslavement."[24]

This is the paradox: after the unspeakable experience of suffering the world alone, and trying to narrate that experience to ourselves, consciously and unconsciously we enter the world of things shared, but here, we realize, communication, full communication, is no longer possible. Through perfunctory verbal excuses we allow ourselves to commit terrible deeds because, we say, others committed them. In the world at large, we repeat the same justifications endlessly, doing violence to the violent and betraying the traitors.

The dark forest is terrible, but it defines itself and its limits, and in doing so frames the world outside and allows us to discern that which we want to attain, whether the seashore or the mountain's peak. But past the forest, the world of experience has no such borders. Everything beyond, like the universe, is simultaneously limited and expanding, not boundless but of boundaries impossible to conceive, utterly unconscious of itself, the stage of both historia rerum gestarum and res gestae. Here we set ourselves up as actors and as witnesses, each a "single individual" and each part of "humanity as a whole." And here we live.

10

How Are We Different?

AMONG THE BOOKS OF MY childhood were many that belonged to a series called La Biblioteca Azul, the Blue Library. In the Blue Library were Spanish translations of the *Just William* stories and several Jules Verne novels, as well as Hector Malot's *Nobody's Boy*, which caused me inexplicable terror. My cousin had the complete companion series, La Biblioteca Rosa, the Pink Library, and she bought every newly published volume month after month with indiscriminate collector's pride. It was an unspoken rule that I, as a boy, could only have access to the titles in the Blue Library, and that she, as a girl, was permitted only those of the Pink. I sometimes envied her a title in her collection—*Anne of Green Gables* or the stories of the comtesse de Ségur — but I knew that if I wanted to read them, I would have to find other editions, not segregated by color.

As so many of the rules that govern our childhood, the distinction between what is appropriate for boys and what is appropriate for girls erects invisible but adamantine barriers between the sexes. Colors, objects, toys, sports were identified according to this unquestioned apartheid that told you who you were according to what you were not. On the other side of the di-

(Opposite) Dante and Beatrice in the Garden of Eden preparing to ascend to Heaven. Woodcut illustrating Canto I of the Paradiso, *printed in 1487 with commentary by Cristoforo Landino. (Beinecke Rare Book and Manuscript Library, Yale University)*

vide lay a gender-defined territory in which the natives did other things, had another language, enjoyed different rights and suffered specific prohibitions. It was an axiom that one side could not understand the other. "She's a girl" or "He's a boy" was sufficient explanation for a certain behavior.

Literature, as usual, helped me subvert the regulations. Reading *The Coral Island* in the Blue Library, I felt repulsed by Ralph Rover's cloying obsequiousness and his absurd talent for peeling coconuts as if they were apples. But reading *Heidi* (in the neutral Rainbow Classics edition), I knew that she and I had many adventurous traits in common, and I cheered when she bravely stole soft rolls to give to her toothless grandfather. In my readings I changed gender with the fluidity of a parrotfish.

Imposed identities breed inequality. Instead of seeing our personalities and bodies as positive features of our singular identities, we are taught to see them as traits that oppose us to the identity of the unknowable, mysterious foreigner, living outside our fortified city walls. From that first negative teaching spring all the others, which end up building a vast shadow mirror of everything that we've been taught we're not. In my early childhood, I wasn't aware of anything being alien, lying outside my world; later, I was aware of little else. Instead of learning that I was a unique part of a universal whole, I became convinced that I was a separate entity and that everyone else was different from the solitary creature that answered to my name.

Men are afraid that women will laugh at them.
Women are afraid that men will kill them.

—Margaret Atwood

Many times in our histories we have proudly declared that each single individual is part of humanity as a whole. And every time this noble proposition has been uttered, we have opposed it, amended it, sought exceptions to it, and in the end defeated it, until such time when it is pronounced again. Then, once more, we allow the notion of an egalitarian society to resurface briefly, and once again let it sink.

For Plato, in the fifth century B.C.E., social equality meant equal rights for male citizens, whose number was limited. Foreigners, women, and slaves were excluded from this privileged circle. In *The Republic,* Socrates proposes to discover the meaning of true justice (or rather, the definition of a truly just man) through a discussion of what is a just society.

Like all of Plato's dialogues, *The Republic* is a rambling conversation with no satisfactory beginning and no obvious conclusion, uncovering on the way new forms to old questions and at times inklings of an answer. In particular, what is remarkable in *The Republic* is its lack of emphasis. Socrates leads the dialogue from one attempt at definition to the next, but none seems definitive to the reader. *The Republic* reads as a sequence of suggestions, sketches, preparations for a discovery that is ultimately never made. When the aggressive Sophist Thrasymachus declares that justice is nothing but "a generous innocence" and injustice a matter of "discretion," we know he isn't right, but Socrates' interrogation will not lead to the incontrovertible proof of Thrasymachus's error: it will lead to a discussion concerning different societies and the merits or demerits of their governments, just and unjust.[1]

According to Socrates, justice must be included in the class of things "that, if one wishes to be happy, one must love as much for their own sake as for what from them may result." But how is that happiness to be defined?

What does it mean to love something for its own sake? What results from that as yet undefined justice? Socrates (or Plato) does not want us to take the time to consider these singular questions: it is the conversational flow of thought that interests him. And so, before discussing what is a just or unjust man, and consequently what is justice, Socrates proposes to investigate the very concept of a just or unjust society (a city or polis). "Are we not saying that there exists a justice proper to a particular man, and yet another, as I believe, proper to an entire city?"[2] Apparently seeking to define justice, Plato's dialogue leads farther and farther away from that ineffable goal, and instead of a straight path from question to answer, *The Republic* proposes a voyage constantly delayed, whose very digressions and pauses grant the reader a mysterious intellectual pleasure.

Faced with *The Republic*'s open questions, what hints of an answer can we offer? If every form of government is somehow nefarious, if no society can boast of being ethically sound and morally fair, if politics is condemned as an infamous activity, if every collective enterprise threatens to crumble into individual villainies and betrayals what hope do we have of living together more or less peacefully, profiting from mutual collaboration and looking after one another? Thrasymachus's pronouncements on the virtues of injustice, however absurd they may seem to the reader, have been repeated throughout the centuries by the exploiters of the social system, whatever that system might be. These were the arguments of the feudal landlords, of the slave traders and their clients, of tyrants and dictators, of the financiers responsible for the recurrent economic crises. The "virtues of egotism" proclaimed by the conservatives, the privatization of public goods and services defended by the multinationals, the benefits of unrestrained capitalism promoted by bankers are different ways of translating Thrasymachus's dictum that "what is just is merely what is convenient for the strongest."[3]

Thrasymachus's ironic conclusions are based on a number of assumptions, principally the idea that what might be perceived as unjust is in fact the consequence of a natural law. Slavery was justified by declaring that the vanquished did not deserve the privileges of the victors or that a different race was inferior; misogyny was justified by extolling the virtues of patriarchy and defining the power and roles assigned to each of the sexes; homophobia was justified by inventing standards of "normal" sexual conduct for men and women. In each of these cases, a vocabulary of symbols and metaphors accompanied the establishment of these hierarchies, so that women, for instance, were assigned the passive role (thereby denigrating or condescendingly praising their domestic activities, a fallacy Virginia Woolf understood when she said that a woman's first task was "to kill the angel in the house") and men the active one (exalting the violence of wars and other social competitions). Although this was not a universal idea—Oedipus, for instance, in Sophocles' *Oedipus at Colonus,* speaks of the difference of the roles of men and women in Greece and Egypt: "For in that country [Egypt] the men sit within doors / working at the loom, while the wives go out / to get the daily bread"—it is from such ingrained symbolic roles that the association of women with speech and men with action derives. Also their perceived opposition, so that in the *Iliad* the fighting stops only when the women speak.[4]

Traditionally however, the speech of women must remain private; public speech is deemed the prerogative of men. In the *Odyssey,* Telemachus tells his mother, Penelope, when she addresses an impertinent bard in public, that as far as speech is concerned, "men will see to that." But at times, the private and the public speech of women in ancient Greece overlapped. In Delphi, the Sibyl spoke seated astride a tripod, taking the vapors of Apollo's prophetic spirit into her vagina, thus making, as the classicist Mary Beard suggests, an explicit connection between the "the mouth that eats and speaks" and the "mouth" of her sexual organs.[5]

Even the identity of a society or city is claimed by patriarchal authority. The legend of the naming of Athens is a fair example. Saint Augustine, citing the authority of the Roman historian Marcus Terentius Varro, retells the story. An olive tree and a water fountain sprang suddenly on the site of the future city of Athens.

> These prodigies moved the king Cecrops to send to the Delphic Apollo to inquire what they meant and what he should do. He answered that the olive signified Minerva [or Athena], the water Neptune [or Poseidon], and that the citizens had it in their power to name their city as they chose, after either of these two gods whose

signs these were. On receiving this oracle, Cecrops convoked all the citizens of either sex to give their vote, for it was then the custom in those parts for the women also to take part in public deliberations. When the multitude was consulted, the men gave their votes for Neptune, the women for Minerva; and as the women had a majority of one, Minerva conquered. Then Neptune, being enraged, laid waste the lands of the Athenians, by casting up the waves of the sea; for the demons have no difficulty in scattering any waters more widely. The same authority said, that to appease his wrath the women should be visited by the Athenians with the three-fold punishment—that they should no longer have any vote; that none of their children should be named after their mothers; and that no one should call them Athenians. Thus that city, the mother and nurse of liberal doctrines, and of so many and so great philosophers, than whom Greece had nothing more famous and noble, by the mockery of demons about the strife of their gods, a male and female, and from the victory of the female one through the women, received the name of Athens; and, on being damaged by the vanquished god, was compelled to punish the very victory of the victors, fearing the waters of Neptune more than the arms of Minerva. For in the women who were thus punished, Minerva, who had conquered, was conquered too, and could not even help her voters so far that, although the right of voting was henceforth lost, and the mothers could not give their names to the children, they might at least be allowed to be called Athenians, and to merit the name of that goddess whom they had made victorious over a male god by giving her their votes. What and how much could be said about this, if we had not to hasten to other things in our discourse, is obvious.

Perhaps "what and how much could said about this" is not as obvious as all that. Gerda Lerner, in an important essay on the origins of patriarchy, argued that what she calls "the enslavement of women" preceded the formation of classes and class oppression by converting, as early as the second millennium B.C.E. in Mesopotamia, the reproductive and sexual capacities of women into

How Are We Different?

commodities. This represented, in her judgment, "the first accumulation of private property." A social contract was established between men and women in which economic support and physical protection were provided by the men and the sexual services and domestic care by the women. Throughout history, though notions of sexual identity vary in the flow of social changes, the contract persisted, and in order to assert the assumption of its validity, commencement stories needed to be told that explained the divine origin of the hierarchical difference between the sexes, as in the legend of the origins of Athens, the tale of Pandora, and the fable of Eve.[6]

Simone de Beauvoir pointed out the danger of reading in patriarchal myths only the sections that can be conveniently reinterpreted from a feminist point of view. And yet reinterpretations and retellings, though they can go in opposite directions, can sometimes be of use in helping us reimagine new identities and new contracts. For example, in Dante's misogynist thirteenth century, certain gaps and tears in the social fabric allowed new versions of the fundamental stories to be imagined—stories that if they did not succeed in effectively subverting the patriarchal norms at least attempted to displace them into different settings that altered their meaning. For Dante, always holding in tension the dictates of Christian theology and his own private ethical notions, the conundrum of how to achieve equal justice is always present, and, within the framework of Christian dogma it concerns all individuals, male and female. Through the voice of Beatrice and other characters, female and male, Dante expresses the belief that the capacity for reason, logical advancement, and enlightenment exists in all, and the different measures of that capacity are determined by grace, not the sex of the individual. Beatrice explains to him:

> In the system of which I speak, by different means,
> all kinds of things tend to be drawn
> in larger or smaller measure towards their essence;
>
> wherein they move to various harbors
> on the great sea of being, and each one
> bearing the instinct that was bestowed upon it.[7]

How Are We Different?

Though in Dante's world the different positions assigned to individuals (peasant or queen, pope or warrior, wife or husband) entail particular rights and obligations to be undertaken or refused according to each person's free will, men and women live under the same moral code and must abide by it or suffer the consequences. The vast questions of human life and the awareness that much of what we want to know is beyond our horizon are shared by women and men alike.

The minor, fleeting, loving soul who calls herself Pia, whom Dante meets in the Purgatory of the late repentant, says, in one of her seven frugal lines, "Siena made me, Maremma unmade me." Historians have argued, with very little to go on, that Pia was perhaps a certain Sapia, murdered by her husband, who had her thrown out of a window, either from jealousy or because he wanted to marry another woman. She speaks to Dante, begging to be remembered, but only after tenderly noting that Dante will be weary after his journey, and that he will need to rest. In Pia's story, what matters is not that she is a woman wronged by a man, but that hers is a compassionate soul seeking to restore a certain balance to a past act of injustice.[8]

This equality of human suffering is made explicit many times in the *Commedia*. In the second circle of Hell, confronted with the fate of the souls punished for excess of love or misplaced love (Cleopatra and Helen, Achilles and Tristan), Dante feels such pangs of pity that he almost faints. Then, out of the whirlwind of the lustful, Francesca speaks both for herself and for her condemned lover, Paolo, with whom she is imprisoned for all eternity, and tells Dante how they fell in love with one another while reading the tale of Lancelot and Guinevere. Hearing the confession, Dante is overcome by the same pity he has experienced earlier, but this time it is so strong that he feels as if he were dying: "And I fell as a dead body falls." Dante's growing pitiful sorrow for the suffering of others turns into compassion (*com-passion,* or shared passion or feeling), reminding him that he himself has been guilty of the same sin as these lovers. As Dante knew, literature is the most efficient instrument for learning compassion, because it helps the reader take part in the emotions of the characters. The secret love of Lancelot and Guinevere in an old Arthurian romance revealed the love that Francesca and Paolo did not yet know they were feeling; Paolo and Francesca's love revealed to Dante the memory of his old loves. The reader of the *Commedia* is the next mirror in this amorous corridor.[9]

One of the most complex ethical dilemmas presented in the *Commedia* is the question of free will in the case of a person forced to suffer or commit an infamous act. At what point does a victim become the accomplice of the victimizer? When does resistance cease and acquiescence start? What are the limits of our own choices and decisions? In Paradise, Dante meets the souls of two women who have been forced by men to break their religious vows. Piccarda, the sister of Dante's friend Forese Donati, is the first soul he encounters in the Heaven of the Moon, and the only one he recognizes unaided (in Heaven, souls acquire an extraterrestrial beauty that changes the appearance they had when alive). Piccarda was forcibly removed from her convent by another of her siblings, Corso Donati, to be married into a powerful Florentine family that could assist Corso in his political career. Piccarda died shortly afterwards, and is now in the lowest of heavens. The second soul is that of Constanza, the grandmother of Manfred, a rebel leader whom Dante met in Purgatory, who will be discussed in Chapter 12, below. She was forced to marry the Holy Roman Emperor Henry VI, after being removed, like Piccarda, from her convent, according to a legend that Dante takes for fact. Piccarda, however, claims that though Constanza was forced to abandon her nun's veil, "she was never freed from the veil of her heart," a willed act that has assured her a place in Paradise. The canto ends with the singing of the Ave Maria, the hymn in praise of Mary, the fundamental Christian symbol of constancy in the heart. With the spiritual weight of her words, Piccarda vanishes, "as something heavy into deep waters."[10]

As these encounters in the *Commedia* suggest, the conviction that the human will can be stronger than the circumstances to which it is subjected enhances the belief in human freedom and equality. Oppression is always an oppression through symbols as well as through material actions, and every revolution is a struggle to gain control over those symbols. "The oppressed group," says Lerner, "while it shares in and partakes of the leading symbols controlled by the dominant, also develops its own symbols. These become, in time of revolutionary change, important forces in the creation of alternatives."[11]

Symbolically, Constanza's and Piccarda's ordeals are conflicts between the female will and the will of the dominant men, and in the dogmatic frame within which the *Commedia* inscribes itself they reflect the larger symbol of the male Trinity. In this symbolic context, however, Dante sets up a personal female trinity that lends power to Piccarda's and Constanza's configurations. The singing of the Ave Maria, the words with which the angel Gabriel greets Mary to announce that she is the bearer of the Messiah in the Gospel of Luke (1:28), places the female divine presence at the cusp of the discussion on free will, the power that makes all human beings equal. Dante, the male protagonist, is saved through the intercession of three female figures: the Virgin Mary "who takes pity / on this [Dante's] impediment"; Saint Lucy, instructed by Mary to help "your faithful one" (faithful because Dante is devoted to Saint Lucy); and Beatrice, whom Lucy seeks out, and asks, "Why don't you rescue one who loved you so?"[12] The saving vision will be granted to Dante by God the Father, by Christ, and by the Holy Spirit, but his salvation itself is devised by the three holy women.

In our time, the symbolic separation of genders is effected not through theological dogma but through the daily instruments of social interaction. Before audiovisual games and activated screens that respond aloud to a child's questions, there were music boxes and talking dolls, dogs that barked, and clowns that giggled. Pull a cord, turn a key, and the toy came to life with sounds that carry meaning. The first talking dolls said things like "Hello," "Play with me," and "I love you." Later, toy soldiers too were given their voice: "Fight!" "You're brave!" "Attack!" Unsurprisingly, toys were made to speak with conventional tags that corresponded implicitly to what was deemed proper for either a boy or a girl. (Sometime in the 1980s, a group of feminist activists purchased a number of talking Barbie dolls and G.I. Joes, exchanged their sound boxes, and returned them to the store. Customers who bought the doctored toys found that when their children activated the doll's voices, G.I. Joe would whine in girlish tones, "I want to go shopping!" while Barbie growled ferociously, "Kill! Kill! Kill!")[13]

These symbolic representations of gender don't grant equality to the sexes. In most of our societies, as is apparent in the defining symbolic language, only the dominant, male sex has existential reality. Grammar confirms this. In French and Spanish, for example, in a sentence where the plural subject is

composed of masculine and feminine elements, the masculine is always privileged. "If you speak of a hundred women and one pig," the poet Nicole
Brossard has remarked, "the pig has the upper hand."[14]

Female identity, outside the roles assigned by society to women, lacks a
vocabulary, even in momentous historical events which supposedly redefine
"humanity as a whole." A notorious example of this can be found in some of
the fundamental texts of the French Revolution.

The revolutionaries by and large believed that in spite of the particular
cultural and political characteristics of every society, all human beings have the
same fundamental needs. Taking as their premise the notion of universal "natural rights" described by Jean-Jacques Rousseau in his *Discourse on Inequality,*
they sought to define these rights in the context of the new society. The duties
of man, Rousseau had argued, are not dictated by reason alone, but by self-
preservation and compassion for his fellow men. Consequently, a society,
composed by men with equal duties and rights, had the right to choose its
own form of government and its own system of laws. In this context, individual freedom is not based on tradition or historical hierarchies but on the
law of nature: man was free because he was human. The French Revolution,
declared Robespierre, "defends the cause of humanity." The particulars of
this defense were set down in the *Declaration of the Rights of Man and of the
Citizen.*[15]

The *Declaration* was a document long in the making. The original version, consisting of seventeen articles that were adopted by the National Assembly in August 1789, became a preamble to the Constitution of 1791.
Later, with some alterations and abbreviated as the *Declaration of the Rights
of Man,* it was used as the preamble to the Constitution of 1793, and later
still, expanded as the *Declaration of the Rights and Duties of Man and the
Citizen,* to that of 1795. The *Declaration* (like the Revolution itself) had "only
one principle: that of reforming abuses. But as everything in this dominion
was an abuse, it resulted from it that everything was changed."[16]

The discussions leading up to its formulation were long and complex.
Two sides confronted each other in the debate: the counterrevolutionaries
who feared the destabilization of the political, social, and moral order and
the ideologues, led by the philosophers who defended a utilitarian theory of

society. Some thirty "declarations" were discussed preceding the adoption in 1789, most of them keyed to the prevention of more urban and rural violence, and a new "plague of despotism." The majority of the group agreed with the leader of the French Protestants, Jean-Paul Rabaut Saint-Etienne, that the language of the *Declaration* should be of "such lucidity, veracity and directness in its principles . . . that everyone should be able to grasp and understand them, that they might become a children's alphabet taught in schools."[17]

The most eloquent of the debaters was the abbé Sieyès. All men, argued Sieyès, are subject to needs and therefore constantly desire comfort and well-being. When in nature, men succeed through their intelligence in dominating the natural world for their benefit. But when they are in a social setting, their happiness depends on whether their fellow citizens are seen as means or obstacles. Relations between individuals, therefore, can take the form of war or of reciprocal utility. The former Sieyès deemed illegitimate because it depended on the power of the strong over the weak. The latter, instead, led to cooperation between all citizens and transformed social obligations from a sacrifice to an advantage. Consequently, the first right of an individual must be "ownership of his person." According to Sieyès, "every citizen has the right to remain, to go, to think, to write, to print, to publish, to work, to produce, to protect, to transport, to exchange, and to consume." The only limitation to these rights was infringement on the rights of others.[18]

But the universality of these rights was undoubtedly not universal. The first distinction established in the *Declaration,* between French citizens deserving civil rights and others who did not, was between the "active" and "passive" male members of society. The Constitution of 1791 defined "active citizens" as all men over the age of twenty-five who possessed independent means (they could not be in domestic service). Property, represented by land, money, and social condition, was deemed the defining feature of citizenship. After 1792 a citizen was defined as a man over twenty-one who earned his living, and owning property was no longer a requisite. But though the distinctions between rich and poor, aristocrats and plebeians were seemingly abandoned, the difference between the sexes was deemed natural and persisted. The chief procurator of the Commune of Paris, Pierre-Gaspard Chaumette, arguing against the right of women to take on a political role, put the question as follows: "Since when is it permitted to give up one's sex? Since when is it decent to see women abandon the pious cares of their households, the cribs of their children, to come to public places and take part in harangues in the galleries or at the bar of the Senate? Is it to men that Nature entrusted domestic cares? Has she given us breasts to feed our children?" To which the marquis de Condorcet, mathematician and philosopher, responded: "Why would beings exposed to pregnancies and temporary indispositions be unable to enjoy the rights that no one has ever imagined to deprive others that suffer from gout every winter and fall easily prey to colds?"[19]

The Revolution granted women certain rights, allowing them to divorce and to administer some of the conjugal property, but these rights were later restricted under Napoleon and revoked by the Bourbons. The Convention of 1893 declared that "children, insane individuals, women, and those condemned to degrading penalties" would not be considered citizens of France.[20] According to the revolutionaries, natural rights did not imply political rights. But there were those who disagreed. Two years after the original *Declaration*, in 1791, a forty-three-year-old playwright, Olympe de Gouges, published *Declaration of the Rights of Woman and of the Female Citizen* to complete what she saw as a faulty and unfair founding document.

Olympe de Gouges was born in Montauban in 1748. To satisfy convention, on her birth certificate her father appears as Pierre Gouze, butcher of Montauban, but she was assumed to be the illegitimate daughter of a mediocre man of letters, the marquis Le Franc de Pompignan, and Anne-Olympe Mouisset. All her life she would idealize the absent marquis, to whom she attributed an "immortal talent." Her contemporaries did not share her high opinion of Pompignan: the aristocratic disdain he showed towards his social inferiors and his indifferent literary style earned him the mockery of Voltaire, who said of Pompignan's *Sacred Poems* that they merited the epithet because "no one would dare touch them."[21]

She was married at sixteen to a much older man ("whom I didn't love, and who was neither rich nor nobly born"), who died when she was twenty. Refusing to be called the Widow Aubry after her husband's death, as custom dictated, she invented for herself a name made up of one of her mother's Christian names and a variation on her surname. She aspired to be a play-

Olympe de Gouges, 1784 (Musée Carnavalet, Paris). (INTERFOTO/Alamy)

wright, but since she was illiterate, like most women of her time who were not brought up in privileged circles, she first had to teach herself to read and write. In 1870, she left Montauban for Paris. She was thirty-two years old.[22]

Almost everyone tried to discourage her from pursuing a writing career. Her father, the old marquis, while refusing to acknowledge her as his daughter, also tried to dissuade her from becoming a playwright. In a letter addressed to her shortly before his death, Pompignan had this to say: "If persons of your sex become logical and profound in your writings, what will we become, we men, who are today so shallow and insubstantial? Farewell the superiority of which we were so proud! Women will dictate to us. . . . Women may be allowed to write, but they are forbidden, for the sake of a happy world, to undertake the task with any pretensions." Nonetheless, she persisted, and wrote over thirty plays, many now lost, but several of which were performed by the Comédie française. So convinced was she of her dramatic talents, boasting that she could write a full-length play in five days, that she challenged the most successful playwright of the day, Pierre Augustin Caron de Beaumarchais, author of *The Marriage of Figaro,* to a writing duel, because he had said that the Comédie française should not perform plays written by women. If Gouges won, she promised to use the money as a dowry to enable six young women to marry. Beaumarchais did not bother to reply.[23]

In her plays, but also in her political tracts, Olympe de Gouges fought for that elusive universal equality vaunted by the revolutionaries. She pleaded for the rights of women as well as men, and also against slavery, arguing that the prejudices that allowed blacks to be bought and sold were only the justifications of greedy white merchants. Slavery was finally abolished by a decree of the Revolutionary Assembly on 4 February 1794; almost fifteen years later, an honor roll was compiled of the "Courageous Men Who Argued or Labored for the Abolition of the Slave Trade." Olympe de Gouges was the only woman listed.[24]

Unlike other revolutionary women such as the ardent Girondin Madame Roland, Gouges maintained that women should have a political voice and be given a place in the Assembly. Whereas Madame Roland had meekly declared, "We don't want another empire than that governed by our hearts, and another throne than that within your hearts," Gouges had argued, "Women have the right to mount the scaffold; they should also have the right to mount the tribune." The nineteenth-century historian Jules Michelet, who recorded these words, at the same time dismissed Gouges as a "hysterical" woman who changed her political position according to her mood: "She was a revolutionary in July 1789, she became a royalist on 6 October after seeing the king made prisoner in Paris. Having then turned republican in June '91, under the impression that Louis XVI had fled and was guilty of treason, she bestowed him again to her favor when he was taken to court."[25]

The *Declaration of the Rights of Woman and the Female Citizen* counters Michelet's misogynistic judgment. It is a document that not only amends and supplements its male counterpart; it adds to the civic liberties listed in the *Declaration of the Rights of Man* the rights of all individuals, proposing, among other things, the recognition of illegitimate children, legal aid for unwed mothers, the right to demand recognition from the biological father, the payment of alimony in case of divorce, and the replacement of marriage vows

How Are We Different?

with a "social contract" that legally recognizes the status of both married and unmarried couples, a forerunner of today's contracts of civil union. Gouges's proposal that all children, whether legitimate or not, be given the right to inherit, had to wait until 1975 to be made a law in France. Perhaps for reasons of diplomacy, Gouges dedicated her *Declaration of the Rights of Woman and the Female Citizen* to Queen Marie Antoinette. It was not a wise decision.

Olympe de Gouges was neither a brilliant playwright nor a profound political theorist; she was a woman who was concerned about a declaration of social equality that was visibly disproved by the facts. To the rules and regulations devised by the lawmakers of the Revolution, Gouges brought her emotional criticism, pointing out their deficiencies and arguing not from a judicial point of view but from a political one, as a conscientious, feeling individual.

In her pamphlets and her speeches, she unwisely expressed sympathy towards the Girondins, a party made up of different factions that had sought the end of the monarchy but resisted the ever-growing violence of the Revolution and whose only common stand was their opposition to the Jacobins in power, who supported a centralized government. To punish her, the Jacobins ordered that she be stripped and flogged in public. (This was a common procedure against rebellious women: at about the same time, Théroigne de Méricourt, another revolutionary, was publically whipped and then locked in the insane asylum of La Salpêtrière, where she died ten years later, having lost her mind because of the brutal treatment she received.) One afternoon, Gouges was attacked in the street as she was coming out of a shop, and her assailant, tearing her dress and grabbing her by the hair, cried out to the mob: "Twenty-four *sols* for the head of Madame de Gouges. Who'll bid?" To which she calmly replied, "My friend, I bid thirty and I claim preference." She was released amid the laughter of the crowd.[26]

Eventually her Girondin sympathies led to her arrest, under the pretext of having printed a subversive poster that appeared in her name. In the fierce summer of 1793, she was detained on the third floor of the infamous Mairie, close to the Palais de Justice. She had a wound in her leg, was running a fever, and had to lie in a lice-infested room for a fortnight, during which time she managed to write a number of letters arguing her case and pleading for mercy, constantly watched over by a gendarme. After her trial, where she was given no real chance to defend herself, she was transferred to other prisons, and finally to the Conciergerie, to the cell reserved for women condemned to death. As a last resort, she claimed to be pregnant because pregnant women were excepted from the guillotine. Her claim was rejected, and the execution was announced for the morning of 3 November; because it was raining, it was postponed until the afternoon. One of the many anonymous witnesses of her death said later that she had died "calm and serene," a victim of Jacobin ambition and of her intention "to denounce the villains."[27]

Olympe de Gouges's determination to seek equality for all was not mere self-serving. Injustice is, or should be, a universal concern, and the gender of those who fight for it should not be a consideration in the argument. "We are ministers of God on earth," says Don Quixote, "and arms through which His justice is executed."[28] Olympe de Gouges would have agreed. Inequality may be principally caused by the efforts of one sex to defend its social or political power, but equality is not a question of gender.

Almost all of us, even those of us who commit unforgiveable atrocities, know, like Socrates and Don Quixote and Gouges and Dante, what justice and equality are, and what they are not. What obviously we don't know is how to act justly on every occasion, individually or collectively, so that we are all treated with justice and equality as citizens and as persons in the society we call ours. Something in each of us draws us toward seeking material and self-satisfying benefits without consideration for our neighbors; an opposite force draws us to the subtler benefits of what we can offer, share, render useful to our community. Something tells us that though ambition for riches, power, and fame can be a strong drive, experience of ourselves and of the world will end up proving that in itself such an ambition is worthless.

In *The Republic's* final pages, Socrates says that when the soul of Odysseus was asked to choose a new life after his death, "leaving aside his ambition with the memory of his previous labors," from all the possible heroic and magnificent lives at his disposal, the legendary adventurer chose the life of "a common and unencumbered man," and "he chose it joyfully."[29] It is possible that this was Odysseus's first true act of justice.

II

What Is an Animal?

IN MY CHILDHOOD, THERE WERE few animals. There were giant tortoises creeping over the dunes in the park in Tel Aviv where I was taken sometimes to play. There were sad animals in the Buenos Aires zoo, their many shapes matched in the biscuits we'd buy to feed the ducks and swans. There were the animals of the Noah's Ark I'd been given for one of my birthdays made out of papier-mâché. It was only much later, as an adult, that I got a dog.

The relationship we have with an animal questions both our identity and that of the animal. Of what consists this relationship? Is it established only through our will or is it determined by the nature of the animal? I know how I feel about and react to the presence of an animal, but how does the animal feel about and react to me? My language has not the elements (except perhaps metaphorically) to express the nature of the other side of the relationship, a side which certainly exists but which I cannot define. Literature is no clearer: Odysseus's dog, which dies at the feet of his returned master in the *Odyssey;* Elizabeth Barrett Browning's dog, which changes as his mistress changes in Virginia Woolf's *Flush;* Bill Sykes's dog, which betrays his master

(Opposite) Dante and Virgil see Cerberus attacking the gluttonous under a storm of hail, foul water, and snow. Woodcut illustrating Canto VI of the Inferno, *printed in 1487 with commentary by Cristoforo Landino. (Beinecke Rare Book and Manuscript Library, Yale University)*

out of faithfulness in Dickens's *Oliver Twist;* the beaten dog of Meursault's neighbor whose death causes his owner such anguish in Camus's *The Outsider*— all are defined through the translation of their actions into the emotional vocabulary of their human companions. But how to speak explicitly from the other bank of the species divide?

I have had two dogs in my life (though the verb "to have," implying possession, is an epistemological blunder). The first dog, named Apple by my son in the days before computers became commonplace, was a clever mongrel, impatient, playful, and vigilant, keen to socialize with the other dogs in our Toronto park. The second, Lucie, is an intelligent, gentle, loving Bernese mountain dog who lives with us in France. Both dogs changed me: their presence forced me to consider my own self beyond the limits of my interior world without falling into the social rituals required in human inter-action. There are rituals, of course, but they are superficial, disguising a cer-tain nakedness that I experience when I am with my dog. In her presence, I feel an obligation of sincerity with myself, as if the dog looking into my eyes were a revelatory mirror of some instinctual buried memory. Barry Lopez, speaking of that ancient relative of the dog, the wolf (the same wolf that for Dante was the symbol of all vices), says that "the wolf exerts a powerful in-fluence on the human imagination. It takes your stare and turns it back on you. The Bella Coola Indians believed that someone once tried to change all the animals into men but succeeded in making human only the eyes of the wolf. People suddenly want to explain the feelings that come over them when confronted with their stare—their fear, their hatred, their respect, their curiosity."

Lucie is a good listener. She sits quietly when I read to her from what-ever book I may have at the moment, and I wonder what holds her attention when she hears the verbal flow: the tone of my voice? the rhythm of the sen-tences? the shadow of a meaning beyond the few words she understands? "To allow mystery, which is to say to yourself, 'There could be more, there could be things we don't understand,'" says Lopez, "is not to damn knowledge."

Puzzled by his own relationship with his dog, the young Pablo Neruda wrote this:

What Is an Animal?

My dog,
If God is in my verses,
I am God.
If God is in your mournful eyes
You're God.
And there is no one in this whole vast world,
That kneels down to either one of us.

The dog, with all its strength and fierceness, when it comes to
bite, if you throw yourself to the ground, will do you no harm;
this, out of mercy.

—FERNANDO DE ROJAS, *La Celestina,* 4.5

Each of Dante's encounters with the souls in the Otherworld entails
an act of justice humanely set against the final justice of God. At
first, Dante is moved by pity for the ordeal of the souls in Hell; as he
advances deeper and deeper within it, recognition of God's unquestionable
justice overrides his human feelings and, as his own soul slowly awakens, as
we have seen, he enthusiastically curses the damned whom God has punished and even takes part in their physical punishment.

Of all the insults and derogatory comparisons Dante uses on both lost
souls and evil demons, one recurs throughout. The wrathful, according to
Virgil, are all "dogs." From then on, in his travel notes through the kingdom
of the dead, Dante echoes his master's ancient vocabulary. Thus, Dante tells us
that the wasteful in the seventh circle are pursued by "famished and fast black
bitches"; the burning usurers running under the rain of fire behave "like dogs
who in the summer fight off fleas and flies with their paws and maw"; a demon
who pursues a barrater is like "a mastiff let loose," and other demons are like
"dogs hunting a poor beggar" and crueler than "the dog with the hare it has
caught." Hecuba's cry of pain is demeaned as a bark "just like a dog"; Dante
apprehends the "doglike faces" of the traitors trapped in the ice of Caïna, the
unrepentant Bocca "barking" like a tortured dog, and Count Ugolino gnawing
at the skull of Cardinal Ruggiero "with his teeth, / which as a dog's were strong
against the bone"; Guido del Duca, in the second terrace of Purgatory, calls
the Aretines "snarling curs."[1] There are several more such instances of canine
invective. Angry, greedy, savage, mad, cruel: these are the qualities that Dante
seems to see in dogs and applies to the inhabitants of Hell.

Human qualities, in Dante's cosmic vision, are fashioned in two ways: by
divine grace, which distributes these qualities to everything in the universe

according to hierarchies of perfection, and by the influence of the heavenly bodies, which mellow or deepen or even change them. This influence, as Carlo Martello explains to Dante in the Heaven of Venus, can alter hereditary traits, so that children often will not follow in their parents' footsteps.[2] These qualities, once given, are dependent for their effects on our individual will: we are all morally responsible for our actions. We choose how to employ our anger, ruled by the planet Mars, for just or merely selfish goals; we decide whether our violence, also under the influence of Mars, will be directed against the enemies of God or against his work.

Theology and astrology, as well as astronomy, were considered in Dante's time worthy sciences that allowed us better to understand our purpose as willed by God and ruled by Mother Church. Astrology was deemed a necessary and practical instrument of ecclesiastical discernment: in 1305, for example, the cardinals assembled in Perugia greeted Clement V, recently elected in France to the papal throne, with the pronouncement: "You who will safely occupy Saint Peter's chair and shine with a radiant light . . . for [now] each of the planets has a great force in its own house."[3] Astrology vouched for Clement as the right choice.

According to medieval cosmogony, human beings are molded, in part at least, by the influence of planets and fixed stars, those that form the constellations of the zodiac and other, lesser stellar formations, since all the heavenly bodies, as Dante reminds us, are moved by the all-determining divine love.[4] Among these lesser constellations that affect our conduct are three that traditionally bear the name of dogs: Canis Major, Canis Minor, and the Canes Venatici (hounds of Venus). Though they are not mentioned by name in the *Commedia,* the third one, the Canes Venatici, is present by implication. Before arriving in the Heaven of the Moon, Dante warns his readers that from this point on, they will have difficulty following him, since, unlike himself, they lack the help of the gods: "Minerva fills my sails, Apollo leads me, / and the nine Muses point me towards the Bears." The constellation of the Great Bear (Ursa Major) is depicted in most cosmographical charts as pursued by two greyhounds, Venus's hunting dogs, a northern hound named Asterion and a southern one named Chara. As creatures of Venus they incarnate desire, the quest for love both earthbound and sacred. Though it is stated that

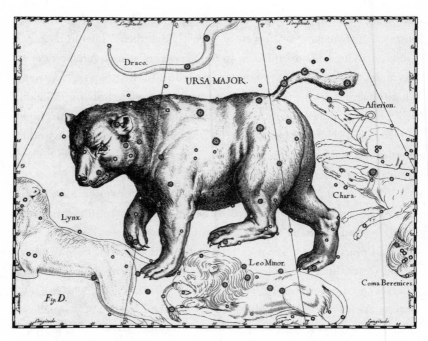

Ursa Major and the hounds of Venus, from Johannes Hevelius's *Uranographia*, 1687. (Photograph © Jay Pasachoff/Superstock)

Dante's ascent through Paradise takes place under his birth sign, Gemini, the entire arrangement of heavenly bodies is revealed to him as he enters the Heaven of Fixed Stars, the sphere whose uttermost north is ruled by Ursa Major, goaded on by the Canes Venatici. These two greyhounds are emblems of that *disio,* "desire," which in the end is transformed by love.[5]

Perhaps as an echo of these greyhounds of the astrological heaven "in whose revolution it seems/that conditions here below are thought to be changed," the only dog mentioned in the *Commedia* as the incarnation of positive canine qualities is the *veltro,* or greyhound, first announced by Virgil at the beginning of their journey and later tacitly invoked by Dante himself: the hound that will one day pursue and kill the evil she-wolf.[6] The omen is traditional: the emperor Charlemagne, in the *Chanson de Roland,* sees such a dog in a dream, while Giovanni Boccaccio, in his commentaries on the first seventeen cantos of the *Commedia* (delivered publicly in 1373), explained that "the greyhound is a breed of dog marvelously inimical to wolves—one of these greyhounds will come 'who will inflict painful death on her [the she-wolf].'" Most commentators identify the greyhound with the emperor Henry VII of Luxembourg, much admired by Dante, who called him "the successor of Caesar and Augustus."[7] In any case, the greyhound is less a dog than the symbol of a hoped-for salvation, a collective or social "disio."

To call a person a "dog" is a common and uninspired insult in almost every language, including, of course, the Italian spoken in Dante's thirteenth- and fourteenth-century Tuscany. But mere commonplaces are absent in Dante: when he uses an ordinary expression, it no longer reads as ordinary. When, for example, he uses the conventional "sapphire-blue" to describe the color of the sky (as in the famous line "sweet color of oriental sapphire"), the epithet carries the contradictory meanings of "hard as stone" and "tender as air," as well as the double meaning of *oriental:* a gem coming physically from the orient and an emblem of the dawning eastern sky.[8] The dogs in the *Commedia* carry connotations other than the merely insulting, but overriding them all is the suggestion of something infamous and despicable. This relentlessness demands a question.

Almost all of Dante's books were written in exile, in houses that he could never consider his own because they were not in his Florence, which in his memory he loved and hated as an unfaithful mistress, both praising her for her beauty and scourging her for her sins. The incipit to his poem reveals the double bind: "Here begins the *Commedia* of Dante Alighieri, Florentine of nationality, not of morals."[9] No doubt his hosts—Cangrande, Guido Novello, and the others—were kind to him and provided him with comfortable rooms and intelligent conversation, but home was always somewhere else, the place of absence. Banned from Florence, he must have felt that the city's gate might have been a parody of the gate of Hell: its sign would be not "Abandon all hope you who enter" but "Abandon all hope you who leave."[10] And yet Dante, like a whipped dog, was unable to give up all hope of returning home.

The Albanian novelist Ismail Kadare remarked that the inhabitants of the *Inferno* "strangely resemble exiled immigrants, including those of our time. The snippets of their stories, their sentimental effusions, their outbursts of anger, the political news from both sides, their thirst for information, their last wishes, everything seems to come from the same clay and the same people. The similarity is such that if we were to mingle them, the reader of today would be hard put to distinguish at first Dante's text from the kind of chronicles or journalistic reports of our present age."[11]

Remembered absence is for every exile, in hell or in a refugee camp, a constant source of pain. "No greater pain," says Francesca in the whirlwind of the lustful, "than to remember happy times / in misery." And the despoiler of Pistoia, Vanni Fucci, questioned by Dante in the serpent-ridden Chasm of the Thieves, as he predicts the sorrows of Florence and the defeat of the White Guelphs makes the intention of inflicting pain explicit: "And I've told you this so that the pain may gnaw you!" Exiles say that their pain comes from a constant feeling of alienation, from living in a place not chosen by them, between walls they haven't erected, surrounded by objects that are borrowed, and in the company of those among whom they are always guests, never hosts. This is the heart of the message delivered by Dante's great-great-grandfather, the crusader Cacciaguida, in the Heaven of Mars, as he describes Dante's (as yet) future banishment:

> You will leave everything you love
> dearest; this is the arrow
> that exile's bow shoots at the start.
>
> To you the alien bread
> will taste like salt; you'll see how hard
> it is to climb up and down unfamiliar stairs.[12]

Exile has the quality of slavery, a state in which nothing belongs to you and you belong to someone else, under the whim of foreign authorities: even your identity is forfeit, subject to your master or benefactor. Exile is a form of loss in which the founding experiences of place and time dissolve into a time and place that exist no more, the memory of which has become something many times removed, a memory remembered, a memory of a memory of a memory, until eventually the dear things lost are nothing but a distant wraith. Perhaps for that reason, the *Commedia* is a catalogue of losses—loss of Florence of course, loss of all the "undone" dead of Dante's past, loss of masters such as Brunetto Latini, loss of his beloved Beatrice when she dies on earth, loss of his beloved guide when Virgil cannot lead him farther and then of the heavenly Beatrice again and forever in the Empyrean—even the loss of Saint Bernard after the old man at last points Dante towards the ineffable and holy center "beyond / what language shows."[13] Nothing remains long in Dante's grasp, except the memorable palimpsest which he must now set down for future readers. Because exiles are allowed only one task: transcription.

Exile is a displaced state, but it is also a perverted form of travel in which the impossible goal of the pilgrim is the one place from which he knows he's barred; his is a pilgrimage towards the unreachable. It is hardly surprising that it is in exile, a state in which Dante defines himself in the *Convivio* as "a bark without sail or rudder," that he dreams his poem of the Otherworld as a cautionary journey through three realms in which he is the absolute foreigner: a prodigy among the departed souls, a freak still possessing a mortal coil, a body casting a shadow in the eternal realms, a being not yet dead. "That which you tell me about my course, I write," he assures, for instance, Brunetto Latini, but he never says, "When I'm back in Florence once more," as if he knew that he would never see his beloved city again. Cacciaguida had told him, "Your life reaches into the future / beyond the punishment of their perfidious acts." In that future, beyond the present infamy of his fellow citizens, there is for Dante the promise of literary recognition but not of return.[14]

Eating bread tasting of tears and climbing unfamiliar stairs, Dante must have many times sought living company that was not that of his well-meaning hosts, someone towards whom he didn't have to act with obsequious gratitude, someone who might distract him from the longing and self-pity. His books and keepsakes (the few that he could carry from place to place), though companionable, merely reminded him of his absent home, and every new object or volume he acquired, like every new experience that came his way, must have seemed a betrayal. How then to bear the slow, relentless reaching into the future of his life, farther and farther away from his dear lost core? Without Virgil, without Beatrice (the icy Beatrice, too forbidding to be amicable company in any case), without the friends with whom he once roamed the streets of Florence discussing philosophy and poetry and the laws of love, how was he to put into writing the vision now unfolding, how to find an ideal listener for the music he was hearing, a first all-pardoning reader on whom to try out the words and images? In such a state, Dante might have looked at one of his host's dogs.

With the easy nostalgia of the elderly, Cacciaguida reminds Dante that in olden times Florence was sober and modest, and the fashion of the day discreet; women were busy with their children and domestic tasks, and keen on telling exemplary stories about the ancient heroes of Troy and Rome.[15] In Dante's time, in spite of Cacciaguida's criticism, life in most Tuscan households continued to be relatively simple and informal. Depictions of interiors in Florence, Siena, and other Tuscan cities in the thirteenth century show sparsely furnished rooms, sometimes decorated with a few tapestries and trompe-l'oeil paintings, often with colorful vases full of flowers. Pets were common. Birds hung in cages by the window, as shown in frescoes by Masaccio and Lorenzetti. Cats snuggled up by the fireplace in the bedroom. (The Florentine Franco Sacchetti advised men rising naked from the bed to make sure that the cat wouldn't mistake "certain pendulous objects" for playthings.) Even geese were sometimes kept indoors; Leon Battista Alberti, in *Il libro della famiglia,* recommends the use of geese to keep watch over one's house.[16] And, of course, there were dogs.

Dogs curled up at the foot of the bed or on the floor by the hearth; dogs watched by the threshold or waited for scraps under the table. Lapdogs kept the ladies company by the spinning wheel, and greyhounds waited patiently for their masters to go hunting. Brunetto Latini noted in his *Livre du trésor* that dogs loved humans more than did any other animals; only dogs born from the union of bitches and wolves were wicked. Most dogs were faithful unto death: it was not uncommon for dogs to guard their master's corpse day and night, and sometimes even to die of grief. According to Latini, the dog is able to understand the human voice. A contemporary of Dante, Pierre de Beauvais, observed in his *Bestiary* that because dogs lick their wounds to heal them, they are like priests who hear our confessions and heal our sorrows. Isidore of Seville, in the *Etymologies,* explained that the dog (*canis*) received its name because the dog's bark was like singing (*canor*) the lyrics that poets composed.[17]

According to ancient lore, dogs are supposed to recognize angelic presences before humans can see them. The dog that accompanied Tobit's son Tobias on the journey with the angel is one such example (and the only good dog in the whole of biblical literature). Dogs can not only be aware of the

The hound Guignefort unjustly killed by his master, from Johannes Pauli, *Schimpf und Ernst* (Strasbourg, 1535), folio XLVI v°. (Bibliothèque nationale de France)

numinous; they themselves can also be saintly. In the thirteenth century, in the region of Lyon, a greyhound was venerated under the name of Saint Guignefort. According to tradition, the dog Guignefort was left to look after an infant in his cradle. A serpent tried to attack the child, and Guignefort killed it. When the master returned, he saw the dog covered in the serpent's blood and thought that it had attacked the child. Furious, he killed the faithful Guignefort, then discovered the infant safe and sound. Vindicated as a martyr, the dog acquired the status of a saint invoked to protect children.[18]

In Verona and Arezzo, Padua and Ravenna, Dante sat at his borrowed table, filled with the vision that he wished to put into words and painfully aware that like the forest of the beginning of his voyage, "to say what it was is hard" because human language, unlike a dog, is an unfaithful creature.[19] The vast and overwhelming systems of theology, astronomy, philosophy, and poetry weighed on him and imposed their rules and tenets. His imagination was free to invent, but always within that incontrovertible cosmic structure, always within the assumption of a universal, God-held truth. The unforgivable sins, the stages of redemption, the nine heavenly spheres over which the godhead holds absolute rule were his facts; his task was to build with words persons and situations and landscapes that would allow him and his readers to enter the vision and explore it, as if it were a geography made of wood, water, and stone. Slowly, around the character that bears his name, Dante conjured up his cast: his best-beloved poet, Virgil; the object of his desire, the dead Beatrice; the men and women who inhabited his past; the pagan heroes who inhabited his books; the saints from the church calendar. Also places and scenes: remembered streets and buildings, mountains and valleys, night skies and dawns, workers in the field and in the village, shopkeepers and artisans, farm animals, wild beasts, and especially the birds that flew among the clouds of Florence—all to illustrate, as best he could, what he knew could not be put exactly into a human tongue.

Observations from thirty-odd years of inquisitive life find their place in the vision: the ox licking his muzzle, once glimpsed perhaps somewhere in the Tuscan countryside, serves to portray the usurer twisting his mouth in the seventh circle; the pilgrims Dante saw in Rome the year of the Jubilee coming and going from Saint Peter's seem like the seducers and panderers in Hell who advance in opposite directions; the surprise of being blinded by a sudden mist in the Alps and feeling the sun gradually clearing its way through the clouds is compared to the slow understanding that reaches Dante on the third cornice of Purgatory; the laborer in the vineyard who must make sure that the vine does not dry out in the summer heat is used to depict Saint Dominic in Paradise, diligently called to serve the Lord.[20]

Overwhelmed by the flood of remembered images, Dante may have looked down once again at the dog. As their eyes met, Dante, for whom every experience was a touchstone for another and every memory a link in an endless chain of memories, might have recalled a dog (or several dogs) that wandered through his parents' house when he was a child, a dog that lay by his side as the five-year-old mourned his mother, and, later, another dog that kept him company as the adolescent Dante watched over the corpse of his emaciated father. A dog trotted alongside his bride four years later on the way to the church where the couple was married; a dog witnessed the birth of his first son, Giovanni; a dog sat quietly in a corner when Dante learned that the fleeting and unforgettable Beatrice Portinari had died as the wife of another man. The dog in front of the exiled Dante might have begotten, in Dante's mind, a pack

Hounds in Andrea di Bonaiuto, *Allegoria della Chiesa militante e trionfante* (Allegory of the Militant and Triumphant Church), detail. (Museo di Santa Maria Novella, Cappellone degli Spagnoli, courtesy of the Musei Civici Fiorentini.)

of remembered dogs: Florentine dogs, Veronese dogs, dogs of Venice and of Ravenna, dogs met on weary roads and in filthy inns, a long line of dogs slowly blending, like the changing shapes of the punished thieves in the eighth circle of Hell, from dog into dog into dog, including his host and protector, Cangrande (Big Dog) della Scala, to whom the *Paradiso* is probably dedicated.[21]

Thomas Aquinas argued that after death, when the soul has left the body, since people would no longer need food, there would be no animals in Heaven. Accordingly, except for a few allegorical beasts—the eagle, the gryphon— Dante's Paradise is devoid of animals of feather and fur. Saint Augustine (who infamously argued that animals do not suffer) suggested that, though dumb animals could not compete with the heavenly beauties, they no doubt contribute to the adornment of our earthly realm. "It would be ridiculous," he wrote, "to regard the defects of beasts, trees, and other mutable and mortal things which lack intelligence, sense, or life, as deserving condemnation. Such defects do indeed effect the decay of their nature, which is liable to dissolution; but these creatures have received their mode of being by the will of their Creator, whose purpose is that they should bring to perfection the beauty of the lower part of the universe by their alteration and succession in the passage of the seasons; and this is a beauty in its own kind, finding its place among the constituent parts of this world." Augustine is echoing Cicero, who found it absurd that the universe could have been created for anything other than man. Could it have been contrived "for the sake of the animals?" asked the aristocratic Roman. "It is no more likely that the gods took all this trouble for the sake of dumb, irrational creatures. For whose sake then shall one pronounce the world to have been created? Doubtless for the sake of those living beings which have the use of reason." In spite of the ever-increasing extinctions, from Augustine's time to ours, there are still 8.7 million species of "dumb, irrational creatures" on earth, most of which are unknown to us; to this day, barely one-seventh of them have been classified.[22]

Popular belief had it that the devil would commonly manifest itself as a "dumb, irrational creature": a serpent, a goat, a dog. Nevertheless, several fathers of the church, such as Saint Ambrose in his *Hexameron,* insisted that we at least learn gratitude from dogs. "What shall I say about dogs who have a natural instinct to show gratitude and to serve as watchful guardians of their masters' safety? Hence Scripture cries out to the ungrateful, the slothful, and the craven: 'Dumb dogs, not able to bark.' To dogs, therefore, is given the ability to bark in defense of their masters and their homes. Thus you should learn to use your voice for the sake of Christ, when ravening wolves attack His sheepfold."[23]

Though experience teaches us that most dogs are grateful servants (we expect in animals virtues often lacking in ourselves), gratitude is an aspect of dogs that appears seldom in popular stories. In the twelfth-century fables of Marie de France (which Dante probably read), only one story shows an example of a loyal dog; in all the others they are quarrelsome, envious, gossipy, and greedy. It is their greed (as commentators point out) that makes them return to their vomit. Dogs also incarnate rage: for that reason, the three-headed Cerberus of ancient mythology, placed by Dante to guard the circle of the gluttons, "claws the souls, flays and tears them to pieces." There was a superstition in Florence that to dream of a dog, especially one nipping at your heels, was a herald of sickness or even death. Also of birth: Saint Dominic's mother, pregnant with the future founder of the Dominican Order, dreamt of a dog carrying a burning torch in its mouth; to confirm the omen, Saint Dominic became the fiery enemy of every heresy, and after his death his order was charged with lighting the flames of the Inquisition.[24]

Dante's *Commedia* is one man's vision but succeeds in being universal. Dante's intimate experiences, his convictions, his doubts and fears, his private notions of honor and civic duty are inscribed in a system not of his making, a universe created by an unquestionable God whose terrible love allows the poet an ineffable glimpse of his creation, identical to God's own tripartite person. Once this vision has been achieved, and though the right words to describe it are lacking—"I declare myself vanquished [by the task]," he confesses—it must be put on paper, and the poem must find a form in which language, in all its irritating and magnificent ambiguity, becomes an epiphany for the reader. To achieve this, Dante threads singular instances of poetic grace with avowals of incompetence, moments of revelation with intermissions of ignorance, the whole within an established, incontrovertible, ideological framework that only theology, rather than art or reason, can approximate. Dante the poet may at times disagree with God's system or be bewildered by it, or even, when overwhelmed by feelings of pity and horror, attempt to soften its adamantine severity. But Dante also knows that for his own passage to be justified and his own voice to be heard, the system must stand firm and, as God's poet, he must write "the matter of which I've been made scribe."[25] To this framing orthodoxy belong the savage examples of God's judgment, the gratuitous demonstrations of God's mercy, the divine hierarchies of bliss, and the infernal gradations of punishment: all beyond human understanding, much as our erratic behavior must be beyond the understanding of dogs.

Even more: for Dante to assert his humanity, God's system must exist beyond any *possibility* of understanding: incomprehension must be part of its very substance, like its eternity and its omnipresence, and as majestic as faith in its evidence of things not seen, as it is written in the Epistle to the Hebrews (11:1). Once God's system appears defined by our incapacity to comprehend and our inability to judge, Dante can resort to the powers that constitute, in essence, his poetic identity: an ability to use words both as incantations and as facts, a sensitivity that allows him to share the suffering and the joy of others, a sensibility that makes him capable of reason and of realizing the limits of that reason. To do all this, Dante must choose from the vast mass of experience, and leave aside certain inspiring and illuminating realities. Nowhere in the *Commedia* are his wife or his children, for example, and these are only a couple of the deliberate absences in a poem that is supposed to hold the poet's whole world. And among the experiences Dante left out, regrettably, is that of the companionable dog.

And yet, not the dog itself but a knowledge of something kind and generous and loyal for which the dog is responsible, something that tries to understand and to follow and to obey, surfaces from time to time in the *Commedia.* As we have seen, Dante seems incapable of using words only in a literal sense to lend the poem nothing but their commonplace meaning. Dogs and their proverbial irascible nature are indeed used to qualify bestiality and infamy in the three realms, but the other, true characteristics of dogs are not altogether absent from the poem.

From the first canto of *Inferno* to the twenty-seventh canto of *Purgatorio,* Dante the protagonist is guided and protected by Virgil, who within the limited capacities of one enlightened not by faith but by intellect teaches his ward to trust his reason, use his memory, and lend meaning to his love. To guide and protect are duties traditionally fulfilled by dogs, but here, in the relationship forged between the lost Christian poet and the poet of ancient Rome, it is the guided one, Dante, who behaves like an errant beast, one of those hounds of Venus that incarnate his disio. And the one who fulfills the guardian functions is Virgil, "my master," as Dante calls him from the start. High on Mount Purgatory, on the threshold of the Earthly Paradise, shortly before their leave-taking, Dante describes himself as a goat kept by Virgil the goatherd. "Goat" fits the bucolic scene, but Dante could also have called himself Virgil's hound because throughout their long and perilous journey, it was always Virgil who gave the orders, Virgil who pronounced the right word or made a clear sign, Virgil who praised or reproved Dante's judgment and actions, Virgil who, so to speak, "owned" Dante, having been charged by Beatrice with looking after him until he could be delivered into the holy presence. Virgil's last words to Dante before parting are those a trainer might address to a well-brought-up dog: "Don't wait again for my word or my sign; your judgment is now free, straight and healthy." Dante, who now knows how to behave, enters "the divine grove" of Eden, of which the ancient poets sang when they spoke of the Golden Age. Like the faithful, loving creature he has become, Dante looks once more at his master, who has remained smiling at the grove's edge, and then he turns obediently towards a beautiful lady who will lead him on to his new, expectant mistress.[26]

The *Commedia* is a poem of evidences and almost invisible subtleties, of explicit and implicit connotations, of orthodox theology and subversive exegesis, of rigorous hierarchies and leveling companionships. To construct its unimaginable edifice, words are borrowed from every available vocabulary, from Latin and Provençal, from common speech and neologistic poetry, from archaic discourse and children's babble, from scientific jargon and the language of dreams—words stripped of their original function and yet echoing ancestral connotations, made to serve and reveal themselves in an almost endless plurality of meaning. Every time curious readers believe they are following one strand of the story, they discover a number of other strands underneath, above, and alongside it: every statement is both subverted and reinforced, every image amplified and reduced to its bare essentials. The wood in which Dante first tells us he has lost his way is an ordinary Tuscan wood, but it is also the wood of our sins, and the wood into which Virgil led Aeneas in his own poem. That first wood encompasses all the woods through which *Commedia* tells its story: the wood of Adam's tree and the wood of Christ's Cross, the wood in which the true path is lost, but also the wood in which the true path can be found again, the wood that leads to the Gates of Hell and the wood above which looms the salutary peak of Mount Purgatory, the wood where the trees hold the living souls of suicides—the shadowy reflection of the luminous wood in the Garden of Eden. Nothing in the *Commedia* is only one thing. Much as the dark wood is not only a wood, Dante is not only Dante, the dog used to curse the wicked is not only the wicked dog: it is also the poem's hero, the pilgrim poet Dante himself, lost like a stray dog in a wild and threatening wood. From the first lines of the *Commedia* (the readers suddenly realized with amazement) the dog at Dante's feet, in all its poetic essence, has surreptitiously entered the poem.

What Is an Animal?

12

What Are the Consequences
of Our Actions?

I HAVE NEVER FIRED A WEAPON. In my last year of high school, one of my friends brought a gun to class and offered to teach us how to use it. Most of us refused. My friend, I later found out, was a member of one of the Argentinian guerrilla movements that fought the military government; his father, whom he loathed, had assisted as a doctor at the government-endorsed torture sessions in the infamous Mechanical School of the Navy.

I left Argentina in 1969, the year in which the atrocities began. I left not for political but for purely private reasons: I wanted to see the world. During the military dictatorship, more than thirty thousand people were kidnapped and tortured, and many were killed. The victims were not only active dissidents; any relative, friend or acquaintance of a dissident could be detained, and anyone who for any reason displeased the Junta was considered a terrorist.

I returned only once to Argentina during the years of the military regime, and while there became aware of the atmosphere of terror that the military had created, but I didn't become part of a resistance group. "During such times of injustice," another friend once told me, "you can do one of two

(Opposite) Virgil and Dante begin the ascent of Mount Purgatory. Woodcut illustrating the Canto IV of the Purgatorio, *printed in 1487 with commentary by Cristoforo Landino. (Beinecke Rare Book and Manuscript Library, Yale University)*

things. You can either pretend that nothing is happening, that the screams you hear next door are the neighbors having a quarrel and that the person who seems to have disappeared is probably on a long and illicit holiday. Or you can learn to fire a gun. There are no other choices." But perhaps becoming a witness is another choice. Stendhal, who thought that politics was a millstone tied to the neck of literature, compared political opinions in a work of fiction to a gun fired at a concert, implicitly endorsing the third option.

The head of the military government, General Jorge Rafael Videla, justified his actions by saying that "a terrorist is not only someone who carries a bomb or a pistol but also someone who spreads ideas contrary to Western Christian civilization. We defended Western Christian civilization." Such justifications for murder are commonplace: defense of the true faith, survival of democracy, protection of the innocent, prevention of greater losses have all been invoked to justify the killing of others. The British engineer and freelance journalist Andrew Kenny, in an article in the London *Spectator,* used just such an argument to defend the dropping of the atomic bomb on Hiroshima, which killed more than 60,000 people instantly and 120,000 more slowly and painfully: "However I look at it, I cannot see other than that the bomb saved millions of lives, Allied and Japanese." On a visit to Hiroshima, Kenny admired the Promotion Hall, a four-story block with a small green dome designed by a Czech architect in 1915, which was close to the center of the target. "The atomic bomb," wrote Kenny, "vastly improved it as an aesthetic object, changing it from a mundanely ugly building into a masterpiece of stricken form."

That day in class, seeing the gun in my friend's hand, I too looked upon it as an aesthetic object. I wondered how such a lovely thing had come into being. I asked myself (like Blake observing the tiger) what its maker had imagined when he wrought it, and whether he had justified his intentions to himself; just as I wondered whether the craftsman who so keenly perfected the military's instruments of torture had dreamt of the precise uses to which his work was to be put. I remembered a legendary account of Joseph-Ignace Guillotin being put to death by his own invention during the French Revolution; that final act must have fulfilled for Guillotin an artist's wish to know the meaning of his art. I thought that my friend's gun was a beautiful thing if one ignored its use. It reminded me of the skull of a small creature I once discovered in Patagonia, polished by the insects and the rain, with an elongated snout and a single gaping socket, like a miniature Cyclops. For the longest time, I kept the skull on my desk as a reminder.

Learning as a dog does the rules of faithfulness and obedience is for Dante a long and painful process. At the foot of Mount Purgatory, not knowing what path to take (in the *Commedia*'s Wonderland there are no signposts), Dante and Virgil meet a group of figures coming slowly towards them. These are the souls of those who, up to the moment of their death, refused spiritual obedience to the church, and then repented with their last breath. Because they rebelled against the Chief Shepherd during their lives, they must now remain shepherdless for thirty times the length of their earthly wandering. Virgil, following Dante's suggestion, asks them courteously if they know "where the mountain slopes down / so that it may be possible to ascend."

> Like little sheep come edging from the pen
> One, then two, then three, the others standing there
> Turning shyly eyes and noses to the ground,
>
> And what the first one does the others do,
> Huddling up to her if she stands still,
> Foolish and humble, and not knowing why,
>
> So I saw, moving on towards us, the forerunner
> Of that fortunate elected flock
> Modest in appearance, and dignified in pace.[1]

Meekly the souls tell Virgil that he and Dante must turn and go ahead of them. Suddenly, one of the flock detaches itself from its companions and asks whether Dante recognizes him. Dante looks carefully and sees that the inquiring soul "was blond and handsome, with a noble look / But one of his eyebrows had been cloven by a blow." Dante, whose memory is, like himself, mortal, denies having met the man. The soul then, pointing to an identifying wound high on his chest, like that made by the Roman lance in the side of the dying Christ, tells Dante that he is Manfred, grandson of the empress Constanza, whom Dante will eventually meet in Paradise.[2]

Manfred, though he identifies himself to Dante only as the grandson of the empress, was in fact the illegitimate son of Frederick II, the emperor condemned with other Epicureans to the circle of the heretics in the *Inferno*. (Later, Frederick would become a Romantic hero; in German folklore, he was supposed to have lived on after the hour of his death, thanks to a magic spell, in an underground castle, away from the world, guarded by ravens.)[3] The historical Manfred was an ambitious, conniving, ruthless character. He became the leader of the Ghibelline cause, opposing the alliance of the pope with the Guelphs and with Charles of Anjou. On his father's death, he was made regent of Sicily until his half-brother Conrad could take the throne; a few years later, when Conrad died, Manfred assumed the regency on behalf of Conrad's son. In 1258, after a false rumor had announced his nephew's death, Manfred had himself crowned king of Sicily and Puglia.

The newly elected pope, Urban IV, proclaimed him a usurper and placed the crown of Sicily on the head of Charles of Anjou. Branded the antichrist because of his fierce opposition to Rome, Manfred was excommunicated twice, once in 1254 by Innocent IV and once in 1259 by Urban. Seven years later, Charles succeeded in killing his rival at the battle of Benevento and, as a gracious victor, had him honorably buried under a cairn of stones, though in unconsecrated ground. With retrospective rancor, however, the new pope, Clement IV, ordered the bishop of Cosenza to have Manfred's body disinterred "with tapers extinct" and thrown into the River Verde, which marked the border with the Kingdom of Naples.[4]

Dante's contemporaries were strongly divided in their judgment of Manfred. For the Ghibellines, he was a heroic figure, a freedom fighter against the tyrannical ambitions of the papacy. For the Black Guelphs, he was a murderer, an infidel who had associated with the Saracens against Pope Alexander IV. Brunetto Latini accused Manfred of killing his father, his half-brother, and two of his nephews, as well as attempting to murder Conrad's infant son. The blond, handsome hero with the cleft eyebrow would later appeal to Byron and Tchaikovsky.

Dante, who sided with the White Guelphs (now associated with the Ghibelline cause), thought of Manfred, the last representative in Italy of the Holy Roman Empire, as a symbolic incarnation of the conflict between empire and church, a leader of the opposition to the church's interference in worldly affairs. In Dante's view, the civil powers of the church had demeaned its spiritual endeavors and turned the institution into a vulgar, politicking arena. No less a presence than Saint Peter, Christ's anointed, in the Heaven of Fixed Stars inveighs against the corruption and abuse of the Holy See:

> He who usurps my place on earth,
> My place, my place which is now vacant
> In the presence of the Son of God,
>
> Has made my burial site a sewer
> Of blood and stench, which the perfidious
> Who fell from here above, delights in below.[5]

Empire and church must follow Christ's dictum of rendering to Caesar what is Caesar's and to God what is God's: Manfred fulfilled the first part of the equation. Just as in the *Inferno* the soul of Muhammad tears open his chest as a symbol of the schism he has caused among Christian believers ("see how I rend myself," he says to Dante), Manfred's wounded chest is the symbol of the wounds in the body of the empire, an empire nevertheless redeemed, in the eyes of God, through Manfred's labors. Manfred is, for Dante, the Christian champion who attempted to mend the disastrous effects of the legendary Donation of Constantine.[6]

According to medieval legend, the emperor Constantine on his deathbed ceded the imperial secular rights to the church, limiting the imperial authority and allowing the pope to meddle in civil affairs. (In the fifteenth century, the humanist Lorenzo Valla proved that the Donation of Constantine was a clever forgery.) Beatrice will later compare Constantine's Donation to a catastrophe as great as Adam's Fall. In spite of what he judges to be the emperor's grievous error, Dante places Constantine in the Heaven of the Just Rulers and, through the voice of the eagle, excuses him because he acted "with good intentions that bore bad fruit."[7]

Manfred is also an example of the limited powers of papal excommunication. God's mercy, Dante repeatedly asserts, is infinite, and even a late repentant, uttering his confession with his dying breath, can be saved when he turns "weeping towards Him who willingly forgives." In Dante's time the church attempted to exclude from the pope's anathema the codicil that acknowledges God's prerogative of pardoning whoever "in the end repents."[8] For Dante, absolute curses were intended to advertise the temporal powers of the pope rather than the overriding quality of God's mercy. A true conclusion to a sinner's life must be not a full stop but an ongoing phrase, an endless questioning of the sinner's own actions, a process of spiritual regeneration driven by the spirit of curiosity towards a better understanding of the self. To emphasize his argument, Dante compares the wounded Manfred to the risen Christ showing his wound to the doubting Thomas in the Gospels of Luke (24:40) and John (20:27). John Freccero, in an enlightening essay on Manfred's wounds, notes that the Gospel text is "filled with signs that demand of the reader the same assent that is demanded of the doubting Thomas. As Christ's scarred body is seen by the disciples, so John's text is read by the faithful." Freccero points out that the same analogy is operative in Dante's poem: "Manfred's wounds, slashed across a body made of thin air, stand for Dante's own intrusion into the course of history. They are, as it were, writing itself, Dante's own markings introduced across the page of history as testimony of a truth which otherwise might not be perceived."[9]

Manfred explains himself to Dante in these words:

> Horrible were my sins;
> But infinite goodness has such wide arms
> That it embraces all who turn to it.
> . . . .
> By their curse a soul is not so lost

What Are the Consequences of Our Actions?

That the eternal love may not return
So long that hope retains a trace of green.

It's true that he who dies scorning the church,
Even though he might repent at last
Must stay upon the outside of this bank

For thirty times as long as he has lived
In his presumption, unless this stern decree
Be not made shorter by kind prayers.[10]

The story of Manfred is one of wounds and bones. Earlier in the canto,
Virgil signifies the hour by noting that it is already evening in Naples where
his mortal body lies after it was taken from Brindisi; Manfred explains that
his bones might still be under the bridge near Benevento had they not been
strewn by the river, washed by the rain, and stirred by the wind. Virgil's
bones were dispersed by order of the empire, Manfred's by that of the church;
in both cases these were temporary displacements, awaiting the promised
Day of Resurrection. In a world in which death by violence was an everyday
occurrence, and war not the exception but the rule, the promise of redemption for the repentant sinner, an answer to the prophet's question "Can these
bones live?," was of the essence.[11]

A near-contemporary of Dante's, the French poet Jean de Meung, argued
that the violence of war was a contest in which we were all pawns; his version
of the story of Manfred presents it in terms of a game of chess. The image
is ancient, going back to Sanskrit texts like the Mahabharata. In the early-
fourteenth-century Welsh epic the *Mabinogion,* two enemy kings play chess
while in a nearby valley their armies clash. At last, one of the kings, seeing that
his adversary will not surrender, crushes the golden chessmen to dust. Shortly
afterwards, a messenger arrives covered in blood and announces that his army
has been slaughtered. So commonplace was the image of war as a game of chess
that Charles of Anjou employed it when referring to the forthcoming battle
with Manfred at Benevento: he promised to checkmate the miscreant "by
moving a pawn which had gone astray in the middle of the chessboard."[12]

The Battle of Benevento, fought on 26 February 1266, is the historical

Giuseppe Bezzuoli, *Discovery of Manfred's Body After the Battle of Benevento, 1266,* 1838. (© DcA Picture Library/Art Resource, NY)

core of Manfred's narrative, and another emblematic episode in the conflict between empire and church. Dante's century had seen several important changes in the art of warfare: increased use of mercenaries, "shock tactics" such as cavalry charges to frighten and scatter the enemy troops, and the deployment of projectile firearms such as bombards, which enabled armies to kill larger numbers of the enemy from a greater distance.[13] At Benevento, both armies employed mercenary forces, but it was Charles who adopted the shock tactics that proved so successful against the confident Manfred. However, neither side made use of projectiles: traditional weapons were enough to inflict on Manfred the wounds that prevented Dante from recognizing the handsome warrior. A fourteenth-century illumination of the *Nuova cronica* shows Charles piercing Manfred with his lance (the depiction is of course allegorical, since we have no historical evidence that this was what happened), while the gash on the eyebrow may have been caused by a sword or by a *doloire* or ax.[14] Swords, lances, and axes were the armies' common weapons; bombards and other projectile firearms were still fairly rare at the time.

Projectile firearms were probably invented in China in the twelfth century, and gunpowder some three centuries earlier. (The formula for gunpowder appears for the first time in a Daoist manual of the ninth century, which warns alchemists not to mix inadvertently the component substances.) Traditionally, Chinese gunpowder was associated with ancient "smoking out" practices, fumigation rituals carried out by law in every home. These practices were used not only as prophylactic measures but also in warfare as early as the fourth century B.C.E. to enable advancing troops to hide behind smokescreens during sieges, as well as to bombard the enemy with toxic fumes produced by pumps and furnaces. In his monumental study of Chinese science and civilization, Joseph Needham noted that "a cardinal feature of Chinese technology and science" was "the belief in action at distance." In warfare, this manifested itself in the use of flame-carrying arrows and the so-called Greek fire, incendiary wagons that used as the inflammatory material a distillation of petroleum (naphtha) first produced in seventh-century Byzantium and probably brought to China by Arab traders.[15]

Although bombards did not make their first appearance in Europe until after Dante's death—in 1343 the Moors of Algeciras used them to attack Christian armies—the first European mention of the composition of gunpowder appears in a text by the English scholar Roger Bacon a century earlier. "We can," Bacon wrote in 1248, "with saltpeter and other substances, compose artificially a fire that can be launched over long distances. . . . By only using a very small quantity of this material much light can be created accompanied by a horrible fracas. It is possible to destroy a town or an army."[16] Bacon, who entered the Franciscan orders and was a friend of Pope Clement IV, might have learned about gunpowder after witnessing a display of Chinese fireworks, which were brought to Europe by other Franciscans who had been to the Far East.

Ironically, the first European bombards or cannons were constructed by the craftsmen who made the traditional symbols of peace: the bell founders. It is likely that the first bombard was a bell, turned upside down and filled with stones and gunpowder. These early cannons were crude, inaccurate, and dangerous to both users and targets. Nor could they be moved with ease: in the fourteenth century, they were mounted on huge blocks and then dismantled when the siege was over.[17]

What Are the Consequences of Our Actions?

Assault of Mara: detail of a tenth-century mural from Dunhuang, Ginsu Province, showing Chinese demons carrying incendiary weapons.
(© RMN-Grand Palais/Art Resource, NY)

Nowhere in the *Commedia* does Dante speak of gunpowder, but in his description of the chasm in which the traffickers in public offices are punished the Arsenal of Venice is mentioned, depicted not as the place in which warships are built but as a repair shop where damaged boats are caulked in wintertime. It is a center of reparation, not of death-mongering, and it contrasts with the hideously farcical scene of the traffickers wallowing in boiling pitch, their flesh torn off by the hooks of angry demons.[18]

The scene bears on Manfred's story in another way. Here Dante shows himself a cowardly onlooker, comically afraid of what the demonic custodians might do to him. Following Virgil's orders, he hides behind a crag to watch undetected the obscene goings-on until, after negotiating with the demons, Virgil calls him forth:

> And my guide said to me: "Oh you that sit
> Squatting and cowering among the splinters of the bridge,
> Securely now return here to my side."[19]

On other occasions, as when crossing the murky Styx where the wrathful and sullen are punished by being plunged into the putrid mud, Dante had been pleased to watch the torture of the sinners. But among the punished traffickers, Dante's curiosity is different. Now he wants to watch but not be seen, and his voyeuristic enjoyment stems from something undefined and archetypal.

In a story that J. Robert Oppenheimer, known as the father of the atomic bomb, later told friends, he was greatly influenced by a similar instance of perverted curiosity in Proust's *Du côté de chez Swann*. He learned by heart the passage in which Mademoiselle Vinteuil goads her lesbian lover to spit on a photograph of her deceased father: "Perhaps she would not have considered evil to be so rare, so extraordinary, so estranging a state, to which it was so restful to emigrate," Proust notes of Mademoiselle Vinteuil, "had she been able to discern in herself, as in everyone, that indifference to the sufferings one causes, an indifference which, whatever names one may give it, is the terrible and permanent form of cruelty."[20] It is this indifference to the suffering of the traffickers that distinguishes Dante's reactions from earlier scenes.

Oppenheimer has been called a modern version of the Romantic hero, who like Byron's Manfred (but not like Dante's) is unable to repent of his sins and is torn between his urge to explore the forbidden unknown and feelings of guilt for having done so. The son of a wealthy Jewish family that had abandoned its faith, Oppenheimer grew up in New York City in a vast apartment where his philanthropic father had accumulated a remarkable art collection. There Oppenheimer grew up among Renoirs and van Goghs, while being instructed by his parents in the obligation to help the less fortunate by funding such organizations as the National Child Labor Committee and National Association for the Advancement of Colored People. Oppenheimer was a precocious, solitary, questioning child, passionately interested in science, especially chemistry. Mathematics, however, was his weak point, and later, when he became known as a brilliant theoretical physicist, his mathematics, by professional standards, were considered by his colleagues to be less than impressive. Like Manfred, the material workings of the substances that made the world interested him more than the abstract rules that governed them.[21]

As a lonely young man, Oppenheimer behaved somewhat erratically. He was sometimes melancholy, refusing to speak or acknowledge the presence of others; sometimes oddly euphoric, reciting lengthy passages of French literature and sacred Hindu texts; a few times he appeared to his friends to be verging on madness. Once, during his year at the University of Cambridge, he left a poisoned apple on his tutor's desk, an affair that was hushed up after his father promised to have his son seen by a psychiatrist. Years later, when Oppenheimer became director of the Los Alamos atomic laboratory, his colleagues found him unnerving. On one hand, he seemed often lost in his own abstractions, silently aloof; on the other, he submitted without compunction to the supervision of military authorities, even though the Intelligence Services suspected him of being a Communist spy because of his liberal opinions and treated him with little regard. When, after the war, Oppenheimer pleaded for the United States and the Soviet Union to share their technological knowledge in order to avoid a nuclear showdown, his opponents found in his conciliatory attitude reason enough to brand him a traitor.

The question of how to make a nuclear bomb, that vastly evolved descendant of the crude early bombard of Dante's time, presented not merely a theoretical problem but one of engineering as well. Because of the fear that the Germans might develop such a bomb before the American scientists, the construction of the Los Alamos site had to proceed rapidly, even while basic problems of physics were still being solved: the strategies for "action at distance" needed to take shape before the question of what that action was to be was fully formulated. When Brigadier General Leslie Groves chose Oppenheimer for the post of director of the Los Alamos lab, what impressed him most was that this scientist understood, far better than his colleagues, the practical aspects of the problem of how to go from abstract theory to concrete construction.

What Are the Consequences of Our Actions?

The situation changed on 7 May 1945 when Germany surrendered, thus ending the threat of a nuclear attack. In July a petition began circulating among Oppenheimer's colleagues urging the government not to use the bomb "unless the terms which will be imposed upon Japan have been made public in detail and Japan knowing these terms has refused to surrender." Oppenheimer was not one of the seventy signatories to the 17 July petition.[22]

The day before, 16 July, the bomb was tested at a site that Oppenheimer had dubbed Trinity. Observing the effects of the controlled explosion behind a protective barrier, Oppenheimer must have looked like Dante behind his crag observing the demonic activity. As the first atomic bomb exploded, unleashing its famous mushroom cloud, Oppenheimer, as he noted two decades later, was reminded of a line from the *Bhagavad Gita,* when the god Vishnu tries to convince the mortal Prince to do his duty, and says to him: "Now I am become Death, the destroyer of worlds."[23]

After the successful test, four Japanese cities were proposed as targets of the bombing: Hiroshima, Kokura, Niigata, and Nagasaki. It was only a few days before the attack that the final decision was made: because it was the only one that did not have an Allied prisoner-of-war camp, the choice fell on Hiroshima. On 6 August, at 8:14 A.M. local time, the *Enola Gay,* a plane named after pilot Paul Tibbets's mother, dropped the bomb. Two shock waves followed a blinding glare, Tibbets recalled. After the second one, "we turned back to look at Hiroshima. The city was hidden by that awful cloud . . . boiling up, mushrooming, terrible and incredibly tall."[24]

The dichotomy that had struck Oppenheimer so strongly in the Proust passage was apparent in his own life. On one hand, he revered scientific pursuit with the intelligent curiosity that led him to question the intimate mechanics of the universe; on the other, he faced the consequences of such curiosity, both in his personal life, where his self-centered ambition verged on a Manfred-like egotism, and in his public life, where, as a scientist, he became the man responsible for the most potent killing machine ever conceived. Oppenheimer never spoke of these consequences in terms of degrees and limits, not to curiosity itself but to the instrumentation of that curiosity.

After the bombing, a Jesuit priest, Father Siemes, who was in the vicinity of Hiroshima at the time, wrote this in a report to his superiors: "The crux of the matter is whether total war in its present form is justifiable, even when it serves a just purpose. Does it not have material and spiritual evil as its consequences which far exceed whatever good might result? When will our moralists give us a clear answer to this question?" Dante's response is given by the eagle in the Heaven of the Just: God's justice is not human justice.[25]

One of Oppenheimer's biographers, quoting the Proust paragraph, compared it to a statement Oppenheimer made towards the end of his life at a conference that was partially sponsored by the Congress for Cultural Freedom, an anti-Communist organization founded after the war (and funded by the CIA):

> Up to now and even more in the days of my almost infinitely prolonged adolescence, I hardly took any action, hardly did anything, or failed to do anything, whether it was a paper on physics, or a lecture, or how I read a book, how I talked to a friend, how I loved, that did not arouse in me a very great sense of revulsion and of wrong. . . . It turned out to be impossible . . . for me to live with anybody else, without understanding that what I saw was only one part of the truth . . . and in an attempt to break out and be a reasonable man, I had to realise that my own worries about what I did were valid and were important, but that they were not the whole story, that there must be a complementary way of looking at them, because other people did not see them as I did. And I needed what they saw, needed *them*.[26]

So does Manfred. His own views are not enough, he must tell his story to Dante, not only to procure the redeeming prayers of his daughter, the "good Constanza," when the poet returns to earth. Manfred, as symbol and as allegory, as a pawn in the game of history and as lines of verse in an immortal poem, needs to know what Dante sees translated into the words of his narrative. In this reflective action Manfred will perhaps feel a redeeming compassion for the victims, understand the import of his full repentance, and believe in the assurance of his salvation, delivered in spite of his undoubtedly "horrible sins."

What Are the Consequences of Our Actions?

13

What Can We Possess?

THE CONCEPT OF MONEY ESCAPES ME. As a child, I never felt that there was a real difference between the bills in my Monopoly set and the ones that came out of my mother's purse except in a conventional sense: one lot was used in the games I played with my friends, the other in the card games my parents played in the evening. The artist Georgine Hu would draw what she called "banknotes" on toilet paper and use them to pay for her psychiatrist's consultations.

As a symbol for the value of goods or services, soon after its invention money universally lost its meaning and became merely equivalent to itself: money equal to money. Literary and artistic symbols, instead, allow unlimited explorations because the things they symbolize are real. On a literal level *King Lear* is the story of an old man who loses everything, but our reading does not stop there: the poetic reality of the story is persistent, echoing throughout our past, present, and future experiences. A dollar bill, instead, is only a dollar bill: whether issued by the United States Federal Reserve or produced by a naïf artist, it has no reality beyond its paper surface. Philip VI of France said that a thing was worth what he said it was worth because he was the king.

(Opposite) Dante, emerging from the dark wood, is threatened by the three beasts. Woodcut illustrating Canto 1 of the Inferno, *printed in 1487 with commentary by Cristoforo Landino. (Beinecke Rare Book and Manuscript Library, Yale University)*

Georgine Hu, *Money Bills* (detail). (*ABCD: Une Collection d'Art Brut* [Actes Sud: Paris, 2000]. Photograph by kind permission of Bruno Decharme.)

Some time ago, a friend savvy in things financial tried to explain to me the truism that the fabulous sums mentioned in national and international transactions don't really exist: they are ciphers taken on faith, supported by abstruse statistics and fortune-tellers' predictions. My friend made it sound as if the science of economics were a more or less successful branch of fantastic literature.

Money is "frozen desire," as James Buchan calls it in his extraordinary book about money's meaning: "the desire incarnate" that offers "a reward to the imagination, as between lovers." In our early centuries, Buchan explains, "money seemed to be guaranteed by rare and beautiful meals, of whose inner nature and capacity men could only dream." Later, that guarantee became merely "the projected authority of a community," first of princes, then of merchants, then of banks.

False beliefs engender monsters. A trust in empty symbols can give rise to financial bureaucracies of chance schemes and red-tape regulations, with convoluted laws and fearful punishments for most, devious strategies of accountancy and obscene wealth for a happy few. The time and energy devoted to tangling and disentangling the world financial apparatus puts to shame the inventions of Gulliver's Academy of Projects, whose bureaucratic members work hard at extracting sunshine from cucumbers. Bureaucracy infects every one of our societies, even those of the Otherworld. In the seventh circle of Hell, those guilty of crimes against nature are made to run incessantly, but as Brunetto Latini explains to Dante, "whoever of this flock stops for a moment, must lie for a hundred years thereafter / without fanning himself when the fire hits him." As in most bureaucratic procedures, no explanation is given.

During the economic crisis in Argentina in 2006, when banks like the Canadian Scotiabank and the Spanish Banco de Santander closed overnight and robbed thousands of people of their savings, whole sections of the Argentine middle class were left without their homes and forced to beg in the streets. Obviously, no one believed any longer in the justice of a civil society. To blame for this loss of ideology and of faith in a legal structure were the international financial giants and their policies of quick gain and institutional corruption. Admittedly, it was not difficult to corrupt the upper classes, the military, even the leaders of the workers' unions, to whom smaller or larger handouts were offered de facto in every business transaction. At the same time, the usurers were mindful of not losing their interest. Even after the horrors of the military dictatorship, when it seemed that Argentina had been bled of all its financial and intellectual powers, the usurers made huge profits. Between 1980 and 2000 (according to the World Bank World Development Indicators of 2011), the private lenders to Latin American governments received $192 billion above their loans. During those same years, the International Monetary Fund lent Latin America $71.3 billion and was reimbursed $86.7 billion, making a profit of $15.4 billion.

What Can We Possess?

More than fifty years earlier, during his long regime as president of Argentina, Perón liked to boast that, like Disney's Uncle Scrooge, he could "no longer walk along the corridors of the Central Bank because they're so crammed full with gold ingots." But after he fled the country, in 1955, there was no gold left to walk on, and Perón appeared on international financial lists as one of the richest men in the world. After Perón, the thefts continued and increased. The money lent to Argentina, several times, by the IMF, was pocketed by the same well-known ruffians: ministers, generals, businessmen, industrialists, congressmen, bankers, senators, their names familiar to every Argentinian.

The IMF's refusal to lend more was based on the safe premise that it would simply be stolen again (thieves know one another's habits all too well). This was no consolation to the hundreds of thousands of Argentinians who were left with nothing to eat and no roof under which to sleep. In many neighborhoods, people resorted to bartering and, for a time, a parallel economy allowed them to survive. Like baking and sewing, poetry became a currency: writers would exchange a poem for a meal or an article of clothing. For a time, the improvised system worked. Then the usurers returned.

And appetite, an universal wolf,
So doubly seconded with will and power,
Must make perforce an universal prey,
And last eat up itself.

—SHAKESPEARE, *Troilus and Cressida*, 1.3.119–24

Historians of the time were less kind to Manfred than Dante was. At the end of the fourteenth century, Leonardo Bruni stressed the fact that Manfred was "the offspring of a concubine who had usurped the royal name against the will of his relations." Manfred's near contemporary Giovanni Villani wrote that "he was as dissolute as his father . . . and delighted in the company of jesters, courtiers and prostitutes, and always dressed in green. He was a spendthrift (and) all his life he was an Epicurean who cared nothing for God nor his saints, but only for bodily pleasure."[1] But Manfred's sin, like that of Statius (of whom more later), seems to have been prodigality, not avarice.

Of the three beasts who stand in Dante's path as he attempts to ascend the beautiful mountain after leaving the dark forest the worst, Virgil will tell him, is the she-wolf. The common inspiration for the three beasts is the biblical book of Jeremiah, where they are summoned to punish the sinners of Jerusalem: "Wherefore a lion out of the forest shall slay them, and a wolf of the evenings shall spoil them, a leopard shall watch over their cities; everyone that goeth out thence shall be torn in pieces: because their transgressions are many and their backslidings are increased" (5:6). But as always in Dante, the creatures he mentions and the places he describes are at once real things and symbols of things that are real. His depictions are never merely emblematic: they always allow for the various levels of reading he recommends in his letter to Cangrande in which he expounds his poetic project, saying that his readers should begin with a literal interpretation, followed by the allegorical, moral, and anagogical or mystical ones.² And even this multilayered reading is not enough.

The first beast, the leopard or panther, "light and very nimble, covered with a spotted coat," is, according to Latin tradition, like the dogs of desire, one of Venus's familiars, and therefore in Dante's bestiary an allegory of lust, the temptation that assaults us in our self-indulgent youth. The second, the lion, "head erect and with rabid hunger," is not Saint Mark's emblematic beast but stands as a symbol of pride, the sin of kings, which comes upon us in our adulthood. The third is the she-wolf.

And a she-wolf that seemed laden
heavily with all cravings in her leanness,
and has made many before now live in distress,

she brought such deep sorrow upon me
with the terror caused by the sight of her,
that I lost all hope of ever ascending.³

Up to this point, Dante's emotions have alternated between hope and fear: fear of the forest followed by the comforting sight of the mountain's glimmering peak; the image of drowning in a high sea, by the sense of being rescued on the shore; dread of the leopard, by the intuition that in the morning light some good might come from meeting the wild beast. But after the encounter with the she-wolf, Dante feels that he can no longer expect to reach the mountaintop in safety. Therefore, just before Virgil appears to guide him, Dante finds himself bereft of hope.

If the sins of the leopard are those of self-indulgence and those of the lion the sins of unreason, the sins of the she-wolf are those of cupidity, the longing for empty things, the pursuit of earthly wealth above all the promises of heaven. Paul's companion Timothy wrote that "the love of money is the root of all evil: which while some coveted after, they have erred from the faith, and pierced themselves through with many sorrows" (1 Timothy 6:10). Dante, on the path of salvation, is threatened by that greedy hunger, tempting him not perhaps with material gain but desire for things that are nevertheless of this world—fame that comes through wealth, recognition that comes through possession, the acclaim of his fellow citizens—and these secret longings drag him back to the edge of the dark forest and weigh him down so heavily that he feels that he can no longer hope for a spiritual ascent. Dante knows that he has been guilty of other sins—his youthful lust, which made him turn from the memory of Beatrice to the desire for another woman; the recurrent pride that is never completely absent, even in his conversations with the dead, until he is shamed by Beatrice in the Garden of Eden. But the sin of the she-wolf is one that threatens not only him but his entire society, even the entire world. To avoid the threat, Virgil tells him, he must take another path:

> Because this beast, because of which you cry out,
> allows no man to pass her way,
> but so strongly she prevents it, that she kills him;
>
> and has a nature so perverse and vicious,
> that she never satiates her craving appetite,
> and after feeding, she's hungrier than before.[4]

But what exactly is this terrible sin of cupidity? No sin is exclusive: all sins intermingle and feed on one another. An excess of love directed towards a mistaken object leads to greed, and greed is at the root of several other vices: avarice, usury, excessive prodigality, overreaching ambition, and, with it all, anger at those who prevent us from getting what we want and envy of those who have more than ourselves. The sin of the she-wolf, therefore, has many names. Saint Thomas Aquinas (once again an unavoidable source for Dante's moral tenets), this time quoting Saint Basil, notes: "It is the hungry man's bread that thou keepest back, the naked man's cloak that thou hoardest, the needy man's money that thou possessest, hence thou despoilest as many as thou mightest succour." And Aquinas adds that cupidity or covetousness, since on the one hand it consists in the unfair taking or retaining of another's property, opposes justice, and since on the other hand it denotes an inordinate love of riches, sets itself above charity. Though Aquinas argues that when covetousness stops short of loving riches more than God it is not a mortal but a venial sin, he concludes that "lust of riches, properly speaking, brings darkness on the soul." If pride is the greatest sin against God, covetousness is the greatest sin against all of humankind. It is a sin against the light.[5]

In Dante's cosmology the covetous are located according to degree. In the fourth circle of Hell can be found the avaricious and the spendthrifts; in the sixth, the tyrants who robbed their people and the violent highwaymen who despoiled them; in the seventh, the usurers and the bankers; in the eighth, the common thieves and those who have sold ecclesiastical and public offices; in the ninth the greatest betrayer of all, Lucifer, who coveted the ultimate power of God himself. In Purgatory the system is reversed (since the ascent leads from worst to best) and new variations and consequences of covetousness are added. On the second cornice of Purgatory the envious are purged, on the third the wrathful, on the fifth the avaricious.

Covetousness is punished and purged in several ways: in the fourth circle of Hell, guarded by Plutus, the god of riches (whom Virgil calls "a cursed wolf"), the avaricious and spendthrifts must push, in large and opposing half-circles, great boulders, which they slam against one another, shouting, "Why do you hoard?" and "Why do you throw away?" Dante notices that a great number of the avaricious are tonsured: Virgil explains that they are priests, popes, and cardinals. Dante fails to recognize any of them, because, says Virgil, "their undiscerning life which has rendered them obscene, / now makes them too obscure for recognition." They mocked, he goes on, the goods that Fortune holds, and now "all the gold that is under the moon, or ever was, could not give rest to a single one of these weary souls." Human beings cannot fathom the wisdom of God that allows Fortune to distribute and redistribute earthly possessions from one person to another, making one rich and another poor in an endless and fluid course.[6]

Avarice is a recurrent theme in the *Commedia;* the sin of the spendthrifts is not much dwelt upon. The case of Statius is the exception. In Purgatory,

Virgil believes that Statius has been condemned for avarice and asks his fellow-poet how was it that a wise man like Statius could fall prey to such an error. Statius smilingly explains that his sin was the opposite.

> Then I realized that our hands could open
> their wings too wide in spending, and I repented
> of that as of the other offences.[7]

The subject of prodigality is then dropped, but avarice is pursued further. Within the mysterious workings of Fortune, there are those who are not only avaricious but try to profit from the misery of others: these Dante meets in Hell three circles below the avaricious. After summoning the winged monster Geryon from the abyss, Virgil tells Dante that while he is giving instructions to Geryon about carrying them down, Dante should speak to a group of people huddled on the edge of the burning sand.

> Through their eyes their grief was bursting forth;
> on this side and that, they attempted to ward off
> sometimes the steam, sometimes the burning soil;
>
> not otherwise do dogs in summertime
> using their muzzle or their paw,
> when they're bitten by fleas, flies or gadflies.[8]

This is the first (and only) time that Virgil has sent Dante on his own to observe a group of sinners, and Dante fails to recognize any of them, as he failed before in the circle of the avaricious. Sitting on the burning sand with their eyes fixed on the ground are the bankers, guilty of the sin of usury: from their necks hang money pouches embroidered with their family arms. One of them, who says he is from Padua, tells Dante that the people surrounding him are all Florentines. The passage is short because it seems unnecessary to dwell on these condemned souls, and Dante treats them with utter scorn. They are like beasts deprived of reason, prisoners of their cupidity. They resemble the animals depicted on their money bags—a gorged goose, a greedy sow—in their gestures, like a Pisan, seen here by Dante, whose final grimace is to lick his snout like an ox.

Usury is a sin against nature because it finds increase in what is naturally sterile: gold and silver. The activity of usurers—making money out of money—is rooted neither in the earth nor in care for their fellow human beings. Their punishment is therefore to stare eternally at the ground from which their treasures were taken and to feel bereft in the company of others. A contemporary of Dante's, Gerard of Siena, wrote that "usury is wicked and bound with vice because it causes a natural thing to transcend its nature and an artificial thing to transcend the skill that created it, which is completely contrary to Nature." Gerard's argument is that natural things—oil, wine, grain—have a natural value; artificial things—coins and ingots—have a value measured by weight. Usury falsifies both, charging more for the former and demanding that the latter unnaturally multiply itself. Usury is the opposite of work. The Spanish poet Jorge Manrique, writing in the fifteenth century, recognized that only death would make equal this world of ours, split as it is between "those who live by their hands, / and the rich."[9]

The church took a stern view of usury. A series of decrees issuing from the Third Lateran Council of 1179 on through the Council of Vienna of 1311 ordered the excommunication of usurers, denied them Christian burial unless they first repaid the interest to their debtors, and forbade local governments to authorize their activities. These religious prescriptions had their roots in ancient Jewish rabbinical law, which prohibited charging interest on loans to fellow Jews (though interest could be charged to Gentiles). Echoing this, Saint Ambrose wrote, somewhat drastically, that "you have no right to take interest, save from him whom you have the right to kill." Saint Augustine thought that charging interest in whatever case was no better than legalized robbery. However, though in theory usury was both a sin and a canonical crime, in practice in the thriving monetary economy of medieval Italy, these prohibitions were hardly ever upheld. The citizens of Florence, for example, were from time to time compelled by decree to lend money to their government at an interest rate of 5 percent. And lawyers and accountants found ways to circumvent the anti-usury laws, providing documents of fictitious sales, presenting the loan as an investment, or finding loopholes in the laws themselves.[10]

The church's laws against usury can be seen as an early systematic attempt to create an economic theory in Europe. It rested on the assumption that the abolition of interest on loans would result in a consumer credit available to all. In spite of these excellent intentions, the practical exceptions, as Dante makes clear, far outdid the theoretical rule. After three centuries of anti-usury policy, the church changed its tactics and lifted the restrictions on moneylending, allowing moderate interest charges. Usury, however, continued to be considered a moral issue as well as a practical one, and in spite of the growing banking practices of the Vatican, it never ceased to be condemned as a sin.[11]

Usury has long been a favorite literary subject and, at least in the Anglo-Saxon world, Dickens's Ebenezer Scrooge is its most famous incarnation. Like the *Commedia, A Christmas Carol* is divided into three parts and, like Dante, Scrooge is guided through each by a spirit. In the *Commedia,* Dante is made to witness the punishment of sinners but also their cleansing and redemption. In *A Christmas Carol,* Scrooge is presented with a similar triple vision: the sinner's punishment, the offer of purgation, and the possibility of salvation. But while in the *Commedia* the sins are many, in Dickens's story the sin is only one, avarice, the root of all others. Avarice makes Scrooge forsake love, betray his friends, reject family ties, withdraw from his fellow human beings. As the young woman to whom he was betrothed tells him, freeing him from his vows, "a golden idol" has replaced her in his heart. To which Scrooge answers with the logic of bankers: "This is the even-handed dealing of the world! . . . There is nothing on which it is so hard as poverty; and there is nothing it professes to condemn with such severity as the pursuit of wealth!"[12]

Scrooge is shunned by everyone, even the friendly dogs who guide the blind. "It was," says Dickens, "the very thing he liked. To edge his way along the crowded paths of life, warning all human sympathy to keep its distance." He is "a squeezing, wrenching, grasping, scraping, clutching, covetous old sinner," and his sin condemns him to be an outcast, like the bankers at the edges of the seventh circle, alone in their singular agonies. His miserable life is a parody of the contemplative life sought by hermits and mystics whom in the fourth century Macarius of Egypt called "drunk with God," and his work (counting money) a parody of true labor.[13]

Dickens was the great chronicler of the working life and an angry critic of the sterile labors of bankers and bureaucrats. One of these financiers, Mr. Merdle in *Little Dorrit*, is "a man of immense resources—enormous capital—government influence." His are "the best schemes afloat. They're safe. They're certain." Only after he has ruined hundreds with his schemes, is Mr. Merdle recognized as "a consummate rascal, of course, . . . but remarkably clever! One cannot help admiring the fellow. Must have been such a master of humbug. Knew people so well—got over them so completely—did so much with them!"[14] A real-life Mr. Merdle, Bernard Madoff, one of the men who made enormous profits out of the economic crisis in 2010, was able to seduce many with his humbug. But unlike the insouciant Madoff, after his schemes fall apart Mr. Merdle cuts his throat in shame. The Mr. Merdles of this world continue to believe in money as a symbol of the good to be attained for the sake of their own selves.

Money is a complex symbol. The Nobel Prize–winning economist Paul Krugman gave, in one of his *New York Times* columns, three examples of its labyrinthine representations.[15] The first is an open pit in Papua New Guinea, the Porgera gold mine, with an infamous reputation for human rights abuses and environmental damage, that continues to be exploited because gold prices have tripled since 2004. The second is a virtual mine, the bitcoin mine in Reykjanesbaer, Iceland, which uses a digital currency, the "bitcoin," which people buy because they believe that others will be willing to buy it in the future. "And like gold, it can be mined," says Krugman. "You can create new bitcoins, but only by solving very complex mathematical problems that require both a lot of computing power and a lot of electricity to run the computers." In the case of the bitcoin mine, real resources are being used to create virtual objects with no clear use.

The third representation is hypothetical. Krugman explains that in 1936, the economist John Maynard Keynes argued that increased government spending was needed to restore full employment. But then, as now, there was strong political opposition to this suggestion. So Keynes, tongue in cheek, suggested an alternative: have the government bury bottles of cash in disused coal mines, and let the private sector spend its own money digging them up. This "perfectly useless spending" would give the national economy "a much-needed boost." Keynes went farther. He pointed out that real-life gold mining was very much like this alternative. Gold miners go to great length to dig cash out of the ground even though unlimited amounts of cash can be created at essentially no cost with the printing press. And no sooner is the gold dug up than much of it is buried again in places like the vault of the Federal Reserve Bank of New York. Money is a symbol bereft of all but virtual significance: it has become self-referential, like the pouches of Dante's bankers that reflect their owners and are reflected back. Money creates usury which creates money.

But where did our obsession with money begin? When was money invented? Our earliest writings mention no coinage, only transactions and lists of goods and livestock. Considering the question, Aristotle argued that money originated in natural bartering: the need for different goods led to the exchange of these goods, and because many were not easily transported, money was invented as a conventional means of exchange. "The amounts were at first determined by size and weight," Aristotle wrote, "but eventually the pieces of metal were stamped. This did away with the necessity of weighing and measuring." Once a currency was established, Aristotle continued, the exchange of goods became trade, and with monetary profit commercial activities became more concerned with coined money than with the products bought and sold. "Indeed," Aristotle concluded, "wealth is often regarded as consisting in a pile of money, since the aim of money-making and of trade is to make such a pile." Though moneymaking can be, for Aristotle, necessary for administrative purposes, if it leads to usury it becomes something noxious because "of all the ways of getting wealth, this is the most contrary to nature." For Aristotle, the absurdity stems from a confusion between means and ends, or between the tools and the job.[16]

Dante, in the *Convivio,* analyzes this absurdity in a different light.[17] Discussing the difference between the two roads to happiness, the contemplative and the active, Dante refers to the example of Mary and Martha from the Gospel of Luke (chap. 10). Unlike the labors of moneymakers, who pretend to be active but don't do any real work, Mary's labors are excellent, even compared to those of her sister, Martha, who busies herself with household chores. Dante refuses to consider manual efforts superior to intellectual ones, and likens both to the labors of the bees that produce wax as well as honey.

According to Luke, six days before the Passover festival in Bethany, Martha and Mary gave a dinner in honor of Jesus who had raised their brother Lazarus from the dead. While Martha was working in the kitchen, Mary sat herself down at the feet of their guest to listen to his words. Overwhelmed by the many tasks to be done, Martha asked her sister to come and help her. "Martha, Martha," said Jesus, "thou art careful and troubled about many things: But one thing is needful: and Mary hath chosen that good part." Dante interprets Christ's words as meaning that every moral virtue stems from choosing the right part, whichever that may be, according to who we are. For Mary, the "good part" is at the feet of her Savior, but Dante does not dismiss the fretting and fussing of Martha.

The scene in the house in Bethany casts its long shadow across our many centuries. Christians and non-Christians alike separate those who tend to menial daily tasks from those who are tended to because the occupations of the latter are supposed to take place on a higher, spiritual plane. At first the dichotomy was understood to be spiritual—between the contemplative and the active life—but this rapidly came to be understood (or misunderstood) as a division between those whom privilege sat at the feet (or in the chair) of divine (or earthly) power, and those who were left to busy themselves in the kitchens and sweatshops of the world.

Mary the sister of Lazarus is exalted in her many guises: as prince and potentate, wise man and mystic, priest and heroic figure, all those to whom fate has allotted "the better part." But Martha is never absent. Accompanying the Egyptian pharaohs in their sumptuous resting places, surrounding the

Chinese emperors as they travel across the magnificent length of a bamboo scroll, embedded in the mosaics of the courtyards of the Pompeian well-to-do, carrying on her unobtrusive life in the background of an Annunciation, pouring wine at Belshazzar's feast, half-hidden in the capitals of Romanesque church columns, framing a seated god on a Dogon carved door, Martha perseveres with her daily task of providing food, drink, and some measure of comfort. Dante never forgets those "who work by their hands": in the *Commedia* we meet masons building bulwarks in the Netherlands, pitch boilers who caulk the damaged ships in the Arsenal of Venice, cooks ordering their kitchen boys to dip the meat into large boilers with their hooks, peasants despairing as the frost covers their early crops, soldiers in the cavalry moving camp just as Dante himself must have done.

The first representations of workers' activities began to emerge in Europe in the late Middle Ages, no longer as accompaniments to depictions of "Vulcan's Forge" or "The Miraculous Catch" to justify the portrayal of a smithy or of fishermen, but as explicit subjects, a change that seems to coincide with the post-feudal society's interest in documentary depictions of itself. The illustration for each month in the famous fifteenth-century illuminated manuscript *Les Très Riches Heures du Duc de Berry* shows farmers, carpenters, shepherds, and reapers all engaged in their particular activities less as signposts for the changing seasons than as self-contained portraits of these members of society. They are among the first specific attempts to single out particular moments of a working life.

Caravaggio is perhaps one of the first painters to turn the convention of literary borrowings on its head. Even though on the surface his proletarian models serve as actors in the biblical dramatic scenes he constructs, the biblical scenes in fact are the excuse for the representations of common working people. So obvious was the device and so shocking the apparent intention, that (legend has it) in 1606, the Carmelites refused his *Dormition of the Virgin,* which they had commissioned, because the painter had used as his model the corpse of a young pregnant prostitute who had drowned herself in the Tiber. What the viewer saw was not, in spite of the title, the Mother of God in her final sleep but the pregnant body of a woman whom society had first exploited and then abandoned. (A similar scandal was provoked by the exhibition, in 1850, of John Everett Millais's *Christ in the House of His Parents,* a painting that was attacked by Charles Dickens, among others, for daring to represent the Holy Family less as a spiritual community of contemplative Marys than as a common flesh-and-blood family of Martha-like carpenters.)[18]

But not until the explorations of the impressionists does work for its own sake, with all its everyday heroic and miserable connotations, become valued as a subject worthy of representation. Vuillard's seamstresses, Monet's waiters, Toulouse-Lautrec's laundry women, and, later, specific depictions of the workers' struggle in the Italian Divisionism school introduce what seems, if not a new subject, then a subject that has at last been granted its own stage. In these images, human labor is shown and commented upon not only in action but also in its consequences (exploitation and exhaustion), causes (ambition or hunger), and attendant tragedies (accidents and armed repression). Many of these images, often sentimentalized or romanticized, acquired after the 1917 October Revolution in Russia decorative, even purely graphic value in Soviet and later in Chinese poster art. On a far larger scale, they lost in Communist aesthetics much of their combative singularity and, in a sense, reverted to the impersonal role given to workers in the earliest medieval depictions. Political and commercial advertising images of work became a parody of Martha's part, much as usury became a parody of Mary's.

Photography, however, the technology that came into being in Monet's time, helped to lend images of Martha's labors the dignity of the viewer's understanding. Manipulating the audience into the position of witness, photography (when outside the field of advertising) framed the activities of the workers both as a document and as an aesthetic object, in images that demanded a narrative political context and, at the same time, followed varying rules of composition and lighting. The minuscule sixteenth-century masons crawling up Breughel's *Tower of Babel* (of which three versions exist) are less, in the viewer's eye, suffering slaves than a collective element in the biblical narrative. Four centuries after Breughel, the Brazilian photographer Sebastião

Sebastião Salgado, Gold-mine workers in Serra Pelada, Brazil, 1986.
(© Sebastião Salgado/Amazonas—Contact Press Images)

Salgado exhibited a Breughelesque series of images that showed destitute gold diggers swarming up and down the walls of a monstrous Amazonian quarry, images which allow hardly any other reading than that of the worker as victim, fellow human beings condemned to hell on earth in our time. In one of his early exhibitions, Salgado quoted Dante's description of the condemned souls gathering on the banks of the Acheron:

What Can We Possess?

As in the autumn the leaves fall off
one after the other, until the branch
sees all its spoils upon the ground,

so the wicked seed of Adam
cast themselves from that shore one by one
at summons, like a bird responding to his call.[19]

Documentary images such as those of Salgado invariably echo established stories that lend them, in metaphorical or allegorical form, a shape and an argument. Salgado's army of workers can be compared to the punished souls in Hell, but they are also the builders of Babylon, the slaves at the pyramids, the allegorical image of all human toil on this earth of sweat and suffering. This does not detract from the viewer's literal reading, from the factual value of Salgado's images, but it allows his photographic depictions to acquire yet another level of story, as Dante would have argued: to reach back into our history and rescue images of Martha that had difficulty in surfacing.

After the birth of his sons Cyril in 1885 and Vyvyan in 1886, Oscar Wilde composed for them a series of short stories which were later published in two collections. The second, *A House of Pomegranates*, begins with a story called "The Young King." A young shepherd boy is discovered to be the heir to the throne and is brought to the royal palace. The night before his coronation he has three dreams in which he sees his crown, scepter, and mantle crafted and woven by "the white hands of Pain" and refuses to wear them. To change his mind, the people tell him that suffering has always been their lot, and that "to toil for a master is bitter, but to have no master to toil for is more bitter still." "Are not the rich and the poor brothers?" asks the young King. "Ay," they answer, "and the name of the rich brother is Cain."[20]

The young King's third dream shows Death and Avarice watching over an army of workers struggling in a tropical forest. Because Avarice won't part with a few seeds that it clutches in its bony hand, Death responds by slaughtering all of Avarice's men. This is Wilde's description of the scene Salgado was to photograph a century later: "There he saw an immense multitude of men toiling in the bed of a dried-up river. They swarmed up the crag like ants. They dug deep pits in the ground and went down into them. Some of them cleft the rocks with great axes; others grabbed in the sand. . . . They hurried about, calling to each other, and no man was idle."[21] Then, outside the frame of Salgado's photograph, in the fifth circle of Hell, Avarice closes her fist.

14

How Can We Put Things in Order?

EVEN AS A CHILD, I GREW accustomed to seeing the world divided into parts, according to the colored patches on my pivoting globe. I learned to say "earth" to mean the clump of dirt I picked up in my hand, and "Earth" to denote the vast clump of dirt, too big to be seen, that my teachers told me circles endlessly around the sun. Every time I move, clumps of earth mark my passage through life like the ticking of a clock, as if time (my time) could be measured in handfuls, each handful unique and distinguishable as part of the place where something has happened to me—where something, quite literally, has taken place. As a place marking time, the earth we tread on acquires, in our symbolic vocabularies, the values of birth, life, and death.

Atlases, maps, encyclopedias, dictionaries attempt to order and label everything we know about the earth and the sky. Our earliest books are Sumerian lists and catalogues, as if giving things names and placing them under various categories allowed us an understanding of them. When I was a child, the ordering of my books suggested to me curious associations by subject, size, language, author, color. All seemed valid upon my shelves and each order transformed the included books into something that I had not noticed

(Opposite) Dante and Virgil contemplate the punishment of the Simonists, whose heads are forced into holes in the rock. Woodcut illustrating Canto XIX of the Inferno, *printed in 1487 with commentary by Cristoforo Landino. (Beinecke Rare Book and Manuscript Library, Yale University)*

before. *Treasure Island* had a place among my books about pirates, among my books with brown covers, among my middle-sized books, among my books written in English. I acknowledged all these labels for my *Treasure Island,* but what did they mean?

Several mythologies see earth as the stuff we are made of, modeled into God's own image by his wizard hand and allotted a specific place and role; earth is also the source of our food and the container of our drink; in the end, earth is the home to which we return and the dust that we become. These categories all define it. A Zen parable which a quirky teacher had us read in high school tells of a disciple who asks his master what is life. The master picks up a handful of earth and lets it sift through his fingers. Then the disciple asks the master what is death. The master repeats the same gesture. The disciple asks what is the Buddha. Again, the master repeats his gesture. The disciple bows his head and thanks the master for his answers. "But those were not answers," says the master. "Those were questions."

The earth does not argue,
Is not pathetic, has no arrangements,
Does not scream, haste, persuade, threaten, promise,
Makes no discriminations, has no conceivable failures,
Closes nothing, refuses nothing, shuts none out,
Of all the powers, objects, states, it notifies, shuts none out.

—WALT WHITMAN, *Leaves of Grass*

Taking time to accustom themselves to the dismal stench that rises from the seventh circle, where the violent are punished, Virgil and Dante take refuge behind a large stone that announces itself as the tomb of Pope Anastasius, punished for his heretical views. Virgil profits from the wait to instruct Dante on the arrangement of the circles of Lower Hell in order to prepare him for the terrible regions that still lie ahead. Coming after the encounter with the heretics who tried to disarrange and confuse the divine laws, Virgil's careful description of the ordered Underworld can be read as a powerful reminder that everything in the universe, as everything in the *Commedia,* has a carefully assigned and singular place. Against this rigorously tidy background all human dramas in the poem are played out, sometimes with detailed reference to the setting, other times with barely a mention of the contextual details. But because everything that occurs in the three realms of the afterlife has a reason and a logical justification (even if it isn't a human logic or a reason that is humanly comprehensible) each punishment, purgation, and reward is strictly and immutably confined to a given place in a preestablished system, mirroring the perfect order of God's mind. The words inscribed on the gate of Hell quoted earlier are valid for the whole of the Otherworld: "Divine Power made me, / Wisdom supreme and primal Love."[1] Hell, because it is God's creation like the rest of universe, cannot be any less than perfect.

Virgil's lesson in geography grounds the nightmarish journey in a landscape of dirt and stone with such precision that Galileo, as we have seen, would later feel able to calculate its measurements. Virgil gives his exposition in two parts: first describing the sections of Hell to come, then responding to Dante's questions about the regions already visited.

After the circle of the heretics lie the circles that lodge the sinners guilty of malice, in which the intellect has a willing part. These damned souls are split into those guilty of perpetrating injustice unthinkingly and those who committed injustice by choice, a much more dreadful fault. The former, lodged in the seventh circle, are in turn divided into three: those who have been violent towards others, towards themselves, and towards God. Those guilty of perpetrating injustice through reason, punished in the next circle, include those guilty of fraud in its various guises. In the ninth and last circle are the traitors; at the very center is the arch-traitor, Lucifer. In answer to Dante's questions, Virgil tells him that the sinners in the second to fifth circles—the lustful, the gluttonous, the avaricious and spendthrifts, and the wrathful—are guilty of the sin of incontinence, a sin (following Aristotle in his *Nicomachean Ethics*) considered less grievous than that of malice, and therefore outside the fiery walls of the City of Dis.[2]

Exactly halfway up Mount Purgatory, Virgil undertakes the same categorical exposition for Dante's (and the reader's) benefit. The source of the arrangement here is not Aristotle but Christian dogma concerning the nature of sins and virtues. Waiting for the sun to rise (since the laws of Purgatory forbid them to travel at night), and before visiting the souls who purge themselves of the sin of sloth, Virgil explains to Dante the cartography of Purgatory. Here, says Virgil, the ruling force is love, both natural and rational, love that moves not only the Creator but his creatures.

> The natural is always without error,
>   but the other one can err through aiming wrongly,
>   or through too little or too much force.[3]

The categories of love are represented by the various sins purged on the mountain. Those who aim their love wrongly are the proud, the envious and the wrathful; those whose love lacks vigor are the slothful; those whose love inclines them too strongly towards earthly things are the avaricious, the gluttons, and the lustful. Each group has a strict place allotted in the ascent. The bureaucracy of Purgatory is very strict.

Paradise is somewhat different from the other two realms because, even if the Celestial Kingdom is partitioned, as we have seen earlier, into several heavens, each blessed soul, wherever it might be, is utterly blissful. As Piccarda tells Dante, after he asks her whether the souls desire a higher position in the grades of heaven:

> Brother, our will is satisfied
> by the quality of love that makes us long
> only for what we have and thirst for nothing else.

Piccarda movingly concludes: "And in his will is our peace." According to God's will, the universe exists in a perfect and immutable order where everything, in Heaven as on Earth (and below it), has been assigned its proper place.[4]

We are tidy creatures. We distrust chaos. Though experience comes to us with no recognizable system, for no intelligible reason, with blind and carefree generosity, we believe despite all evidence to the contrary in law and order, and portray our gods as meticulous archivists and dogmatic librarians. Following what we believe to be the method of the universe, we put everything away into files and compartments; feverishly we arrange, we classify, we label. We know that what we call the world has no meaningful beginning and no understandable end, neither a discernible purpose nor a method in its madness. But we insist: it must make sense, it must signify something. So we divide space into regions and time into days, and again and again we are bewildered when space refuses to hold to the borders of our atlases and time overflows the dates of our history books. We collect objects and build houses for them in the hope that the walls will give the contents coherence and a meaning. We will not accept the inherent ambiguity of any object or collection that charms our attention by saying, like the voice in the burning bush, "I am that I am." "All right," we add, "but you are also a thornbush, *Prunus spinosa*," and give it its place in the herbarium. We believe that location will help us understand events and their protagonists, and that all the chattel they

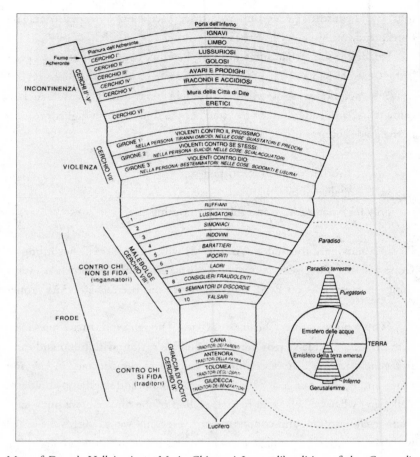

Map of Dante's Hell in Anna Maria Chiavacci Leonardi's edition of the *Commedia* (Milan: Mondadori, 2007), vol. 1, pp. xlx–xlxi. (Used with permission.) Reading from top to bottom, left to right: (*first section*) Gate of Hell; The Plains of Acheron: Neutrals; Acheron River; INCONTINENCE/CIRCLES II–V: Circle I: Limbo; Circle II: The Lustful; Circle III: Gluttons; Circle IV: Spenders and Hoarders; Circle V: The Wrathful and Sullen; The Walls of the City of Dis; Circle VI: Heretics; (*second section*) VIOLENCE/CIRCLE VII: Cornice I: Violent Toward Others, Toward People: Tyrants and Murderers, Toward Things: Robbers and Plunderers; Cornice II: Violent Toward Self, Toward People: Suicides, Toward Things: Squanderers; Cornice III: Violent Toward God, Toward People: Blasphemers, Toward Things: Sodomites and Usurers; (*third and fourth sections*) FRAUD (*third section*) AGAINST THE UNTRUSTWORTHY (FRAUDS)/MALEBOLGE: CIRCLE VIII: 1. Flatterers; 2. Seducers; 3. Simoniacs; 4. Diviners; 5. Barrators; 6. Hypocrites; 7. Thieves; 8. False Counselors; 9. Schismatics; 10. Falsifiers; (*fourth section*) AGAINST THOSE WHO BETRAY TRUST (TRAITORS)/THE LAKE OF ICE: CIRCLE IX: Caina: Traitors to Kin; Antenora: Traitors to Country; Ptolemea: Traitors to Guests; Judecca: Traitors to Benfactors; Lucifer. *Right-hand schema:* Paradise; Earthly Paradise; Purgatory; EARTH: Hemisphere of Water, Hemisphere of Emerged Land, Hell, Jerusalem. (Translation by Will Schutt.)

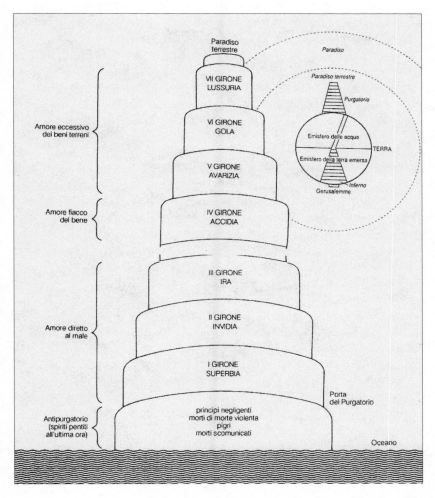

Map of Dante's Purgatory in Anna Maria Chiavacci Leonardi's edition of the *Commedia* (Milan: Mondadori, 2007), vol. 2, pp. xlviii–xlix. (Used with permission.) Reading from top to bottom, left to right: Earthly Paradise; (*first section*) EXCESSIVE LOVE OF WORLDLY GOODS: Cornice VII: Lust; Cornice VI: Gluttony; Cornice V: Avarice; (*second section*) DEFECTIVE LOVE: Cornice IV: Sloth; (*third section*) MISDIRECTED LOVE: Cornice III: Wrath; Cornice II: Envy; Cornice I: Pride; Gate of Purgatory; (*fourth section*) ANTE-PURGATORY (SOULS WHO REPENTED AT THE FINAL HOUR): Negligent Rulers; Those Who Died by Violence; The Lethargic; Excommunicates; Ocean. *Right-hand schema:* Paradise; Earthly Paradise; Purgatory; EARTH: Hemisphere of Water, Hemisphere of Emerged Land, Hell, Jerusalem. (Translation by Will Schutt.)

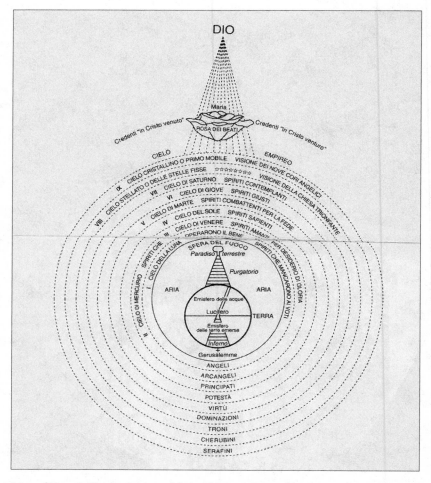

Map of Dante's Heaven in Anna Maria Chiavacci Leonardi's edition of the *Commedia* (Milan: Mondadori, 2007), vol. 3, pp. lviii–lix. (Used with permission.) Reading from top to bottom, left to right: God; Believers in Christ; Mary/Rose of the Blessed; Believers in Christ; (*upper rings*) HEAVEN/EMPYREAN: IX (*Heaven*) Crystalline Heaven or Primum Mobile (*Empyrean*) Vision of the Nine Angelic Choirs; VIII (*Heaven*) Starry Heaven or Fixed Stars (*Empyrean*) Vision of the Church Triumphant; VII (*Heaven*) Heaven of Saturn (*Empyrean*) Contemplative Souls; VI (*Heaven*) Heaven of Jupiter (*Empyrean*) Just Souls; V (*Heaven*) Heaven of Mars (*Empyrean*) Souls Who Fought for the Faith; IV (*Heaven*) Heaven of Sun (*Empyrean*) Wise Souls; III (*Heaven*) Heaven of Venus (*Empyrean*) Souls of Lovers; II (*Heaven*) Heaven of Mercury (*Empyrean*) Souls Who Worked for Glory; I (*Heaven*) Heaven of Moon (*Empyrean*) Souls Who Failed to Keep Their Vows; (*center schema*) CIRCLE OF FIRE; Earthly Paradise; Purgatory; AIR/AIR; EARTH: Hemisphere of Water, Lucifer, Hemisphere of Emerged Land, Hell, Jerusalem; (*lower rings*) Angels; Archangels; Principalities; Powers; Virtues; Dominions; Thrones; Cherubim; Seraphim. (Translation by Will Schutt.)

take on their adventures and misadventures will be defined by the place we assign it. We trust maps.

Vladimir Nabokov, prior to delivering his Harvard lectures on the novel, used to prepare charts of the locations in which the novels he taught took place, just like the ones found in the "scene of the crime" plans that used to accompany detective novels in the pocket editions of the forties and fifties: a map of Great Britain with the sites of *Bleak House,* the layout of Sotherton Court in *Mansfield Park,* the Samsa family's flat in *The Metamorphosis,* Leopold Bloom's path through Dublin in *Ulysses.*[5] Nabokov understood the inextricable relationship between a setting and its narrative (a relationship that is of the essence in the *Commedia*).

A museum, an archive, a library are each a species of map, a place of defining categories, an organized realm of predetermined sequences. Even an institution that houses an apparently heterogeneous collection of objects, assembled, it would seem, without a clear purpose, becomes identified by a label that is not that of any of its several pieces: the name of their collector, for instance, or the circumstances of their assembly, or the overall category within which the objects are inscribed.

The first university museum—the first museum built for the purpose of facilitating study of a specific group of objects—was the Ashmolean Museum in Oxford, founded in 1683. At its core was a collection of strange and wonderful things amassed by two seventeenth-century botanists and gardeners, father and son, both called John Tradescant, and sent to Oxford by barge from London. Several of these treasures are listed in the museum's earliest catalogue:

- A Babylonian Vest.
- Diverse sorts of Egges from Turkic; one given for a Dragons egge.
- Easter Egges of the Patriarchs of Jerusalem.
- Two feathers of the Phoenix tayle.
- The claw of the bird Rock: who, as Authors report, is able to trusse an Elephant.
- Dodar, from the island Mauritius; it is not able to fly being so big.
- Hares head, with rough horns three inches long.
- Toad fish, and one with prickles.

How Can We Put Things in Order?

- Divers things cut on Plum-stones.
- A Brazen-balle to warme the Nunnes hands.[6]

A phoenix's feather and a nun's warming-ball, a toad fish and hare's horned head have little in common: what holds them together is the fascination these objects produced, three centuries ago, in the minds and hearts of the two Tradescants. Whether these objects represented the Tradescants' greed or curiosity, whether they were real or fabulous, their vision of the world or a reflection of the dark map of their souls, those who visited the Ashmolean in the late seventeenth century would enter a space ordered, so to speak, by the Tradescants' ruling passion. Private imagination can lend the world coherence and a semblance of order.

And yet no order, as we know, however coherent, is ever impartial. Any categorical system imposed on objects or souls or ideas must be suspect since, of necessity, it contaminates with meaning those very ideas, people, objects. The Babylonian vest and the Easter eggs of the Ashmolean formulate a seventeenth-century notion of private property; the sinners in Hell and the blessed in Heaven enact their singular dramas, collectively representing both a thirteenth-century Christian cosmogony and Dante's intimate vision of the world. The *Commedia* is in this sense an imaginary universal museum, a stage for the performance of unconscious fears and desires, a library of everything that was one poet's passion and vision, arranged and displayed for our enlightenment.

In the Middle Ages such eclectic collections were amassed by the church and the nobility, but the habit of exposing one's private passions to public view can be traced, in Europe, to the late fifteenth century. At a time when heads of state had begun to amass some of the world's greatest collections of art in Vienna, the Vatican, Spain's El Escorial, Florence, and Versailles, smaller, more personal collections were also being formed by private individuals. One such collection was that of Isabella d'Este, wife of the marquis of Mantua, who, rather than purchasing art for devotional reasons or to furnish a house, began collecting works of art for the sake of the objects themselves. Up to that time, the wealthy collected artwork mainly to lend a domestic space beauty or prestige. Isabella reversed the process and set aside a room that would instead provide a frame to the objects she had collected. In her *camerino,* or "small chamber" (which was to become famous in the history of art as one of the earliest private museums), Isabella exhibited "paintings with a story" by the best contemporary artists. She had a good eye: she instructed her agents to approach Mantegna, Giovanni Bellini, Leonardo, Perugino, Giorgione, Raphael, and Michelangelo in order to obtain artwork for her camerino. Several of these artists complied.[7]

A century later the collecting passion took over the houses not only of aristocrats like Isabella but also of the rich bourgeoisie, and owning a private collection became an indication of social status, financial or scholarly. What Francis Bacon called "a model of the universal nature made private" could be seen in the parlors of many lawyers and physicians. The French word *cabinet,* referring to a piece of furniture with lockable drawers or a small wood-paneled room like the camerino, became commonplace in wealthy homes. In England, the cabinet was called a closet, from the Latin *clausum,* or "closed," indicating the private nature of the space. In the rest of Europe, the private collection of heterogeneous objects came to be known as a *cabinet de curiosités* or *Wunderkammer.* Some of the most famous, assembled during the following centuries, were those of Rudolph II in Prague, Ferdinand II in Ambras Castle at Innsbruck, Ole Worm in Copenhagen, Peter the Great in Saint Petersburg, Gustaf Adolphus in Stockholm, and the architect Sir Hans Sloane in London. Fostered by men like these, curiosity was officially given its place in the household.[8]

Sometimes, when cash was lacking, curiosity collectors resorted to ingenious devices. In 1620, the scholar Cassiano dal Pozzo assembled in his house in Rome not the original works of art, the authentic handcrafted models of famous buildings, the natural-history specimens sought after by his wealthier peers, but drawings commissioned from professional draftsmen of all kinds of strange objects, creatures, and antiquities. He called this his Paper Museum. Here again, as in Isabella's camerino and in the Tradescants' collection, the ruling design, the imposed order, was personal, a Gestalt created by one person's private history—with an added characteristic: the objects themselves were no longer required to be the real thing. These could now be replaced by their imagined representations. And since these reproductions were much cheaper and easier to come by than the originals, the Paper Museum allowed

How Can We Put Things in Order?

even those of moderate means to become collectors. Borrowing the notion of surrogate reality from literature, where the representation of an experience is equivalent to the experience itself, the Paper Museum enabled the collector to possess a shadow model of the universe under his or her roof. Not everyone approved, echoing the criticism of the Neoplatonist scholar Marsilio Ficino, who in the fifteenth century spoke of "those who in their wretchedness prefer the shadows of things to things themselves."[9]

The idea of collecting shadows is very ancient. The Ptolemaic kings, conscious of the impossibility of gathering the whole of the known world within the borders of Egypt, conceived the idea of collecting in Alexandria, within the walls of one building, every representation of whatever knowledge of the world they could lay their hands on, and so sent out orders to bring to their universal library every scroll or tablet that could be found, acquired, copied, or stolen. Every ship docking at the port of Alexandria had to give up any book it carried so a copy could be made, after which the original (or sometimes the copy) would be returned to its owner. It is surmised that at the height of its fame the Library of Alexandria held a collection of over half a million scrolls.[10]

Setting up an ordered space for displaying information is always a dangerous enterprise, since, as in the case of any scaffolding or frame, the arrangement, however neutral its intention, always affects the contents. An all-encompassing poem, read as religious allegory, fantastical adventure, or autobiographical pilgrimage, much as a universal library of incised, handwritten, printed, or electronic texts, translates each of the elements collected under its roof into the language of the framework. No structure is innocent of meaning.

A spiritual heir of the Alexandrian Ptolemies was an extraordinary man called Paul Otlet, born in Brussels on 23 August 1868 to a family of financiers and city planners. As a child, Otlet showed a remarkable interest in ordering things: his toys, his books, his pets. His favorite game, in which his younger brother took part, was bookkeeping, listing debits and credits in neat columns, and filing timetables and catalogues. He also liked drawing plots for the plants in the garden and building rows of pens for the barnyard animals. Later, when the family moved for a time to a small Mediterranean island off the French coast, Otlet began a collection of bits and pieces—shells, minerals, fossils, Roman coins, animal skulls—with which he built his own cabinet de curiosités. At the age of fifteen, he founded with several school friends the Private Society of Collectors and edited a magazine for its members severely titled *La Science*. About the same time, Otlet discovered in his father's library the *Encyclopédie Larousse,* "a book," he later said, "that explains everything and gives all the answers."[11] And yet the many-volumed *Larousse* was for the ambitious young man too modest in its scope, and Otlet began a project that would see the light several decades later: the preparation of a universal encyclopedia that would include not merely answers and explanations but the totality of human questioning.

In 1892, the young Otlet met Henri Lafontaine, who was to receive in 1913 the Nobel Peace Prize for his efforts toward an international peace movement. The two men became inseparable, and like Bouvard and Pécuchet, Flaubert's endless seekers of information, Otlet and Lafontaine would together scour libraries and archives to compile an enormous collection of bibliographical resources in every field of knowledge. Inspired by the decimal system of library classification invented by the American Melvin Dewey in 1876, Otlet and Lafontaine decided to use Dewey's system on a worldwide bibliographical scale, and wrote to Dewey for permission. The result was the creation of the Office international de Bibliographie in 1895, centered in Brussels but with correspondents in many countries. In the first few years of the institute's existence, an army of young female employees went through the catalogues of libraries and archives, transcribing the data onto 7.5 × 12.5–centimeter index cards at an approximate rate of two thousand cards a day. In 1912, the number of cards of the Office reached more than ten million; an additional hundred thousand iconographical documents included photographic images, as well as transparencies, film stills, and movie reels.

Otlet believed that cinema, together with the recently invented (but not yet made public) television, was the way in which information would be transmitted in the future. To foster this idea, he developed a revolutionary machine (similar to microfilm) that copied books photographically and projected the pages onto a screen. He called his invention a *bibliophote,* or "projected book," and he imagined the possibility of spoken books, of books transmitted from a distance, and of books made visible in three dimensions—fifty years before the invention of the hologram—that would all be available to private citizens in their own homes, like today's Internet. Otlet called these gadgets "substitutes for the book."[12]

To visualize the extent to which Dewey's decimal system could be put to use in the vast maze of documentation, Otlet drew a chart comparing Dewey's system to a sun whose rays spread and multiply as they retreat from the center, embracing every branch of human knowledge. The diagram uncannily resembles Dante's final vision of three luminous circles in one, spreading their combined light throughout the universe, containing everything and being everything.

> Oh light eternal, that in yourself abide,
> only yourself understands, and, self-understood
> and self-understanding, loves yourself and laughs![13]

Otlet was always a keen collector, and the universal archive he imagined would not neglect anything. Like the Jews who preserved in the Cairo Geniza every scrap of paper in case it might contain, unbeknownst, the name of God, Otlet kept everything.[14] A small example: before leaving on his honeymoon in 1890, the young Otlet and his bride went to weigh themselves in the Grands Magasins du Louvre in Paris. The tickets, indicating that Otlet weighed 70 kilos and his wife 55, were carefully preserved by Otlet in cellophane envelopes and can been seen today in a cardboard box containing his assorted cards and papers. "You see the essential in what is accessory," a friend remarked to Otlet, a useful way of explaining Otlet's omnivorous curiosity.[15]

Collecting led to cataloguing and classifying. Otlet's grandson Jean recalled that one day, as they were strolling together on the beach, they came upon a number of jellyfish washed up on the sand. Otlet stopped, gathered the jellyfish into a pyramid, took out a blank card from the pocket of his vest, and wrote the creature's classification according to the Office international de Bibliographie: "5933." The number 5 indicated the category of general sciences, followed by 9, it was narrowed down to zoology, with a 3 added, to coelenterates, and with another 3, to jellyfish, 5933. Then he fixed the card to the top of the gelatinous compilation, and they continued their stroll.[16]

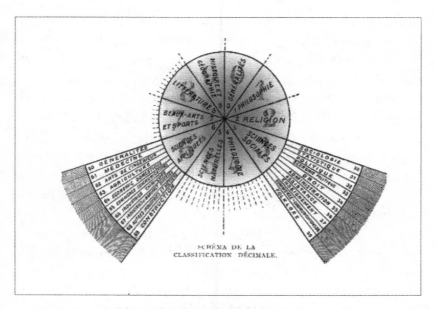

Otlet's chart depicting the division of all branches of knowledge, from Françoise Levie, *L'Homme qui voulait classer le monde: Paul Otlet et le Mundaneum* (Bruxelles: Les Impressions Nouvelles, 2006). (Illustration © Collections Mundaneum [Belgium])

Otlet's organizational passion led him to support the utopian project of a Norwegian architect, Hendrik Andersen, for an ideal city that was to serve as the World Centre for Peace and Harmony. Several sites were suggested: Tervuren in Flanders, Fiumicino near Rome, Constantinople, Paris, Berlin, and somewhere in New Jersey. The ambitious dream provoked much skepticism among politicians as well as among intellectuals. Henry James, who was a good friend of Andersen and admired the Norwegian's sculptures, abhorred the idea of such an elephantine plan. In a letter addressed to Andersen, James called his friend a megalomaniac. "How can I throw myself on your side," he wrote, "to the extent of employing to back you a single letter of the Alphabet when you break to me anything so fantastic or out of relation to any reality of any kind in all the weary world???" James should not have been surprised: as a novelist, he had shown how deeply he understood the megalomaniac character. In 1897 his *Spoils of Poynton* had dissected Mrs. Gereth's obsession with the bric-à-brac collected over the years in her splendid house, Poynton. "To have created such a place," James had written, "was to have had dignity enough; when there was a question of defending it the fiercest attitude was the right one." The Ideal City of Andersen, like the mountains of data collected by Otlet in the Office, were, like Poynton for Mrs. Gereth, a totality of things too precious to admit reproof of any kind. "There are things in the house that we almost starved for!" says Mrs. Gereth. "They were our religion, they were our life, they were *us!*" As James made clear, these "'things' were of course the sum of the world; only, for Mrs. Gereth, the sum of the world was rare French furniture and oriental china. She could at a stretch imagine people's not having, but she couldn't imagine their not wanting and not missing."[17] Andersen, like Otlet, was of a similar mind. James's criticism went unheeded.

Otlet became obsessed with the project, which he now named his Mundaneum, and which, in his vision, would comprise a museum, a library, a large auditorium, and a separate building devoted to scientific research. He proposed that the Mundaneum be built in Geneva under the motto "Classification of everything, by all and for all." The most famous architect of the time, Charles-Edouard Jeanneret-Gris, better known as Le Corbusier, supported the project and drew up an audacious plan for Otlet's city; Andrew Carnegie, the Scottish-American millionaire, offered to help finance it. But in October 1929, the crash of Wall Street put an end to all hopes for American financial support, and Otlet's utopian project was all but forgotten.[18]

Yet the basic concept of the Mundaneum, of various collections "conceived as parts of one universal body of documentation, as an encyclopedic survey of human knowledge, as an enormous intellectual warehouse of books, documents, catalogues and scientific objects," survived immutable in their catalogued sequences, stowed away in the Palais du Cinquantenaire in Brussels, until 1940.[19] On 10 May of that year, the German army invaded Belgium, and Otlet and his wife were forced to abandon their precious collection and seek refuge in France. Desperate to save his classified universe, Otlet wrote pleading letters to Marshall Pétain, to President Roosevelt, even to Hitler. But his efforts proved useless. The Palais that lodged his collection was dismantled, the furniture he lovingly designed was transferred to the Palais de Justice, and the books and documents put away in boxes. When Otlet returned home after the liberation of Brussels, on 4 September 1944, he discovered that the card indexes and iconographic files had been replaced by an exhibition of "new art" from the Third Reich, the Nazis had destroyed sixty tons of periodicals catalogued in the institute, and two hundred thousand volumes of the carefully assembled library had disappeared. Paul Otlet died, heartbroken, in 1944.

After his death, the remains of his colossal project were stored in Brussels's insalubrious Institute d'Anatomie. After a few more displacements, in 1992 the dismembered collection found at last a secure place in a renovated 1930s department store in the Belgian city of Mons, where, after being painstakingly reorganized, the new Mundaneum opened its doors in 1996.[20]

Perhaps an explanation for Otlet's obsession can be found in a diary entry of 1916. There Otlet says that after an illness suffered in his adolescence (a mixture, according to him, of scarlet fever, diphtheria, meningitis, and typhus), he lost his textual memory and could no longer learn by heart poems or sections of prose. To remedy this, he explains, "I learned to correct my memory through reason."[21] Unable to memorize facts and figures by himself, Otlet perhaps imagined his Office international de Bibliographie or Mundaneum as a sort of surrogate memory that could be constructed through index cards, images, books, and other documents. It is certain that Otlet loved the world and longed to know everything about the things of the world, and yet, like the sinners described by Virgil, he erred by directing his love towards a mistaken goal, or with too much vigor. It is to be hoped that the God in whom he believed found it in his heart to forgive a fellow cataloguer.

In 1975, Jorge Luis Borges, perhaps inspired by the character of Otlet, wrote a long story called "The Congress" in which a man tries to compile an encyclopedia from which nothing on earth should be excluded.[22] This virtual version of the world proves in the end to be impossible or, as the narrator concludes, useless, since the world, to our joy and sorrow, already exists. In the last pages, the ambitious encyclopedist takes his fellow researchers on a horse-and-buggy ride through Buenos Aires, but the city they now see, with its houses, trees, and people, is not alien and individual: it is the researchers' own creation, the one they had bravely attempted and which now, suddenly and full of wonder, they realize has always been there.

How Can We Put Things in Order?

15

What Comes Next?

SOME TIME IN THE NINETIES, when I was visiting Berlin, the writer Stan Persky took me to see Lucas Cranach the Elder's painting of the Fountain of Youth at the Gemäldegalerie. It is a medium-sized canvas that depicts, in great detail, a rectangular swimming pool, seen in perspective, full of happily cavorting men and women. Old people are arriving from the left in carts and wheelbarrows; youths emerge naked from the other side, where a series of red tents await them, like those bathing-machines of which Lewis Carroll's Snark was so inordinately fond.

The Cranach painting led Stan and me into a discussion of whether we would like to extend the length of our lives, if such a thing were possible. I said that the foreseeable end did not frighten or worry me; on the contrary, I liked the idea of living with a conclusion in mind, and compared an immortal life to an endless book which, however charming, would end up being tiresome. Stan, however, argued that living on, perhaps forever (provided he were free of sickness and infirmities), would be an excellent thing. Life, he said, was so enjoyable, that he never wanted it to end.

When we had that conversation, I was not yet fifty; more than fifteen years later, I am more convinced than ever that an endless life is not worth

(Opposite) Minos consigning each sinner to his place in Hell. Woodcut illustrating Canto V of the Inferno, *printed in 1487 with commentary by Cristoforo Landino. (Beinecke Rare Book and Manuscript Library, Yale University)*

Lucas Cranach the Elder, *Fountain of Youth*, 1546 (Gemäldegalerie). (Staatliche Museen, Berlin, Germany. © Leemage/Bridgeman Images.)

living. It is not that I think I have many decades left to go: it is difficult to be certain without holding the entire volume in my hands, but I'm fairly sure that I'm on one of the last chapters. So much has occurred, so many characters have come and gone, so many places have been visited that I don't suppose the story can continue for many more pages without petering out into an incoherent and incontinent babble.

"The days of our age," the Psalmist tells us, "are threescore years and ten; and though men be so strong that they come to fourscore years: yet is their strength then but labour and sorrow; so soon passeth it away, and we are gone." I am now less than a decade away from that figure, which until recently seemed to me as remote as the last digit of pi. I realize that in what I must now call my old age, my body is constantly shuffling its weight upon my conscious mind, as if jealous of the attention I give my thoughts and trying to edge them out by brute force. Up to a short time ago, I had imagined that my body ruled only over my youth, and that with maturity, my mind would take the privileged place. And because of the hold I believed

What Comes Next?

each one, body and mind, had upon a distinct half of my life, I imagined that they would reign unobtrusively and fairly, one in quiet succession after the other.

In the beginning, I suspect, that is how it was. In my adolescence and early adulthood, my mind seemed like a jumbled, uncertain presence, clumsily intruding upon the carefree life of the ruling body, which took pleasure wherever it found it. Paradoxically, my body felt then less solid than my thoughts, and made its presence felt only through my eclectic senses, smelling the cool air of the morning or walking through a city at night, eating breakfast in the sunshine or holding my lover's body in the dark. Even reading was a bodily activity: the touch, the smell, the look of the words on a page were an essential part of my relationship to books.

Now pleasure comes mainly through thinking, and dreams and ideas seem richer and clearer than ever before. The mind wants to come into its own, but the old body, like a deposed tyrant, refuses to withdraw and insists on constant attention: biting, scratching, pressing, howling, or falling into a state of numbness or unwarranted exhaustion. A leg burns, a bone chills, a hand seizes up, an anonymous bluntness prods me somewhere in the gut, distracting me from books and conversation and even from thought itself. In my youth, I always felt as if I were on my own, even in the company of others, because my body never nagged me, never appeared as something separate from me, as a shameful Doppelgänger. It was absolutely and indivisibly my whole self, singular, invincible, casting no shadow, like the body of Peter Schlemiel. Now even when I'm alone my body is always there like an unwelcome visitor, making noises when I want to think or sleep, elbowing my side when I sit or walk about.

In a Brothers Grimm tale I liked as a child, Death is struck down on a country road and is rescued by a young peasant. To thank him for his deed, Death makes his rescuer a promise: since he cannot exempt him from dying, for all men must die, before coming for him Death will send his messengers. Several years later, Death appears at the peasant's door. The terrified man reminds Death of his promise. "But have I not sent you my messengers?" Death asks. "Did not Fever come and smite you, and shake you, and cast you down? Has Dizziness not bewildered your head? Have not Cramps twitched your limbs? Did not Toothache bite your cheeks? And besides that, has not my own brother Sleep reminded you every night of me? Did you not lie by night as if you were already dead?"

My body seems to welcome these messengers daily, preparing to receive their master. The prospect of a longer sleep doesn't trouble me, and that too has changed. In my youth, death was merely part of my literary imagination, something that happened to evil stepmothers and stout-hearted heroes, to evil Professor Moriarty and brave Alonso Quijano. The end of a book was conceivable and (if the book was good) lamented, but I could not picture the possibility of my own end. Like all young people, I was immortal, and time had been granted to me without term of expiration. As May Swenson put it:

> Can it be there was only one
> summer that I was ten? It must
> have been a long one then—

Today, summers are so short that barely have we put out the garden chairs when we are storing them away again; we hang up the Christmas lights for what seems only a few hours, while the new year comes and goes, and a new decade follows. This rush doesn't unsettle me: I'm accustomed to the accelerated pace of the final pages in a story I've enjoyed. I feel some mild regret, yes. I am aware that the characters I grew to know so well will have to say their few last words, perform their last gestures, circle just one more time around the inaccessible castle, or drift away into the sea fog strapped onto the back of a whale. But everything that needed to be tidied up is tidied up, and anything that must remain unresolved will remain unresolved. I know that my desk is ordered to my satisfaction, my letters mostly answered, my books in their right places, my writing more or less finished (not my reading, but that, of course, is the nature of the beast). My list of "Things to Do," propped up in front of me, still has a number of uncrossed items on it; but they have always been there and they always will, however many times I reach the bottom of the list. Like my library, my list of "Things to Do" is not meant ever to be exhausted.

Talmudists say that the stern injunction to make certain, through thoughts and deeds, that one's name is written in the Book of Life means that we ourselves must become responsible for that inscription, that we must be our own scribes. In that case, for as long as I can remember, I have been writing my name in the words of others, taking dictation, as it were, from those authors (such as Stan Persky) whom I've had the fortune to make mine through their books. Petrarch, in one of his letters, confesses that he has read Virgil, Boethius, and Horace not once but thousands of times, and that if he stopped reading them now (he is writing at the age of forty), for the rest of his life their books would still remain within him, "since they have dug their roots into my heart, so deeply that often I forget who wrote them and, like someone who because of having owned and made use of a book for so long, I become myself its author and hold it for my own." I echo his words. As Petrarch understood it, the intimate conviction of readers is that there are no individually written books: there is only one text, infinite and fragmented, through which we leaf with no concern for continuity or anachronism or bureaucratic property claims. Since I first started reading, I know that I think in quotations and that I write with what others have written, and that I can have no other ambition than to reshuffle and rearrange. I find great satisfaction in this task. And at the same time, I'm convinced that no satisfaction can be truly everlasting.

I find it easier to imagine my own death than to imagine the death of everything. In spite of theology and science fiction, the end of the world is difficult to conceive from our egocentric viewpoint: what is the stage like once the audience has departed? What does the aftermath of the last universal moment look like once there is no one left to see it? These seemingly trite conundrums show up to what point our capacity to imagine is bound by the consciousness of the first-person singular.

Seneca tells the story of the ninety-year-old Sextus Turannius, an administrator under Caligula, who, when the emperor relieved him of his post, "ordered his household to lay him out and start wailing about his bed as if he were dead. The household went into mourning for the unemployment of their aged master and did not lay their mourning aside until his work was restored to him." With this stratagem, Turannius achieved what appeared to be impossible and became a witness to his own funeral. Seventeen centuries later, and for less practical reasons, the eccentric American businessman "Lord" Timothy Dexter faked his own death in order to see how people would react. Since the apocryphal widow didn't show enough signs of distress at the funeral, upon restoring himself to life, the disappointed Dexter gave her a tremendous beating.

My imagination is more modest: I simply see myself concluded, devoid of decisions, of thoughts, fears and emotions, no longer here and now in any perceptible sense, unable to use the verb "to be."

The world is always here, but we are not. However, in the *Commedia* there is no death. Or rather, the death of the souls that Dante meets has taken place before the story starts. After that, every human soul in the three terrible kingdoms is alive until the Day of Judgment. As Dante finds, the death of the body has stripped the individuals of very little except perhaps a will of their own. And language is still theirs, so that both the lost and the saved can put into words who they were and who they are, and relive the moment of their death now translated into words. The fleeting references to individual deaths are many: among the most prestigious, that of Virgil, who tells Dante that his body, "within which I made shadow," was moved from Brindisi and lies buried in Naples; that of Beatrice, who accuses Dante of betraying her when she "was on the threshold / of my second age" (she died at the age of twenty-five); the terrible death of Count Ugolino, immured in the Tower of Hunger by his enemy Cardinal Ruggiero and condemned to die of starvation and devour his own children (according to Borges, in the historical reality he must have done one or the other, but in the poem he does both); the suicides in the bloody forest; the briefly announced death of Peter Damian; and that of Manfred discussed earlier.[1] The *Commedia* is an exercise not in death but in the memory of death. To know what awaits him, the mortal Dante asks questions of those who have undergone the experience of mortality. That is where his curiosity leads him.

In the "awful place," Virgil tells him, he will see "the ancient suffering souls / each crying out for a second death," begging for the ultimate annihilation announced in the book of the Apocalypse (the Revelation of Saint John in the English-language canon).[2] According to its author, John of Patmos, on that dreadful day the dead will arise to be judged, and will seek their name in the Book of Life: if it does not appear in the inconceivable pages, they are condemned to the flames for all eternity. "And death and hell were cast into the lake of fire," says John. "This is the second death" (Rev. 20:14).

Allegorically, in Christian Europe, the iconography of Death has ancient roots: the animated skeleton represented, for example, in a Pompeian mosaic begins its first macabre dance in the early Middle Ages, calling all people to join him (or her, because in the Latin languages Death is a woman), the young and old, the rich and poor. This terrifying image of Death is not universal. For instance, Yukio Mishima, writing in 1967, observed,

> The Japanese people have always been conscious of the fact that death lies in wait behind all everyday actions. But their idea of death is straightforward and joyful. A different idea from the abominable and horrendous notion of death that foreigners have. The concept of a personified death in the guise of a skeleton carrying a scythe, like that imagined by the Europeans in the Middle Ages, did not exist in Japan. It is also different from the idea of death as lord and master that is prevalent in those countries where, to this day, next to modern cities and under the blazing sun, stand ancient ruins covered by a luxuriant vegetation. I mean those of the Aztec and Toltec people of Mexico. No, ours is not an aggressive death, but a sort of fountain of pure water from which streams are born that run endlessly throughout the world, and that, for a long time now, have nurtured and enriched the art of the Japanese people.[3]

Whether death is to be happily expected or tremblingly dreaded, the question remains: What lies beyond the last threshold, if threshold it is? Buddhists believe that the four noble truths taught by the Buddha provide an escape from the endless circle of dying and rebirth, a deliverance first experienced by the Buddha himself. After his death (or *Parinibbana*, meaning "all-round completion of earthly existence"), the Buddha continued to exist as what believers call "a presence in the absence." A later Buddha, the Maitreya or Metteyya, in order to enlighten his disciples about the world to come, composed a poetic text, *The Sermon of the Chronicle-To-Be,* announcing "five disappearances" that will follow the death of the last Buddha: "the disappearance of attainments, the disappearance of method, the disappearance of learning, the disappearance of symbols, the disappearance of relics." This multiple absence shall proclaim an age in which the truth will no longer be attainable by humankind. The end of all things shall see the last priest break the sacred precepts, the memory of the sacred texts fade, the vestments and attributes of the monks lose their meaning, and the destruction of all holy Buddhist relics by fire. "Then the Kappa or World-Cycle shall be annihilated," reads this solemn document.[4]

For the Zoroastrians, death is a creation of the Evil Spirit, Angra Mainyu. In the beginning, the world existed in two consecutive ages of three thousand years each, first in spiritual form, then in material form, before it was attacked by the Evil Spirit, who created disease to oppose health, ugliness to beauty, death to life. Three thousand years later, sometime between 1700 and 1400 B.C.E., the prophet Zarathustra (or Zoroaster) was born in Persia, heralding the divine revelation that would allow humankind to do battle against Angra Mainyu. According to the Zoroastrian sacred book, the *Zend-Avesta,* the present age will last another three thousand years from the date of Zoroaster's death, at the end of which evil will be defeated for ever. Until then, each individual death leads a step closer to that blessed hour which Zoroastrians call *Frashokereti.*[5]

In the Judeo-Christian tradition, the earliest apocalyptic literature can be traced to the end of the fifth century B.C.E., when, according to the Talmud, classical Jewish prophecy came to an end with the last of the prophets, Malachi, Haggai, and Zechariah.[6] But prophetic visions continued to be recorded, no longer as an individual voice, with the prophet proclaiming his own name, but anonymously or under the borrowed names of ancient sages. With the exception of the book of Daniel, the rest of this new prophetic literature came to form part of the Aggadah, the Jewish corpus of mainly Talmudic texts that deals with nonlegal topics. Classical prophetic literature described events that would result from human misconduct and would take place when time came to an end, heralding an eternal Golden Age. These cataclysms would bring about the fall of heathen kingdoms, the redemption of the chosen people, the return from their exile to the Promised Land, and the establishment of universal peace and justice. While admitting these visions, the new prophets announced a battle: not only a mortal conflict between God's people and the unbelievers, but a vast otherworldly war between the hosts of good and those of evil. In the early biblical prophecies, the Redeemer was God himself; the newer ones announced the coming of a Messiah whose nature would be both human and divine. These later prophetic writings were to nourish, of course, the nascent beliefs of the followers of Christ.

The Old Testament taught that a relationship with God is possible only during a person's lifetime. After death—the realm from which in the Jewish tradition language is excluded—all contact with the divine is severed. "The dead praise not the Lord, neither any that go down into silence," wrote the Psalmist (Ps. 115:17). Whatever a person could do to please God had to be accomplished on earth or not at all. But during the first century B.C.E., different, more hopeful notions began to thrive among the Jewish people. The existence of an afterlife, retribution for bad and good behavior, and the concept of the resurrection of the body (though all these, in rudimentary form, can be traced back to canonical texts) became fundamental tenets of Jewish belief. With them God's reach was reaffirmed even after the death of the flesh, and humankind was assured an immortality that lent tremendous importance to whatever a person did in the here and now. These ancient certainties, assimilated and transformed in successive exegetical readings culminating in the Apocalypse, are at the core of Dante's *Commedia*. For Dante, we, the living, are responsible for our actions and our life, on earth and beyond, and we forge our own rewards and punishments as we travel along the road of life to our certain end. They constitute the fundamental declaration of the duty of the individual-to-be. For Dante, after life we are not condemned to silence: the dead retain the gift of language so they may reflect through words on what came to pass.

Islam promises that after death there will be punishments for the miscreants and rewards for believers. "For the unbelievers We have prepared chains and fetters and a blazing Fire. But the righteous shall drink of a cup tempered at the Camphor Fountain, a gushing spring at which the servants of God will refresh themselves: they who keep their vows and dread the far-spread terrors of Judgment day; who, though they hold it dear, give sustenance to the destitute, the orphan, and the captive, saying: 'We feed you for God's sake only; we seek of you neither recompense nor thanks: for we fear from our Lord a day of anguish and of woe.'" This fear will prove fruitful: after the death of the body, God will reward believers with robes of silk, reclining couches, shady trees, offers of fruit, silver dishes, and cups of ginger-flavored water served by eternally young boys sparkling like sprinkled pearls. In the twelfth century, Ibn 'Arabi explained that the condemned "shall be gathered in such ugly forms that apes and swine would look better." The accumulation of wealth is an obstacle to eternal bliss: according to the Prophet's companion, Abu Huraryra, the Prophet said that believers who are poor will enter Paradise half a day before the rich.[7]

The Day of Resurrection, or *Al-yawm al-qiyama* (also called *Al-yawm al-fasal,* or Day of Sorting Out, and *Al-yawm al-din,* or Day of Religion), in which humankind shall bear witness against itself, is mentioned more specifically in sura 75 of the Qur'an. "On that day there shall be joyful faces, looking towards their Lord. On that day there shall be mournful faces, dreading some great affliction." The exact date of that awful event is not given (it is known only to God, and even the Prophet cannot change it), but on that day the dead will be resurrected, "whether you turn to stone or iron, or any other substance you may think unlikely to be given life." The Day of Resurrection will be announced by a number of major signs: the appearance of Masih ad-Dajjal, the false messiah; the desertion of Medina; the return of Isa (Christ in Islamic nomenclature), who will defeat Masih ad-Dajjal and all false religions; the release of the tribes of Gog and Magog; the assault on Mecca and the destruction of the Kaaba; and the death of all true believers caused by a sweet southern breeze. At this time all the verses of the Qur'an will be forgotten, all knowledge of Islam will fall into oblivion, a demonic beast will emerge to address the survivors, who will take part in a frenzied sexual de-bauch, a vast black cloud will cover the earth, the sun will rise in the west, and the angel Israfil will sound the first trumpet, causing the death of all living creatures. Finally, the second trumpet will sound, and the dead will be resurrected.[8]

The Spanish scholar Miguel Asín Palacios argued that Islamic eschatol-ogy may have been known to Dante through Latin translations of the *hadith* made in Córdoba. Though Asín Palacios's theories regarding Islamic influ-ences in the *Commedia* have been largely discredited, his critics have been forced to accept the possibility of "an intrusion of Islamic themes in medi-eval Christian religious thought." Once suggested, Asín Palacios's basic argu-ment appears obvious: that from Al-Andalus (a civilization which fostered a fluid dialogue between the three cultures of Spain: Islamic, Christian, and Jewish) the Islamic texts, translated into Latin, could easily have traveled to the cultural centers of Italy, where they would have certainly attracted the attention of an omnivorous reader such as Dante. Notable among these texts is the *Epistle of Forgiveness,* a satirical excursion through heaven and hell written by the eleventh-century Syrian poet Abu l-'Ala' al-Ma'arri, which irresistibly evokes for a Western reader the conversational Otherworld of Dante's *Commedia*. In the *Epistle,* the author makes fun of an obscure and pedantic grammarian of his acquaintance, who, after death, having overcome the difficulties of otherworldly bureaucracy, engages in a dialogue with fa-mous poets, philosophers, and heretics from the past, and even speaks with the devil himself.[9]

Distinguishing the "second death" from the first, Islamic authors have argued that dying is the crowning, positive act of a true believer's life. A col-lection of writings from the tenth century penned by the anonymous mem-bers of an esoteric fraternity based in Basra and Baghdad known as the Ikhwan al-Safa, or Brethren of Purity or Sincerity, contains a text called "Why We Die" that describes the act of dying through a series of extended metaphors. The body is a ship, the world the sea, death the coast we are headed for; the world is a racecourse, the body a noble horse, death the goal where God is the king who gives out the prizes; the world is a plantation, life is the succession of the seasons, the hereafter is the threshing floor that separates the grain from the chaff. "Therefore," reads the text, "death is a wise thing, a mercy, and a blessing, since we can only arrive at our Lord after we have left this physical structure and have departed from our bodies."[10]

No doubt the Islamic Day of Resurrection shares certain features of its Christian counterpart. According to Iranaeus, a leader of the Christian church in the second century, John of Patmos was granted his vision in the last years of the reign of Domitian, 95 or 96. Traditionally (and erroneously), John of Patmos is identified as John the Evangelist, Jesus's beloved disciple, who in his old age, it was supposed, retired to Patmos's rocky wilderness to put his vision into words.[11]

John's Apocalypse is a haunting, mysteriously poetic text that portrays death not as the end but as a stage in the struggle between good and evil. It is structured around the numinous number seven: seven letters, seven seals, seven trumpets, seven visions, seven vials, and finally seven more visions. To the anguished question "What is to become of us?" John's book responded with a wealth of terrible images of "things that must shortly come to pass" (Rev. 1:1) and enticed readers to decipher them. The mysteries of revelation were depicted as closed book secured with seven seals, the promise of understanding as an open book that the Angel gives John to eat, mirroring a metaphor from the book of Ezekiel (2:10), in which the prophet is also given a book "written within and without: and there was written therein lamentations, and mourning, and woe." Thus the vision granted by God was both unintelligible (sealed) to the unbeliever and intelligible (ingestable) by those who believed. This is one of the oldest and most enduring images of the act of reading: devouring the text in order to apprehend it, making it part of one's own body.

The earliest known Latin interpretation of the Apocalypse was written in the fourth century by Victorinus, bishop of Pettau, in Styria (now Austria), who was martyred under the emperor Diocletian. Victorinus composed commentaries on the Bible, of which none survives except fragments of his readings of the first and last books, Genesis and the Apocalypse. Believing that the persecution suffered by the Christians was proof that the end of the world

An illuminated fifteenth-century manuscript of the Apocalypse depicting (*top*)
the Beast and Dragon and (*bottom*) Worship of the Beast and Dragon.
(The Pierpont Morgan Library, New York, MS M.0524, fol. 10v, 1.
Photograph © The Pierpont Morgan Library/Art Resource, NY.)

was approaching, Victorinus saw in John's Apocalypse the announcement of contemporary events that were to culminate (he thought) a thousand years after the beginning of Christ's reign.[12]

Victorinus's reading proved convincing. Long after the year 1000, readers continued to interpret John's vision as a chronicle of present history. As late as 1593, John Napier, a Scottish mathematician who invented the decimal point and the logarithm, published *A Pleine Discoverie of the Whole Revelation of St. John* that echoed Victorinus's commentaries. Fiercely anti-Catholic, Napier developed in this book a timeline based on his reading of the Apocalypse. Using the defeat of the Spanish Armada as proof that God sided with the Protestant cause, he explained that the seventh and last age of history had started with a blast of the final trumpet in 1541, the year John Knox began the Scottish Reformation, and would end, according to his calculations, in the year 1786. Modern-day inheritors of these tidy readings are American evangelical revivalists such as Billy Graham who see in John's vision the threat or promise of Armageddon.[13]

But in the fourth century, Victorinus's historical reading of the Apocalypse was not found acceptable by the ecclesiastical authorities, especially in light of the growing power of the church after Constantine. The commentaries of Saint Jerome on the commentaries of Victorinus, though granting the martyred scholar a distinguished place among ecclesiastical writers, suggested that his interpretation was misguided and the Apocalypse required an allegorical, not a literal reading. Ingeniously, Jerome found a solution that embraced Victorinus's ideas but did not negate the present existence of the church triumphant. Jerome suggested that the Apocalypse presented a series of typological events that recurred throughout history, periodically reminding us that the Day of Judgment is nigh: the trumpets that began sounding in Babylon are sounding yet today. The second death still awaits us.[14]

In *The City of God,* Saint Augustine seems to agree with Jerome's inclusionary interpretation. The Apocalypse, according to Augustine, reveals to its intended readers the history of the true church, and also their own personal conflicts, by means of a series of images that might seem baffling to some but that, read in the light of certain clarifying passages, speak to each reader of a private struggle to overcome the darkness and go towards the light. Augustine is severely critical of those who believe that the end of the thousand-year kingdom announces a bodily resurrection in order to enjoy "most unrestrained material feasts." This first resurrection, Augustine says, will enable those to whom it is granted "not only [to come] to life again from the death of sin, but [to continue] in this new condition of new life." Augustine concludes: "This coming to life again would have made them sharers in the first resurrection; and then the second death would have had no power over them."[15] Dante's emergence from the dark forest and his pilgrimage to the final vision follows Augustine's reading.

Nourished by these commentaries, medieval Christian eschatologists assumed that death is not the end: there is an afterlife of the souls. But even that is not the final stage of being. The ultimate moment will come when the last trumpets are sounded and, in one final ordering, the souls will know the true conclusion to their stories. In expectation of a just retribution, true Christians were supposed to face their last moments with ritual equanimity, quietly trusting their soul to their Maker, the Aristotelian Supreme Good to whom all things must return.

According to the historian Philippe Ariès, this meek attitude towards death can be traced to the end of the first millennium. Christian Europe conceived death as "domesticated"—that is to say, controlled by a system of rituals that allowed the dying person to be the conscious protagonist of his or her last moment.[16] The agonizing person was supposed to await death with active resignation, placing the body in a preordained position, lying on the back with the face turned towards heaven, and accepting his or her participation in conventional ceremonies that transformed the death chamber into a public space.

Death came to be understood as a consolation, a hopeful notion that prevailed until perhaps the skepticism of the Enlightenment; it was seen as a safe haven, a final resting place from the toils of life on earth. To the Islamic images of death as the longed-for harbor, the threshing floor after harvest, the finish line of a race, the Christian imagination added that of the inn, waiting at the end of life's journey. "Mad, my lady, is the traveler who annoyed by the day's fatigues wants to go back to the beginning of the journey and return to the same place," we read in *La Celestina*, "for all those things in life that we possess, it is better to possess them than to expect them, because nearer is the end when we have more advanced from the beginning. There is nothing sweeter or more pleasant to the weary man than an inn. So it is that, although youth be merry, the truly wise old man does not wish for it, because he who lacks reason and good sense loves almost nothing else but what he has lost."[17]

The end of the first millennium, according to Ariès, marked yet another change in our dealings with death: the acceptance of the dead within the realm of the living. In ancient Rome, civic law forbade the burial *in urbe,* within the city walls. This convention changed, says Ariès, not because of a reconsideration of European rituals but through the North African custom of venerating the remains of martyrs and burying them in churches, first on the outskirts of the city and then wherever the church stood.[18] Church and graveyard became one and the same place, and part of the neighborhood of the living.

With the incorporation of the dead into the world of those still alive, the ritual of dying took on a double sense: an "acting out" of death, the performance of a first-person-singular Day of Judgment concluding with the end of "I," and a witnessing of that act by those who remain alive, who acquire the duty of mourning and of memory, and shift the paraphernalia of death into the realm of the erotic, as, for example, in the art and literature of the Romantic movement. Death acquired a gothic beauty. Edgar Allan Poe judged the death of a beautiful woman "unquestionably, the most poetical topic in the world."[19]

The industrialized societies of the twentieth and twenty-first centuries tend to exclude death. Death in our time occurs in hospitals and nursing homes, far from the domestic or public eye. Death "becomes shameful and forbidden," argues Ariès, hiding even from the patient the proximity of the final moment. And modern war, up to a point, deprives death of its singularity. The two world wars and the slaughters they engendered that continue up to this day made death plural, swallowing up each individual death in interminable statistics and conglomerate memorials. It was to this erasure by numbers that Christopher Isherwood referred when speaking to a young Jewish movie producer. Isherwood had mentioned that six hundred thousand homosexuals were killed in the Nazi concentration camps. The young man was not impressed. "But Hitler killed six million Jews," he said sternly. Isherwood looked back at him and asked: "What are you? In real estate?"[20]

In spite of dying offstage, in spite of dying anonymously or as part of a multitude, in spite of the possibility of consolation and the assurance of closure, it seems that we still don't want to die absolutely. In 2002, Jeremy Webb, editor of the *New Scientist,* offered a prize to its readers: after the death of the winner, his or her body would be prepared and slowly cooled to an astonishingly low temperature at the Cryonics Institute of Michigan, where it would be held indefinitely in liquid nitrogen. "Though sperm, embryos, viruses and bacteria have been frozen and then returned to life, large volumes of flesh and bone and brain and blood present more of a challenge. There is no decay process, no biological action below $-196°$ C," explained Webb. "The whole emphasis of cryonics is that you put yourself into deep freeze until technology has gained the expertise to bring you back."[21]

The questions "What is to become of us?" "Do we disappear forever?" "Can we return from the grave?" imply many different conceptions of death. Whether we conceive death as the last chapter or imagine it as the beginning of a second volume, whether we fear it because we can't know it or believe that beyond it lies retribution for our conduct on earth, whether we become prematurely nostalgic at the thought of no longer existing or empathize with those whom we'll leave behind, our picture of death as a state of being (or not being) determines our notion of death as an act, final or perambulatory. "Even if I am mistaken in my belief that the soul is immortal," wrote Cicero in the first century B.C.E. with unusual simplicity, "I make the mistake gladly, for the belief makes me happy, and is one which as long as I live I want to retain."[22]

Beyond the impossible realization of our own death, as we grow older we are made persistently aware of the increasing absence of others. We find it hard to say good-bye. Every farewell haunts us with the secret suspicion that this might be the last; we try to remain waving at the door for as long as possible. We don't resign ourselves to definitive absences. We don't want to believe in the absolute power of dissolution. This incredulity is a consolation to believers. When Saint Bernard prays to the Virgin for Dante's salvation, he asks her to "scatter for him every cloud of his mortality with your prayers, / so that joy supreme may unfold for him."[23]

Seneca (whom Dante certainly read but merely acknowledged with a single epithet, "moral Seneca," in the Noble Castle of Limbo) had studied the Greek Stoics but did not follow in his own life their excellent advice. In his writings, however, he notes with stoic sobriety that death must not frighten us: "It is not that we have so little time," he writes in banker's terms to his friend Paulinus, supervisor of Rome's grain supply, "but that we lose so much. Life is long enough and our allotted portion generous enough for our most ambitious projects if we invest it all carefully."[24] These ideas, of course, were not new in the Rome of the first century C.E. Since the earliest times, the Romans had conceived of an afterlife conditioned by how well (or how badly) we had administered this one.

The idea that there is a sequel to this life, a continuum, an ingrained immortality, is beautifully summed up in an inscription collected in the *Corpus Inscriptionum Latinarum,* the great collection of Latin epitaphs: "I am ashes, ashes are earth, the earth is a goddess, therefore I am not dead."[25] Religious dogmas, civil legislations, aesthetics and ethics, philosophies highbrow and low, mysticism: everything relies on this limpid syllogism.

If the dead do not vanish utterly, then it might be convenient to maintain with them some sort of a relationship: a chance to speak with them and, above all, an opportunity for them to speak, as they do in the *Commedia.* The earliest literary examples of such dialogues can be seen in ancient tombstones inscribed with words attributed to the dead, like the ones mentioned by Dante after entering the infernal City of Dis.[26] Among the oldest tombs in the Italian landscape were those built by the Etruscans, elegantly decorated with festive funeral scenes and portraits of the departed. The Romans continued the customs of the vanished Etruscan civilization by adding inscriptions to their tombstones. At first these merely either announced the name of the dead, praised the departed with sober words, and wished his or her souls a painless voyage to the next ("May the earth be light on you!") or politely addressed passing strangers ("Greetings, you who go by!"). Though brevity continued to be a feature of epitaphs, with time these became less conventional, more lyrical, simulating a conversation with the absent friend or relative, or establishing a link of common mortality between the dead and those still living. And yet, translated into words, the most heartfelt sentiments and the deepest sorrow can become artificial. In the end, the epitaph became a literary genre, the elegy's younger brother.

In the first chapter of Giorgio Bassani's *The Garden of the Finzi-Contini*, a group of people visit an Etruscan cemetery north of Rome. A young girl asks her father why it is that tombs that are ancient make us less sad than more recent graves. "That is easily understood," says the father. "Those who have died recently are nearer to us, and precisely for that reason we love them more. While the Etruscans, they have been dead for so long that it is as if they never had lived, as if they had been dead *forever*."[27]

Whether near to us or far removed in time, the dead arouse our curiosity because we know that, sooner or later, we will join them. We want to know how things begin, but we also want to know how they will end. We try to imagine the world without us, in a disturbing effort to conceive a story without a narrator, a scene without a witness. Dante ingeniously inverted the procedure: he imagined the world not without him but without the others, or, rather, with him alive and all the others dead. He granted himself the power to explore death from the point of view of the living, wandering among those for whom the final question has been dreadfully or joyously answered.

The *Commedia* is a poem with no end. Its conclusion is also its beginning, since it is only after the final vision, when Dante at last sees the ineffable, that the poet can begin to tell the chronicle of the journey. Borges, shortly before his death in Geneva in 1986, conceived a short story (which he did not have a chance to write) about Dante in Venice, dreaming of a sequel to the *Commedia*. Borges never explained what that sequel might have been, but perhaps in that second volume of his pilgrimage, Dante would have returned to earth to die and, as if in a mirror of his masterpiece, his soul would have roamed the world of flesh and blood engaging his contemporaries in conversation. After all, in his weary exile, he must have felt as exiles do, like a ghost among the living.

16
Why Do Things Happen?

My governess escaped Nazi Germany in the early forties and, after a difficult voyage with her family, arrived in Paraguay to be greeted by swastika banners waving on the dock at Asunción. (This was during Alfredo Stroessner's military regime.) Eventually she came to Argentina, and there was engaged by my father to accompany us as my governess on his diplomatic mission to Israel. She seldom spoke of her years in Germany.

A melancholy, quiet person, in Tel Aviv she didn't make many friends. Among the few she had was a Swiss woman with whom she would go from time to time to the movies, who bore on her forearm a tattooed number, somewhat blurred. "Never ask Maria what that is," she warned me, but added no explanation. I never asked.

Maria didn't hide her tattoo, but she avoided looking at it or touching it. I tried to keep my eyes away, but it was irresistible, like a line of writing seen under water, taunting me to decipher its meaning. It was not until I was much older that I learned about the system used by the Nazis to identify their victims, mainly at Auschwitz. An old Polish librarian in Buenos Aires,

(Opposite) Dante and Virgil meet the evil counselors. Woodcut illustrating Canto XXVI of the Inferno, *printed in 1487 with commentary by Cristoforo Landino. (Beinecke Rare Book and Manuscript Library, Yale University)*

also an Auschwitz survivor and also the bearer of such a tattoo, said to me once that it reminded him of the call numbers in the books he used to sort out in the Lublin Municipal Library, where he had worked as a helper in his distant adolescence.

I believe I'm in Hell, therefore I am.

—ARTHUR RIMBAUD, *Nuit de l'enfer*

There are places on this earth from which those who return, return to die.

On 13 December 1943, the twenty-four-year-old Primo Levi was arrested by the Fascist Militia and detained at a camp in Fossoli, near Modena. Nine weeks later, having admitted to being an "Italian citizen of Jewish race," he was sent to Auschwitz along with all the other Jewish prisoners. All, he says, "even the children, even the old, even the ill."[1]

In Auschwitz, one of the tasks assigned to Levi and five others in his Kommando was to scrape out the inside of an underground petrol tank. The work was exhausting, brutal, and dangerous. The youngest of the group was an Alsatian student called Jean, a twenty-four-year-old who was given the job of *Pikolo,* or messenger-clerk, in the mad bureaucracy of the camp. During one of the assignments, Jean and Levi were obliged to spend an hour together, and Jean asked Levi to teach him Italian. Levi agreed. As he remembers the scene years later in his memoir *Se questo è un uomo (If This Is a Man,* retitled for the U.S. edition *Survival in Auschwitz),* suddenly the Ulysses canto of the *Commedia* comes to his mind, how or why he does not know. As the two men walk towards the kitchens, Levi tries to explain to the Alsatian, in his bad French, who Dante was and what the *Commedia* consists of, and why Ulysses and his friend Diomedes burn eternally in a double flame for having deceived the Trojans. Levi intones for Jean the admirable verses:

> The greater horn of the ancient flame
> Began to shake itself, murmuring,
> Just like a flame that struggles with the wind;

Then carrying to and fro the top
As if it were the tongue that spoke
Threw forth a voice, and said: "When . . . "

After that, nothing. Memory, which at the best of times betrays us, at the worst of times serves us no better. Fragments, tatters of the text return to him, but it is not enough. Then Levi remembers another line, "ma misi me per l'alto mare aperto . . .":

I launched forth on the deep open sea . . .[2]

Jean has traveled by sea, and Levi believes that the experience will allow him to understand the force of "misi me," so much stronger than "je me mis" in Levi's rough French translation; "misi me," the act of throwing oneself on the other side of the barrier, towards "sweet things, ferociously far away." Hurried by the approaching end of their brief respite, Levi remembers a little more:

Consider your origins:
You were not made to live like brutes,
But to follow virtue and knowledge.[3]

Suddenly, Levi hears the verses in his head as if he were hearing them for the first time, "like the blast of a trumpet," he says, "like the voice of God." For a moment, he forgets what he is and where he is. He tries to explain the lines to Jean. Then he recalls:

when there appeared to us a mountain,
Dark because so far away, and to me it seemed higher
Than any I had ever seen before.[4]

More lines go missing. "I would give today's soup," Levi says, "to know how to connect 'than any I had ever seen before,' with the final lines." He closes his eyes, he bites his fingers. It is late, the two men have reached the kitchen. And then memory throws him the lines, like coins to a beggar:

Three times it made her whirl with all the waters;
At the fourth it made the poop rise up
And the prow go down, as pleased Another.[5]

Levi holds Jean back from the soup line: he feels that it is vitally necessary for the young man to listen, to understand the words "as pleased Another" before it is too late; tomorrow one of them might be dead, or they
might never meet again. He must explain to him, says Levi, "about the
Middle Ages, about the so human and so necessary and yet unexpected
anachronism, but still more, something gigantic that I myself have only just
seen, in a flash of intuition, perhaps the reason for our fate, for our being
here today."

They arrive at the queue, among the sordid, ragged soup carriers of
other Kommandos. An official announcement is made that that day's soup
will be of cabbages and turnips. The last line of the canto comes back to Levi:

Till the sea was closed over us.[6]

Under Ulysses' engulfing wave, what is that "something gigantic" that
Levi realizes and wants to communicate?

Primo Levi's experience is perhaps the ultimate experience a reader can
have. I hesitate to qualify it in any way, even as ultimate, because there are
things that lie beyond language's capacities to name. Nevertheless, without
ever being able to convey the entirety of any experience, language can, in
certain moments of grace, touch upon the unnamable. Many times throughout his journey Dante says that words fail him; that lack is precisely what
allows Levi to seize in Dante's words something of his own incomprehensible
condition. Dante's experience is in the words of his poem; Levi's in the words
made flesh, or dissolved into flesh, or lost in flesh. The inmates of the camps
were stripped and shorn, their bodies and faces emaciated, their names replaced by a number tattooed on their skin; the words briefly restored something of what had been torn away.

If the inmates of Auschwitz wished to keep their names, that is, if they
wished to still be human, they have to find in themselves (says Levi) the

Primo Levi. (Photograph © Gianni Giansanti/Sygma/Corbis)

strength to do so, "to manage somehow so that behind the name something of us, of us as we were, still remains." This conversation with Jean was the first time (Levi says) that he became aware that language lacks words to express the offence of demolishing a man. The term "extermination camp" acquires here a double meaning, but even that is not enough to name what is taking place. This is the reason why Virgil cannot open for Dante the doors of the City of Dis in the ninth canto of the *Inferno:* because Hell, absolute Hell, cannot be known by reason, as most things are known through language—not even through the silver words of the master poet Virgil. The experience of Hell escapes language because it can only be submitted to the ineffable, to what Ulysses means when he says "as pleased Another."

But there is one essential, all-important difference between Auschwitz and Dante's Hell. Beyond the innocent first circle where the only suffering is expectation without hope, Hell is a place of retribution, where each sinner is responsible for the punishment that he or she bears. Auschwitz, instead, is a place of punishment without fault or, if there is a fault (as there is in every one of us), it is not the fault for which the punishment is meted out. In Dante's Hell, all the sinners know why they are punished. When Dante asks them to tell their stories, they can put into words the reason for their suffering; even if they don't agree that they have earned it (as in the case of Bocca degli Abati), that is only due to their pride or anger, or the desire to forget. The need of man, says Dante in *De vulgari eloquentia,* is to be heard rather than to hear, "out of the joy we feel in translating into an orderly act our natural affections."[7] That is why the sinners speak to Dante, so that he may hear them out; that is why the dead are left language, against the opinion of the Psalmist. It is the living Dante who, over and over, lacks the words to describe the horrors and later the glories, not the condemned, who, stripped of all comfort and peace, are miraculously in possession of a tongue to speak of what they have done in order to continue to be. Language, even in Hell, grants us existence.

In Auschwitz, however, language was useless either to explain the non-existent fault or to describe the senseless punishments, and words took on other, perverted and terrible meanings. There was a joke told in Auschwitz (because even in the place of agony there is humor): "How does one say 'never' in camp slang?" "*Morgen früh,* 'Tomorrow morning.'"

For the Jews, however, language—specifically the letter beth—was the instrument with which God effected his Creation and therefore could not be debased, however much it was ill-used.[8] The intellect, the seat of language, was humankind's driving force, not the body, its vessel. Accordingly, Orthodox Jews believed that the concept of heroism was inextricably linked to that of spiritual courage, and the notion of "bravery with holiness" or, in Hebrew, *Kiddush ha-Shem* (the sanctification of God's name) was at the root of their resistance to the Nazis. They believed that evil should not be fought physically by mortals because evil cannot be defeated through physical action: only Divine Providence can decide whether evil is to triumph or not. The true weapons of resistance were, for most Orthodox Jews, conscience, prayer, meditation, and devotion. "They believed that the reciting of a chapter of the Psalms would do more to affect the course of events than would the killing of a German—not necessarily immediately but at some point in the infinite course of relations between the Creator and His creatures."⁹

Ulysses, like the other souls in Dante's Hell, suffers a punishment that he himself has fashioned during his own limited course of his relations with his Maker. In Dante's imagination, we, not God, are responsible for our actions and for their consequences. Dante's world is not the world of Homer, where whimsical gods play with our human destinies for their entertainment or private purpose. God, Dante believes, has given each of us certain abilities and possibilities, but also the gift of free will, which allows us to make our own choices and assume the consequences of those choices. Even the quality of the punishment itself is, according to Dante, determined by our transgression. Ulysses is condemned to burn invisibly in the forked flame because his sin, counseling others to practice fraud, is furtive, and since he has committed it through speech, through the tongue, it is in tongues of flame that he is eternally tortured. In Dante's Hell, every punishment has a reason.

But Auschwitz is a very different kind of hell. Soon after Levi's arrival in the midst of a terrible winter, sick with thirst, locked up in a vast, unheated shed, he sees an icicle hanging outside the window. He sticks out a hand and breaks the icicle off, but a guard snatches it from him, throws it away, and pushes Levi back into his place. "*Warum?*" asks Levi in his poor German, "Why?" "*Hier ist kein warum,*" the guard replies, "Here is no why."¹⁰ This infamous response is the essence of the Auschwitz hell: in Auschwitz, unlike in Dante's realm, there is no "Why."

In the seventeenth century, the German poet Angelus Silesius, trying to speak of the beauty of a rose, wrote, "Die Rose ist ohne warum," "The rose is without why."¹¹ This, of course, is a different "why": the "why" of the rose lies merely beyond the descriptive capabilities of language, but not beyond language's epistemological scope. Auschwitz's "why" is beyond both. To understand this, we must, like Levi and like Dante, remain stubbornly curious because our relationship to language is always a dissatisfying one. To put our experience into words again and again falls short of our aim: language is too poor to conjure up experience fully: it disappoints us when the events are happy and pains us when they are not. For Dante, "to tell it as it was is hard," and yet he says he must attempt to do so, "to address the good I found there." But, as Beatrice tells him, "will and instrument among mortals . . . are unequally feathered in their wings."[12] Try as Dante might and try as we, so much less gifted, might to assert our will, the instrument of language creates its own semantic field.

That semantic field is always a multilayered one because our relationship to language is always a relationship with the past as well as with the present and the future. When we use words, we are making use of the experience accumulated before our time in words; we are making use of the multiplicity of meanings stored in the syllables we employ to render our reading of the world comprehensible to ourselves and others. The uses that have preceded our own nourish and alter, sustain and undermine our present use: whenever we speak, we speak in voices, and even the first-person singular is in fact plural. And when we speak with tongues of fire, many of those tongues are ancient flames.

The early Christian fathers, keen on finding a strategy to bring the wisdom of the pagans into accord with the tenets of Jesus, decided, after reading in the Acts of the Apostles that "Moses was learned in all the wisdom of the Egyptians, and was mighty in words and deeds" (7:22), that it was from Moses that the Greeks had learned their philosophy. Moses had been taught by the Egyptians, and it was through his words that the precursors of Plato and Aristotle received inklings of the truth. By a change of vowels, it was said, the name Moses had become Musaeus, a legendary pre-Homeric poet who had been a disciple of Orpheus.[13] For this reason, in the twelfth century, the learned Richard of Saint-Victor, whom Dante placed next to Saint Isidore of Seville and the Venerable Bede in Paradise, declared that "Egypt is the mother of all arts."[14]

In the late fourth century, Saint Jerome defended himself from the accusation of favoring the ancient flames of pagan poetry over the redeeming Christian fire by arguing that in order fully to explore the word of God, the best instruments must be used. Cicero and his brethren, though deaf to the true word, had perfected the instrument of language, which Christian writers could now use for their benefit. But there should be no doubt as to which was the better source of wisdom. Writing to the cloistered Héloise towards

1160, Peter the Venerable praised her for having entered the cloister after her tragic love affair with Peter Abelard. "You have changed your studies of various disciplines," he wrote, "for others that are far better, and instead of Logic you have chosen the Gospel, instead of Physics, the Apostle, instead of Plato, Christ, instead of the academy, the cloister. You are now a wholly and truly philosophical woman."[15]

A thousand years after Jerome, Dante argued that not only the language and early ideas but the entire pagan *imaginaire* could serve that higher purpose, and throughout the *Commedia* Christian saints and ancient gods, citizens of Florence and heroes of Greece and Rome share the long tripartite adventure in which anachronism has no place. In the first circle of Hell, Virgil is greeted by the poets who have preceded him, and Homer himself welcomes Virgil back to the Noble Castle with a solemn "Honor the very great poet." Dante too is welcomed into this "fine school" by Homer's companions, and even though Virgil smiles at this perhaps exaggerated estimation of the Florentine, Dante's art now forms part of that same great ageless circle of poetry, and shares with the work of his masters the same verbal triumphs and defeats.[16]

It is a question of shared inheritance. The same "traces of the ancient flame" confessed by Dido in the *Aeneid* burn again in Dante's address to Virgil in Purgatory upon finally seeing Beatrice: "I recognize the traces of the ancient flame," says Dante in awe.[17] And the identical image serves Dante to depict, in a very different context and no longer as a metaphor, the forked flame from which the soul of Ulysses speaks to him in Hell: a flame colored by its amorous antecedents. We should not forget, however, that the ancient flame that embraces the soul of Ulysses embraces that of Diomedes as well. The ancient flame is double-tongued, but only one tip, the greater one, is allowed to make itself heard. It is therefore licit, perhaps, to ask how Diomedes, the silent one, would have told the shared story.

Recalling the tongues of the ancient flame in Auschwitz, Primo Levi hears in the railing words "fatti non foste a viver come bruti" (you were not made to live like brutes) a reminder of his own abused humanity, a warning not to give up even now, a life-giving draft of words that not Virgil, not Dante, but the intrepid and over-ambitious Ulysses (dreamt up of course by Dante) addresses to his men in order to convince them to follow him "beyond the sun, to the world without people." But Levi does not remember these last, precise words of Ulysses' speech. The verses that dance in Levi's head bring memories of another life: the mountain, "dark because so far away," reminds him of other mountains seen in the dusk of evening as he returned by train from Milan to Turin, and the awful "as pleased Another," compels him to make Jean understand, in a flash of intuition, why they are where they are.[18] But the revelation goes no further. Memory, which dives into our sunken libraries and rescues from the long-past pages only a few seemingly random paragraphs, chooses better than we know, and perhaps selecting wisely prevented Levi from the realization that even though he might have followed Ulysses' cry and refused to live like a brute, he has nevertheless reached, like Ulysses and his men, the world beyond the gentle sun, a condemned place inhabited by beings who have been incomprehensibly thrust below the human condition.

Diomedes in the *Iliad* is the reliable man, a courageous and bloodthirsty warrior, a disciplined strategist willing to fight to the end if he believes his cause to be just. "Not a word of retreat," he says when alerted of the danger of an advancing Trojan chariot. "You'll never persuade me. / It's not my nature to shrink from battle, cringe in fear / with the fighting strength still steady in my chest." Diomedes is more reasonable than Ulysses, more dependable than Achilles, a better soldier than Aeneas. Diomedes is driven by an almost unconscious curiosity to know whether our fate depends on ourselves or entirely on the will of apparently all-powerful gods; this drives him to attack even the gods themselves. The War of Troy is a war in which both men and gods take equal part. When Aphrodite sweeps down to rescue her son Aeneas from a huge boulder thrown at him by Diomedes, he slashes her wrist with his spear, then charges against Apollo, so that the god of the sun has to appeal to Ares, the god of war, to stop him. "That daredevil Diomedes, he'd fight Father Zeus!" Then Diomedes strikes against the god of war as well. "The gods are bloodless, so we call them deathless," says Homer, but they can be wounded, and when they bleed, they bleed not human blood but an ethereal fluid known as ichor.[19] By attacking the immortal gods, Diomedes discovers that they too suffer pain, and that they can therefore know and understand what humans suffer: this wounding of the ancient gods foreshadows another god's torture and death, centuries later, on a cross on Mount Golgotha. A god that can suffer and who allows the suffering he himself understands: that is the paradox.

Martin Buber tells this story:

The emperor of Vienna issued an edict which was bound to make thoroughly miserable the already oppressed Jews in Galizia. At that time, an earnest and studious man by the name of Feivel lived in Rabbi Elimelekh's House of Study. One night he rose, entered the zaddik's room, and said to him: "Master, I have a suit against God." And even as he spoke he was horrified at his own words.

But Rabbi Elimelekh answered him: "Very well, but the court is not in session by night."

The next day, two zaddikim came to Lizhensk, Israel of Koznitz and Jacob Yithak of Lublin, and stayed in Rabbi Elimelekh's house. After the midday meal, the rabbi had the man who had spoken to him called and said: "Now tell us about your lawsuit."

"I have not the strength to do it now," Feivel said falteringly.

"Then I give you the strength," said Rabbi Elimelekh.

And Feivel began to speak. "Why are we held in bondage in this empire? Does not God say in the Torah: 'For unto Me the children of Israel are servants.' And even though he has sent us to alien lands, still, wherever we are, he must leave us full freedom to serve him."

To this Rabbi Elimelekh replied: "We know God's reply, for it also is written in the passage of reproof through Moses and the prophets. But now, both the plaintiff and the defendant shall leave the courtroom, as the rule prescribes, so that the judges may not be influenced by them. So go out, Rabbi Feivel. You, Lord of the world, we cannot send you out, because your glory fills the earth, and without your presence, not one of us could live for even a moment. But we herewith inform you that we shall not let ourselves be influenced by you either."

Then the three sat in judgment, silently and with closed eyes.

After an hour, they called in Feivel and gave him the verdict: that he was in the right. In the same hour, the edict in Vienna was cancelled.[20]

If Diomedes could speak from the forked flame, aware as he must have been that the gods are fallible, this is perhaps what he would have told Dante: that being human does not prevent us from suffering inhuman torture, that every human enterprise has its unspeakable shadow, that in this "brief vigil" of our life we may be made to capsize in sight of the longed-for mountain for no intelligible reason, merely because of the whim or the will of Something or Someone.[21] Diomedes might have spoken to Dante with Ulysses' same words, but if they came from the other fork of the flame, Dante might have heard them differently, not as proud ambition but as despair and rage, and Levi might have then recalled the speech not as a promise of redemption but as a sentence both unjust and incomprehensible. Perhaps Diomedes' unspoken words are part of the "something gigantic" that Levi suddenly understands and wants to communicate to Jean.

Literature promises nothing except that however hard we may try to reach its farthest horizon we will fail. But even though no reading is ever complete, and no page is ever quite the last, coming back to a text we are familiar with, either reread or recalled, allows us a wider sailing, and our "mad flight," as Dante describes Ulysses' quest, will take us always a little farther into meaning.[22] And as Ulysses discovers, whatever understanding we may reach at last, it will not be the expected one. Centuries of words transform Virgil's ancient flame into a forest of meanings, none lost, none definitive, and it may be that when the words come back to us in our hour of need, they will indeed save us, but only for the time being. Words always hold yet another meaning which escapes us.

Franz Kafka imagined in "The Penal Colony" a machine that punishes prisoners by inscribing on their bodies a mysterious script.[23] Only once the needle has dug deep into the flesh are the prisoners able to make out the nature of their fault and the reason for their punishment, in the instant before the last. Kafka died sixteen years before Auschwitz was built, and his machine, though implacable and deadly, delivers nevertheless some sort of answer to the question "Why?"—an answer however crabbed, however late. Auschwitz did not. After Levi's liberation in January 1945, he lived on for a time as a writer among new readers. But no understanding came to him, however hard he tried to lead a normal life again, no understanding of the "why." And yet, catching traces of the other voice hidden somewhere in the double flame, Levi must have reached a better understanding of why no "why" ever existed there.

Less than a year before his death, in a letter addressed to the Latin poet Horace, Levi wrote this: "Our life is longer than yours, but it is neither gayer nor more secure, nor do we have the certainty that the gods will grant a tomorrow to our yesterdays. We too shall join our father Aeneas, Tullus, Ancus, and you in the realm of shadows; we too, so insolent, so self-assured, will return to dust and shadows."[24] To dust and shadows Levi returned, like Dante and Virgil, and Horace too, and like theirs, Levi's flame continues to speak to us. Perhaps that perseverance of a voice is poetry's only true justification.

Poetry offers no answers, poetry cannot erase suffering, poetry will not bring the beloved dead back to life, poetry does not protect us from evil, poetry does not grant us ethical strength or moral courage, poetry does not avenge the victim or punish the victimizer. All poetry can do, and only when the stars are kind, is lend words to our questions, echo our suffering, assist us in recalling the dead, put a name to the works of evil, teach us to reflect on deeds of revenge and punishment, and also of goodness, even when goodness is no longer there. An ancient Jewish prayer humbly reminds us: "Lord, remove the stone from the middle of the road, that the thief may not stumble at night."[25]

This power of poetry is something we know from old, or perhaps always knew since the beginnings of language, a knowledge made wonderfully evident in the first cantos of *Purgatorio*. Subtly overshadowing these cantos is the shadow of Ulysses' failed attempt to reach the solitary mountain. Following the instructions of Cato, the guardian of Purgatory, Virgil girdles Dante with the reed "as pleased Another" (the same words Ulysses used in the tale of his adventure). Standing with Virgil on the beach, Dante sees, on either side of the approaching ship of souls, "an I-knew-not-what white" that proves to be the wings of the piloting angel; in Ulysses' account, he and his men "made wings out of oars." Ulysses' powerful defense of his burning curiosity is countered by the angel's cold and eloquent silence, admonishing all errant souls to return to the true path. And even before the arrival of the ship, Dante implicitly opposes his expectations to those of the intrepid Ulysses, who physically sailed forth but whose soul remained landlocked:

> We stood still by the edge of the sea
> Like those who think about the road they'll take
> And go with their heart, but with their body stay.[26]

And then an extraordinary scene takes place.

Among the souls descending from the ship, Dante recognizes his friend Casella, who in happier days had put to music some of Dante's verses. Dante, to soothe his soul, "which, with its body / traveling to this place, is so very weary," asks Casella to sing for him once again—that is unless "a new law has not deprived / your memory or skill in the art of love songs / that used to calm all my longings." Casella consents, and begins to sing the words of a poem composed by Dante himself during the years of their friendship. The beauty of Casella's voice in the pure air of Purgatory's beach makes Virgil and the other newly arrived souls gather around to listen, enraptured. They stand there, "fixed and intent on his notes," until ancient Cato rushes towards them, angrily calling them back to their sacred business, reminding them of the tremendous purpose of their journey with echoes of God's admonition to Moses: "Neither let the flocks nor the herds feed before that mount."[27]

The abashed souls disperse like a flock of startled doves, putting an end to Casella's song, but not before Dante has shown us, so humanely, so delicately, so truly, that even in the all-important moments of our life's journey, even when the very salvation of our soul is in question, art will still be of the essence. Even in Auschwitz, where nothing seemed any more to have had importance or meaning, poetry could still stir in inmates such as Levi the remnants of life, could offer the intuition of "something gigantic," light in the ashes a spark of the old curiosity, and make it burst once more into everlasting flames.

17

What Is True?

SOMETIME IN THE LATE 1980S, the Canadian magazine *Saturday Night* sent me to Rome to report on a curious story. Two Quebecois sisters in their mid-fifties, the younger a widow with a son and a daughter, the elder unmarried, had traveled together from their village in Quebec to India, on what they insisted was an exotic holiday. During a stopover in Rome, they were found to be carrying several kilos of heroin in one of their suitcases and were detained by the Italian police. The sisters explained that the suitcase had been given to them in India by a friend of the daughter, the man who had arranged for their travel and had taken them on a guided tour of several Indian cities. The police, however, were unable to trace the man; the daughter explained that he was a casual acquaintance who had kindly offered to help her mother and her aunt to arrange the holiday of a lifetime.

In Rome, I was allowed to interview both sisters. They had been spared the prison cell and had been lodged in a religious residence under the supervision of Benedictine nuns. Both gave a coherent, believable account of their ordeal, saying that they had been completely unaware of the fact that the suitcase given to them had contained drugs. After all the man had done for

(Opposite) After riding Geryon into the abyss, Dante sees the punished usurers with their armorial pouches. Woodcut illustrating Canto XVII of the Inferno, *printed in 1487 with commentary by Cristoforo Landino. (Beinecke Rare Book and Manuscript Library, Yale University)*

them, they felt that they couldn't very well have refused his simple request to take a suitcase back to Canada. In Quebec, the daughter confirmed their story.

During the interviews, conducted in the Benedictine residence under the supervision of a smiling nun, I noticed in the older sister a puzzled look and a tone of voice that I read as disbelief or anger. There was something in her attitude that made me think that perhaps she suspected her sister of having had a hand in the plot, maybe with the help of the daughter. Or that she suspected the daughter of having set them up, and that now the mother was protecting her child by not telling the full story. Or perhaps I misinterpreted the look and tone, and both the sisters were guilty. Perhaps they had planned the smuggling together, perhaps the daughter knew nothing about it. Or perhaps they were both innocent, and they were telling the simple truth. The older sister's attitude meant something that I was unable to decipher. What had really taken place? It was impossible to know.

In the end, after a somewhat chaotic trial, the judge found both women not guilty, and they were allowed to return to their village. Nevertheless, the doubt remained. Several years later, the younger sister declared that their lives had become unbearable because so many people still suspected them of a crime they had not committed.

We all know that the events we experience, in their fullest, deepest sense, escape the boundaries of language. That no account of even the smallest occurrence in our life can truly do justice to what has taken place, and that no memory, however intense, can be identical to the thing remembered. We try to relate what happened but our words always fall short, and we learn, after many failures, that the closest approximation to a truthful version of reality can be found only in the stories we make up. In our most powerful fictions, under the web of the narrative the complexity of reality can be discerned, like a face behind a mask. Our best way of telling the truth is to lie.

*"What is truth?" said jesting Pilate, and would not stay
for an answer.*

—FRANCIS BACON, "Of Truth"

According to the seventeenth-century Kabbalist Nathan of Gaza, the light that bursts from the everlasting flames of the deity is twofold, like the forked tongue that holds Ulysses and Diomedes: one is a light "pregnant with thought," the other is "void of thought," and both qualities are present in the same fire, in dialogue one with the other. "This," wrote Gershom Scholem, "is the most radical and extreme affirmation of the process of dialectical materialism in God Himself."[1]

The light of Dante's God embodies as well this apparent opposition. This becomes clear when, guided by Virgil, Dante arrives at the brink of the second cornice of the seventh circle of Hell. After circling the incandescent sands where the violent against nature are punished, Virgil leads Dante close to a loud waterfall. There Virgil has Dante loosen the cord from around his waist (the same cord with which, he says now, he tried to catch the leopard that first crossed his path outside the dark forest) and casts it into the abyss. On that signal, from the depths of the abyss rises the emblem of fraud, the winged monster Geryon.

The significance of this cord has worried commentators from the first. Most of the early readers of the *Commedia* understood the cord to be a symbol of fraud, but the explanation is not convincing: fraud is not capable of subjugating lust (the leopard) but rather is used to incite it (because lust entails deceit, just as false promises are part of the art of the seducer). Virgil must employ something good to counter evil, not a sin against another sin. The critic Bruno Nardi suggested that the cord has a twofold biblical symbolic meaning: in both the Old and the New Testaments, the cord is the girdle of justice worn against fraud and a chastity belt worn against lust.[2]

Whatever its symbolic significance, Dante realizes that Virgil's gesture

Geryon conveying Dante and Virgil down towards Malebolge, one of the 102 watercolors produced by William Blake between 1824 and 1827 to illustrate the *Commedia*. (National Gallery of Victoria, Melbourne, Australia, Felton Bequest/Bridgeman Images)

will bring up a "novità," something new, in response to the "nuovo cenno," the new sign given by his guide. And Dante adds this warning to the reader:

> Ah, how cautious ought men to be
> with those who not only perceive the deed
> but see also the thoughts, with their sense![3]

About to enter the circle of fraud, Dante reminds the reader that though the enlightened Virgil can read his thoughts, most ordinary people judge others by their actions only, and are incapable of seeing the thought behind the deed. Too often, actions that are taken to be proof of a truth are shown to be false.

Summoned from the abyss, the monster Geryon appears as the incarnation of fraud, a creature with the face of an honest man,[4] hairy paws, a body covered with whirls and circles like an Oriental carpet, and a scorpion's deadly tail. But before describing this prodigious vision to the reader, Dante pauses, and says:

> Always about the truth that has an air of falsehood
> A man should seal his lips, as far as he is able,
> For even blameless, he'll be put to shame;

> But here I can't be silent; and by the notes
> Of my *Commedia,* Reader, I do swear,
> So that they may not be deprived of lasting fame,

> I saw . . .[5]

And then Dante tells us about Geryon.

The reader who has followed Dante's story up to this point and heard about many prodigies and marvels (not the least being the journey of Dante himself) is, for the first time, faced with a marvel so great that the poet feels the need to stop and swear by his own work that what he will now tell is true. That is to say, almost exactly halfway through Hell, Dante swears by the truth of his poem, indeed of his fiction, that the forthcoming episode in the poem truly happened. In a vertiginous logical circle, Dante informs the reader, his accomplice in this elaborate fabrication, that the poetic lie he will tell has the weight of a factual truth, and he offers as proof of this the very fictional edifice: the web of poetic lies from within which he addresses the reader. Whatever belief the reader has accorded the poet up to this point is now put to the test: if the reader has felt that there really was a forest, and a lofty mountain in the distance, and a ghostly companion, and a dreadful, eloquent portal leading into the circular landscape of Hell (and few are the readers who have not felt, verse after verse, the solid reality of Dante's story), then now that same reader must admit the truth of what the poet is about to tell or forfeit everything. Dante is not demanding from the reader the kind of faith demanded by the Christian religion; he is demanding poetic faith, which, unlike the tenets of divinely revealed truth, exists merely through words.

However, Dante allows both truths to coexist in the *Commedia.* When

What Is True?

at the summit of Purgatory, accompanying the divine pageant, Dante sees the four beasts of the Apocalypse advancing towards him, he describes their appearance—"each was plumed with six wings"—and adds, for the benefit of the reader: "read Ezekiel, who depicts them," "except . . . as to the wings, / where John and I differ from him."[6] Dante claims for his side the authority of John of Patmos, who said that the wings were six (Rev. 4:8), while Ezekiel, in his vision, claimed they had four (1:6). Dante is not shy of placing himself in the same authorial plane as the author of the Apocalypse: he, the poet of the *Commedia,* certifies John's divine authority.

And Virgil certifies the authority of Dante. When first encountering the shade of Virgil come to guide him, Dante addressed the author of the *Aeneid* as "my master, and my author," confessing, "You alone are he from whom I took / the sweet style that has brought me honor."[7] From Virgil's poetry Dante learned to express his own experience, and "mio autore" carries the double sense of "writer of the book I admire most" and "the one who made me." Words, syntax, music: all lies through which the reader's mind receives and reconstructs an experience of the world.

One of Dante's most lucid commentators, John Freccero, asks whether "a human author can imitate theological allegory . . . by imitating reality." He goes on: "In fact, mimesis has the opposite effect, short-circuiting allegory and transforming it into irony. Instead of reaching out for meaning allegorically, realism turns significance back on itself by repeatedly affirming and then denying its own status as fiction. In Dante's terms, we might say that realism is alternately truth with the face of a lie, and a fraud that looks like the truth."[8]

In his famous letter to Cangrande della Scala, Dante, explicitly quoting Aristotle, notes that according to how far from or how near its being something is, we can say that it is far from or near the truth.[9] He is referring to the literary form that Freccero mentions, the allegory, whose truth depends on how close the poet has managed to bring the image to the subject allegorized. Dante compares the relationship to one of dependency: son to father, servant to master, singular to double, a part to the whole. In all these cases, the "being" of something depends on something else (we can't know what a double is if we ignore the singular), and therefore the truth of that something is dependent on something else. If that something else is fraudulent, the thing considered is also infected by fraud. Deceit, as Dante keeps reminding us, is contagious.

Saint Augustine, in the earliest of his two long treatises on lying (with which Dante may well have been familiar), argued that a person who says something false is not telling a lie if the teller believes or is convinced of its truth. Augustine distinguishes between "believing" and "being convinced": those who believe may recognize that they don't know much about what they believe in without doubting its existence; those who are convinced think that they know something without realizing that that they don't know much about it. According to Augustine, there is no lie without an intent to lie: lying is a question of the difference between appearance and truth. A person, he says, can be mistaken in supposing that a tree, for instance, is a wall, but there will be no fraud unless there is a will to commit it. "Fraud," says Augustine, "lies not in things themselves but in the senses." Satan, the arch-deceiver, "liar and father of lies" (as Virgil is reminded by a condemned soul in Hell), was aware of committing fraud when he deceived Adam and Eve, whose sin was to choose what they knew was forbidden. Our forefathers, through their willing senses, could have chosen not to be accomplices in the fraud; instead, they distanced themselves from the truth, and used their free will to take the wrong path. Every traveler can choose the path he will take. Dante, who had lost his way in the dark forest, which Augustine had called "this immense forest, so full of snares and dangers," chose to follow Virgil's advice and is now on the true path.[10]

The source of Augustine's argument on the question of lying is a controversial passage in Paul's Epistle to the Galatians. "Now the things which I write unto you, behold, before God, I lie not" (1:20), says Paul, to establish a vantage point for his arguments. And as an example of deceit, Paul then tells a story drawn from his own experience, describing a moment when he was confronted with the peculiar behavior of a fellow apostle. Saul (as Paul was then called) had been a zealous Jew, notorious for his determined pursuit of Jews who had converted to Christianity. On the way to Damascus, he saw a blinding light and heard the voice of Jesus asking why he was persecuting him. Saul fell to ground and found that he could no longer see. After three days, his sight was restored by Ananias, who baptized him with the name of Paul (Acts 8:9). Following his conversion, Paul divided his missionary efforts with the apostle Peter: Peter would preach to the Jews while Paul would address himself to the Gentiles.

Fourteen years later, the leaders of the Christian church, gathered in Jerusalem, decided that Gentiles were not required to be circumcised (that is, to become Jews) before converting to the faith of Jesus. After the conference, Paul went to Antioch, where Peter joined him some time later. At first, Peter ate with the Gentiles of the Antioch church, but when Jewish members from the Jerusalem church arrived, he withdrew from the Gentile table, because "them which were of the circumcision" (the Jewish members) had insisted that Gentile Christians observe Jewish dietary laws. Paul, upset at Peter for not recognizing that the only thing that was required to sit at Christ's table was faith, "withstood him to his face, because he was to be blamed": "If thou, being a Jew, livest after the manner of Gentiles, and not as do the Jews, why compellest thou the Gentiles to live as do the Jews?" (Gal. 2:12, 11, 14).

Saint Jerome, in his commentary on Paul's epistle, as well as in a letter to Augustine written in the year 403, argued that this passage did not represent an authentic dispute between the two apostles. Without going so far as to say that the two leaders staged a didactic scene for the benefit of their audience, Jerome refused to see a doctrinal opposition between them. According to Jerome, the dispute was a question of different points of view in which neither of the apostles acted deceitfully but merely took opposing stances in order to illustrate the argument.[11] Augustine thought otherwise. To admit that even a slight dissimulation had taken place during the meeting at Antioch, would be, he says, to admit a lie in the exposition of religious dogma, and therefore in Scripture. Furthermore, Paul's criticism of Peter was well founded because the old Jewish rites had no significance for a convert to the new faith; therefore it would have been useless for either man to dissemble. What happened, according to Augustine, was that Peter was not aware of his dissemblance until Paul exposed the truth to him. A deceit, under whatever circumstance, is never justified in the behavior of a true Christian.

What Is True?

In that light, are the lies of fiction really disguised truths? Or are they fraudulent stories that distract us from the truth that should be our main concern? In the *Confessions,* Augustine says that, in his adolescence, reading the Latin classics in school, "I was obliged to memorize the wanderings of a hero named Aeneas, while in the meantime I failed to remember my own erratic ways. I learned to lament the death of Dido, who killed herself for love, while in the midst of these things, I was dying, separated from you, my God and my Life, and I shed no tears for my own plight." The young Augustine, if he were forbidden to read these books, "was sad not being able to read the very things that made [him] sad." The old Augustine thought that the curtains hung over the entrance of the classrooms where literature was taught were "not so much symbols in honour of mystery as veils concealing error."[12]

When Dante first sees Geryon, the monster's appearance seems to him "marvelous to every steadfast heart." Only when Virgil has explained to him who the monster really is does Dante understand the truth of Geryon's being.

> Behold the beast with the sharp pointed tail,
> That crosses mountains and breaks through walls and arms!
> Behold him who pollutes the entire world!

Virgil's references are historical: through deceit, Tomyris, queen of the Massagetae, crossed the mountains and defeated Cyrus, king of the Persians; through deceit, the Greeks breached the walls of Troy. But the deceit of Geryon is worse. Legend has it that he was an Iberian king with three gigantic bodies united at the waist, who welcomed travelers in order to despoil and then kill them. Dante retains the name but changes his shape: Geryon is made to resemble the serpent from the Garden of Eden, who deceived Eve and thus caused the fall of all humankind.[13]

A discussion of the relation of fiction to truth takes place on the third cornice of Purgatory: Dante meets a learned Venetian courtier, Marco Lombardo, who is cleansing himself of the sin of wrath in a cloud of suffocating smoke. Lombardo lectures Dante on the problem of free will. If everything is predetermined, then a sin cannot be judged right or wrong, and wrath is simply a mechanical response to an unavoidable situation. But however fully things may be ordained in advance by universal laws, within this framework human beings are free to choose. The stars may have some influence on our conduct, but they are not responsible for our ultimate decisions.

> You, the living, refer all causes
> only to the heavens, as if they alone
> must move everything in their course.

> If it were this way, free will would
> be destroyed and it would not be fair
> that good be joyous and evil mournful.

> The heavens set your impulses in motion;
> I don't say all, but suppose I said it,
> a light is granted you to know good and evil,

> and free will, if it endure
> its first struggles with the heavens,
> wins everything, if it is nourished well.

> To a better strength and a better nature
> you are subject in your freedom, which in your mind
> creates what the heavens are unable to control.[14]

What Marco Lombardo is arguing is that the universe is almost indifferent to our actions: we create in our minds the laws that we are constrained to follow. If this is so, then fiction (the world created by our imagination, that of the *Aeneid* for Augustine and Dante, and that of the *Commedia* for us) has the power of shaping our vision and our understanding of the world. And language, the instrument through which imagination presents itself to us and communicates our thoughts to others, not only assists our efforts but re-creates the very reality we attempt to communicate.

Four centuries after Dante, David Hume (whom we encountered at the beginning of this book) would reconsider the question from the viewpoint of the Enlightenment. In his *Treatise of Human Nature* he argued that human beings invented the "fundamental laws of the nature, when they observ'd the necessity of society to their mutual subsistence, and found, that 'twas impossible to maintain any correspondence together, without some restraint on their natural appetites," but then he went on to say that we could not have invented other laws but these: these are the laws required to explain the universe we inhabit.[15] Like any law, the laws of nature can be broken, but they can't be broken indiscriminately, or at any arbitrary time.

Hume's reasoning concerns the matter of truth. Truth is like a law that can be disregarded, but it is impossible for someone to disregard it continually. If I disregard the truth by saying "white" every time the truth is "black," my "white" will eventually be interpreted as "black," and the words with which I lie will simply change their meaning through my constant usage. In the same way, moral laws must stem from a perception of what is true, rooted in our consciousness and expressed in a commonly accepted way: what Hume calls "any *natural* obligation of morality."[16] Otherwise, morality is nothing but a relative concept, and arguments in favor of torture, for instance, according to the particular "natural law" of a Stalin or a Pinochet, would be as valid as the arguments against it. Free will allows for the question of whether an action is good or bad based on the "natural obligation of morality," and is independent of whether the person committing the action is guilty or not guilty.

The question becomes more complex in the case of an act that can be judged bad in itself but is committed for a cause that is deemed good. When Nelson Mandela died, on 5 December 2013, politicians all over the world praised the man who had ended apartheid in South Africa and had stood for a moral law common to all. A handful of conservative British MPs, however, recalling that Margaret Thatcher had described Mandela's African National Congress as "a typical terrorist organisation" that wanted to establish "a Communist-style black dictatorship," refused to mourn Mandela and continued to argue that Mandela had been a terrorist who had thrown bombs from speeding motorcycles. And the Tory MP Sir Malcolm Rifkind declared that "Nelson Mandela was not a saint, as we have heard" but "a politician to his fingertips. He actually believed in the armed struggle in the earlier part of his career and perhaps to some degree for the rest of his career." Saints, in the opinion of Rifkind, who had obviously never heard of Saint Francis Xavier or Saint Joan of Arc, could not be politicians.[17]

In 1995, five years after the official abolition of apartheid, the people of South Africa set up what was called the Truth and Reconciliation Commission, a judicial body assembled to allow victims of human rights abuses to give testimony. Not only were the victims called to testify; the abusers as well could defend themselves and request an amnesty from both civil and criminal prosecution. In 2000, the Commission was replaced by the Institute for Justice and Reconciliation. The change in nomenclature was seen to represent an evolution from the establishment of truth to the establishment of justice. Recognition of guilt without a system within which it can be judged was deemed a sterile exercise. "Guilt," declared Nadine Gordimer in 1998, "is and was unproductive."[18]

Mandela had said at his 1963 trial that he wanted to live for and achieve the ideal of a democratic and free society, but it was also an ideal for which he was prepared to die. "I, who had never been a soldier, who had never fought in a battle, who had never fired a gun at an enemy, had been given the task of starting an army," he wrote in his autobiography.[19] With a warrant out for his arrest, Mandela went underground, learning how to make bombs and moving through Africa in disguise. After he was caught and sentenced to prison in 1963, he rejected offers of freedom until the South African government had removed all obstacles to a proper judicial hearing. He later said that what sustained him throughout the ordeal was "a belief in human dignity." The activities that the conservative MPs called "terrorist acts" were necessary for the attainment of this dignity. To break an unjust law, to commit the so-called terrorist acts, was for Mandela a just act and a moral obligation.

Gordimer, whose fiction offers a long and profound record of the injustice of the apartheid regime, argued that in a society of unjust laws, crime and punishment (as well as truth and deceit) become aleatory moral concepts. "If you're black," she said, "and you've lived during apartheid time, you're accustomed to people going in and out of prison all the time. They didn't carry the right documents in their pockets when they went out. They couldn't move freely from one city to another without acting against the law and being subject to imprisonment. So that there's no real disgrace about going to prison, because you didn't have to be criminal to go to prison."[20] But are terrorist-like acts committed under a criminal regime themselves criminal?

The question is not a simple one, as Dante knew. When Dante takes part in the torture of Bocca degli Abate in the frozen pit of Hell, is he morally justified in his action merely because Dante is contaminated by Bocca's sin of treason, and by the inscrutability of divine judgment? Or has he been tempted into an immoral action by a setting in which betrayal of those one trusted has rendered all social conventions arbitrary, and language is no longer able to communicate what is true? Is Dante acting truthfully within the natural moral laws of humankind, or is he breaking those laws as the now suffering sinners had done before their punishment?

Free will is, for Dante, an intellectual choice based on a given reality, but a reality that is transformed by our intelligence, imagination, dreams, and physical senses. We are free to choose, but at the same time we are bound by the acquired knowledge of the world translated into our understanding. To understand this paradox, Dante offers the metaphor of civil law, which necessarily curbs a citizen's absolute freedom but allows simultaneously a choice of how to act within the terms of that law. Because the soul, as an infant, indulges at first in the pleasures offered to it and then, unless guided by a teacher, seeks them out with the avidity of a spoilt child, a certain restraint must be placed on human desire. Ulysses and Nimrod are chastised examples. On the third cornice of Mount Purgatory, Marco Lombardo explains:

> Therefore laws are necessary as a curb;
> necessary to have a ruler who might discern
> at least the tower of the True City.[21]

The Celestial City is unattainable in this life, but a just ruler might help the polis live by its tenets by having even a distant glimpse of it, a notion of that ideal. Laws, then, and good government will back our moral choices. Unfortunately, according to Dante, no such government existed in his time (and no such government exists in ours). Between the hopeful city founded by Aeneas and the divided Rome of the fourteenth century, with a corrupt pope who demeaned his holy office to preside over the base kingdom of this earth, Dante claimed our natural right to a society that does not foster deceit.

A century after Hume, Percy Bysshe Shelley wrote that, against a deceitful society, what we must do is "to hope, till Hope creates / From its own wreck the thing it contemplates."[22] This too, was Mandela's conviction.

Five centuries after Dante, another Italian sought to inquire into the nature of truth and the art of lying. Of all the adventures that Carlo Collodi imagined for his wooden puppet, one in particular has become part of universal folklore: when Pinocchio lies to the Blue Fairy, his nose grows longer. After Pinocchio has been taken down from the oak tree where he had been left hanging by the wicked Cat and Fox, he is put to bed by the kind Blue Fairy, who asks him what happened. But Pinocchio is too afraid or ashamed to tell the truth, and, as we all know, after each lie his nose grows a little longer. "Lies, my dear boy," the Fairy explains to him, "are quickly discovered; because they are of two kinds. There are lies with short legs, and lies with long noses."[23] Pinocchio's are obviously of the latter variety.

But what does the Fairy's distinction mean? Pinocchio's long-nosed lies are stubborn means to avoid confessing something he has done. As a result, his extensive nose becomes an impediment to moving freely, and even prevents him from leaving the room. These are the lies of the status quo, fibs that nail him to one spot, from which, because he won't acknowledge the truth of his own deeds, he is forbidden to go forward and advance in his life story. Like the lies of politicians and financiers, Pinocchio's lies undermine his own reality and destroy even that which he is supposed to treasure. As Pinocchio's adventures and Dante's *Commedia* make explicit, the acknowledgement of our reality leads us on, from chapter to chapter, and from canto to canto, towards the revelation of our true self. The denial of that reality renders any true telling impossible.

Of the short-legged lies, the Blue Fairy gives us no examples, but we can imagine what they might look like. In Canto V of *Paradiso,* in the inconstant Heaven of the Moon, Beatrice explains to Dante the way in which charity proceeds, "moving its foot to the apprehended good." Freccero noted that Thomas Aquinas, in one of his commentaries to Peter Lombard's *Sentences,* argued that the mind must move to God through intellect and affection, but because of our fallen state, our intellect is stronger in understanding than our affections are in loving. And since our ability to see the good has outdistanced our ability to do good on our own, we travel through life with one foot lagging behind. That is exactly how Dante describes his own progress at the beginning of the *Commedia,* after leaving the dark wood and seeing the mountain peak lit in the dawn light:

> After I had rested a little my weary body
> I took again the path along the desert strand,
> So that the firm foot was always the lowest.[24]

Boccaccio, in his commentary on the *Commedia,* lends a literal explanation to this limping advancement, describing merely the process of an ascent that naturally causes one foot to be always lower than the other. However Freccero, in his learned discussion of the symbolic function of the parts of the body, reads Dante's image as depicting the soul advancing on the twin "feet" of intellect and affect, just as our feet of flesh and blood allow us to move forward. Following the Scholastic thinkers of Dante's time, who thought that the strongest foot (*pes firmior*) was the left, Freccero associates the right foot with intellect ("the beginning of choice, the apprehension, or the reason") and the left one with affect.[25] Rooted still to the earth, the left foot prevents the traveler from advancing properly, from disengaging himself from earthly concerns and setting his mind on higher things.

Unable, without the help of divine grace, to reach the good perfectly, the poet struggles on, hobbled by the eager love of his left foot, which wishes to remain attached to the world of sensation, and urged by the intellect of his right to press ahead with the journey of metaphysical discovery; Dante must, as best he can, use his intellect to fashion something coherent out of his blurred perceptions and uncertain intuitions. He knows he sees now "through a glass, darkly, but then face to face," in the words of Saint Paul, and believes in the promise that "then shall I know even as also I am known" (1 Cor. 13:12). Saint Paul's words are from his discourse on charity, the same charity that Beatrice described with the image of the moving feet and that now binds

Dante to earthly things. To be faithful to what he has been allowed to see and understand, Dante must, on one hand, not be distracted from the charity, the "warmth of love" that has been granted him, and, on the other, sharpen his intellect to put the forthcoming vision into words. Beatrice tells him:

> I see distinctly how in your intellect
> the eternal light shines brightly,
> which once seen, kindles love forever.[26]

As he approaches his intended goal, Dante's love will have to turn to the ineffable Supreme Good, and his intellect will have to reach down to his fellow pilgrims on earth. And both to embrace the vision and to report it, Dante understands that he must lie, lie truthfully, admit "non-false errors,"[27] construct a monster much like Geryon, but one that will exalt and not betray its matter. And so, like all true poets who acknowledge their faulty intellect and their restraining affect, Dante offers us, his readers, short-legged lies so that we too can share something of the journey and follow hopefully our ongoing quests.

The knowledge writers seek, through both affect and intellect, lurks in the tension between what they perceive and what they imagine, and that fragile knowledge is passed on to us, their readers, as a further tension between our reality and the reality of the page. The experience of the world and the experience of the word compete for our intelligence and love. We want to know where we are because we want to know who we are: we magically believe that context and contents explain one another. We are self-conscious animals—perhaps the only self-conscious animals on the planet—and we are capable of experiencing the world by asking questions, putting our curiosity into words, as literature proves. In a continuous process of give-and-take, the world provides us with the puzzling evidence that we turn into stories, which in turn lend the world a doubtful sense and an uncertain coherence that lead to further questions. The world gives us the clues that allow us to perceive it, and we order those clues in narrative sequences that seem to us truer than the truth, making them up as we go, so that what we tell about reality becomes for us reality. "By the very fact that I get to know them, things cease to exist," says the Devil in Flaubert's *Temptation of Saint Anthony.* "Shape is perhaps an error of your senses, substance a fancy of your thoughts. Unless, since the world is in a constant flow of things, appearance, on the contrary, is the truest of truths, and illusion the only reality."[28] Illusion is the only reality: this is perhaps what we mean when we say that a writer knows.

NOTES

Unless otherwise noted, all translations are mine. All biblical quotations are from the King James Bible.

Introduction

1. "Infants talk, in part, to re-establish 'being-with' experiences . . . or to re-establish the 'personal order'": Daniel N. Stern, *The Interpersonal World of the Infant: A View from Psychoanalysis and Developmental Psychology* (New York: HarperCollins, 1985), p. 171.

2. Michel de Montaigne, "An Apology for Raymond Sebond," 2.12, in *The Complete Essays,* trans. and ed. M. A. Screech (Harmondsworth, U.K.: Penguin, 1991), p. 591. According to Pausanias (2nd century C.E.), the sayings "Know Thyself" and "Nothing Too Much" were inscribed on the front of the Temple of Delphi and dedicated to Apollo. See Pausanias, *Guide to Greece,* vol. 1: *Central Greece,* trans. Peter Levi (Harmondsworth, U.K.: Penguin, 1979), 10.24, p. 466. There are six Platonic dialogues which discuss the Delphic saying: *Charmides* (164D), *Protagoras* (343B), *Phaedrus* (229E), *Philebus* (48C), *Laws* (2.923A), *I. Alcibiades* (124A, 129A, and 132C). See *The Collected Dialogues of Plato,* ed. Edith Hamilton and Huntington Cairns (Princeton: Princeton University Press, 1973).

3. Michel de Montaigne, "On Physiognomy," 3.12, in *Complete Essays,* p. 1176.

4. Michel de Montaigne, "On Educating Children," 1.26, in *Complete Essays,* p. 171.

5. Job 28:20. The book of Job provides no answers but poses a series of "real questions" that are, according to Northrop Frye, "stages in formulating better questions; an-

(Opposite) Dante and Virgil meet Plutus, the ancient god of riches. Woodcut illustrating Canto VII of the Inferno, *printed in 1487 with commentary by Cristoforo Landino. (Beinecke Rare Book and Manuscript Library, Yale University)*

swers cheat us of the right to do this." See Frye, *The Great Code: The Bible and Literature,* ed. Alvin A. Lee, volume 19 in the *Collected Works* (Toronto: University of Toronto Press, 2006), p. 217. Michel de Montaigne, "On Democritus and Heraclitus," 1.50, in *Complete Essays,* p. 337.

6. See Richard Dawkins, *The Selfish Gene,* 30th anniversary ed. (Oxford: Oxford University Press, 2006), pp. 63–65.

7. Samuel Beckett, *Worstward Ho* (London: John Calder, 1983), p. 46.

8. Honoré de Balzac, *Le Chef-d'oeuvre inconnu* (Paris: Editions Climats, 1991), p. 58.

9. Francis Bacon, *New Atlantis,* in *The Advancement of Learning and New Atlantis,* ed. Arthur Johnston (Oxford: Oxford University Press, 1974), p. 245.

10. Putting a question into words distances our own experience and allows it to be explored verbally. "Language forces a space between interpersonal experience as lived and as represented": Stern, *Interpersonal World of the Infant,* p. 182.

11. MS lat. 6332, Bibliothèque nationale, Paris, reproduced in M. B. Parkes, *Pause and Effect: An Introduction to the History of Punctuation in the West* (Berkeley: University of California Press, 1993), pp. 32–33.

12. *Paradiso,* XXV:2, "al quale ha posto mano e cielo e terra."

13. Giovanni Boccaccio, *Trattatello in laude di Dante,* ed. Luigi Sasso (Milan: Garzanti, 1995), p. 81; Jorge Luis Borges, "Prólogo," in *Nueve ensayos dantescos,* ed. Joaquín Arce (Madrid: Espasa-Calpe, 1982), pp. 85–86; Giuseppe Mazzotta, *Reading Dante* (New Haven: Yale University Press, 2014), p. 1; Osip Mandelstam, "Conversation on Dante," in *The Selected Poems of Osip Mandelstam,* trans. Clarence Brown and W. S. Merwin (New York: New York Review of Books, 2004), p. 151; Olga Sedakova, "Sotto il cielo della violenza," in *Esperimenti Danteschi: Inferno 2008,* ed. Simone Invernizzi (Milan: Casa Editrice Mariett, 2009), p. 107.

14. This text was never written, but in 1965 I witnessed Borges and Bioy discuss their intention to write it as part of their collection of mock essays, *Crónicas de Bustos Domecq* (Buenos Aires: Losada, 1967).

15. *Paradiso,* XVIII:20–21, "Volgiti e ascolta; / ché non pur ne' miei occhi è paradiso."

16. Martin Buber, *Tales of the Hasidim,* vol. 1, trans. Olga Marx (Oxford: Oxford University Press, 1948), p. 76.

17. *Inferno,* I:91, "A te convien tenere altro vïaggio."

18. Montaigne, "Apology for Raymond Sebond," 2.12, p. 512, quoting *Purgatorio* XXVI:34–36, "così per entro loro schiera bruna / s'ammusa l'una con l'altra formica, / forse a spïar lor via e lor fortuna."

19. Michel de Montaigne, "On Educating Children," 1.26, in *Complete Essays,* p. 170; *Inferno* XI:93, "Non men che saver, dubbiar m'aggrata."

20. *Paradiso* II:1–4, "O voi che siete in piccioletta barca, / desiderosi d'ascoltar, seguiti / dietro al mio legno che cantando varca, // tornate a riveder li vostri liti."

I
What Is Curiosity?

Chapter opener: Sir Arthur Conan Doyle, *The Hound of the Baskervilles* (1902) (London: John Murray, 1971), p. 28.

1. Roger Chartier, "El nacimiento del lector moderno. Lectura, curiosidad, ociosidad, raridad," in *Historia y formas de la curiosidad,* ed. Francisco Jarauta (Santandor: Cuadernos de la Fundación Botín, 2012), pp. 183–210; *The Jerusalem Bible: Reader's Edition,* gen. ed. Alexander Jones (Garden City, N.Y.: Doubleday, 1966), p. 905.

2. Plato, *Theaetetus* 149A–B, trans. F. M. Cornford, in *The Collected Dialogues of Plato,* ed. Edith Hamilton and Huntington Cairns (Princeton: Princeton University Press, 1973), pp. 853–54.

3. *Inferno,* VIII:1, "Io dico, seguitando, che assai prima."

4. Giovanni Boccaccio, *Trattatello in laude di Dante,* ed. Luigi Sasso (Milan: Garzanti, 1995), p. 70.

5. Ibid., pp. 71–72. Luigi Sasso notes that these verses come from the letter from Brother Ilaro to Uguccione della Faggiuola preserved in Boccaccio's own *Zibaldone Laurenziano;* the letter itself is most probably the creation of Boccaccio himself.

6. Francesco Petrarca, *Familiares,* 21:15, quoted in John Ahern, "What Did the First Copies of the Comedy Look Like?" in *Dante for the New Millennium,* ed. Teodolina Barolini and H. Wayne Storey (New York: Fordham University Press, 2003), p. 5.

7. Gennaro Ferrante, "Forme, funzioni e scopi del tradurre Dante da Coluccio Salutati a Giovanni da Serravalle," in *Annali dell'Istituto Italiano per gli Studi Storici,* 25 (Bologna: Il Mulino, 2010), pp. 147–82.

8. *Inferno* I:114, "per loco etterno"; II:31–32, "Ma io, perché venirvi? o chi 'l concede? / Io non Enea, io non Paulo sono."

9. *Apocalypse de Pierre,* 16:2–3, and *Apocalypse de Paul,* 32 a–b, in *Écrits apocryphes chrétiens,* vol. 1, ed. François Bovon and Pierre Geoltrain (Paris: Gallimard, 199), pp. 773, 810.

10. Dante Alighieri, *Vita nova,* II:5, in *Le opere di Dante: testo critico della Società dantesca italiana,* ed. M. Barbi et al. (Florence: Bemporad, 1921), p. 3.

11. Dante Alighieri, *Questio de aqua et terra,* I:3, in *Opere di Dante,* p. 467.

12. *Paradiso,* XXXIII:33, "sì che 'l sommo piacer li si dispieghi"; *Convivio* III:XI, 5, in *Opere di Dante,* p. 229.

13. *Paradiso* X:89, "la tua sete"; X:90, "se non com'acqua ch'al mar non si cala."

14. G. K. Chesterton, *Saint Thomas Aquinas* (New York: Doubleday, 1956), p. 59.

15. Ibid., p. 21.

16. Thomas Aquinas, *Summa Theologica, prologue,* 5 vols., trans. Fathers of the English Dominican Province (1948; repr. Notre Dame, Ind.: Christian Classics, 1981), vol. 1, p. xix.

17. Aristotle, *Metaphysics,* 980.a.21; Thomas Aquinas, "Exposition of *Metaphysics,*" 1.1–3, in *Selected Writings,* ed. and trans. Ralph McInerny (Harmondsworth, U.K.: Penguin, 1998), pp. 721–24.

18. Saint Augustine, *The Retractions*, 2.24, in *The Fathers of the Church*, vol. 60, ed. and trans. Sister Mary Inez Bogan (Washington, D.C.: Catholic University of America Press, 1968), p. 32; Saint Augustine, *De Morib. Eccl.* 21, quoted in Aquinas, *Summa Theologica*, pt. 2.2, q. 167, art. 1, vol. 4, p. 1868.

19. Aquinas quotes Jerome (*Epist.* XXI *ad Damas*): "We see priests forsaking the Gospels and the prophets, and reading stage-plays, and singing the love songs of pastoral idylls" (*Summa Theologica*, pt. 2, art. 1, vol. 4, p. 1869).

20. Bernard de Clairvaux, *Sermones super Canticum Canticorum, Ser. 36*, in *S. Bernardi Opera II*, ed. J. Leclerq (Rome: Editiones Cistercienses, 1958), p. 56; Alcuin, *De Grammatica*, PL 101, 850 B, quoted in Carmen Lozano Guillén, "El concepto de gramática en el Renacimiento," *Humanistica Lovaniensia: Journal of Neo-Latin Studies* 41 (1992): 90.

21. Bruno Nardi, "L'origine dell'anima umana secondo Dante," in *Studi di filosofia medievale* (Rome: Edizioni di Storia e Letteratura, 1960), p. 27.

22. *Paradiso* XXXIII:142–45, "All' alta fantasia qui mancò possa;/ ma già volgeva il mio disiro e il velle,/sì come rota ch' egualmente è mossa,/l'amor che move il sole e l'altre stelle."

23. David Hume, "My Own Life" (1776), quoted in Ernest C. Mossner, "Introduction," in Hume, *A Treatise of Human Nature*, ed. Ernest C. Mossner (Harmondsworth, U.K.: Penguin, 1969), p. 17.

24. David Hume, *A Treatise of Human Nature* (London, 1739), title page; Hume, "My Own Life," quoted in Mossner, "Introduction," p. 17.

25. Hume, "My Own Life," quoted in Mossner, "Introduction," p. 17.

26. Isaiah Berlin, *The Age of Enlightenment: The Eighteenth Century Philosophers* (1956), quoted in Mossner, "Introduction," p. 7; Hume, *Treatise of Human Nature*, ed. Mossner, p. 41.

27. Hume, *Treatise of Human Nature*, ed. Mossner, pp. 499–500; Aquinas, *Summa Theologica*, pt. 2.2, q. 167, vol. 4, p. 1870.

28. Hume, *Treatise of Human Nature*, pp. 495, 497.

29. The chevalier de Jaucourt, "Curiosité," in Denis Diderot and Jean Le Rond d'Alembert, *Encyclopédie; ou, Dictionnaire raisonné des sciences, des arts et des métiers* (Paris, 1751), vol. 4, pp. 577–78.

30. *Inferno*, XXVIII:139–41, "Perch' io partii così giunte persone,/ partito porto il mio cerebro, lasso!/ dal suo principio ch' è in questo troncone."

31. Boccaccio, *Trattatello in laude di Dante*, p. 51.

32. *Inferno*, XX:19–21, "Se Dio ti lasci, lettor, prender frutto/ di tua lezione, or pensa per te stesso/ com' io potea tener lo viso asciutto."

33. See Denise Heilbronn, "Master Adam and the Fat-Bellied Lute," *Dante Studies* 101 (1983): 51–65.

34. *Inferno*, XXX:131–32, "Or pur mira!/ che per poco è teco non mi risso"; 148, "ché voler ciò udire è bassa voglia."

35. Seneca, "On Leisure," 5.3, in *Moral Essays*, vol. 2, trans. John W. Basore (Cambridge: Harvard University Press, 1990), pp. 190–91. I have slightly altered the translation.

2
What Do We Want to Know?

Chapter opener: Jean-Jacques Rousseau, *Emile; ou, De l'éducation,* bk. 1, ed. Charles Wirz and Pierre Burgelin (Paris: Gallimard, 1969), p. 89.

1. *Inferno,* XXVI:25, 29, "Quante 'l villan ch'al poggio si riposa, / . . . vede lucciole giù per la vallea"; 52–53, "chi è 'n quel foco che vien sì diviso / di sopra"; 82, "quando nel mondo li alti verse scrissi"; 93, "prima che sí Enea la nomasse."

2. Ibid., 97–98, "dentro a me l'ardore / ch'i' ebbi a divenir del mondo esperto"; Alfred, Lord Tennyson, "Ulysses" (1842), in *Selected Poems,* ed. Michael Millgate (Oxford: Oxford University Press, 1963), p. 88.

3. Torquato Tasso, *Gerusalemme liberata,* ed. Lanfranco Caretti, XV:25 (Milan: Mondadori, 1957), p. 277.

4. 'Abd-ar-Rahmân b. Khaldûn Al-Hadramî, *Al-Muqaddina: Discours sur l'Histoire Universelle,* translated from the Arabic and edited by Vincent Monteil, 3rd ed., 6.39 (Paris: Sinbad/Actes Sud, 1997), p. 948. Ibn Khaldun quotes Qur'an 2:142.

5. *Inferno,* XI:60, "e simile lordura"; XXVI:58–63, "e dentro da la lor fiamma si geme / l'agguato del caval che fé la porta / onde uscì de' Romani il gentil seme. // Piangesvisi entro l'arte per che, morta, / Deîdemìa ancor si duol d'Achille, / e del Palladio pena vi si porta." Leah Schwebel, "'Simile lordura,' Altra Bolgia: Authorial Conflation in Inferno 26," *Dante Studies* 133 (2012): 47–65.

6. See Giuseppe Mazzotta, *Dante, Poet of the Desert: History and Allegory in the "Divine Comedy"* (Princeton: Princeton University Press, 1979), pp. 66–106.

7. It is not clear whether Dante's Ulysses left on his last fatal journey after his return to Ithaca (as Tennyson believed) or whether he never returned and kept on traveling after his Homeric adventures.

8. Oscar Wilde, *The Importance of Being Earnest* (London: Nick Hern Books, 1995), p. 32.

9. "Philo," in Louis Jacob, *The Jewish Religion: A Companion* (Oxford: Oxford University Press, 1995), p. 377.

10. Saint Augustine, *On Genesis* (Hyde Park, N.Y.: New City Press, 2002), p. 83.

11. Hesiod, *Theogony* and *Works and Days,* trans. Dorothea Wender (Harmondsworth, U.K.: Penguin, 1973), pp. 42, 61; Joachim du Bellay, *Les Antiquitez de Rome,* quoted in Dora and Erwin Panofsky, *Pandora's Box: The Changing Aspects of a Mythical Symbol,* 2nd rev. ed. (New York: Harper and Row, 1962), pp. 58–59.

12. Robert Louis Stevenson, Letter to Mrs. Thomas Stevenson, December 26, 1880, in *The Letters of Robert Louis Stevenson to His Family and Friends,* vol. 1, ed. Sidney Colvin (New York: Scribner's, 1899), pp. 227–29.

13. *Paradiso* XXXIII:94–96, "Un punto solo m'è maggior letargo / che venticinque secoli a la 'mpresa / che fé Nettuno ammirar l'ombra d'Argo."

14. Cited in "Questions," in Jacob, *Jewish Religion,* p. 399.

15. *Paradiso,* XXXIII:85–87, "Nel suo profondo vidi che s'interna, / legato con amore in un volume, / ciò che per l'universo si squaderna."

16. See Agostino Ramelli, *Diverse et artificiose macchine* (Paris, 1588). Discussed in Lina Bolzoni, *La stanza della memoria: modelli letterari e iconografici nell'età della stampa*, (Milan: Einaudi, 1995), p. 64.

17. Orazio Toscanella, *Armonia di tutti i principali retori* (Venice, 1569). Discussed in Bolzoni, *Stanza della memoria*, pp. 69–73.

18. "La scienza del perché," quoted in Bolzoni, *Stanza della memoria*, p. 48.

19. *Purgatorio*, II:11–12, "gente che pensa suo cammino / che va col core, e col corpo dimora." The canto ends with a simile of the opposite impulse: "come uom che va, nè sa dove riesca" (132), "like a man who goes, but doesn't know where he'll come out."

20. Carlo Ossola, *Introduzione alla Divina Commedia* (Venice: Marsilio, 2012), p. 40.

21. Dante Alighieri, *Epistola* XIII:72, in *Le opere di Dante: testo critico della Società dantesca italiana*, ed. M. Barbi et al. (Florence: Bemporad, 1921), p. 440; *Inferno*, I:91, "A te convien tenere altro viaggio"; V:22, "Non impedir lo suo fatale andare."

22. Seneca, *Epistulae morales*, ed. and trans. R. M. Gummere, vol. 1, *Ep.* 88 (Cambridge: Harvard University Press, 1985); Héraclite, *Allégories d'Homère*, 70:8, translated from the Greek by Félix Buffière (Paris: Belles Lettres, 1962), p. 75; Dio Chrysostom, "Discourse 71," in *Discourses 61–80*, trans. H. Lamar Crosby (Cambridge: Harvard University Press, 1951), p. 165; for Epictetus see Silvia Montiglio, *From Villain to Hero: Odysseus in Ancient Thought* (Ann Arbor: University of Michigan Press, 2011), pp. 87–94.

23. See Raymond Klibansky, Erwin Panofsky, and Fritz Saxl, *Saturn and Melancholy* (London: Nelson, 1964), p. 77.

3
How Do We Reason?

Chapter opener: Fernando de Rojas y "Antiguo Autor," *La Celestina: Tragicomedia de Calisto y Melibea*, 3.3, ed. Francisco J. Lobera, Guillermo Serés, Paloma Díaz-Mas, Carlos Mota, Iñigo Ruiz Arzaluz, and Francisco Rico (Madrid: Real Academia Española, 2011), p. 110; Simone Weil, quoted in Roberto Calasso, *I quarantanove gradini* (Milan: Adelphi, 1991), p. 121.

1. *Paradiso*, XXIV:25–27, "Però salta la penna e non lo scrivo: / ché l'imagine nostra a cotai pieghe, / non che 'l parlare, è troppo color vivo."

2. Ibid., 40, "ama bene e bene spera e crede"; 46–51, "Sí come il baccilier s'arma e non parla / fin che l'maestro la question propone, / per approvarla, non per terminarla, // così m'armava io d'ogne ragione / mentre ch'ella dicea, per esser presto / a tal querente e a tal professione."

3. Ibid., 79–81, "Sé quantunque s'acquista / giú per dottrina, fosse così 'nteso, / non lí avria loco ingegno di sofista."

4. Bonaventure, *Les Sentences 2*, in *Les Sentences; Questions sur Dieu: Commentaire du premier livre de sentences de Pierre Lombard*, translated from the Latin by Marc Ozilou (Paris: PUF, 2002), p. 1.

5. See Etienne Gilson, *History of Christian Philosophy in the Middle Ages* (New York: Random House, 1955), pp. 246–50.

6. Aristotle, *Topics, Books I and VIII with Excerpts from Related Texts*, trans. Robin Smith (Oxford: Clarendon, 1997), p. 101 (slanderers and thieves); Aristotle, *On Sophistical Refutations; On Coming-to-be and Passing Away; On the Cosmos*, trans. E. S. Forster and D. J. Furley (Cambridge: Harvard University Press, 2001), esp. pp. 13–15 (leading others into error); Aristotle, *Topics*, p. 127 (irrelevant premise).

7. G. B. Kerferd, *The Sophistic Movement* (Cambridge: Cambridge University Press, 1981), p. 1.

8. Thomas Mautner, *The Penguin Dictionary of Philosophy*, 2nd ed. (Harmondsworth, U.K.: Penguin, 2005), p. 583; Martin Heidegger, *Plato's Sophist*, trans. Richard Rojcewicz and André Schuwer (Bloomington: Indiana University Press, 2003), p. 169; Lucian, "The Passing of Peregrinus," in *Lucian*, ed. and trans. A. M. Harmon (Cambridge: Harvard University Press, 1936), vol. 5, chap. 13.

9. Quoted in Marcel Bataillon, *Erasmo y España*, translated from the French by Antonio Alatorre (Mexico City: Fondo de Cultura Económica, 2007), p. 506.

10. François Rabelais, *Gargantua and Pantagruel*, bk. 1, chap. 19, trans. Sir Thomas Urquhart and Pierre Le Motteux (New York: Knopf, 1994), p. 66.

11. See Lucien Febvre, *Le problème de l'incroyance au XVIe siècle: La religion de Rabelais* (Paris: Albin Michel, 1942).

12. See Mikhail Bakhtin, *Rabelais and His World*, trans. Helene Iswolsky (Bloomington: Indiana University Press, 1984), pp. 362–63.

13. Rabelais, *Gargantua and Pantagruel*, bk. 5, chap. 48, p. 806; chap. 37, p. 784; chap. 48, p. 807.

14. Deleuze, quoted in Barbara Cassin, *L'Effet sophistique* (Paris: Gallimard, 1995), p. 20.

15. See W. K. C. Guthrie, *A History of Greek Philosophy*, vol. 3 (Cambridge: Cambridge University Press, 1969), p. 282.

16. See Kerferd, *Sophistic Movement*, p. 38.

17. *The Greek Sophists*, ed. and trans. John Dillon and Tania Gregel (Harmondsworth, U.K.: Penguin, 2003), pp. 119–32.

18. Plato, *Lesser Hippias*, 363c–d, trans. Benjamin Jowett, in *The Collected Dialogues of Plato*, ed. Edith Hamilton and Huntington Cairns (Princeton: Princeton University Press, 1973), p. 202.

19. W. K. C. Guthrie, *The Greek Philosophers from Thales to Aristotle* (London: Routledge, 1960), p. 66.

20. I. F. Stone, *The Trial of Socrates* (Boston: Little, Brown, 1988), pp. 41–42; Harry Sidebottom, "Philostratus and the Symbolic Roles of the Sophist and the Philosopher," in *Philostratus*, ed. Ewen Bowie and Jas Elsner (Cambridge: Cambridge University Press, 2009), pp. 77–79.

21. Xenophon, "On Hunting" 13, quoted in Jacqueline de Romilly, *Les Grands Sophistes dans l'Athène de Périclès* (Paris: Editions de Fallois, 1988), p. 55.

22. Philostratus, quoted in Sidebottom, "Philostratus and the Symbolic Roles of the Sophist and the Philosopher," p. 80; Lucian of Samosata, *The Rhetorician's Vade Mecum*, 15, in *The Works of Lucian of Samosata*, trans. H. W. and F. Fowler (Oxford: Oxford University Press, 1905), p. 52.

23. See Mario Untersteiner, *I sofisti* (1948; repr. Milan: Mondadori, 2008), p. 280.

24. Plato, *The Republic*, bk. 5, 462c–e, 463a–e, trans. Paul Shorey, in *Collected Dialogues of Plato*, pp. 701–3.

25. Plato, *Protagoras*, trans. W. K. C. Guthrie, in *Collected Dialogues of Plato*, pp. 319–20.

26. Plato, *Lesser Hippias*, 365b, p. 202.

27. Ibid., 376a–b, p. 214.

28. Ibid., 376c, p. 214.

29. Stone, *Trial of Socrates*, p. 57.

30. Michel de Montaigne, "An Apology for Raymond Sebond," 2.12, in *The Complete Essays*, trans. and ed. M. A. Screech (Harmondsworth, U.K.: Penguin, 1991), p. 656.

31. George Steiner, "Where Was Plato?" *Times Literary Supplement*, 26 July 2013, p. 11.

32. Plato, *Theaetetus*, 149A–B, trans. F. M. Cornford, in *The Collected Dialogues of Plato*, pp. 853–54.

4
How Can We See What We Think?

Chapter opener: Dante Alighieri, *De vulgari eloquentia*, edited and translated from the Latin by Vittorio Coletti (Milan: Garzanti, 1991), p. 25.

1. R. H. Charles, *The Apocrypha and Pseudepigrapha of the Old Testament* (Oxford: Clarendon, 1913), p. 75.

2. *Paradiso*, XVIII:73–78, "E come augelli surti di rivera, / quasi congratulando a lor pasture, / fanno di sé or tonda or altra schiera, // sí dentro ai lumi sante creature / volitando cantavano, e faciensi / or D, or I, or L in sue figure."

3. In Fariduddin Attar's *Conference of the Birds* (twelfth century), the birds set out to seek their king, the Simurgh. After many adventures, they realize that they all are the Simurgh and the Simurgh is all of them. Jorge Luis Borges made the association between the two birds in "El Simurgh y el águila," in *Nueve ensayos dantescos* (Madrid: Espasa-Calpe: 1982), pp. 139–44.

4. *Purgatorio*, X:95, "visibile parlare"; *Inferno*, III:1–9, "Per me si va ne la città dolente, / per me si va ne l'etterno dolore, / per me si va tra la perduta gente. // Giustizia mosse il mio alto fattore; / fecemi la divina podestate, / la somma sapïenza e 'l primo amore. // Dinanzi a me non fuor cose create / se non etterne, e io etterno duro. / Lasciate ogne speranza, voi ch'intrate."

5. *Inferno*, III:17, "genti dolorose"; 21, "dentro alle segrete cose."

6. *Purgatorio*, IX:112–14; 131–32, "Intrate; ma facciovi accorti / che di fuor torna chi 'n dietro si guata."

7. Saint Augustine, *De Magistro*, 8, in *Les Confessions, précédées de Dialogues philosophiques*, bk. 1, ed. Lucien Jerphagnon (Paris: Gallimard, 1998), p. 370.

8. Julian Jaynes, *The Origin of Consciousness in the Breakdown of the Bicameral Mind* (New York: Houghton Mifflin, 1976).

9. Plato, *Phaedrus*, 274d–e, trans. R. Hackforth, in *The Collected Dialogues of Plato*, ed. Edith Hamilton and Huntington Cairns (Princeton: Princeton University Press, 1973), p. 520; G. K. Chesterton, "A Defense of Nonsense," in *The Defendant* (London: Dent, 1901), p. 14.

10. Nic Dunlop, *The Lost Executioner: A Journey to the Heart of the Killing Fields* (New York: Walker, 2005), p. 82.

11. Inca Garcilaso de la Vega, *Comentarios reales*, in *Obras completas del Inca Garcilaso*, vol. 2 (Madrid: Colección Rivadeneira, 1960).

12. Ibid., p. 67.

13. All the information on Sansevero comes from the superb edition of Sansevero's *Apologetic Letter*, translated into Spanish and edited by José Emilio and Lucio Adrián Burucúa: Raimondo di Sangro, *Carta Apologética* (Buenos Aires: UNSAM Edita, 2010).

14. This is true in both written and oral societies. "All societies known as 'oral' employ two different and parallel communication systems: one based on language, the other on sight": Anne-Marie Christin, *L'Image écrite ou la déraison graphique* (Paris: Flammarion, 1995), p. 7.

15. Robert Bringhurst, *The Elements of Typographic Style* (Vancouver: Hartley and Marks, 1992) p. 9.

16. See Marcia and Robert Ascher, *Code of the Quipu: A Study in Media, Mathematics and Culture* (Ann Arbor: University of Michigan Press, 1981), p. 102.

17. Pedro Cieza de León, *Crónica del Perú: Cuarta parte*, vol. 3, ed. Laura Gutiérrez Arbulú (Lima: Pontificia Universidad Católica del Perú y Academia Nacional de la Historia, 1994), p. 232.

18. Bringhurst, *Elements of Typographic Style*, p. 19.

5
How Do We Question?

Chapter opener: Solomon Volkov, *Conversations with Joseph Brodsky: A Poet's Journey Through the Twentieth Century*, trans. Marian Schwartz (New York: Free Press, 1998), p. 139; Joseph Brodsky, "The Condition We Call Exile," in *On Grief and Other Reasons: Essays* (New York: Farrar, Straus and Giroux, 1995), p. 33; Brodsky, "Venetian Stanzas I," in *To Urania* (New York: Farrar, Straus and Giroux, 1988), p. 90.

1. *Purgatorio*, III:34–42, "Matto è chi spera che nostra ragione / possa trascorrer la infinita via / che tiene una sustanza in tre persone. // State contenti, umana gente, al quia: / ché, se potuto aveste veder tutto, / mestier no era parturir Maria; // e disïar vedeste sanza frutto / tai che sarebbe lor disio quetato, / ch' etternalmente è dato lor per lutto."; 43–44, "io dico d'Aristotile e di Plato / e di molt' altri."

2. Thomas Aquinas, *Summa Theologica*, pt. 1, q. 2, art. 2, 5 vols., trans. Fathers of the English Dominican Province (1948; repr. Notre Dame, Ind.: Christian Classics, 1981), vol. 1, p. 12; Francis Bacon, *The Advancement of Learning*, I:v.8, in *The Advancement of Learning and New Atlantis*, ed. Arthur Johnston (Oxford: Oxford University Press, 1974), p. 35.

3. *Paradiso*, XXVI:115–17, "non il gustar del legno / fu per sé la cagion di tanto esilio, / ma solamente il trapassar del segno"; 124–32, "La lingua ch'io parlai fu tutta spenta / innanzi che a l'ovra iconsummabile / fosse la gente di Nembròt attenta: // ché nullo effetto mai razïonabile, / per lo piacere uman che rinovella / seguendo il cielo, sempre fu durabile. // Opera naturale 'ch'uom favella; / ma cosí o cosí, natura lascia / poi fare a voi secondo che v'abbella."

4. Ibid., 132–38.

5. Dante Alighieri, *De vulgari eloquentia*, edited and translated from the Latin by Vittorio Coletti (Milan: Garzanti, 1991), pp. 14–15.

6. See Louis Ginzberg, *The Legends of the Jews*, 7 vols., vol. 1: *From the Creation to Jacob*, trans. Henrietta Szold (Baltimore: Johns Hopkins University Press, 1998), pp. 5–8.

7. Quoted in Gershom Scholem, *Kabbalah* (New York: Dorset, 1974), p. 12. In the Jewish tradition, the *Mishnah* is held to be infallible.

8. Cf. Matthew 6:22–23: "The light of the body is the eye: if therefore thine eye be single, thy whole body shall be full of light."

9. Jorge Luis Borges, "La biblioteca de Babel," in *Ficciones* (Buenos Aires: Sur, 1944), pp. 85–95.

10. The ten *sefirot* are the Crown, wisdom, understanding, loving kindness, power or judgment, beauty, victory, splendor, foundation, and sovereignty. There are said to be 613 mitzvot, of which 365 are negative ("do not") and 248 positive ("do this"). See Louis Jacobs, *The Jewish Religion: A Companion* (Oxford: Oxford University Press, 1995), pp. 450, 350.

11. *Purgatorio*, XXII:137–38, "cadea de l'alta roccia un liquor chiaro / e si spandeva per le foglie suso." In Dante's condemnation of the Epicureans in *Inferno* VI, only their notion that the soul dies with the body is mentioned, not the Epicurean exaltation of pleasure.

12. On the spring, see *Purgatorio*, XXII:65; *Purgatorio*, XXI:97–98, "mamma / fumi, e fummi nutrice, poetando."

13. *Purgatorio*, XXI:131–32, "Frate / non far, ché tu se' ombra e ombra vedi"; 136, "trattando l'ombre come cosa salda"; *Inferno*, I:82–84, "lungo studio e 'l grande amore / che m' ha fatto cercar lo tuo volume."

14. See Sandra Debenedetti Stow, *Dante e la mistica ebraica* (Florence: Editrice La giuntina, 2004), pp. 19–25.

15. Umberto Eco, *La ricerca della lingua perfetta* (Rome: Laterza, 1993), pp. 49–51.

16. See Stow, *Dante e la mistica ebraica*, pp. 41–51; *Paradiso*, XXXIII:140, "la mia mente fu percossa."

17. See Plato, *The Republic*, bk. 2, 376d–e, trans. Paul Shorey, in *The Collected Dialogues of Plato*, ed. Edith Hamilton and Huntington Cairns (Princeton: Princeton University Press, 1973), p. 623; *Purgatorio*, XV:117.

18. See Giovanni Carlo Federico Villa, *Cima da Conegliano: Maître de la Renaissance vénitienne,* translated from the Italian by Renaud Temperini (Paris: Réunion des musées nationaux, 2012), p. 32.

19. H. Strack and G. Stemberger, *Introducción a la literatura talmúdica y midrásica* (Valencia: Institución San Jerónimo, 1988), p. 76.

20. See B. Netanyahu, *Don Isaac Abravanel, Statesman and Philosopher,* 5th ed., rev. (Ithaca: Cornell University Press, 1998), p. 122.

21. See Herbert A. Davidson, *Moses Maimonides: The Man and His Works* (Oxford: Oxford University Press, 2005), p. 72.

22. *Pirke de Rabbi Eliezer: The Chapters of Rabbi Eliezer the Great According to the Text of the Manuscript Belonging to Abraham Epstein of Vienna,* trans. Gerald Friedlander (New York: Sepher Hermon Press, 1981), p. 63.

23. See Eco, *Ricerca della lingua perfetta,* p. 50.

24. See Attilio Milano, *Storia degli ebrei in Italia* (Turin: Einaudi, 1963), p. 668; Rainer Maria Rilke, "Eine Szene aus dem Ghetto von Venedig," in *Geschichten vom lieben Gott* (Wiesbaden: Insel Verlag, 1955), p. 94.

25. The mathematically backed promise of salvation conjured up by Abravanel (which no doubt Abravanel himself would have repudiated with horror) cast its lengthy shadow over the next centuries of Jewish patience, so that, as late as 1734, the rabbinical council of Venice had to issue a decree of excommunication against a certain Mosè Chaím Luzzatto for proclaiming one of his associates to be the expected Messiah, his arrival inexplicably delayed for 231 years since Abravanel's calculation. See Riccardo Calimani, *The Ghetto of Venice,* trans. Katherine Silberblatt Wolfthal (New York: M. Evans, 1987), pp. 231–35.

26. Gideon Bohak, *Ancient Jewish Magic: A History* (Cambridge: Cambridge University Press, 2008), pp. 358–59.

27. See Marvin J. Heller, *Printing the Talmud: A History of the Earliest Printed Editions of the Talmud* (Brooklyn, N.Y.: Im Hasefer, 1992), p. 7.

28. Bomberg, quoted in Calimani, *Ghetto of Venice,* pp. 81–82.

29. *Editoria in ebraico a Venezia,* catalogo de la mostra organizzata da Casa di Risparmio di Venezia, Comune di Sacile (Venice: Arsenale Editrice, 1991).

30. Heller, *Printing the Talmud,* pp. 135–82.

31. Quoted ibid., p. 142.

32. Marc-Alain Ouaknin, *Invito al Talmud,* trans. Roberto Salvadori (Turin: Bottati Boringhieri, 2009), p. 56; for the map, see the front endpaper in Calimani, *Ghetto of Venice.*

33. Gilbert K. Chesterton, *Orthodoxy* (New York: John Lane, 1909), p. 108.

34. I am grateful to Arthur Kiron, of the Jewish Institute Collections at the University of Pennsylvania, for this information. Mr. Kiron referred me to George M. Stratton, "The Mnemonic Feat of the 'Shass Pollak,'" *Psychological Review* 24, no. 3 (May 1917): 181–87.

35. Saint Bonaventure, *Collationes in Hexaemeron,* 13.12, quoted in Hans Blumenberg, *Die Lesbarkeit der Welt* (Frankfurt-am-Main: Suhrkamp, 1981), p. 73.

36. See, e.g., Marina del Negro Karem, "Immagini di Potere: Il Leone Andante nel

Battistero di San Marco di Venezia," *Atti dell'Istituto Veneto di Scienze, Lettere ed Arte* 162 (2003–4): 152–71.

37. *Mishneh Torah: The Book of Knowledge by Maimonides*, edited according to the Bodleian codex, with introduction, Biblical and Talmudical references, notes, and English translation by Moses Hyamson (Jerusalem: Feldheim, 1981).

6
What Is Language?

Chapter opener: Lewis Carroll, *Through the Looking-Glass and What Alice Found There*, in *The Annotated Alice*, ed. Martin Gardner (New York: Clarkson Potter, 1960), p. 269; *Paradiso*, XXXIII:140–41, "la mia mente fu percossa / da un fulgore in che sua voglia venne"; *Inferno*, XXVIII:139–41.

1. See, e.g., *Inferno*, XXX:130–32; *Purgatorio*, XIII:133–41.

2. *Inferno*, XXVIII:4–6, "Ogne lingua per certo verria meno / per lo nostro sermone e per la mente / c'hanno a tanto comprender poco seno."

3. Ovide, *Les Métamorphoses*, 6.382–400, bilingual edition, edited and translated from the Latin by Danièle Robert (Paris: Actes Sud, 2001), pp. 246–49; *Paradiso*, I:19–21, "Entra nel petto mio, e spira tue / sí come quando Marsïa traesti / de la vagina de le membra sue."

4. *Inferno*, I:1–7.

5. Though there is no proof that Cervantes read the *Commedia*, some of its episodes were well known in the seventeenth century, and the scene in which Don Quixote attacks the towering windmills which he believes are giants may have been inspired by the episode in which Dante believes that the giants are towers.

6. Genesis 6:4; Dante's source for the story, other than Genesis itself, is Saint Augustine's commentary; see *The City of God*, 15.23, trans. Henry Bettenson (Harmondsworth, U.K.: Penguin, 1984), p. 639. *Inferno*, XXXI: 76–81, "Elli stessi s'accusa; / questi è Nembrotto per lo cui mal coto / pur un linguaggio nel mondo non s'usa. // Lasciànlo stare e non parliamo a vòto; / ché cosí è a lui ciascun linguaggio / come 'l suo ad altrui, ch'a nullo è noto."

7. Domenico Guerri, *Di alcuni versi dotti della "Divina Commedia"* (Città di Castello: Casa Tipografica-Editrice S. Lappi, 1908), pp. 19–47.

8. Jorge Luis Borges, "La muerte y la brújula," in *La muerte y la brújula* (Buenos Aires: Emecé Editores, 1951), p. 131.

9. *Inferno*, VII:1. A brief history of the various interpretations of the line is to be found in Anna Maria Chiavacci Leonardi's edition of the *Commedia* (Milan: Mondadori, 1994), p. 233. (Following medieval tradition, Dante may have confused Pluto, god of the Underworld, and Plutus, god of riches.) *Inferno* VII:14, "l'alber fiacca."

10. Herodotus, *The Histories*, II:2, trans. Aubrey de Sélincourt, revised, with an introduction and notes by A. R. Burn (Harmondsworth, U.K.: Penguin, 1972), pp. 129–30.

11. Salimbene de Adam, *Chronicle of Salimbene de Adam*, ed. and trans. Joseph L. Baid, B. Giuseppe, and J. R. Kane (Tempe: University of Arizona Press, 1986), p. 156.

12. Oliver Sacks, *Awakenings*, rev. ed. (New York: Dutton, 1983), pp. 188–89; Rainer Maria Rilke, "The Panther," in *The Selected Poetry of Rainer Maria Rilke*, ed. and trans. Stephen Mitchell (New York: Random House, 1982), pp. 24–25.

13. *Inferno*, XXXI:127–29, "Ancor ti può nel mondo render fama, / ch'el vive, e lunga vita ancor aspetta / se 'nnanzi tempo grazia a sé nol chiama"; 142–43, "al fondo che divora / Lucifero con Giuda"; 145, "come albero in nave."

14. Louis Ginzberg, *The Legends of the Jews*, 7 vols., vol. 1: *From the Creation to Jacob*, trans. Henrietta Szold (Baltimore: Johns Hopkins University Press, 1998), pp. 177–80. Ginzberg lists rabbinical sources giving God, at the time of the Creation, as the first ruler. God was followed by seven mortals: Nimrod, Joseph, Solomon, Ahab, Nebuchadnezzar, Cyrus, and Alexander of Macedon. These in turn will be followed by the ninth and last universal ruler, the Messiah. Ginzberg, *Legends of the Jews*, vol. 5: *From the Creation to Exodus*, p. 199.

15. Ginzberg, *Legends of the Jews*, vol. 1, p. 180.

16. Michael A. Arbib, *How the Brain Got Language: The Mirror System Hypothesis* (Oxford: Oxford University Press, 2012), p. ix.

17. Ibid., pp. 84–85.

18. Franz Kafka, "Ein Bericht für eine Akademie," in *Die Erzählungen,* ed. Roger Hermes (Frankfurt-am-Main: Fischer Tagebuch Verlag, 2000), pp. 322–33. In 1906, the Argentine writer Leopoldo Lugones imagined a story in which a man tries to teach an ape to speak, convinced that apes are able to speak but that for thousands of years they have not done so in order not to be forced to work for humans. In the story, the man first tries a method for teaching deaf-mutes, then resorts to threats and punishments; nothing succeeds. The efforts end up by weakening the poor beast to the point where the man understands that it is dying. Suddenly, in his agony, the ape cries out ("how to explain the tone of a voice that had not spoken for ten thousand centuries?") the words "Master, water, master, my master." For Lugones, in the beginning humans and apes shared a common language: Leopoldo Lugones, "Yzur," in *Las fuerzas extrañas* (Buenos Aires: Arnoldo Moen y hermanos, 1906), pp. 133–44.

19. *Paradiso*, I:70–71, "Trasumanar significar per verba / non si poria"; Thomas Aquinas, *Summa Theologica,* pt. 1, q. 12, art. 6, 5 vols., trans. Fathers of the English Dominican Province (1948; repr. Notre Dame, Ind.: Christian Classics, 1981), vol. 1, p. 53.

20. From the *Nîti Sataka* of Bhartrihari. Quoted in Barbara Stoler Miller, ed. and trans., *The Hermit and the Love-Thief: Sanskrit Poems of Bhartrihari and Bilhana* (New York: Columbia University Press, 1978), p. 3.

21. I-Tsing, quoted in Amartya Sen, "China and India," in *The Argumentative Indian: Writings on Indian Culture, History and Identity* (London: Allen Lane, 2005), p. 161.

22. See R. C. Zaehner, ed. and trans., *Hindu Scriptures* (New York: Knopf, 1992), p. x.

23. *The Upanishads*, trans. Swami Paramananda (Hoo, U.K.: Axiom, 2004), p. 93; Ralph Waldo Emerson, "Brahma," in *Selected Writing of Ralph Waldo Emerson*, ed. William H. Gilman (New York: New American Library, 1965), p. 471.

24. See Romila Thapar, *A History of India*, vol. 1 (Harmondsworth, U.K.: Pelican, 1966), pp. 140–42.

25. K. Raghavan Pillai, ed. and trans., *The "Vâkyapadîya": Critical Text of Cantos I and II, with English Translation, Summary of Ideas and Notes* (Dehli: Motilal Banarsidass, 1971), p. 1.

26. B. K. Matilal, *The Word and the World: India's Contribution to the Study of Language* (Delhi: Oxford University Press, 1992), p. 52.

27. Jorge Luis Borges, "La biblioteca de Babel," in *El jardín de los senderos que se bifurcan* (Buenos Aires: Sur, 1941), pp. 85–95;. Cicero, *De natura deorum*, 2.37.93, trans. H. Rackham (Cambridge: Harvard University Press, 2005), p. 213, quoted in Jorge Luis Borges, "La biblioteca total," *Sur* 59 (August 1939): 13–16.

28. Carroll, *Through the Looking-Glass*, p. 251.

29. See Tandra Patnaik: *Sabda: A Study of Bhartrihari's Philosophy of Language* (New Delhi: D. K. Print World, 1994).

30. Italo Calvino, *Se una notte d'inverno un viaggiatore* (Turin: Giulio Einaudi, 1979), p. 72.

31. Dante Alighieri, *De vulgari eloquentia*, edited and translated from the Latin by Vittorio Coletti (Milan: Garzanti, 1991), p. 23.

32. Ibid., p. 99.

7

Who Am I?

Chapter opener: Inferno, XIII:105, "chè non è giusto aver ciò ch'om si toglie."

1. *Inferno*, I:66, "qual che tu sii, od ombra od omo certo!"

2. Craig E. Stephenson, "Introduction," *Jung and Moreno: Essays on the Theatre of Human Nature* (London: Routledge, 2014), p. 14.

3. *Purgatorio*, XXII:127–29, "Elli givan dinanzi, ed io soletto / diretro, ed ascoltava i lor sermoni / h'a poetar mi davano intelletto"; XXIII:32–33, "Chi nel viso de li uomini legge 'omo' / ben avria quivi conosciuta l'emme"; Pietro Alighieri, *Il "Commentarium" di Pietro Alighieri nelle redazioni Ashburnhamiana e Ottoboniana*, ed. Roberto della Vedova and Maria Teresa Silvotti (Florence: Olschki, 1978).

4. See Diogenes Laertius, *Lives of the Philosophers*, 3.6, trans. R. D. Hicks (Cambridge: Harvard University Press, 1995), vol. 1, p. 281; Plato, "Cratylus," trans. Benjamin Jowett, in *The Collected Dialogues of Plato*, ed. Edith Hamilton and Huntington Cairns (Princeton: Princeton University Press, 1973), p. 422.

5. *Paradiso*, VI:10, "Cesare fui, e son Giustiniano"; XII:68–69, "quinci si mosse spirito a nomarlo / dal possessivo di cui era tutto"; Vincenzo Presta, "Giovanna," in *Enciclopedia Dantesca*, vol. 9 (Milan: Mondadori, 2005), p. 524; *Paradiso*, XII:79–81, "Oh padre suo veramente Felice! / oh madre sua veramente Giovanna, / se, interpretata, val come si dice!"

6. *Purgatorio*, XXX: 62–63, "quando mi volsi al suon del nome mio, / che di necessità qui si registra"; 73–75, "Guardaci ben! Ben son, ben son Beatrice. / Come degnasti d'accedere al monte? / non sapei tu che qui è l'uom felice?"

7. Ibid., 76–78, "Li occhi mi cadder giú nel chiaro fonte; / ma veggendomi in esso, i trassi a l'erba, / tanta vergogna mi gravò la fronte."

8. William Shakespeare, *All's Well That Ends Well*, 4.1.48–49 and 4.3.371–74, in *The Complete Works of Shakespeare*, ed. W. J. Craig (London: Oxford University Press, 1969).

9. William Butler Yeats, "A Woman Young and Old," in *The Collected Poems of W. B. Yeats* (London: Macmillan, 1979), p. 308; Plato, *Symposium*, trans. Michael Joyce, in *Collected Dialogues of Plato*, pp. 542–45.

10. David Macey, "Mirror-phase," in *The Penguin Dictionary of Critical Theory* (Harmondsworth, U.K.: Penguin, 2000), p. 255; Arthur Rimbaud, Lettre à Georges Izambard, 13 mai 1871, in *Correspondance*, ed. Jean-Jacques Lefrère (Paris: Fayard, 2007), p. 64. An almost identical expression is used in Rimbaud's letter to Paul Demeny, 15 mai 1971.

11. Carl Gustav Jung, "Conscious, Unconscious and Individuation" in *The Archetypes and the Collective Unconscious*, trans. R. F. Hull (Princeton: Princeton University Press, 1980), p. 279; Saint Augustine, *Confessions*, 11.28, trans. R. S. Pine-Coffin (Harmondsworth, U.K.: Penguin, 1961), p. 278.

12. Jung, "Conscious, Unconscious and Individuation," p. 275; Carl Gustav Jung, *Memories, Dreams, Reflections*, recorded and ed. Aniela Jaffé, trans. Richard and Clara Winston, rev. ed. (New York: Vintage, 1965), p. 359.

13. Jung, *Memories, Dreams, Reflections*, p. 318.

14. Carroll, *Alice's Adventures in Wonderland*, in *The Annotated Alice*, ed. Martin Gardner (New York: Clarkson Potter, 1960), p. 22.

15. Ibid., pp. 22–23; Osip Mandelstam, "Conversation on Dante," in *The Selected Poems of Osip Mandelstam*, trans. Clarence Brown and W. S. Merwin (New York: New York Review of Books, 2004), p. 117.

16. *Purgatorio*, XXVIII:139–41.

17. Herman Melville, *Moby-Dick; or, The Whale*, ed. Luther S. Mansfield and Howard P. Vincent (New York: Hendricks House, 1962), p. 54.

18. Carroll, *Alice's Adventures in Wonderland*, p. 158.

19. William Shakespeare, *Hamlet*, 2.2.93, in *Complete Works*; Carroll, *Alice's Adventures in Wonderland*, 30, 31.

20. Carroll, *Alice's Adventures in Wonderland*, p. 161.

21. Ibid., p. 67.

22. Ibid., p. 32; Carroll, *Through the Looking-Glass*, p. 238.

23. Carroll, *Alice's Adventures in Wonderland*, pp. 37–38, 59, 75; Carroll, *Through the Looking-Glass*, pp. 201, 287; Oscar Wilde, "Narcissus," in *Poems in Prose*, in *The Works of Oscar Wilde*, ed. G. F. Maine (London: Collins, 1948), p. 844.

24. Carroll, *Alice's Adventures in Wonderland*, p. 39.

8
What Are We Doing Here?

Chapter opener: Peter Levi, *Virgil: His Life and Times* (London: Duckworth, 1998), p. 35; Drieu La Rochelle, *L'Homme à cheval* (Paris: Gallimard, 1943), p. 15; José Hernández, *El gaucho Martín Fierro* (Buenos Aires: Ediciones Pardo, 1962), pp. 44, 10 (ellipsis in the original).

1. John Ruskin, *Modern Painters,* in *The Complete Works of John Ruskin,* vol. 3 (London: Chesterfield Society, n.d.), pp. 208, 209; *Purgatorio,* XXVIII:2, "foresta spessa"; *Inferno,* I:2, "selva oscura"; Ruskin, *Modern Painters,* p. 214.

2. *Inferno* XIII:1–11, "Non ra ancor di là Nesso arrivato, / quando noi ci mettemmo per un bosco / che da neun sentiero era segnato. // Non fronda verde, ma di color fosco, / non rami schietti, ma nodosi e 'nvolti; / non pomi v'eran, ma stecchi con tòsco. // Non han sì aspri sterpi né sí folti / quelle fiere selvagge che 'n odio hanno / tra Cecina e Cornetto i luoghi cólti."

3. *Inferno,* XIII:21, "cose che torrien fede al mio sermone"; 32, "Perché mi schiante?"; 35–39, "ricomociò a dir: 'Perché mi scerpi? / non hai tu spirto di pietade alcuno? // Uomini fummo, e or siam fatti sterpi: / ben dovrebb' esser la tua man piú pia / se state fossimo anime di serpe."; Virgil, *Aeneid,* 3.19–33, in *Eclogues, Georgics, Aeneid,* 2 vols., trans. H. Rushton Fairclough (Cambridge: Harvard University Press, 1974), vol. 1, pp. 348–50.

4. *Inferno,* XIII:52–53, "'n vece / d'alcun' ammenda"; 72, "ingiusto fece me contra me giusto."

5. Saint Augustine, *City of God,* 1.20, trans. Henry Bettenson (Harmondsworth, U.K.: Penguin, 1972), p. 32.

6. *Inferno,* XIII:37, "uomini fummo"; Olga Sedakova, "Sotto il cielo della violenza," in *Esperimenti Danteschi: Inferno 2008,* ed. Simone Invernizzi (Milan: Casa Editrice Marietti, 2009), p. 116; Dante Alighieri, *De vulgari eloquentia,* edited and translated from the Latin by Vittorio Coletti (Milan: Garzanti, 1991), p. 9.

7. See Sir Paul Harvey, *The Oxford Companion to Classical Literature* (Oxford: Clarendon, 1980), p. 194.

8. Ruskin, *Modern Painters,* p. 212.

9. *Inferno,* I:39–40, "quando l'amor divino / mosse di prima quelle cose belle." *Contrapasso* is a term Dante borrowed from Thomas Aquinas to describe the punishment or purgation of a specific sin. For example, thieves, who take what does not belong to them, are punished by losing everything that does belong to them, including their human shape.

10. Virgil, *Georgics,* 1.155–59, in *Eclogues, Georgics, Aeneid,* vol. 1, pp. 90–91.

11. Porphyry, *De abstinentia,* 1.6, and Pliny the Elder, *Naturalis historia,* 16.24.62, quoted in J. Donald Hughes, "How the Ancients Viewed Deforestation," *Journal of Field Archeology* 10, no. 4 (winter 1983): 435–45.

12. Alfred Wold, "Saving the Small Farm: Agriculture in Roman Literature," *Agriculture and Human Values* 4, nos. 2–3 (spring–summer 1987): 65–75. In eighteenth-century England, Samuel Johnson mocked his contemporaries' bucolic interests. Commenting on a certain Dr. Grainger's "The Sugar-Cane, a Poem," he remarked to his biographer and friend James Boswell: "What could he make of a sugar-cane? One might as well write the 'Parsely-bed, a Poem,' or 'The Cabbage-garden, a Poem'": see James Boswell, *The Life of Samuel Johnson* (London: T. Cadell and W. Davies, 1811), vol. 3, p. 170. In South America, the classic nineteenth-century example is the Chilean Andrés Bello's "Silva a la agricutura en la zona tórrida," "Ode to Agriculture in the Torrid Zone."

13. *Inferno,* XI:48, "spregiando Natura, e sua bontade."

14. Linda Lear, "Afterword," in Rachel Carson, *Silent Spring* (Harmondsworth, U.K.: Penguin, 1999), p. 259; Charles Williams, *The Figure of Beatrice: A Study in Dante* (Woodbridge, U.K.: Boydell and Brewer, 1994), p. 129. Traditionally, the "sinners against nature" are sodomites, who have wilfully forgone intercourse, the "lawful" purpose of sexual congress. However, a number of scholars, notably André Pézard (*Dante sous la pluie de feu* [Paris: Vrin, 1950]), suggest that the "sinners against nature" have sinned in a different way, through "blindness of judgment" of what is natural. Neither "sodomy" nor "sodomites" are mentioned in the *Commedia*. In *Purgatorio* XXVI:40, however, a group of souls cries out, "Sodom and Gomorrah," in reference to the "great sin" of the Cities of the Plain (Genesis 18:20), to which another group responds in the next two lines with a reference to Pasiphaë, wife of Minos, who copulated with a bull and gave birth to the Minotaur. Both groups belong to the excessively lustful, homosexual and heterosexual, and since they are found on the highest cornice of the mountain (the closest to Eden), they represent for Dante the least serious of the seven sins.

15. Carson, *Silent Spring*, p. 257.

16. Aristotle, *The Politics*, 1.8, trans. T. A. Sinclair (Harmondsworth, U.K.: Penguin, 1962), pp. 38–40.

17. "Assessing Human Vulnerability to Environmental Change: Concepts, Issues, Methods, and Case Studies" (Nairobi: United Nations Environmental Programme, 2003), www.unep.org/geo/GEO3/pdfs/AssessingHumanVulnerabilityC.pdf; "Social Issues, Soy, and Defenestration," *WWF Global,* http://wwf.panda.org/about_our_earth/about_forests/deforestation/forest_conversion_agriculture/soy_deforestation_social/.

18. Theodore Roszak, *The Voice of the Earth* (Grand Rapids, Mich.: Phanes, 1992), p. 2; Ruskin, *Modern Painters,* p. 155; Anita Barrows, "The Ecological Self in Childhood," *Ecopsychology Newsletter* 4 (Fall 1995), quoted in David Suzuki (with Amanda McConnell), *The Sacred Balance: Rediscovering Our Place in Nature* (Vancouver: Greystone/Toronto: Douglas and McIntyre, 1997), p. 179.

19. *Inferno*, XXIV:1–15, "In quella parte del giovanetto anno / che 'l sole i crin sotto l'Aquario tempra / e già le notti al mezzo dí sen vanno, // quando la brina in su la terra assempra / l'imagine di sua sorella bianca, / ma poco dura a la sua penna tempra, // lo villanello a cui la roba manca, / si leva, e guarda, e vede la campagna / biancheggiar tutta; ond' ei si batte l'anca, // ritorna in casa, e qua e là si lagna, / come 'l tapin che non sa che si faccia; / poi riede, e la speranza ringavagna, // veggendo 'l mondo avec cangiata faccia / in poco d'ora, e prende suo vincastro / e fuor le pecorelle a pascer caccia." Virgil, *Georgics,* 1.145–46, in *Eclogues, Georgics, Aeneid,* vol. 1, pp. 90–91; *Georgics* 2.9–16, ibid., pp. 116–17.

20. Working Group II, AR5, Final Drafts, IPCC, available at http://ipcc-wg2.gov/AR5/report/final-drafts/ (accessed November 2013). The intergovernmental panel was not the first group of world-renowned scientists to issue such a warning. On November 18, 1992, five months after an Earth Summit in Rio de Janeiro, the largest gathering of heads of state in history, 1,600 scientists from all over the world, many of them Nobel Prize winners, issued their "World Scientists' Warning to Humanity," which laid out the dan-

ger in strong language: "Human beings and the natural world are on a collision course. Human activities inflict harsh and often irreversible damage on the environment and on critical resources. If not checked, many of our current practices put at serious risk the future that we wish for human society and the plant and animal kingdoms, and may so alter the living world that it will be unable to sustain life in the manner that we know. Fundamental changes are urgent if we are to avoid the collision our present course will bring about. . . . No more than one or a few decades remain before the chance to avert the threats we now confront will be lost and the prospects for humanity immeasurably diminished. We the undersigned, senior members of the world's scientific community, hereby warn all humanity of what lies ahead. A great change in our stewardship of the Earth and life on it is required, if vast human misery is to be avoided and our global home on this planet is not to be irretrievably mutilated." In *The Sacred Balance* (pp. 4–5), the ecologist David Suzuki remarks that when the document was released to the press, few papers took notice. Both the *Washington Post* and the *New York Times* rejected it as "not newsworthy"; the papers' editors wilfully avoided recognition of the warning and of their responsibility in the lack of response that followed it.

21. *Inferno* IV:131, "maestro di color che sanno."

9
Where Is Our Place?

Chapter opener: Derek Walcott, "The Star-Apple Kingdom," in *Selected Poems,* ed. Edward Baugh (New York: Farrar, Straus and Giroux, 2007), p. 129; James Joyce, *A Portrait of the Artist as a Young Man* (New York: Random House, 1928), pp. 11–12; Johann Wolfgang Goethe, *Die Wahlverwadtschaften,* ed. Hans-J. Weitz (Frankfurt-am-Main: Insel Verlag, 1972), p. 174; Lawrence Durrell, *Constance; or, Solitary Practices* (London: Faber and Faber, 1982), p. 50; Tayeb Salih, *Season of Migration to the North,* trans. Denys Johnson-Davies (Harmondsworth, U.K.: Penguin, 2003), p. 30; Lewis Carroll, *The Hunting of the Snark,* ed. Martin Gardner (Harmondsworth, U.K.: Penguin, 1967), p. 55; Northrop Frye, "Haunted by Lack of Ghosts: Some Patterns in the Imagery of Canadian Poetry" (26 April 1976), in *Northrop Frye on Canada,* ed. Jean O'Grady and David Staines (Toronto: University of Toronto Press, 2003), p. 476.

1. *Inferno*, I:5, "selvaggia e aspra e forte"; 7, "amara"; 21, "la notte, ch'i' passai con tanta pieta."

2. See *Purgatorio* II:146, *Convivio* II:1, 6–8, and *Epistola* XIII:21, in *Le opere di Dante: testo critico della Società dantesca italiana,* ed. M. Barbi et al. (Florence: Bemporad, 1921), pp. 172, 438, respectively.

3. The only exception is when Virgil sends his ward off on his own to observe the punishment of the usurers in *Inferno*, XVII:37–78.

4. Henry James, *Substance and Shadow; or, Morality and Religion in Their Relation to Life* (Boston: Ticknor and Fields, 1863), p. 75.

5. *Inferno*, XXXII:100–102, "Ond' elli a me: 'Perchè tu mi dischiomi, / nè ti dirò ch'io

sia, nè mostrerolti, / se mille fiate in sul capo tomi'"; 104, "più d'una ciocca"; 106, "Che hai tu, Bocca"?

6. Ibid., XXXIII:94, "Lo pianto stesso lí pianger non lascia"; 112, "i duri veli"; 116–17, "s'io non ti disbrigo, / al fondo de la ghiaccia ir mi convegna"; 150, "e cortesia fu lui esser villano."

7. Ibid., VIII:45, "benedetta colei che 'n te s'incinse."

8. Thomas Aquinas, *Summa Theologica,* pt. 1.2, q. 47, art. 2, 5 vols., trans. Fathers of the English Dominican Province (1948; repr. Notre Dame, Ind.: Christian Classics, 1981), vol. 2, p. 785. Among Dante's defenders are Luigi Pietrobono, "Il canto VIII dell' *Inferno,*" *L'Alighieri* 1, no. 2 (1960): 3–14, and G. A. Borgese, "The Wrath of Dante," *Speculum* 13 (1938): 183–93; among his detractors, E. G. Parodi, *Poesia e storia nella "Divina Commedia"* (Vicenza: Neri Pozza, 1965), p. 74, and Attilio Momigliano, *La "Divina Commedia" di Dante Alighieri* (Florence: Sansoni, 1948), pp. 59–60, but there are innumerable voices on both sides of the question.

9. Giovanni Boccaccio, *Il Decamerone,* 9.8 (Turin: Einaudi, 1980), pp. 685–89.

10. *Inferno,* V:141–42.

11. Aquinas, *Summa Theologica,* pt. 1, q. 21, art. 2, vol. 1, p. 119.

12. Ricardo Pratesi, introduction to Galileo Galilei, *Dos lecciones infernales,* translated from the Italian by Matías Alinovi (Buenos Aires: La Compañía, 2011), p. 12.

13. Galileo Galilei, *Studi sulla Divina Commedia* (Florence: Felice Le Monnier, 1855); see also Galileo, *Dos lecciones infernales,* and Galileo Galilée, *Leçons sur l'Enfer de Dante,* translated from the Italian by Lucette Degryse (Paris: Fayard, 2008).

14. *Inferno,* XXXI: 58–59 (Nimrod's face); XXXIV:30–31 (Lucifer's arm).

15. Nicola Chiaromonte, *The Worm of Consciousness and Other Essays,* ed. Miriam Chiaromonte (New York: Harcourt Brace Jovanovich, 1976), p. 153.

16. Homer, *The Odyssey,* 8.551, trans. Robert Fagles (New York: Viking Penguin, 1996), p. 207.

17. See François Hartog and Michael Werner, "Histoire," in *Vocabulaire européen des philosophies,* ed. Barbara Cassin (Paris: Editions du Seuil, 2004), p. 562; Georg Wilhelm Friedrich Hegel, *Lectures on the Philosophy of World History,* trans. Hugh Barr Nisbet (Cambridge: Cambridge University Press, 1975), pp. 27, 560.

18. László Földényi, *Dostoyevski lee a Hegel en Siberia y rompe a llorar,* translated from the Hungarian by Adan Kovacsis (Madrid: Galaxia Gutenberg, 2006); Max Brod, *Franz Kafka* (New York: Schocken, 1960), p. 75.

19. Földényi, *Dostoyevski lee a Hegel en Siberia y rompe a llorar,* p. 42.

20. See John Hendrix, *History and Culture in Italy* (Lanham, Md.: University Press of America, 2003), p. 130.

21. Al-Biruni, *Le Livre de l'Inde,* edited and translated from the Arabic by Vincent Mansour-Monteil (Paris: Sinbad/UNESCO, 1996), pp. 41–42; Virgil, *The Aeneid,* 6.847–53, trans. C. Day Lewis (Oxford: Oxford University Press, 1952), p. 154.

22. Claude Lévi-Strauss, *Tristes tropiques,* trans. John and Doreen Weightman (London: Jonathan Cape, 1973), p. 411.

23. *Inferno*, II:121–23, "Dunque: che è? perché, perché restai,/perché tanta viltà nel core allette?/perché ardire e franchezza no hai?"

24. Lévi-Strauss, *Tristes tropiques*, p. 414.

10

How Are We Different?

1. Plato, *The Republic*, 1.20, trans. Paul Shorey, in *The Collected Dialogues of Plato*, ed. Edith Hamilton and Huntington Cairns (Princeton: Princeton University Press, 1973), p. 597.

2. Ibid., 2.1, p. 605; 2.10, p. 614.

3. Ibid., 1.12, p. 589.

4. Virginia Woolf, "Speech to the London and National Society for Women's Service," in *The Essays of Virginia Woolf*, vol. 5: *1929–1932*, ed. Stuart N. Clarke (London: Hogarth, 2009), p. 640; Sophocles, *Oedipus at Colonus*, ll. 368–70, in *The Theban Plays*, trans. David Grene (New York: Knopf, 1994), p. 78. The argument about men's and women's roles in the *Iliad* is made by Alessandro Baricco, *Omero, Iliade* (Milan: Feltrinelli, 2004), pp. 159–60.

5. Homer, *The Odyssey*, 1.413, trans. Robert Fagles (New York: Viking Penguin, 1996), p. 89; Mary Beard, "Sappho Speaks," in *Confronting the Classics* (London: Profile, 2013), p. 31. (In the afterword to her collection, Beard noted that, in retrospect, she may have been "perhaps a bit over-enthusiastic" about the different mouths of the Delphic priestess [p. 285].)

6. Saint Augustine, *The City of God*, 18.9, trans. Henry Bettenson (Harmondsworth, U.K.: Penguin, 1984), pp. 771–72; Gerda Lerner, *The Creation of Patriarchy* (New York: Oxford University Press, 1986), p. 213.

7. Simone de Beauvoir, *Le Deuxième Sexe* (Paris: Gallimard, 1949), p. 31; *Paradiso*, I:109–14, "Ne l'ordine ch'io dico sono accline/tutte nature, per diverse sorti,/più al principio loro e men vicine;//onde si muovono a diversi porti/per lo gran mar de l'essere, e ciascuna/con istinto a lei dato che la porti."

8. *Purgatorio*, V:130–36, "Siena mi fé, disfecemi Maremma."

9. *Inferno*, V:142, "E caddi come corpo morto cade." The thirteenth-century romances *Lancelot du lac* and *Mort Artu* have both been suggested as possibilities for Paolo and Francesca's book.

10. *Paradiso*, III:117, "non fu dal vel del cor già mai disciolta"; 123, "come per acqua cupa cosa grave."

11. Lerner, *Creation of Patriarchy*, p. 222.

12. *Inferno*, II:94–95, "che si compiange/di questo'mpedimento"; 98, "il tuo fedele"; 104, "ché non soccori quei che t' amò tanto."

13. Marina Warner related this story in a personal communication.

14. "S'il y a cent femmes et un cochon, le cochon l'emporte." Nicole Brossard, "The Volatility of Meaning," the Paget/Hoy lecture delivered on 11 March 2013 at the University of Calgary.

15. Robespierre, "Discours du 15 mai," in *Oeuvres de Maximilien Robespierre*, 10 vols. (Paris: Armand Colin, 2010), vol. 6, p. 358.

16. J.-P. Rabaut Saint-Etienne, *Précis historique de la Révolution* (Paris, 1792), p. 200, quoted in Jeremy Jennings, "The *Déclaration des Droits de l'Homme et du Citoyen* and Its Critics in France: Reaction and *Idéologie,*" *Historical Journal* 35, no. 4 (1992): 840.

17. The comte d'Antraigues, quoted ibid., p. 841; Archives parlementaires, VIII (Paris, 1875), p. 453, quoted ibid.

18. Ibid., pp. 842–43.

19. Chaumette, quoted in Joan Wallach Scott, "French Feminists and the Rights of 'Man,'" *History Workshop* 28 (Autumn 1989): 3; Marquis de Condorcet, *Sur l'admission des femmes au droit de cité* (1790), in *Oeuvres*, ed. A. Condorcet O'Connor and A. F. Arago, 3 vols. (Paris: Firmin Didot, 1847), vol. 2, pp. 126–27.

20. Convention of 1893, quoted in Benoîte Groult, *Ainsi soit Olympe de Gouges* (Paris: Grasset, 2013), p. 57.

21. Ibid., p. 50; *Voltaire en sa correspondence*, ed. Raphaël Roche, vol. 8 (Bordeaux: L'Escampette, 1999), p. 65.

22. Olympe de Gouges, *Mémoire de Mme de Valmont* (Paris: Côté-Femmes, 2007), p. 12.

23. Pompignon, quoted in Groult, *Ainsi soit Olympe de Gouges*, pp. 25–26.

24. The anti-slavery movement in America read in the *Commedia* arguments to sustain their struggle, and in the nineteenth and twentieth centuries, African American writers found in it inspiration and guidance. See Dennis Looney, *Freedom Readers: The African American Reception of Dante Alighieri and the "Divine Comedy"* (Notre Dame, Ind.: University of Notre Dame Press, 2011).

25. Jules Michelet, *Les Femmes de la Revolution*, 2nd rev. ed. (Paris: Adolphe Delahays, 1855), p. 105.

26. Groult, *Ainsi soit Olympe de Gouges*, pp. 75–77.

27. Ms 872, fols. 288–89, Bibliothèque historique de la Ville de Paris, quoted in Olympe de Gouges, *Écrits politiques, 1792–1793*, vol. 2 (Paris: Côté-femmes, 1993), p. 36.

28. Miguel de Cervantes, *El Ingenioso Hidalgo Don Quijote de la Mancha*, 1.13.

29. Plato, *The Republic*, 10.15, p. 835.

II
What Is an Animal?

Chapter opener: Barry Holstun Lopez, *Of Wolves and Men* (New York: Scribner's, 1978), pp. 4, 284; Pablo Neruda, "Si Dios está en mi verso," in *Crespuculario (1920–1923)*, in *Obras Completas*, vol. 1 (Barcelona: Galaxia Gutenberg, Círculo de Lectores, 1999), pp. 131–32.

1. *Inferno*, VIII:42, "via costà con li altri cani"; XIII:125, "nere cagne, bramose e correnti"; XVII: 49–51, "non altrimenti fan di state i cani / or col ceffo or col piè, quando son morsi / o da pulci o da mosche o da tafani"; XXI:44, "mastino sciolto"; XXI:68, "cani a

dosso al poverello"; XXIII:18, "'l cane a quella lievre ch'elli acceffa"; XXX:20, "sì come cane"; XXXII:71, "visi cagnazzi"; XXXII:105, latrando"; XXXIII:77–78, "co' denti, / che furo a l'osso, come d'un can, forti"; *Purgatorio*, XIV:46–47, "botoli . . . ringhiosi."

2. *Paradiso*, VIII:97–148.

3. Guillaume Mollet, *Les Papes d'Avignon*, 9th rev. ed. (Paris: Letouzey and Ané, 1950), p. 392.

4. *Paradiso*, XXXIII:145.

5. Ibid., II:8–9, "Minerva spira, e conducemi Appollo, / e nove Musi mi dimostran l'Orse"; XXII:152; XXXIII:143.

6. *Purgatorio*, XX:13–14, "nel cui girar par che si creda / le condizion di qua giù tras-mutarsi"; *Inferno*, I:101; *Purgatorio*, XX:13–15.

7. "D'enz de sale uns veltres avalat": *La Chanson de Roland*, 57.730, edited and trans-lated into modern French by Joseph Bédier (Paris: L'Edition d'art, 1922), p. 58; Giovanni Boccaccio, *Esposizioni sopra la Comedia di Dante*, ed. Giorgio Padoan, in *Tutte le opere di Giovanni Boccaccio*, ed. Vittore Branca (Milan: Mondadori, 1900), vol. 6, p. 73; *Inferno*, I:102, "che la farà morir con doglia"; Dante Alighieri, *Epistola* VII:5, in *Le opere di Dante: testo critico della Società dantesca italiana*, ed. M. Barbi et al. (Florence: Bemporad, 1921), p. 426.

8. *Purgatorio* I:13, "dolce color d'oriental zaffiro."

9. Dante Alighieri, *Epistola* XIII:10, in *Opere di Dante*, p. 437.

10. *Inferno*, III:9, "Lasciate ogne speranza, voi ch'intrate."

11. Ismail Kadare, *Dante, l'incontournable*, translated from the Albanian by Tedi Pa-pavrami (Paris: Fayard, 2005), pp. 38–39.

12. *Inferno*, V:121–23, "Nessun maggior dolore / che ricordarsi del tempo felice / ne la miseria"; XXIV:151, "E detto l'ho perché doler ti debbia!"; *Paradiso*, XVII:55–60, "Tu lascerai ogne cosa diletta / più caramente; e questo è quello strale / che l'arco de lo essilio pria saetta. // Tu proverai sì come sa di sale / lo pane altrui e come è duro calle / lo scendere e 'l salir per l'altrui scale."

13. Ibid., XXXIII:55–56, "maggio / che 'l parlar mostra."

14. Dante Alighieri, *Convivio* I:3, in *Opere di Dante*, p. 147; *Inferno*, XV:88, "Ciò che narrate di mio corso scrivo"; *Paradiso*, XVII:98–99, "s'infutura la tua vita / via più là che 'l punir di lor perfidie."

15. *Paradiso*, XV:97–126.

16. Franco Sacchetti, *Trecentonovelle* (Rome: Salerno, 1996), p. 167; Leon Battista Al-berti, *Il libro della famiglia*, ed. Ruggiero Romano and Alberto Tenenti; rev. ed., ed. Fran-cesco Furlan (Turin: Giulio Einaudi, 1996), p. 210.

17. Brunetto Latini, *Li Livres dou tresor* (The Book of the Treasure), trans. Paul Barrette and Spurgeon Baldwin (New York: Garland, 1993), pp. 133–34; Pierre de Beauvais, *Besti-aire*, in *Bestiaires du Moyen Age*, set in modern French by Gabriel Bianciotto (Paris: Edi-tions Stock, 1980), p. 65; San Isidoro de Sevilla, *Etimologías*, chap. 12, ed. J. Oroz Reta and M. A. Marcos Casquero (Madrid: Biblioteca de Autores Cristianos, la Editorial Católica, 2009).

18. Tobit 5:16 and 11:4; David Gordon White, *Myths of the Dog-Man* (Chicago: University of Chicago Press, 1991), p. 44.

19. *Inferno*, I:4, "dir qual era è cosa dura."

20. *Inferno*, XVII:74–75; XVIII:28–33; *Purgatorio*, XVII:1–9; *Paradiso*, XII:86–87.

21. *Inferno*, XXV:58–66.

22. Thomas Aquinas, *Summa Theologica*, pt. 1, q. 102, art. 2, 5 vols., trans. Fathers of the English Dominican Province (1948; repr. Notre Dame, Ind.: Christian Classics, 1981), vol. 1, p. 501; Saint Augustine, *On the Free Choice of the Will*, 3.23.69, in *On the Free Choice of the Will, On Grace and Free Choice, and Other Writings*, ed. and trans. Peter King (Cambridge: Cambridge University Press, 2010), p. 52 (animals do not suffer); Saint Augustine, *The City of God*, 2.4, trans. Henry Bettenson (Harmondsworth, U.K.: Penguin, 1984), p. 475; Cicero, *De natura deorum*, 2.53.133, trans. H. Rackham (Cambridge: Harvard University Press, 2005), p. 251; Pierre Le Hir, "8,7 millions d'espèces," *Le Monde*, 27 August 2011.

23. Saint Ambrose, *Hexameron*, chap. 4, trans. John. J. Savage (Washington, D.C.: Catholic University of America Press, 1961), p. 235.

24. Marie de France, "Le Lai de Bisclavret," in *Lais*, ed. G. S Burgess (London: Bristol Classical Press, G. Duckworth, 2001); *Inferno*, VI:18, "graffia li spiriti ed iscoia ed isquatra"; *Paradiso*, XII:58–60.

25. *Paradiso*, XXX:22, "vinto mi concedo"; X:27, "quella materia ond'io son fatto scriba."

26. *Inferno*, I:85, "lo mio maestro"; *Purgatorio*, XXVII:86; XXVII:139–40, "Non aspettar mio dir più né mio cenno; / libero, dritto e sano è tuo arbitrio"; XXVIII:2, "la divina foresta."

12
What Are the Consequences of Our Actions?

Chapter opener: Stendhal, *Le Rouge et le noir*, ed. Henri Martineau (Paris: Editions Garnier Frères, 1958), p. 376; obituary of General Jorge Rafael Videla, *El País*, 17 May 2013; Andrew Kenny, "Giving Thanks for the Bombing of Hiroshima," *The Spectator*, 30 July 2005.

1. *Purgatorio*, III:76–77, "dove la montagna giace, / sì che possibil sia l'andare in suso"; 79–87, "Come le pecorelle escon del chiuso / a una, a due, a tre, e altre stanno / timedette atterando l'occhio e l'muso; // e ciò che fa la prima, e l'altre fanno, / addossandosi a lei, s'ella s'arresta, / semplici e quete, e lo 'mperché non sanno; // sí vid' io muovere a venir la testa / di quella mandra fortunata allotta, / pudica in faccia e ne l'andare onesta."

2. Ibid., 107–8, "biondo era e bello e di gentile aspetto / ma l'un de' cigli un colpo avea diviso"; *Paradiso*, III:109–20.

3. *Inferno*, X:119. Friedrich Rückert, "Barbarossa" (1824), in *Kranz der Zeit* (Stuttgart: Cotta, 1817), vol. 2, pp. 270–71.

4. *Purgatorio*, III:132, "a lume spento." "Sine croce, sine luce" (without cross, without light) was a medieval incantation used for the burial of excommunicants.

5. *Paradiso,* XXVII:22–27, "Quelli ch'usurpa in terra il luogo mio, / il luogo mio, il luogo mio che vaca / ne la presenza del Figliuol di Dio, // fatt' ha del cimitero mio cloaca / del sangue e de la puzza; onde 'l perverso / che cadde di qua sú, là giú si placa."

6. Christ's injunction appears three times: Mark 12:17, Matthew 22:21, and Luke 20:25; *Inferno,* XXVIII:30, "vedi com'io mi dilacco."

7. Lorenzo Valla, *On the Donation of Constantine,* trans. G. W. Bowersock (Cambridge: Harvard University Press, 2007); *Purgatorio,* XXXIII:55–57; *Paradiso,* XX:56, "sotto buona intenzion che fé mal frutto."

8. *Purgatorio,* III:120, "piangendo, a quei che volontier perdona"; 137, "al fin si penta." The *Catholic Encyclopedia* defines *anathema* thus: "The Roman Pontifical distinguishes three sorts of excommunication: minor excommunication, formerly incurred by a person holding communication with anyone under the ban of excommunication; major excommunication, pronounced by the Pope in reading a sentence; and anathema, or the penalty incurred by crimes of the gravest order, and solemnly promulgated by the Pope. In passing this sentence, the pontiff is vested in amice, stole, and a violet cope, wearing his mitre, and assisted by twelve priests clad in their surplices and holding lighted candles. He takes his seat in front of the altar or in some other suitable place, and pronounces the formula of anathema which ends with these words: 'Wherefore in the name of God the All-powerful, Father, Son, and Holy Ghost, of the Blessed Peter, Prince of the Apostles, and of all the saints, in virtue of the power which has been given us of binding and loosing in Heaven and on earth, we deprive N— himself and all his accomplices and all his abettors of the Communion of the Body and Blood of Our Lord, we separate him from the society of all Christians, we exclude him from the bosom of our Holy Mother the Church in Heaven and on earth, we declare him excommunicated and anathematized and we judge him condemned to eternal fire with Satan and his angels and all the reprobate, so long as he will not burst the fetters of the demon, do penance and satisfy the Church; we deliver him to Satan to mortify his body, that his soul may be saved on the day of judgment.' Whereupon all the assistants respond: '*Fiat, fiat, fiat.*' The pontiff and the twelve priests then cast to the ground the lighted candles they have been carrying, and notice is sent in writing to the priests and neighboring bishops of the name of the one who has been excommunicated and the cause of his excommunication, in order that they may have no communication with him" ([New York: Appleton, 1905–14], vol. i).

9. John Freccero, "Manfred's Wounds," in *Dante: The Poetics of Conversion,* ed. Rachel Jacoff (Cambridge: Harvard University Press, 1986), pp. 200–201.

10. *Purgatorio,* III:121–41, "Orribili furon li peccati miei; / ma la bontà infinita ha sí gran braccia, / che prende ciò che si rivolge a lei. // . . . Per lor maladizion sí non si perde, / che non possa tornar, l'etterno amore, / mentre che la speranza ha fior del verde. // Vero è che quale in contumacia more / di Santa Chiesa, ancor ch'al fin si penta, / star li convien da questa ripa in fore, // per ognun tempo ch'elli è stato, trenta, / in sua presunzïon, se tal decreto / piú corto per buon prieghi non diventa."

11. *Purgatorio,* III:25–27, 124–32; Ezekiel 37:3.

12. Guillaume de Lorris and Jean de Meung, *Le Roman de la rose,* Continuation par Jean

de Meung, vv. 6705–6726, ed. Daniel Poition (Paris: Garnier-Flammarion, 1974), p. 204; *The Mabinogion*, trans. Lady Charlotte Guest (London: Dent, 1906), pp. 142–50; Charles of Anjou, quoted in Arno Borst, *Medieval Worlds: Barbarians, Heretics and Artists*, trans. Eric Hansen (Chicago: University of Chicago Press, 1992), p. 209.

13. See Charles W. C. Oman, *The Art of War in the Middle Ages, A.D. 378–1515*, rev. and ed. John H. Beeler (Ithaca: Cornell University Press, 1953), pp. 7–9.

14. Giovanni Villani, *Nuova cronica*, ed. Giovanni Porta (Parma: Ugo Guanda, 1991).

15. Joseph Needham, with the collaboration of Ho Ping-Yü, Lu Gwei-Djen, and Wang Ling, *Chemistry and Chemical Technology: Military Technology; The Gunpowder Epic*, vol. 5, pt. 7 of *Science and Civilisation in China* (Cambridge: Cambridge University Press, 1986), pp. 1–7 and 579.

16. Francis Bacon, *The Works of Francis Bacon*, 10 vols. (London: W. Baynes and Son/ Dublin: R. M. Tims, 1824), vol. 9, p. 167.

17. James Burke, *Connections* (London: Macmillan, 1978), p. 70.

18. *Inferno*, XXI:7–18.

19. Ibid, 88–90, "E 'l duca mio a me: 'O tu che siedi / tra li scheggion del ponte quatto quatto, / sicuramente omai a me to riedi.'"

20. Proust, quoted in Ray Monk, *J. Robert Oppenheimer: A Life Inside the Center* (New York: Anchor, 2012), p. 114.

21. Kai Bird and Martin J. Sherwin, *American Prometheus: The Triumph and Tragedy of J. Robert Oppenheimer* (New York: Knopf, 2005).

22. "A Petition to the President of the United States," 17 July 1945, U.S. National Archives, Record Group 77, Records of the Chief of Engineers, Manhattan Engineer District, Harrison-Bundy File, folder 76, available at http://www.dannen.com/decision/45-07-17.html.

23. Oppenheimer, quoted in Robert Jungk, *Brighter than a Thousand Suns: A Personal History of the Atomic Scientists*, trans. James Cleugh (Harmondsworth, U.K.: Penguin, 1960).

24. Tibbets, quoted in Monk, *J. Robert Oppenheimer*, p. 462, ellipsis in original.

25. Father Siemes, quoted in John Hersey, *Hiroshima* (New York: Knopf, 1946), pp. 117–18; *Paradiso*, XVIII:91–93.

26. Oppenheimer, quoted in Monk, *J. Robert Oppenheimer*, p. 115, ellipsis in original.

13
What Can We Possess?

Chapter opener: Bruno Ducharme, Estelle Lemaître, and Jean-Michel Fleury, eds., *ABCD: Une collection d'Art Brut*, ouvrage réalisé à l'occasion de l'exposition "Folies de la beauté," au Musée Campredon de l'Isle-sur-la Sorgue, du 8 juillet au 22 octobre 2000 (Arles: Actes Sud, 2000), pp. 282–83; James Buchan, *Frozen Desire: The Meaning of Money* (New York: Farrar, Straus and Giroux, 1997), pp. 18, 269; *Inferno*, XV:37–39, "qual di questa gregga / s'arresta punto, giace poi cent' anni / sanz' arrostarsi quando 'l foco il feggia"; World Bank indicators in *Le Monde diplomatique,* February 2002, p. 13; Félix Luna, *Argentina: de Perón a Lanusse, 1943–1973* (Buenos Aires: Planeta, 2000), p. 43.

1. Leonardo Bruni, *History of the Florentine People,* 1.2.30, ed. and trans. James Hankins (Cambridge: Harvard University Press, 2001), p. 141; Giovanni Villani, *Nuova cronica,* ed. Giovanni Porta (Parma: Ugo Guanda, 1991), vol. 2, p. 52.

2. Dante Alighieri, *Epistola* XIII, in *Le opere di Dante: testo critico della Società dantesca italiana,* ed. M. Barbi et al. (Florence: Bemporad, 1921), pp. 436–46.

3. *Inferno,* I:32–33, "leggera e presta molto, / che di pel macolato era coverta"; on the leopard as Venus's familiar see Virgil, *Aeneid,* 1.323; *Inferno,* I:47, "con la test' alta, e con rabbiosa fame"; 49–54, "Ed una lupa, che di tute brame / sembiava carca ne la sua magrezza, / e molte genti fé già viver grame, // questa mi porse tanto di gravezza / con la paura ch'uscia di sua vista, / ch'io perdei la speranza de l'altezza."

4. Ibid., 94–99, "ché questa bestia, per la qual tu gride, / non lascia altrui passar per la sua via, / ma tanto lo 'mpedisce che i'uccide; // e ha natura sì malvagia e ria, / che mai non empie la bramosa voglia, / e dopo 'l pasto ha più fame che pria."

5. Thomas Aquinas, *Summa Theologica,* pt. 2, q. 32, art. 5, 5 vols., trans. Fathers of the English Dominican Province (1948; repr. Notre Dame, Ind.: Christian Classics, 1981), vol. 3, p. 1322.

6. *Inferno,* VII:8, "maledetto lupo"; 30, "'Perchè tieni?' e 'Perchè burli?'"; 53–54, "la sconoscente vita che i fé sozzi, / ad ogne conoscenza or li fa bruni"; 64–66, "tutto l'oro ch'è sotto la luna / e che già fu, di quest' anime stanche / non potrebbe fare posare una."

7. *Purgatorio,* XXII:43–45, "Allor m'accorsi che troppo aprir l' ali / potean le mani spendere, e pente' mi / così di quel come de li altri mali."

8. *Inferno,* XVII:46–51, "Per li occhi fora scoppiava lor duolo; / di qua, di là soccorrien con le mani / quando a' vapori, e quando al caldo suolo: // non altrimenti fan di state i cani / or col ceffo o col piè, quando son morsi / o da pulci o da mosche o da tafani."

9. Gerard of Siena, "On Why Usury Is Prohibited," translated from MS 894, fol. 68r–68v, Leipzig, Universitätsbibliothek, quoted in *Medieval Italy,* ed. Katherine L. Jansen, Joanna Drell, and Frances Andrews (Philadelphia: University of Pennsylvania Press, 2009), p. 106; Jorge Manrique, "Coplas a la muerte de su padre," in *Obras completas,* ed. Augusto Cortina (Madrid: Espasa-Calpe, 1979), p. 117.

10. John T. Gilchrist, *The Church and Economic Activity in the Middle Ages* (New York: Macmillan, 1969), p. 218.

11. Ibid., p. 221.

12. Charles Dickens, *A Christmas Carol,* in *The Complete Works of Charles Dickens,* vol. 25 (New York: Society of English and French Literature, n.d.), p. 34.

13. Ibid., pp. 5, 4; Pseudo-Macarius, *Spiritual Homilies,* quoted in Jacques Lacarrière, *Les Hommes fous de Dieu* (Paris: Fayard, 1975), p. 1.

14. Charles Dickens, *Little Dorrit,* in *Complete Works of Charles Dickens,* vol. 25, pp. 171, 352.

15. Paul Krugman, "Bits and Barbarism," *New York Times,* 22 December 2013.

16. Aristotle, *The Politics,* 1.8 and 1.11, trans. T. A. Sinclair (Harmondsworth, U.K.: Penguin, 1962), pp. 42–43, 46.

17. Dante Alighieri, *Convivio,* IV:XVII, 10, in *Opere di Dante,* p. 285.

18. Helen Langdon, *Caravaggio: A Life* (London: Chatto and Windus, 1998), pp. 250–51; Peter Ackroyd, *Dickens* (London: Sinclair-Stevenson, 1990), p. 487.

19. Sebastião Salgado, *Trabalhadores: Uma arqueologia da era industrial* (São Paulo: Companhia das Letras, 1997), pp. 318–319; *Inferno,* III:112–17, "Come d'autunno si levan le foglie / l'una appresso de l'altra, fin che 'l ramo / vede a terra tutte le sue spoglie, // similmente il mal seme d'Adamo / gittansi di quel lito ad una ad una / per cenni come augel per suo riciamo." The image appears in Homer; Dante probably took it from Virgil.

20. Oscar Wilde, "The Young King," in *A Garden of Pomegranates* (1891), in *The Works of Oscar Wilde,* ed. G. F. Maine (London: Collins, 1948), p. 232.

21. Ibid., p. 229.

14

How Can We Put Things in Order?

1. *Inferno,* III:5–6, "fecemi la divina podestate, / la somma sapïenza e 'l primo amore."

2. Aristotle, *Nicomachean Ethics,* 7.1–6.

3. *Purgatorio,* XVII:94–96, "Lo naturale è sempre sanza errore, / ma l'altro puote errar per mal obietto / o per troppo o per poco di vigore."

4. *Paradiso,* III:70–72, "Frate, la nostra volontà quïeta / virtù di carità, che fa volerne / sol quel ch'avemo, e d'altro non ci asseta"; 85, "E 'n la sua volontade è nostra pace."

5. Vladimir Nabokov, *Lectures in Literature,* ed. Fredson Bowers (New York: Harcourt Brace Jovanovich, 1980), pp. 62, 31, 257, 303.

6. Ashmolean Museum catalogue, quoted in Jan Morris, *The Oxford Book of Oxford* (Oxford: Oxford University Press, 1978), pp. 110–11.

7. George R. Marek, *The Bed and the Throne: The Life of Isabella d'Este* (New York: Harper and Row, 1976), p. 164.

8. Francis Bacon, *Gesta Grayorum* (1688) (Oxford: Oxford University Press, 1914), p. 35; Roger Chartier, ed. *A History of Private Life,* vol. 3: *Passions of the Renaissance,* trans. Arthur Golhammer (Cambridge: Harvard University Press, 1989), p. 288; Patrick Mauriès, *Cabinets of Curiosities* (London: Thames and Hudson, 2011), p. 32.

9. Lorenza Mochi and Francesco Solinas, eds. *Cassiano dal Pozzo: I segreti di un Collezionista* (Rome: Galleria Borghese, 2000), p. 27; Marsilio Ficino, *Book of Life,* trans. Charles Boer (Irving, Tex.: Spring, 1980), p. 7.

10. Luciano Canfora, *La biblioteca scomparsa* (Palermo: Sellerio, 1987), p. 56; Mustafa El-Abbadi, *La antigua biblioteca de Alejandría: Vida y destino,* translated from the Arabic by José Luis García-Villalba Sotos (Madrid: UNESCO, 1994), p. 34.

11. Otlet, quoted in Françoise Levie, *L'Homme qui voulait classer le monde: Paul Otlet et le Mundaneum* (Brussels: Impressions Nouvelles, 2006), p. 33.

12.Ibid., pp. 107, 271.

13. *Paradiso,* XXXIII:124–126, "O luce etterna che sola in te sidi, / sola t'intendi, e da te intelleta / e intendente te ami e arridi!"

14. See Adina Hoffman and Peter Cole, *Sacred Trash: The Lost and Found World of the Cairo Geniza* (New York: Schocken, 2011).

15. Quoted in Levie, *L'Homme qui voulait classer le monde,* p. 72.

16. Ibid., pp. 69–70.

17. Henry James, Letter of 4 April 1912, in *Letters,* vol. 4, ed. Leon Edel (Cambridge: Harvard University Press, 1984), p. 612; Henry James, *The Spoils of Poynton* (London: Bodley Head, 1967), pp. 38, 44.

18. Levie, *L'Homme qui voulait classer le monde,* p. 225.

19. Quoted in W. Boyd Rayward, "Visions of Xanadu: Paul Otlet (1868–1944) and Hypertext," *Jasis* 45 (1994): 242.

20. Levie, *L'Homme qui voulait classer le monde,* pp. 293–308.

21. Ibid., pp. 47–48.

22. Jorge Luis Borges, "El congreso," in *El libro de arena* (Buenos Aires: Emecé, 1975).

15
What Comes Next?

Chapter opener: The Book of Common Prayer (1662), 90:10 (Cambridge: Cambridge University Press, 2003), p. 463; Jakob und Wilhelm Grimm, "Die Boten des Todes," *Die Märchen der Brüder Grimm* (Leipzig: Insel Verlag, 1910), pp. 294–95; May Swenson, "The Centaur," in *To Mix with Time: New and Selected Poems* (New York: Scribner's, 1963), p. 86; Francesco Petrarca, *Le familiari,* vol. 3: *bks. 12–19,* 22:2, ed. Vittorio Rossi (Florence: Casa editrice Le Lettrere, 2009), p. 68; Seneca, "On the Shortness of Life," in *The Stoic Philosophy of Seneca,* trans. Moses Hadas (Garden City, N.Y.: Doubleday, 1958), p. 73; Samuel L. Knapp, *The Life of Lord Timothy Dexter, with Sketches of the Eccentric Characters That Composed His Associates, Including His Own Writings* (Boston: J. E. Tilton, 1858).

1. *Purgatorio,* III:26, "dentro al quale io facea ombra"; *Purgatorio,* XXX:124–25, "su la soglia fui / di mia seconda etade"; *Inferno,* XXXIII: 13–75; "The famous verse 75 of the penultimate canto of the *Inferno* has created [for Dante's commentators] a problem that stems from a confusion between art and reality. . . . In the gloom of his Tower of Hunger, Ugolino devours and does not devour the beloved corpses, and that wavering imprecision, that uncertainty, is the strange matter of which he is made. Thus, with two possible agonies, Dante dreamt him and thus shall dream him the generations to come" (Jorge Luis Borges, "El falso problema de Ugolino," in *Nueve ensayos dantescos* [Madrid: Espasa Calpe, 1982]), pp. 105 and 111; *Inferno,* XIII:31–151; *Paradiso,* XXI:124; see Chapter 12, above.

2. *Inferno,* I:116–17, "li antichi spiriti dolenti / ch'a la seconda morte ciascun grida."

3. Yukio Mishima, *La ética del samurái en el Japón moderno,* translated from the Japanese by Makiko Sese y Carlos Rubio (Madrid: Alianza Editorial, 2013), p. 108.

4. *Anagata Vamsadesance: The Sermon of the Chronicle-To-Be,* trans. Udaya Meddagama, ed. John Clifford Holt (Delhi: Motilal Banarsidass, 2010), p. 33.

5. Mary Boyce, *Zoroastrians: Their Religious Beliefs and Practices* (London: Routledge, 2001), pp. 56–70.

6. *Talmud Megillah* 15a.

7. *The Koran,* sura 76, trans. N. J. Dawood, rev. ed. (Harmondsworth, U.K.: Penguin, 1993), p. 413–14; Ibn 'Arabi, quoted in Mahmoud Ayoub, *The Qur'an and Its Interpreters* (Albany: State University of New York Press, 1984), vol. 1, p. 125; Abu Huraryra, quoted ibid., vol. 1, p. 89.

8. *Koran,* sura 75, p. 412; sura 33, p. 299; sura 6, p. 97; sura 17, p. 200; Imam Muslim, *Sahih Muslim,* vols. 1–4, trans. Abdul Hamid Sidiqi (Dehli: Kitab Bharan, 2000), p. 67.

9. Miguel Asín Palacios, *Dante y el Islam* (1927) (Pamplona: Urgoiti, 2007), p. 118; Louis Massignon, "Les recherches d'Asín Palacios sur Dante," *Ecrits mémorables,* vol. 1 (Paris: Robert Laffont, 2009), p. 105; Abu l-'Ala' al-Ma'arri, *The Epistle of Forgiveness,* vol. 1: *A Vision of Heaven and Hell,* ed. and trans. Geert Jan van Gelder and Gregor Schoeler (New York: New York University Press, 2013), pp. 67–323.

10. "Why We Die," in *Rasa'il Ikhwan al-Safa* (The Epistles of the Sincere Brethren), in *Classical Arabic Literature: A Library of Arabic Literature Anthology,* select. and trans. Geert Jan van Gelder (New York: New York University Press, 2013), pp. 221–22.

11. G. B. Caird, *A Commentary on the Revelation of St. John the Divine* (New York: Harper and Row, 1966), p. 11.

12. "Victorinus," in *The New Catholic Encyclopedia* (Farmington Hills, Mich.: CUA Press and the Gale Group, 2002).

13. See Crawford Gribben and David George Mullan, eds., *Literature and the Scottish Reformation* (Cape Breton, Canada: Ashgate, 2009), p. 15. The Scientologist L. Ron Hubbard and his followers also adopt this apocalyptic reading,

14. See E. Ann Matter, "The Apocalypse in Early Medieval Exegesis," in *The Apocalypse in the Middle Ages,* ed. Richard K. Emmerson and Bernard McGinn (Ithaca: Cornell University Press 1992), pp. 38–39.

15. Saint Augustine, *The City of God,* trans. Henry Bettenson (Harmondsworth, U.K.: Penguin, 1984), pp. 906–18, 907, 918.

16. Philippe Ariès, *Essais sur l'histoire de la mort en Occident du Moyen Age à nos jours* (Paris: Editions du Seuil, 1975), p. 21.

17. Fernando de Rojas y "Antiguo Autor," *La Celestina: Tragicomedia de Calisto y Melibea,* 4.5, ed. Francisco J. Lobera, Guillermo Serés, Paloma Díaz-Mas, Carlos Mota, Iñigo Ruiz Arzalluz, and Francisco Rico (Madrid: Real Academia Española, 2011), p. 110. The image of the inn also appears in Cicero's "On Old Age" (*De senectute*): "When I leave life, therefore, I shall feel as if I am leaving a hostel rather than a home." In Cicero, *Selected Works,* trans. Michael Grant, rev. ed. (Harmondsworth, U.K.: Penguin, 1971), p. 246.

18. Ariès, *Essais sur l'histoire de la mort en Occident,* p. 30.

19. Edgar Allan Poe, "The Philosophy of Composition," in *On Poetry and the Poets,*

vol. 6 of *The Works of Edgar Allan Poe,* ed. E. C. Stedman and G. E. Woodberry (New York: Scribner's, 1914), p. 46.

20. Ariès, *Essais sur l'histoire de la mort en Occident,* p. 67; Isherwood, quoted in Gore Vidal, "Pink Triangle and Yellow Star," *Nation,* 14 October 1981.

21. Tim Radford, "A Prize to Die For," *The Guardian,* 19 September 2002. For those winners who preferred not to wait for the resurrection prize, the alternative was a trip to Hawaii. Freezing the body to be resurrected in the future is the subject of a Howard Fast story, "The Cold, Cold Box," in *Time and the Riddle* (Pasadena, Calif.: Ward Ritchie Press, 1975), pp. 219–31.

22. Cicero, "On Old Age," p. 247.

23. *Paradiso,* XXXIII:32–33, "ogne nube li disleghi / di sua mortalità co' prieghi tuoi."

24. *Inferno,* IV:141, "Seneca morale"; Seneca, "On the Shortness of Life," p. 48.

25. The *Corpus Inscriptionum Latinarum* (*CIL*) is a comprehensive collection of ancient Latin inscriptions from all corners of the Roman Empire. Public and personal inscriptions throw light on all aspects of Roman life and history. The *Corpus* continues to be updated with new editions and supplements by the Berlin-Brandenburgische Akademie der Wissenschaften, and can be accessed at http://cil.bbaw.de/cil_en/index _en.html.

26. *Inferno,* IX:112–20.

27. Giorgio Bassani, *Il giardino dei Finzi-Contini* (Turin: Giulio Einaudi, 1962), p. 3.

16
Why Do Things Happen?

1. Primo Levi, *Se questo è un uomo* (Milan: Einaudi, 1958), p. 10.

2. *Inferno,* XXVI:85–90, "Lo maggior corno de la fiamma antica / cominciò a crollarsi mormorando / pur come quella cui vento affatica. // Indi, la cima in qua e in là menando / come fosse la lingua che parlasse, / gittò voce di fuori e disse: 'Quando . . . '"; 100 ("ma misi . . .").

3. Levi, *Se questo è un uomo.* The episode appears in pages 102–5; *Inferno,* XXVI:118–20, "Considerate la vostra semenza: / fatti non foste a viver come bruti, / ma per seguir virtute e conoscenza."

4. *Inferno,* XXVI:133–35, "quando n'apparve una montagna, bruna / per la distanza, e parvemi alta tanto / quanto veduta non avëa alcuna."

5. *Inferno,* XXVI:139–41, "Tre volte il fé girar con tutte l'acque; / a la quarta levar la poppa in suso / e la prora ire in giù, com' altrui piacque."

6. *Inferno,* XVI:142, "infin che 'l mar fu sovra noi richiuso."

7. Dante, *De vulgare eloquentia,* I:v, edited and translated from the Latin by Vittorio Coletti (Milan: Garzanti, 1991), pp. 10–11.

8. Louis Ginzberg, *Legends of the Jews,* 7 vols., vol. 1: *From the Creation to Jacob,* trans. Henrietta Szold (Baltimore: Johns Hopkins University Press, 1998), pp. 5–8. For more on this legend of creation, see Chapter 5, above.

9. Philip Friedman, *Roads to Extinction: Essays on the Holocaust,* ed. Ada June Friedman (New York: Jewish Publication Society of America, 1980), p. 393.

10. Levi, *Se questo è un uomo,* p. 25.

11. Angelus Silesius, *Cherubinischer Wandersmann,* bk. 1, sect. 289, ed. Louise Gnädinger (Stuttgart: Philipp Reclam, 1984), p. 69.

12. *Inferno,* I:4, "dir qual era è cosa dura"; 8, "per trattar del ben ch'i' vi trovai"; *Paradiso,* XV: 79–81, "Ma voglia e argomento ne' mortali . . . diversamente son pennuti in ali."

13. Henri de Lubac, *Medieval Exegesis: The Four Senses of Scripture,* vol. 1, trans. Mark Sebac (Grand Rapids, Mich.: Eerdmans, 1998), p. 41. Lubac says that Musaeus was Orpheus's master, not his disciple.

14. *Paradiso,* X:131; Richard de Saint-Victor, *Liber exeptionum,* pt. 1, bk. 1, chap. 23, p. 3, ed. Jean Châtillon (Paris: Vrin: Paris, 1958), p. 12.

15. Giles Constable, *The Letters of Peter the Venerable,* 2 vols., vol. 1, bk. 4:21 (Cambridge: Harvard University Press, 1967).

16. *Inferno,* IV:80, "Onorate l'altissimo poeta"; 94, "bella scuola."

17. Virgil, *Aeneid,* 4.23, " veteris vestigia flammae"; *Purgatorio,* XXX:48, "cognosco i segni de l'antica fiamma."

18. *Inferno,* XXVI:117, "di retro al sol, del mondo sanza gente"; 133–34, "bruna / per la distanza."

19. Homer, *The Iliad,* 5.279–81, 526, 384, trans. Robert Fagles (Harmondsworth, U.K.: Viking/Penguin, 1990).

20. Martin Buber, *Tales of the Hasidim,* trans. Olga Marx (New York: Schocken, 1991), pp. 258–59.

21. *Inferno,* XXVI:114, "picciola vigilia."

22. Ibid., 125, "folle volo."

23. Franz Kafka, "In der Strafkolonie," in *Die Erzählungen und andere ausgewählte Prosa,* ed. Roger Hermes (Frankfurt-am-Main: Fischer Verlag, 2000).

24. Primo Levi, "Caro Orazio," in *Racconti e saggi* (Turin: La Stampa, 1986), p. 117.

25. "Lord, let Your light," in George Appleton, ed., *The Oxford Book of Prayer* (Oxford: Oxford University Press, 1985), p. 275.

26. *Purgatorio,* I:133, "com' altrui piacque"; II:23, "un non sapeva che bianco"; *Inferno,* XXVI:125, "de' remi facemmo ali"; *Purgatorio,* II:10–12, "Noi eravam lunghesso mare ancora, / come gente che pensa a suo cammino, / che va col cuore e col corpo dimora."

27. *Purgatorio,* II:110–11, "l'anima mia, che, con la sua persona / venendo qui, è affannata tanto!"; 106–8, "Ed io: 'Se nuova legge non ti toglie / memoria o uso a l'amoroso canto / che mi solea quetar tutte mie voglie"; the poem is in *Convivio,* bk. 3: "Amor che ne la mente mi raggiona"; *Purgatorio,* II:118–19, " . . . tutti fissi e attenti / a le sue note"; Exodus 34:3.

17
What Is True?

Chapter opener: The sisters told their story a few months after their release. See Laurence and Micheline Levesque, *Les Valises rouges* (Ottawa: Editions JCL, 1987).

1. Gershom Scholem, *Dix propositions anhistoriques sur la Cabale* (Paris: Editions de l'éclat, 2012), p 43.

2. Bruno Nardi, *Saggi e note di critica dantesca* (Milan: Riccardo Ricciardi Editore, 1966), p. 333; see, for example, Isaiah 11:5: "And righteousness shall be the girdle of his loins, and faithfulness the girdle of his reins." In the Catholic Church, before mass the priest puts on the girdle and prays, "Gird me, O Lord, with the girdle of purity."

3. *Inferno,* XVI: 118–120, "Ahi quanto cauti li uomini esser dienno / presso a color che non veggion pur l'ovra, / ma per entro i pensier miran col senno!"

4. Boccaccio speaks of Geryon in the feminine, "daughter of Erebus and Night" (*Genealogy of the Pagan Gods,* bk. 1, chap. 21, ed. and trans. Jon Solomon [Cambridge: Harvard University Press, 2011], pp. 137–39). William Blake, in one of his illustrations for the *Commedia,* gave Geryon a beardless, androgynous face.

5. *Inferno,* XVI:124–30, "Sempre a quel ver c'ha faccia di menzogna / de' l'uom chiuder le labbra fin ch'el puote, / però che sanza colpa fa vergogna; // ma qui tacer non posso; e per le note / di questa comedìa, lettor, ti giuro, / s'elle non sien di lunga grazia vòte, // ch'i' vidi . . ."

6. *Purgatorio,* XXIX:94, "ognuno era pennuto di sei ali"; 100, "ma leggi Ezechïel, che li dipigne"; 104–5, "salvo ch'a le penne, / Giovanni è meco e da lui si diparte."

7. *Inferno,* I:85, "lo mio maestro, e il mio autore"; 86–87, "tu se' solo colui da cu'io tolsi / lo bello stilo che m'ha fatto onore."

8. John Freccero, "Allegory and Autobiography," in *The Cambridge Companion to Dante,* 2nd ed., ed. Rachel Jacoff (Cambridge: Cambridge University Press, 2007), pp. 174–75.

9. Dante Alighieri, *Epistola* XIII:5 in *Le opere di Dante: testo critico della Società dantesca italiana,* ed. M. Barbi et al. (Florence: Bemporad, 1921), p. 436.

10. *Inferno,* XXIII:144, "bugiardo e padre di mensogna"; Saint Augustine, *Confessions,* 10.35, trans. R. S. Pine-Coffin (Harmondsworth, U.K.: Penguin, 1961), p. 242.

11. Jerome, quoted in Jean-Yves Boriaud, note to "Le Mensonge" in Saint Augustin, *Les Confessions, précédées de Dialogues philosophiques,* vol. 1, édition publiée sous la direction de Lucien Jerphagnon (Paris: Pléiade, 1998), p. 1363.

12. Augustine, *Confessions,* 1.13, pp. 33, 34.

13. *Inferno,* XVI:132, "meravigliosa ad ogni cor sicuro"; XVII:1–3, "Ecco la fiera con la coda aguzza, / che passa i monti e rompe muri e l'armi! / Ecco colei che tutto 'l mundo apuzza!"; Herodotus, *The Histories,* 1.205–16, trans. Aubrey de Sélincourt, revised, with an introduction and notes, by A. R. Burn (Harmondsworth, U.K.: Penguin, 1972), pp. 123–26; for the legend of Geryon see Boccaccio, *Genealogy of the Pagan Gods,* bk. 1, chap. 22, vol. 1, p. 139.

14. *Purgatorio,* XVI:67–81, "Voi che vivete ogne cagion recate / pur suso al cielo, pur come se tutto / movesse seco di necessitate. // Se così fosse, in voi fora distrutto / libero arbitrio, e non fora giustizia / per ben letizia, e per male aver lutto. // Lo cielo i vostri movimenti inizia; / non dicco tutti, ma posto ch'i 'l dica, / lume v'è dato a bene e a malizia, // e libero voler; che, se fatica / ne le prime battaglie col ciel dura, / poi vince tutto, se ben si notrica. // A maggior forza e a miglior natura / liberi soggiacete; e quella cria / la mente in voi, che 'l ciel non ha in sua cura."

15. David Hume, *A Treatise of Human Nature,* 3.2.8, ed. Ernest C. Mossner (Harmondsworth, U.K.: Penguin, 1969), p. 594.

16. Ibid., p. 594.

17. Julian Borger, "World Leaders Not Ready for Reconciliation with Mandela," *Guardian,* 6 December 2013; Jason Beattie, "Tory Grandee Smears Nelson Mandela," *Daily Mirror,* 9 December 2013.

18. Dwight Garner, "An Interview with Nadine Gordimer," *Salon,* 9 March 1998.

19. Nelson Mandela, *Long Road to Freedom* (New York: Holt, Rinehart and Winston, 2000), p. 176.

20. Garner, "Interview with Nadine Gordimer."

21. *Purgatorio,* XVI:94–96, "Onde convenne legge per fren porre; / convenne rege aver, che discernesse / de la vera cittade almen la torre."

22. Percy Bysshe Shelley, *Prometheus Unbound,* 4.573–74, in Shelley, *The Major Works,* ed. Zachary Leader and Michael O'Neill (Oxford: Oxford University Press, 2003), p. 313.

23. Carlo Collodi, *Le avventure di Pinocchio,* bilingual edition, trans. Nicolas J. Perella (Berkeley: University of California Press, 1986), p. 211.

24. *Paradiso,* V:6, "così nel bene appreso move il piede"; John Freccero, "The Firm Foot on a Journey Without a Guide," in *Dante: The Poetics of Conversion,* ed. Rachel Jacoff (Cambridge: Harvard University Press, 1986), pp. 29–54.

25. *Inferno,* I:28–30, "Poi ch'èi posato un poco il corpo lasso, / ripresi via per la pieaggia diserta, / sì che 'l piè fermo sempre era 'l più basso"; Freccero, "Firm Foot on a Journey Without a Guide," p. 31.

26. *Paradiso,* V:1, "caldo d'amore"; 7–9, "Io veggio ben sì come già resplende / ne l'intelletto tuo l'etterna luce, / che, vista, sola e sempre amore accende."

27. *Purgatorio,* XV:117, "non falsi errori."

28. Gustave Flaubert, *La Tentation de Saint Antoine,* ed. Claudine Gothot-Mersch (Paris: Gallimard, 1983), p. 214.

ACKNOWLEDGMENTS

TO WRITE THIS BOOK, I've used many editions and commentaries of Dante's *Commedia.* The best Italian edition in my view is the one by Anna Maria Chiavacci Leonardi, first published by Mondadori in 1994. In English, the version that to my taste comes closest to the music and power of the original is that of W. S. Merwin, who unfortunately translated only the *Purgatorio* and two cantos of the *Inferno* because he said he didn't like Saint Bernard and did not wish to suffer his company throughout much of the *Paradiso.* Other than Dante, *duca, signore e maestro,* I notice that several other writers have led me through these pages: Plato, Augustine, Aquinas, Montaigne, Hume, and the secret authors of the Talmud seem to be more present in this book than in all my previous ones, whose presiding deities were Lewis Carroll, Flaubert, Cervantes, and Borges.

Several of my editors have faithfully helped me with their comments and corrections. Among them, Hans-Jürgen Balmes, Valeria Ciompi, John Donatich, Luiz Schwarcz, and Marie-Catherine Vacher: to them my deepest thanks. Also to Fabio Muzi Falconi, Françoise Nyssen, Guillermo Quijas, Arturo Ramoneda, Javier Setó, and Güven Turan for their trust in a book that, for the longest time, consisted simply of a one-word title. And to Lise Bergevin, for her constancy, friendship, and generosity.

My deepest thanks to the book designer, Sonia Shannon, to the picture researcher, Danielle D'Orlando, to the indexer, Alexa Selph, and the proofreader, Jack Borrebach, and to the eagle-eyed Susan Laity, whose meticulous copyediting pointed out my *errori falsi.*

My deepest gratitude, as always, to my old friend and agent Guillermo Schavelzon, from the days when our conversations were not about illnesses. And also to Bárbara Graham, for all her efforts on my behalf.

A number of other friends helped with support and information: Professor Shaul Bassi, Professor Lina Bolzoni, Father Lucien-Jean Bord, Professors José and Lucio Burucúa, Professor Ethel Groffier, Professor Tariq S. Khawaji, Piero Lo Strologo, Dr. José Luis Moure, Lucie Pabel, Gottwalt Pankow, Ileene Smith (with whom the project was first discussed and who encouraged me to pursue it), Dr. Jillian Tomm, Dr. Khalid S. Yahya, and Marta Zocchi.

I was greatly assisted by a few vastly efficient librarians, especially Donatino Domini, director of the Biblioteca Classense in Ravenna; Patricia Jaunet of the Bibliothèques départementales de la Vienne; Arthur Kiron, director of the Jewish Institute Collections of the University of Pennsylvania; and Guy Penman, Amanda Corp, and Emma Wigham at the London Library. They justify the definition that, according to Diodorus Siculus, was inscribed above the door of the ancient Egyptian libraries: "Clinic of the Soul." Thanks also to C. Jay Irwin for his help in the first stages of the project.

A few pages of this book, in various early forms, were published in *Descant, Geist,* the *New York Times, Parnassus, La Repubblica,* the *Threepenny Review,* and *Théodore Balmoral.* To Thierry Bouchard, Kyle Jarrard, Herbert Leibowitz, Wendy Lesser, Karen Mulhallen, Stephen Osborne, and Dario Pappalardo many thanks.

Dante believed that during our voyage through life, if grace allows, we'll find a fellow soul to assist us on our way beyond the dark wood, to reflect back our questions and to help us discover whatever it is we are meant to be; above all, one whose love keeps us alive. To Craig, *dolce guida e cara,* as ever.

Alberto Manguel
MONDION, 5 MAY 2014

INDEX

Abelard, Peter, 304
Abravanel, Isaac, 93–97, 339n25
Abu Huraryra, 283
Abulafia, Abraham, 89–91
Acts of the Apostles, 303, 318
Adam, 38, 86–87; Ulysses as, 35–36
Aeneid (Virgil), 14, 19, 28–29, 33
Aeolus, 46–47
afterlife. *See* death and the afterlife
Aggadah, 281
agriculture: in ancient Rome, 158; and humans' responsibility towards nature, 157–59
Akiva ben Yoseph, 98
Alberti, Leon Battista, 210
Albertus Magnus, 22
Al-Biruni, 179
Alboino della Scala, 17
alchemy, 76
Alcidamas, 59
Alcuin of York, 23–24
Alembert, Jean Le Rond d', 26
Alexander, Pope, 223–24
Alexandria, Library of, 266
Alice's Adventures in Wonderland. See Carroll, Lewis
All's Well That Ends Well (Shakespeare), 134
al-Ma'arri, Abu l-'Ala', 284

alphabet: combinatory possibilities of, 123; Hebrew, 88
Al-Rashid, Haroun, 66
Ambrose, Saint, 214, 244
Anastasius, Pope, 257
anathema, 225, 352n8
Andersen, Hendrik, 269–70
animals: Augustine's view of, 213–14; as constellations, 205–6; devil manifested as, 214. *See also* dogs
Antaeus, 116
Apocalypse (Revelation): as described in the *Commedia,* 316; interpretations of, 285–88
Apocalypse of Paul, 20
Apocalypse of Peter, 20
Aquinas, Saint Thomas. *See* Thomas Aquinas, Saint
Arabian Nights, 66, 120
Argenti, Filippo, 171
Argentina: economic crisis in, 237; military atrocities in, 219–20; under Perón, 238
Ariès, Philippe, 288, 289
Aristophanes, 135
Aristotle, 21, 22, 54, 108–9, 173, 316; on money, 247; nature as viewed by, 158, 159, 161, 162, 163; *Nicomachean Ethics,* 258

artistic endeavor, as "false image," 91–92. *See also* literature; poetry, power of; stories

Ashmolean Museum, 263, 264

Asín Palacios, Miguel, 284

astrology, as science in Dante's time, 205–6

Athens, naming of, 187–88

atomic bomb, building of, 230–33

Attar, Fariduddin, 336n3

Atwood, Margaret, 185

Auden, W. H., 84, 85

Augustine, Saint, 23, 38, 136, 154, 168, 187; animals as viewed by, 213–14; *City of God,* 287–88; *Confessions,* 319; on lying, 317, 318–19

Augustus, Emperor, 158

Auschwitz, 307–8, 309; as distinguished from hell, 302; language as instrument of resistance at, 301–2; Primo Levi at, 297–300, 304–5

automata, 76

avarice, sin of, 242–43

Babel, Tower of, 21, 45; curse of, 86

Bacon, Francis, 4, 86, 265, 313

Bacon, Roger, 228

Barbari, Jacopo de', 101, 102

Barrows, Anita, 161

Bartolomeo della Scala, 17

Basil, Saint, 241

Bassani, Giorgio, 292

Beard, Mary, 187

Beatrice: as Dante's guide in the *Commedia,* 7, 21, 24, 52, 67, 130, 133–34, 145, 189, 208–9, 241, 325–26; as venerated in the *Vita nova,* 19, 20

Beaumarchais, Pierre Augustin Caron de, 197

Beauvais, Pierre de, 210

Beauvoir, Simone de, 189

Beckett, Samuel, 151

beekeeping, 147–48

Bellay, Joachim du, 40

Benedict XI, Pope, 17

Benevento, Battle of, 226–27

Berlin, Isaiah, 25

Bernard of Clairvaux, Saint, 21, 23, 209, 291

Bertran de Born, 27–28

Bezzuoli, Giuseppe, 227

Bhagavad Gita, 232

Bhartrihari, 120–25

Biblia rabbinica, 99

bitcoins, 246

Boccaccio, Giovanni, 6, 14, 16, 18, 28, 86, 171, 206, 325

Boethius, 16

Bomberg, Daniel, 99–101

Bonaiuto, Andrea di, 213

Bonaventure, Saint, 53, 103, 133

Bonet de Lattes, 97

Boniface VIII, Pope, 17

bonobo apes, 118–19

books: alternative forms of, 267–68; arranging of, 255–56; as oracles, 83–84. *See also* Jewish books, published in Venice; literature; reading

Borges, Jorge Luis, 6, 89, 113, 279, 292–93, 336n3; "The Congress," 271; Universal Library of, 123

Bragadin, Pietro, 99

Breughel, Pieter the Elder, *Tower of Babel,* 250

Bringhurst, Robert, 80, 81

Brod, Max, 119, 178

Brodsky, Joseph, 84

Browning, Elizabeth Barrett, 201

Bruni, Leonardo, 239

Buber, Martin, 306–7

Buchan, James, 236–37

Buddha, 280–81

Buddhism, and death, 280–81

deforestation, 160. *See also* forests; nature

Deleuze, Gilles, 57

delle Vigne, Pier, 153, 154

Delphi, 178–79

Deuteronomy, book of, 96, 98

De vulgari eloquentia (Dante), 65–66, 86–88, 125, 154, 301

Dewey, Melvin, 267

Dewey decimal system, 267, 268

Dexter, Timothy, 278

Dickens, Charles, 250; *A Christmas Carol,* 245–46; *Little Dorrit,* 246; *Oliver Twist,* 201–2

Diderot, Denis, 26

Dio Chrysostom, 45

Diocletian, Emperor, 285

Diomedes, 33, 305–6, 307

Dodgson, Charles Lutwidge. *See* Carroll, Lewis

dogs: in the *Commedia,* 204, 207, 212–13, 217; as constellations, 205; "dog" as term of insult, 204, 207; as faithful companions, 210–11; in literature, 201–3; as omen, 215; rage embodied by, 214–15

Dominic, Saint, 215

Donati, Corso, 17

Donati, Forese, 191

Don Quixote (Cervantes), 49, 109, 135, 199, 340n5

Dostoyevsky, Fyodor, 177–78

Doyle, Arthur Conan, 13

Duckworth, Robinson, 138, 139–40

Dürer, Albrecht, 176

Durrell, Lawrence, *Constance,* 166

Dürrenmatt, Friedrich, 222

Ecclesiasticus, 13, 26

Eco, Umberto, 91

ecopsychology, 160–61

educational institutions, 3–4, 8

Einstein, Albert, 222

Eliezer ben Hyrcanus, Rabbi, 94–95, 98

Encyclopédie (Diderot and Alembert), 26–27,

Encyclopédie Larousse, 267

Epictetus, 45

Epistle of Forgiveness (al-Ma'arri), 284

Erasmus, 55, 63

Este, Isabella d', 264–65

Etruscan tombs, 291–92

Eve, as Pandora, 39–40

Exodus, book of, 94

Ezekiel, book of, 94, 285, 316

Faulkner, Barry, 95

Felice da Prato, 99

Ferdinand, King, 96

Ficino, Marsilio, 174, 266

Flaubert, Gustave, 327

Florence, domestic life in, 210

Földényi, László, 177–78

forests: in the *Commedia,* 151–56, 168–70; as metaphor, 169–70. *See also* nature

Francesca, 154, 172, 190–91

Francesco da Barberino, 18

Freccero, John, 225, 316, 324–25

Frederick II, Emperor, 115, 153, 223

free will, 190, 192, 319–20; and civil law, 323; dilemma of, 191, 317; as gift of God, 302, 320; and morality, 321, 323

French Revolution, 220–21; equality for women in, 193–99

Freud, Sigmund, 137

Frost, Robert, 84

Frye, Northrop, 167

Fucci, Vanni, 208

Galatians, Epistle to the, 317–18

Galileo Galilei, 174–76, 257–58

Garcilaso de la Vega, the Inca, 74–75, 77

Horace, 308
Hu, Georgine, 235, 236
humanism, 53
Hume, David, 29; *A Treatise of Human Nature*, 25–26, 320–21
Huns, 122

Ibn ʿArabi, 283
Ibn Khaldun, 35
identity, 127–29; adolescents' search for, 49–50; children's awareness of, 135; name as, 132–33; and place, 165–67. *See also* gender identity
Ikhwan al-Safa, 284–85
imagination: and humans' sense of place, 178–79; as tool for survival, 3; truth embodied in, 315–27; of the writer, 9
individuation, Jung's concept of, 136–37
injustice: justifications for, 219–20; Thrasymachus on, 185, 186
Intergovernmental Panel on Climate Change (IPCC), 162–63, 345–46n20
International Monetary Fund (IMF), 237–38
Irenaeus, Saint, 40, 285
Isherwood, Christopher, 290
Isidore of Seville, 210
Islam, and death, 283–85
I-Tsing, 120–21

Jacopo Alighieri (Dante's son), 16, 18
James, Henry, 169; *Spoils of Poynton*, 269–70
Japan: concept of death in, 280; as target of atomic bomb, 220, 232
Jason (captain of the Argonauts), 40–41
Jaucourt, chevalier de, 27
Jaynes, Julian, 71–72
Jeremiah, book of, 239

Jerome, Saint, 92, 287, 318
Jewish books, published in Venice, 98–101
Jews, persecution of, 295–96; and language as instrument of resistance, 301–2. *See also* Auschwitz; Judaism, principles of
Job, book of, 2–3, 171
John, Gospel of, 225
John of Patmos, 279, 285, 287, 316
Johnson, Samuel, 344n12
John the Baptist, Saint, 92
John the Evangelist, Saint, 88, 92
Joyce, James, 34; *Portrait of the Artist as a Young Man* (Stephen Dedalus character in), 165–66
Judah the Prince, Rabbi, 89
Judaism, principles of, 93–98. *See also* Kabbalah; Talmud; Talmudic tradition; Torah, as word of God
Judeo-Christian beliefs, about death, 281–82, 285–88
Julius Caesar (Shakespeare), 154
Jung, Carl Gustav, 136–37
justice. *See* God's justice; Socrates: on justice and equality
just society, 199; Socrates' concept of, 185–86. *See also* natural rights

Kabbalah, 88–89, 97–98
Kabbalists, 79–80
Kadare, Ismail, 207–8
Kafka, Franz, 16, 119, 141, 178; "The Penal Colony," 307–8
Kalidasa, 121
Kant, Immanuel, 177
Keats, John, 16
Kenny, Andrew, 220
Kerford, G. B., 54
Keynes, John Maynard, 247

Thomas Aquinas, Saint (*continued*)
    influence on, 22–23; *Summa
    Theologica*, 22, 85–86
thought processes, mapping of, 109–10
Thrasymachus, on injustice, 185, 186
Tibbets, Paul, 232
Timothy, first book of, 240
Toland, John, 76
Torah, as word of God, 88–89, 93–97,
    104. *See also* Talmud
Toscanella, Orazio, 42–44
Tradescant, John (father and son),
    263–64
translation: concept of, 65; writing as,
    66, 70–71
Très Riches Heures du Duc de Berry, 249
Troilus and Cressida (Shakespeare), 33,
    239
Trojan Horse, 29
Trojan War, 35, 305. *See also* Homer: *Iliad*
truth: in the *Commedia*, 315–17, 319–20;
    Hume's perspective on, 321; poetic lie
    as, 315–27; stories as, 312
Truth and Reconciliation Commission
    (South Africa), 322
Tsevetaeva, Marina, 84
Turannius, Sextus, 277–78
Tuscany, political factions in, 16–17,
    223–24
typography, 80, 81

Ugolino, Count, 279
Ulysses: as character in the *Commedia*,
    33–34, 36, 40–41, 44–46, 297–99, 302,
    304–5; curiosity of, 44–47; and the
    gift of language, 35; literary incarna-
    tions of, 34–35, 41; sins committed by,
    35–36
unconscious, Jung's concept of, 136
United Nations Environmental Pro-
    gramme (UNEP), 160

universe, models of, 173–77. *See also*
    center of the universe, as perceived
    by various cultures
Upanishads, 121
usury, sin of, 243–45, 247

Valla, Lorenzo, 224–25
Valmiki, 111
Varro, Marcus Terentius, 158, 187
Vedas, 121, 122
Vellutello, Alessandro, 174, 176
Veltwyck, Gerard, 99
Venice: imaginative and historical roots
    of, 104–5; Jewish books published in,
    98–101; Jewish community in, 96, 97,
    100–101
Victorinus, 285, 287
Videla, Jorge Rafael, 220
Villani, Giovanni, 239
violence, to nature, 154–56
Virgil: *Aeneid*, 14, 19, 28–29, 33, 83, 153,
    179, 304; as Dante's guide in the
    Commedia, 19, 27–29, 36, 44, 68–70,
    113, 116, 130, 145, 152–53, 170–71, 180,
    216–17, 222–23, 230, 257–58, 300,
    308–9, 313–14, 316; *Georgics*, 157, 162;
    as model for José Hernández, 148;
    and the natural world, 157–58
Vita nova (Dante), 19, 20
Viviano, Vincenzo, 176
Volkov, Solomon, 84
Voragine, Jacop de, *Golden Legend*, 20

Walcott, Derek, 165
war: death in, 289–90; as game of chess,
    226–27; moral justification for, 232–33
Webb, Jeremy, 290
Weil, Simone, 50
Weissmuller, Johnny, 120
Whitman, Walt, *Leaves of Grass*, 257

Wilde, Oscar, 143–44; *A House of Pomegranates,* 252; *The Importance of Being Earnest,* 38; "The Young King," 252–53
Williams, Charles, 159
wolves, 202. *See also* she-wolf, sins of
women: in ancient Greece, 187–88; as commodities, 188–89; in Dante's world, 189–92; during the French Revolution, 193–99; rights of, 195–99; "subservient" function of, 38; traditional role of, 187–89. *See also* gender identity
Wood of Suicides, 151, 152
woods. *See* forests; nature
Woolf, Virginia, 187, 201
words: and meaning, 123–24; as representation of thoughts, 66. *See also* language; translation; writing
workers, as represented in art and literature, 249–53

writing: aesthetics and utility of, 73; invention of, 71–73; as translation of the visual, 66, 70–71. *See also* language
Wunderkammer, 265

Xenophon, 57, 58, 59

Ya'akov ben Asher, 98
Yeats, William Butler, 134–35
Yi Jing. *See* I-Tsing
Yitzhak, Rabbi Levi, 93
Yitzhaki, Rabbi Shlomo. *See* Rashi

Zend-Avesta, 281
Zeno's paradox, 93
Zephyr, the West Wind, 47
Zoroastrianism, and death, 281